Juvenile justice in Britain and the United States

Library of social work

General Editor:
Noel Timms
Professor of Social Work Studies
University of Newcastle upon Tyne

Juvenile justice in Britain and the United States

The balance of needs and rights

Phyllida Parsloe
Professor of Social Work
University of Bristol

Routledge & Kegan Paul
London, Boston and Henley

First published in 1978
by Routledge & Kegan Paul Ltd
39 Store Street,
London WC1E 7DD,
Broadway House,
Newtown Road,
Henley-on-Thames,
Oxon RG9 1EN and
9 Park Street,
Boston, Mass. 02108, USA
Reprinted in 1980
Printed in Great Britain by
Redwood Burn Ltd
Trowbridge and Esher

British Library Cataloguing in Publication Data

Parsloe, Phyllida
    Juvenile justice in Britain and the United
    States. – (Library of social work).
    1. Juvenile delinquency – Great Britain –
    History   2. Juvenile delinquency – United
    States – History   3. Criminal justice,
    Administration of – Great Britain – History
    4. Criminal justice, Administration of –
    United States – History
    I. Title   II. Series
    345'.41'08   KD8445   77–30714

ISBN 0 7100 8772 1

Contents

Acknowledgments

Many people made this book possible although none can be blamed for its shortcomings. I am grateful to my personal travel agent, Kevin Leddy, who made my visit to Indiana School of Law a possibility. In Indiana I was helped by many of the faculty but especially by two deans, Burnett Harvey and Douglas Boshkoff and by three professors, Dan Hopson, Edwin Greenebaum and Bill Popkin. They are responsible for my interest in many legal matters but not for my failures in understanding. In Britain so many social workers and teachers have helped me that they defy naming. Finally my thanks go to my family; my father who reversed roles and became my research assistant, my mother who, with Ena Rae, Mary Dinnie, Irene Strachan and Claudia Duncan, typed and re-typed my many drafts and my lawyer brother, John, who put his logical mind at my service and - so far as I would let him - edited my manuscript.

Preface

The purpose of this book is to explore the ideas which led
to the establishment of systems of juvenile justice in the
US, England and Wales, and Scotland and which affect their
continued existence. Three sets of ideas can be distinguished, and these I am calling ideas of welfare, ideas of
criminal justice and ideas of community concern and responsibility. Each set of ideas would, were it implemented
alone, lead to very different systems of juvenile justice.
However, it is a feature of the three systems with which
we are concerned that ideas of welfare, criminal justice
and community concern co-exist, and it is the balance between them which determines the actual form of the system
of juvenile justice. This balance is created, maintained
and changed by a number of different factors. First the
history of the systems will be explored, since their nineteenth-century beginnings are a powerful determinant of
their twentieth-century form. Chapters four, seven and
eight will consider the statutes and rules which provide
the framework within which the present systems operate.
Despite the influence of history and control provided by
law, the way the balance between the three sets of ideas is
held seems ultimately to rest with the people who work in
the juvenile justice system. A large part of their behaviour is not the result of rules but of the way they exercise their discretion. The factors which influence the
nature and use of this discretion by judges, magistrates
and panel members, probation officers and social workers
and by prosecutors, police and defence lawyers will be
considered.

Chapter one

Juvenile justice systems

In Britain and the United States juvenile justice systems have recently attracted public, political and scholarly attention. In the United States the attention has been largely critical and many people consider that the system has failed.(1) In Britain the emphasis was first upon restructuring,(2) a process which found legislative expression in the Social Work (Scotland) Act(3) in 1968 and the Children and Young Persons Act 1969,(4) in England.* Now there is growing discontent with the new structures and, in particular, with what is seen as the powerlessness of juvenile courts and children's Hearings.

The demands made on the systems are similar on both sides of the Atlantic but in some ways their recent development has been in opposite directions. In the United States, where juvenile courts have no criminal jurisdiction, there is movement away from the informality, which often amounted to procedural sloppiness and arbitrariness, towards a more legalistic approach. The procedures for the protection of adults charged with criminal offences have been extended to juveniles facing the possibility of a finding of delinquency. A child alleged to be a delinquent now has almost the same right to trial by due process of law as has an adult charged with an offence. In Britain the trend has been in the opposite direction. Starting from a much more legalistic base, the move has been to extend the civil category of children in need of care and reduce the number of children who are charged with a criminal offence. In theory at least the aim in England was to treat children according to their underlying needs and not in response to specific acts. Scotland went further and took decisions concerning the disposition of juveniles away from the

* England will be used to include England and Wales.

1

courts, making them the responsibility of the newly created children's hearings.(5)

These changes suggest a difference between Britain and the United States, but, while there is a difference in the direction of their development, the result is that the juvenile justice systems, particularly in the United States and England, are becoming more alike. English juvenile courts were, and still are, courts with a criminal jurisdiction, but over the years they have gradually incorporated ideas drawn from a welfare approach. The juvenile courts in the United States were established as civil courts offering a gateway for children to welfare services. Only gradually has their law-enforcement function been acknowledged. Each country is now moving towards a central point where ideas drawn from a welfare approach and those from criminal justice are finely balanced.

England and Wales, Scotland and the United States also share an uncertainty about their ability to control or to help troubled or troublesome children and a growing awareness of the unintended effects of intervention into children's lives. It is recognised that juvenile courts, and even the new Scottish children's hearings, may be stigmatising rather than helping children. This failure of confidence is characteristic of the 1960s and 1970s in relation not only to juvenile justice but to other social problems. Recognition of the stigmatising effects of treatment is perhaps the most important contribution our century has made to an understanding of juvenile justice. It has led to a concern to keep children out of the court and hearing system. All three countries are placing legislative and financial emphasis upon what in the United States is known as 'diverting children from the juvenile courts' and what in Britain is called 'prevention'. Government and voluntary agencies are charged with responsibility to provide help for young people and their families outside the court system. The juvenile court and the children's hearings are to be places of last resort, and compulsion is to be used only when no other way of meeting a child's needs seems possible. This is a considerable change, particularly in the United States where, as Paulsen explains, the reformers who established the first juvenile court saw it(6):

as a gateway through which children would pass into a rich supermarket of salvation services: a probation officer here, a medical doctor there, a dentist there, a psychiatrist here, a psychologist there. The court would be the means whereby the community brought services to bear in respect of youngsters who need them.

THE FUNCTIONS OF THE JUVENILE JUSTICE SYSTEM

To understand the present trends in juvenile justice it is
necessary to consider what functions the system fulfils for
society and what different sets of ideas meet and influence the decisions and actions of the people in the systems.

The juvenile justice system is one of a number of institutions which society has developed for the purpose of so-
cialising and controlling children, and particularly lower-
class city children. All societies have developed some
such institutions, since the future of society and the culture it develops depend upon socialisation processes. Most
have placed a primary responsibility for socialisation upon
the family unit but, where the family has proved inadequate,
other institutions have been developed to supplement, support or supplant the parents. The twentieth century has
seen in the US and Britain the development of this special
agent of socialisation and control: the juvenile court.

Theoretically there are many forms which a system designed to handle troublesome behaviour in children might
take. The form depends upon the way the behaviour is defined. Such behaviour can be seen as part of growing-up,
and so a matter for internal management by the family, or
as a wider educational matter and therefore the concern and
responsibility of the schools. It may be regarded as a
social problem to be dealt with by voluntary social service agencies or welfare departments of the local or national government. In some countries it can be seen as
behaviour directed against the State and therefore a political matter to be corrected by local political groups.
Other possibilities are to regard the behaviour as a moral
matter and thus the concern of religious bodies or as a
manifestation of illness, either mental or physical, and
therefore a medical matter. In certain circumstances each
of these definitions is used and also the corrective measures which the definition entails, but the master definition in our society is that of law breaker. The ultimate
and residual responsibility for controlling troublesome behaviour is therefore vested in a court.

All these choices may in theory have been open to the
nineteenth-century reformers, but looking back on history
one can see how much choice was limited by social pressures
and preceding events. Juvenile courts did not appear out
of a clear blue sky one day in Illinois in 1898. They
evolved gradually and inevitably from earlier developments
in criminal law and welfare provisions. It would have been
impossible, then at least, for children who committed offences to be dealt with outside some court structure.

Various social pressures combined to ensure that a court was the institution. A strong belief in punishment and deterrence as necessary and successful was as characteristic of the nineteenth as of all previous centuries. Such beliefs led naturally to a definition of troublesome behaviour as bad, unlawful, and therefore requiring punishment, which is a prerogative of parents and courts. There was also a belief that an offender had a right to a fair hearing before being judged and punished, perhaps by removal from the community. This belief contributed to the choice of a court and, in Britain more than in the United States, had a strong influence on the form of procedure inside the court.

Other pressures contributed to the establishment of courts which were very unlike any existing court and ensured that the juvenile court had a complex function. Concern for the children as children had grown during the nineteenth century and their special needs were beginning to be acknowledged. Such concern was based in part upon humanitarian ideas, but also upon a belief that poverty and criminality in adults were best prevented by segregating, educating and correcting children who showed the first signs of such conditions. By the end of the century these ideas were firmly backed by legislation, and thus courts for children were required to give expression to humanitarian as well as punitive beliefs. They were also to express society's belief in education. The reformers had a profound faith in the strength of educative measures and in the reformative effect of family life. The juvenile court, particularly in the United States, was to provide a gateway to a changed environment, and the result would be a changed child. In 1900 Freud had not yet loosed on the world the idea of a personal internal world resistant to external manipulation, nor had society grasped the problems of managing a spoiled identity, which concern us today. So the reformers gave the juvenile court the task of changing children, with more belief in the possibilities of success than we might have now.

These trends alone would have ensured that the juvenile justice system had multiple functions and aims. From the beginning it was concerned both with protecting society and with serving the best interests of the child, with meeting the child's needs while also protecting his rights, although in the United States the concept of a child's right differed from that held today.(7) The complexity was compounded because society is concerned with controlling behaviour in children which goes far beyond the commission of criminal acts. In addition to jurisdiction over incorrigible children, beggars and vagrants, which the juvenile codes took

over from the Poor Laws, new legislation in both countries
gave the courts jurisdiction over children who truant and
were promiscuous, juvenile drinkers and curfew breakers,
the sexually assaulted and the physically abused;(8)   all
these in addition to those children who committed crimes.
Besides extending the State's control, this had important
implications for the future of the juvenile court, since it
ensured its welfare function. Without the presence of these
children the juvenile court might have developed more clearly as an arm of criminal justice. The inclusion of non-
offenders(9) prevented this and provided for the children
who had committed, what in an adult is a crime, some of the
attitudes and actions associated with a welfare system. The
corollary is that, in so far as the juvenile court is also
an agent of criminal justice, it functions as such towards
children who are non-offenders as well as towards those who
are offenders, and some of the stigma of criminality attaches to these non-offenders as well as to those who commit crimes.

HOW CHILDREN'S BEHAVIOUR IS CLASSIFIED

The types of behaviour which bring children within the
jurisdiction of the juvenile justice system are similar in
Britain and the United States, although there is some difference in the legal groupings of these types. The behaviour and needs of children which these societies see as
the concern of their juvenile justice system are:
   1 Acts which, if committed by an adult, would be criminal acts. These acts are specified not in juvenile codes
but in general criminal legislation.
   2 Acts which are not illegal for adults but which society has made illegal for children and young persons. The
most important are probably sexual acts between persons below legislatively established age limits. Also in this
group are failure to attend school and entering premises
where alcohol is sold. In some parts of the United States
being out after curfew(10) or drinking alcohol(11) come
into this category.
   3 Being beyond the control of parents or guardians.
This is phrased in various ways - being unruly, incorrigible or ungovernable - but implies a breakdown of the
usual family controls on behaviour.
   4 Children who are physically or sexually abused or neglected or treated in ways likely to impair their health.
   5 Children whose emotional development is neglected or
impaired, including those who are in moral danger.
   6 Children to whom 4 or 5 might happen because they live

in a home where other children have been found to have suffered in those ways.

7   Children who are deserted, deprived or abandoned.
The judicial grouping of these acts and needs is indicated in Table 1.1. Each State of the United States has its own law relating to children, but most States use similar categories, although the actual word to describe them may vary.

TABLE 1.1

	Classification		
	in US	in England	in Scotland
1 Acts which if committed by adults are crimes	Delinquent	In need of care or control. If over 12 can be found to have committed an offence	In need of compulsory measures of care if under 16 years
2 Acts illegal only if committed by children	Delinquent or persons in need of supervision	In need of care or control	In need of compulsory measures of care if under 16 years
3 Incorrigible	Delinquent or persons in need of supervision	In need of care or control	In need of compulsory measures of care if under 16 years
4 Physically or & emotionally 5 neglected	Neglected	In need of care or control	In need of compulsory measures of care if under 16 years
6 Potentially neglected	No such category included under neglect	In need of care or control	In need of compulsory measures of care if under 16 years
7 Deserted, deprived or abandoned	Dependent	Usually dealt with outside court system, but could be brought as in need of care or control	Usually dealt with outside court system, but could be in need of compulsory measures of care if under 16

The major difference is that the term delinquent in the
United States has a legal meaning and can (but does not always) cover criminal acts, incorrigibility and acts illegal
only for children. In Britain, when it is used, it does not
describe a legal category and is usually taken to refer only
to those children who have committed acts which are criminal
if committed by an adult. The British category of 'in need
of care' is wider than the United States category of delinquent (or delinquent plus persons in need of supervision),
because it includes neglected children, who form a separate
group in many United States juvenile codes, and also includes a category of potentially neglected children, which
is not common in the United States. Finally, the British
system, with a much more comprehensive local government
child care system outside the courts, has no category of
dependent child, although the local authority can take
action to retain children already in its care.(12)
    Treatment of neglected and dependent children in the
United States raises many of the same problems, in terms
of their rights and needs, as does the treatment of those
in the other categories, but much less is known about the
way the law operates towards them. Perhaps they will soon
come under the spotlight of public concern, and it is probable that they need to do so. We, however, will concentrate
on those aspects of juvenile justice which relate to children who fall into categories 1, 2 and 3. These children
are those who are said to have acted in ways which contra-
vene society's view of what is proper behaviour in children.
We will not be concerned with the other aspect of the juvenile courts' work, which relates to children who are victims of ill-treatment by others.

APPROACHES TO JUVENILE JUSTICE

The reader will already be aware that different ideas are
operating in the juvenile justice systems, and it is to
these ideas that we now turn. There is a growing interest
amongst sociologists and political scientists in the sets
or patterns of ideas which people hold about social problems. These sets influence what comes to be defined as a
social problem, what laws are passed to deal with it and
how these laws are implemented in practice. It is perhaps
a particular feature of laws relating to social problems
that, while they establish a system within which to alle-
viate or control the problem, they also leave wide scope
for decision making in individual instances by those who
operate the system. Such a situation is necessary because social problems are the problems of distinct human

beings who ultimately require individualised treatment.
The discretion exercised by those who decide what this
treatment shall be, is influenced not only by their role
and by the available resources but also by the set of ideas
they hold about the human situation with which they are
dealing.   They do not rethink situations anew each time but
carry with them a relatively consistent set of interlocking
ideas about causes and solutions, which guide their actions.
Such ideologies are an essential feature of situations
where people have to act without certainty and with incom-
plete understanding and they serve to legitimate authority
as well as to give meaning to behaviour.   There are two
fundamental sets of ideas and actions found in the juvenile
justice system and these I am characterising as the welfare
approach and the criminal justice approach.   We shall also
find another set of ideas and, to a lesser extent, actions
which we will discuss under the title of the community
approach.   The last approach, although not new, seems to be
taking a new form and is gaining momentum, although it
remains largely theoretical, having as yet less practical
application than have the welfare and criminal justice approaches.

Each approach comprises ideas about a number of different
issues and emphasises different values.   All three approaches
offer means by which humans try to explain and to manage the
fundamental tension between the individual and the group
without denying the place of either.   The individual can
exist only as a member of the group and yet the group inevitably imposes limits upon his individuality.   The approaches emphasise different aspects of this dilemma and
in so doing give primacy to different values.   At a less
abstract level the approaches offer different explanations
for human behaviour and for deviant behaviour in particular.
As a consequence they support different means of bringing
about change in people as well as holding different ideas
about who should be required to change.   Here values and
explanations are interwoven and provide the base on which
each approach offers prescriptions for the future and interpretations of the past.

These approaches have a long history.   Not only do they
influence the way people use their discretion in the juvenile justice systems today, but they have influenced the
way the systems developed in the past.   Their influence extends far beyond the area of juvenile justice into most social institutions.   One way to explore these approaches is
to examine those institutions which reflect in almost pure
form the ideas and values inherent in one approach, and
for this purpose a criminal trial might serve for the criminal justice approach and a child guidance for the welfare

approach. The community approach has as yet no such clear expression in action, although the Youth Service Bureau may come to fill this role.

These approaches find expression not only in social institutions but in the professions, so that another means of understanding the criminal justice approach is to consider the accepted values, training and methods of the legal profession. Social workers are the group who corporately stand for the ideas and values of the welfare approach. The community approach, which is itself anti-professional, has no such group through whom the approach is translated into action.

THE CRIMINAL JUSTICE APPROACH

The criminal justice approach is concerned with the maintenance of a stable society, and therefore with particular actions on the part of individuals which threaten to upset this fragile stability. The individual is potentially dangerous and, as Mead(13) has suggested, the criminal justice approach represents the cohesion of a group against an enemy. An unlawful act disturbs the equilibrium between the individual and the group and weakens the rule of law which maintains the balance. The rule of law needs to be re-established and the chosen means is by trial and then sentencing. This means also ensures that individual freedom, on which the approach places a high value, is protected.

The approach involves the assumption that behaviour is within the control of the individual. Apart from young children and the severely mentally ill, people do what they do because they decide they want to. Thus breaking a rule or committing a crime are acts within the control of the individual which occur as a result of his free choice. Neither unconscious forces nor sociological influences are important. Roscoe Pound(14) sets this view of man in a historical perspective:

It is one which has governed from the seventeenth to the nineteenth century, getting what is likely to prove its final form in the latter. It is a picture in which relation is ignored and each man is made to stand out by himself as an economically, politically, morally and hence legally self-sufficient unit.

These assumptions about the causes of behaviour entail other assumptions about changing deviant behaviour. If the criminal is a rational man, then the law must ensure that he and the rest of society realise that crime does not pay. Since crime is freely chosen, it can be dealt with by punishment,

because offenders as rational people will dislike the pain
of a fine or imprisonment and the next time will choose to
avoid rule breaking. Even more important, others, seeing
them suffer, will be deterred from breaking the law. Deterrence is not the only aim of sentencing according to the
criminal justice approach. It also meets the desire for
retribution or vengeance, which is justified when criminal
acts have been freely chosen. In addition, failure to provide an institutionalised outlet for vengeance might lead to
individuals taking vengeance into their own hands and thus
endangering the existence of society.(15)

> The first requirement of a sound body of law is that it
> should correspond with the actual feeling and demands of
> the community, whether right or wrong. If people would
> gratify the passion of revenge outside the law, if the
> law did not help them, the law has no choice but to
> satisfy the craving itself, and thus avoid the greater
> evil of private retribution. At the same time, this
> passion is not one which we encourage, whether as pri-
> vate individuals or as law-makers.

The criminal justice approach also requires that 'the punishment fits the crime'. As Rosenheim points out, 'Justice
implies some relationship between a person's actions and
the consequences the state assigns to them.'(16)

The criminal justice approach is seen in its clearest
form in a criminal trial, although this is by no means the
only social institution influenced by this approach, nor
are other influences entirely lacking in a modern trial.
Because the approach sees the deviant individual as the
enemy of the group, the essence of the situation is one of
conflict. Stapleton and Teitelbaum(17) point out:

> Mechanisms for handling legal disputes (and particu-
> larly those between the state and the individual) adopt
> conflict as a normative theme. . . . The essence of this
> system is challenge; . . . It is in its conception based
> upon the assumption that the primary interest of the
> accused lies in avoiding conviction and that the state's
> interest lies in securing that result; thus, conflict
> is necessary to the system.

Criminal courts in the United States are probably more
obviously conflict orientated than are English courts, the
difference being most clearly seen in the role of the prosecutor, who in England is usually a lawyer in private
practice who prosecutes occasionally, but whose future does
not depend upon his success as a prosecutor, as is the case
with his full-time United States counterpart. In contrast,
a United States prosecutor aims at getting a conviction and
at influencing the sentence which is passed, although he is
constrained by certain rights allowed to the defendant. The

situation in Scotland is more like that existing in the
United States, although the atmosphere probably more closely
resembles that of English courts, since one seldom hears
complaints against the procurator fiscal, the Scottish prosecutor, for being unduly eager to obtain convictions.
Nevertheless, while the British system may have the parties
in the battle less clearly aligned, there can be no doubt
that the model is one of conflict. Certainly, any accused
person experiences a trial as such.

The criminal justice approach values individual freedom
and, because the court pits the State against the individual in a conflict situation, rules have been developed to
control the behaviour on both sides, but especially the
behaviour of the prosecutor. Stapleton and Teitelbaum,(18)
who compare the court situation to a sporting event in
which each side must play to win, point out: 'As with
sporting events this element of conflict exists within a
framework bounded by norms which may be more rigid and
carefully observed than those of groups formed for co-operative purposes.' Thus, defendants in criminal trials in the
United States are entitled under the Constitution to trial
by due process of law. This means they are presumed innocent until the State proves them guilty and are allowed
procedural protection, such as a right to notice of hearing
and of the charge against them, to representation by attorneys, to protection against illegal search and seizure,
coerced confessions, and self-incrimination. The proof
must be established beyond reasonable doubt and, in many
instances, to the satisfaction of a jury. British courts
offer defendants similar protection. Besides such procedural rights, the systems operate in principle, however
little in practice, upon an assumption of equal justice
for all. What is at issue is whether or not a rule has
been broken, and individual attributes of the accused,
such as wealth, education, race, religion and intelligence
and to some extent past criminal history, are irrelevant.
The criminal justice system is concerned largely with external facts, and operates on the assumption that there is
an external reality which can be identified, irrespective
of the feelings of those who perceive it. The justice with
which it is concerned is equal justice.

The criminal justice approach is institutionalised in the
legal profession, which ensures for society the continuous
socialisation of some of its members into this particular
approach and provides prosecutors and defenders, as well
as judges, to man the trial by law. Although the legal
profession has other ways of handling conflicts, which are
based on co-operation, its popular image is that of the
advocate who fights for his client. Such behaviour would

be disfunctional in many situations, but it serves the
special needs of the criminal justice system to establish
the facts of a past event, through the medium of a conflict
in which each side presents those aspects most favourable
to themselves or their viewpoint. It also leads inevitably to a decision. There is no place in the criminal
justice approach for agreeing to differ or being unable to
decide. As Hazard has pointed out, in contrast to science
which 'requires the agreement of minds . . . legal processes begin with their disagreement', and the concerns of
'law men . . . are for immediate, cheap and significant
decision making. For them there are continuing attractions
in the Delphic Oracle.'(19)

Medicine and social work are among the professions or
semi-professions institutionalising the welfare approach,
and the contrast between their methods, which are based
upon consensus, and those of lawyers are pointed out in
these quotations:(21)

> The doctor confesses that there are some questions to
> which he has no answers and acknowledges that some mat-
> ters must be left open to await scientific proof. But
> no trial court can do that. Eventually, right or wrong,
> some judge will (have to) say: 'This is the answer; this
> is the end of the litigation.' The physician can say
> with honesty: 'I just don't know.' The judge can never
> say that.(20)

> while practising lawyers and social workers are both
> 'helping professions' dealing with conflict resolution,
> there are fundamental differences in their objectives
> and methodology. One appeals as a representative of
> the client to the adversary system of conflict reso-
> lution; the other establishes and uses a professional
> relationship with the client to effect change in the
> client and/or his environment as a basic problem-solving
> method.

THE WELFARE APPROACH

The welfare approach is concerned with the failure of individuals to develop their full potential, a failure which
involves a loss to society as well as a loss to the individual. Ideally the stable society is one composed of
mature, fully-functioning individuals, and the welfare
approach is more concerned with what people are than with
what they do. Specific acts are important, not in their
own right but as indicators of the problems of the individual. In this way a criminal offence is interpreted as
an expression of social or psychological malaise.

Like the criminal justice approach, the welfare approach
relies upon particular assumptions about the causes of criminal behaviour. David May(22) lists these assumptions in
his article, 'Delinquency control and the treatment model':
  (1) that explanations of delinquency are to be found in
  the behavioural and motivational systems of delinquents,
  and not in the law and its administration.
  (2) that in some identifiable way delinquents are different from non-delinquents. Earlier theories stressed
  the physical and visible nature of the differences but
  these have long since been superseded by more sophisticated statements that seek to locate the differences
  in systems of norms and values, socialisation experience
  or psychological disorders . . . .
  (3) that the delinquent is constrained and cannot ultimately be held responsible for his actions. The constraints might be physiological, psychological or sociological.
  (4) that delinquent behaviour *per se* is not the real
  problem. It possesses 'significance only as a pointer
  to the need for intervention'. It is the presenting
  symptom that draws attention to the more intractable
  disease. 'Sometimes it is a response to unsatisfactory
  family or social circumstances, a result of boredom in
  and out of school, an indication of maladjustment or
  immaturity, or a symptom of a deviant, damaged or abnor-
  mal personality' ('Children in Trouble', para. 6).
The emphasis is upon the state of the individual rather than
upon past acts. It may not even be important whether an
individual has committed an act, so long as his state of
being suggests that he needs help. Such a point is apparently made by Lou(23) in describing the Chicago Boys' Court
(which was not a juvenile court) and regretting the number of dismissals.
  During 1921 the number of cases filed in the Chicago
  Boys' Court was 8,521, of which 62 per cent resulted in
  discharges. Doubtless, many of those would have been
  found delinquent and dealt with accordingly if the procedure had been that of the juvenile court.
The means by which one discovers whether or not someone
needs help in no way resemble a battle. The method is one
of co-operation. The supporters of the early juvenile
courts, who were influenced by the welfare approach, often
pointed out that the pattern to be followed is that of the
family.(24)
  The fundamental idea of the Juvenile Court law is that
  the state must step in and exercise guardianship over a
  child found under such adverse social or individual
  conditions as develop crime. . . it proposes a plan

whereby he may be treated, not as a criminal, or legally
charged with a crime, but as a ward of the state, to
receive practically the care, custody and discipline
that are accorded the neglected and dependent child,
and which, as the Act states, 'shall approximate as
nearly as may be that which should be given by its
parents.'
If there is to be any battle, it is one in which the individual and those who treat him unite in a fight against
delinquency.(25)
the framers of our Bill of Rights, with all their learning and wisdom, were familiar with only one type of lit-
igation - the traditional adversary type. They could
hardly have intended the Bill to apply in a hitherto
unheard-of type of court that was designed to eliminate
the ancient, accusatory, prosecutive, punitive approach;
to depose the state from its aggressive, hostile role;
and to substitute a nonadversary, nonpunitive, solici-
tous approach aimed to protect and correct the child
malefactor. This new court aimed to protect the child
from evils likely to be met in the criminal process and
prison, perhaps in his own home and neighbourhood, and
to correct his malevolent attitudes by diagnosing and
either removing or rectifying, as far as possible, the
causal factors through application of the social
sciences - such as medicine, psychology, psychiatry,
counselling, education, social casework - and, most of
all, through benevolent personal contact. In short, this
court aimed not to fight the delinquent but to fight
delinquency, and not with a legal bludgeon, but with
knowledge, science, skill and devotion.
The model here is that of the doctor and patient fighting
disease.
Within such an approach the individual needs no protection. The emphasis is not upon his rights but upon his
needs, and so the welfare approach has few recognised rules
of procedure to protect the client or patient. It is not
correct that it has no rules, since confidentiality is at
times referred to as a right of the client in receipt of
welfare services. However, this is not a right in the same
sense as is the right to jury trial in the criminal field.
It arises from the value placed upon the individual which
is the basis of the welfare approach. It is also a necessary technique for developing the trust and co-operation
upon which change in the individual is thought to depend.
The same is true for all the so-called principles of social
work. The right of a client to a non-judgmental attitude
in the worker, to self determination, and to be respected
as an individual, are not legally enforceable rights but

statements about underlying philosophy. They serve as
ideals by which social workers will attempt to shape their
behaviour.
    Justice within a welfare approach can never be equal.
Individual justice is the only justice which can embody
ideas of fairness, because people are not equal in the
point from which they start. Not only are they unequal
in wealth, education, racial and religious background,
but in personality, potential and resources. Treatment
must be tailored to the individual's needs, and the act
which brought these needs to the attention of the helping
agency cannot be used alone as the basis for a treatment
decision. An act which may be defined as a crime by the
law is in welfare philosophy the sign of a social problem
which must be assessed and treated. The decision about
treatment is related only to the needs of the individual.
Rehabilitation is the main concern of the welfare approach
and retribution, vengeance and deterrence of others play
no part in it.
    One of the major problems within the welfare approach
is how far it is practicable to coerce people into changing. On the one side is the model of the family in which
the parents, knowing what is best for their children,
punish and coerce them for their own good. Punishment
must never be for the sake of revenge but can be used to
train the child in more acceptable and healthy modes of
behaviour. Learning theory supports the view that behaviour can be changed by negative reinforcement, although
studies suggest that it is more permanently established
by positive reinforcement on an intermittent basis. On
the other hand, many treatment theories suggest that
lasting change only takes place when a person is engaged
in changing himself and that, unless this desire to
change develops, any behavioural change may be short-
lived. This view does not preclude the need for some
coercion to start an individual on the road to change,
and the authority inherent in the welfare approach is
now receiving more attention in social work literature.
Despite these variations, what separates any punishment
within the welfare approach from punishment in the criminal justice approach is that it can never be inflicted
on one person in order to deter others. Punishment, if
it occurs within the welfare approach at all, can be
justified only by the needs of the person punished.
    The welfare approach in its present secular form has
a shorter history than the criminal justice approach and
is less clearly expressed in our social institutions,
professions or language. Doctors, particularly psychiatrists, and social workers are the professional groups on

whom society places considerable responsibility for a
welfare approach to social problems. The child guidance
clinic probably illustrates the working of the approach
in its purest form. Here behaviour is seen as a response
to faulty past and present relationships, and change is
effected by means of a corrective therapeutic relationship
entered into on a voluntary basis. Children are frequently
protected from prosecution while their needs for treatment
are met. There is little or no attention paid to rights,
because the assumption is that the doctor or social worker
will be able to engage the healthy part of the child or
parents in working towards their own increased maturity.
The only conflict may be an internal one for the patient.

THE COMMUNITY APPROACH

This is much less well developed than are the two earlier
approaches. Instead of the individual being seen as a
threat to society or his under-development being regarded
as society's loss, in the community model the person who
breaks the laws is seen as the victim of society. The
older version of this theory saw individuals as victims of
poverty, poor education and lack of job opportunities.
This view was expressed by Lou in 1924.(26)

> Juvenile delinquency is not a problem of the courts
> only but, in its causes, its consequences, and its
> treatment, is also a problem of the community. It is
> largely the community which provides for its youth
> their attitude, their philosophy of life, their example,
> their contacts, and their incentives. Juvenile delin-
> quency, in its last analysis, is nothing but the result
> of the maladjustment of the child to the community stan-
> dards and the failure on the part of the community to
> provide for his wholesome development. The community,
> therefore, must take upon itself the responsibility for
> the child's social maladjustments in the community,
> whether they arise in home, in school, in industry, in
> recreation, or elsewhere. The community must also de-
> tect and treat early symptoms of maladjustments and
> other difficulties in the child's physical, mental, or
> moral development. This conception of community res-
> ponsibility in regard to juvenile delinquency is com-
> paratively recent. The adequate fulfilment of this
> responsibility will result in the prevention of a con-
> siderable amount of juvenile delinquency and in the
> subsequent reduction of the number of children who come
> before the courts. It can be accomplished only by crea-
> ting an informed public opinion, an individual respon-

sibility, and an intelligent community action.
There was also the recognition that the social background
of a juvenile affected the treatment he received, and this
had important implications for his future. Alexander
Thompson,(27) in a book published in 1857, says:

There is a very remarkable contrast in the manner in
which the same acts are treated in the case of the
cherished and that of neglected juveniles; and the
results throw no small light on the manner in which the
one class grows up to be the useful and honoured members of society, while the other becomes its reproach
and its torment. . . .

He adds in a footnote:

It has been lately stated in a public meeting in London
that when Lord Chancellor Eldon was a boy at school, he
was caught robbing an orchard. His father was prosecuted and had to pay full compensation, and very wisely
administered a sound flogging to the culprit, thereby
doubtless laying the foundation of his son's future
eminence as a lawyer and a statesman. Had little John
Scott been himself prosecuted, and convicted, and re-
corded as a thief for life, how could he ever have become Lord Chancellor of England?

Later, theorists like Cloward and Ohlin(28) and Cohen
(29) in their studies of gangs and delinquent boys, stressed
the reaction of lower-class youth to the inequalities of society. They suggested that boys were raised with expectations that they would succeed in achieving the American
dream, but opportunities for doing so were denied to them.
These writers saw the community in which a child grew up
acting in a general and unspecified way upon some children
to bring about delinquent behaviour. This view of the community as creating delinquency still exists, but another
viewpoint has been developing recently which ascribes to
the community a far more specific and active role. According to this theory, society makes deviants, not only as an
unintended by-product of its social and political systems,
but because it needs them to exist. Without deviants cohesion is an impossibility. People are drawn together not
only because of an inherent wish to unite, but also because
they unite against an outsider. Politicians facing trouble
at home pray for a foreign war, or they did until the Viet-
nam war served to splinter rather than unite the American
people. Witch hunts in the middle ages, and law and order
cries today, give society a cause to which to rally and so
sink their differences in order to combat some other evil.
Criminals are needed by society, and especially by its
middle-class members.
Psychologically as well as sociologically, deviants are

needed by society. Karl Menninger(30) explains this need:
>   The vicarious use of the criminal for relieving the
>   guilt feelings of 'innocent' individuals by displace-
>   ment is no recent theory, but it constantly eludes
>   public acceptance. The internal economics of our
>   own morality, our submerged hates and suppressed aggres-
>   sions, our fantasied crimes, our feeling of need for
>   punishment - all these can be managed in part by the
>   scapegoat device. To do so requires this little man-
>   oeuver of displacement, but displacement and projection
>   are easier to manage than confession or sublimation.

He also explains the psychological functions served for the
general public by accusations and criminal trials:
>   'Distrust', said Nietzsche, 'all in whom the impulse to
>   punish is strong'. No one is more ferocious in demand-
>   ing that the murderer or the rapist 'pay' for his crime
>   than the man who has felt strong impulses in the same
>   directions. No one is more bitter in condemning the
>   'loose' woman than the 'good' women who have on occa-
>   sion guiltily enjoyed some purple dreams themselves.
>   It is never he who is without sin who casts the first
>   stone.
>
>   Along with the stone, we cast our own sins onto the
>   criminal. In this way we relieve our own sense of
>   guilt without actually having to suffer the punishment -
>   a convenient and even pleasant device, for it not only
>   relieves us of sin, but makes us feel actually virtu-
>   ous. A criminal trial, like a prizefight, is a public
>   performance in which the spectators work off in a so-
>   cially acceptable way aggressive impulses of much the
>   same kind that the man on trial worked off in a socially
>   unacceptable way.

Furthermore, 'labelling theory', which is the general
name given to the sociological aspects of this approach,
suggests that individuals are selected and then turned into criminals. The road to becoming a deviant is marked by
a number of steps and at each step there is a choice, made
by the representatives of society, as to whether this particular individual shall be sent back into the general
population or marked for further deviant processing. The
steps society takes with regard to juveniles probably begin in school, but are clearly taken in the police decision
to arrest, and in the decision by the police to warn and
dismiss or refer on to local authority or probation department. Further steps occur when the social work agency
decides to go to a court or panel hearing and when the
disposition is commitment to an institution. During this
process a child becomes re-defined as a delinquent; a role
which has the characteristics of a master status. Being

delinquent now defines and explains all past history - 'he really was a thief all along' - and it predicts future behaviour. It is present all the time in all situations and the child begins to think of himself as a delinquent and to adjust his self image to this new label. Having once acquired the label, he is much more likely to be arrested a second time, not, it is contended, because he commits more criminal acts than other people, but because he is now known as a delinquent by public and police, and sees himself in this light.

The community approach sees the juvenile court as one, perhaps the primary one, of a number of agencies whose function it is to label and stigmatise selected children. A juvenile court hearing serves the purposes of a degradation ceremony. Lemert develops this viewpoint:(31)

> Stigmatization is a process which assigns marks of moral inferiority to deviants; more simply it is a form of degradation which transforms identities and status for the worse. It is both implicit and explicit in formal procedures in the court.

Children subjected to processing are not randomly selected. They come from the poorer and more disadvantaged groups in society, whose values and behavioural patterns may run counter to those of the prevailing middle-class establishment. In addition they suffer from powerlessness and do not have access to the methods of rebutting deviant labelling which better educated, better housed and more adequately financed families usually have.

Within such an approach the court can have no positive function, and the only treatment possible for so-called juvenile delinquents is to prevent their further labelling and to divert them as soon as possible out of the system. If criminals are just ordinary citizens selected as victims, rather as in more primitive societies some members were selected for human sacrifices, then the way to reduce crime is to stop labelling people criminals. Children must be referred to non-stigmatising agencies such as the youth service bureaux of the United States, social work departments in Scotland and social service agencies in England. This, however, is only in the nature of first aid, since the real focus of attention must be the community itself. If delinquency is not an individual phenomenon, but a status created by society to serve its need for a scapegoat, then society must change. How such change is to be brought about and who will take responsibility for it is still unclear, but, as Lemert, here with reference to children, suggests:(32)

> it seems safest to hold that diversion of children and youth from the official court system is a state of mind;

once it is established as a predominant social value,
the question of adaptation of means to the end should
be more easily answered.

People who are the servants of the community approach do
not fall into any recognised professional grouping. They
may be politicians or revolutionaries, academic sociologists
or community workers. This illustrates the point, which is
less obvious in relation to the criminal justice and welfare
approaches, that we are considering are attitudes of mind
and that no one professional group has the monopoly of any
one attitude.

These approaches consist of values, ideas and actions
which hold together logically. However, it would be a mistake to assume that any individual person is likely to hold
all, and only, the ideas characteristic of one approach.
Human beings, because of their essential ambivalence, rational and emotional, conscious and unconscious, often believe in ideas which are rationally contradictory. Most
people, however, most of the time, are likely to feel more
comfortable with one of these approaches; but on special
issues or at particular points in their lives, they may
change their position and be influenced by another approach.
Walter Miller,(33) who has considered the ideology of criminal justice policy, suggests that, rather than distinct
ideologies, one should think of a continuum from radicalism
to conservatism, with general assumptions and crusading issues ranged on each side of a central point. While his suggestion of a continuum is hard to sustain, because the
assumptions chosen are not logically connected to each other
but rest on different value bases, his idea that people hold
different ideas on different issues seems a useful one.

The classification of sets of ideas which I have used
has similarities with those used in other recent writing.
Gilbert Smith,(34) in discussing ideology and the Scottish
children's panels, writes of 'three consistent sub-ideo-
logies': of law enforcement, social work and community
involvement. He does not define these in any detail, but
they appear to refer to groups of ideas similar to those
contained in the criminal justice, welfare and community
approaches. Schur(35) uses a slightly different division
of what he calls reactions to delinquency: those of individual treatment, liberal reform and radical non-intervention. He dismisses a fourth, 'a get tough anti-permis-
sive approach', because he claims, strangely I consider,
that it does not exert a significant influence on delinquency policies in the United States. I have grouped together within the welfare approach the ideas contained in
Schur's first two categories. The individual treatment
orientation has as its central organising feature the

assumption that delinquents are biologically or psychologically different from non-delinquents. This assumption
distinguishes it from the liberal reform orientation, which
maintains that delinquents can be distinguished from non-
delinquents by the social conditions to which they have
been exposed. However, Schur admits that research and
policy-making in the field of delinquency have reflected
the combined influence of these two orientations and that
'the line between them is actually rather hazy.'(36) The
much more important distinction is between these approaches,
which are grounded in assumptions about the basic difference
of delinquents, and the radical non-intervention orientation,
which resembles my community approach. This repudiates the
idea that delinquents are basically different, except that
they have been processed by the juvenile justice system.

    Apart from those who have classified a number of ap-
proaches, a variety of names are being used to describe the
groups of ideas and actions which make up the individual
approaches. The term justice model has begun to appear in
recent writings(37) about the parole board, and this model
resembles my criminal justice approach, particularly in
the stress upon rights. There are several names used for
what I have called the welfare approach. In the United
States the early juvenile court movement used the doctrine
of *parens patriae* - the State as father of the people - to
suggest a family model for the juvenile court. The term
guardianship has some of the same connotations. David May,
(38) relying heavily on the work of an American legal scho-
lar, F.A. Allen,(39) makes use of the term treatment model
to describe the same general set of ideas which are also
included in the term rehabilitative ideal. Finally, a recent work on the role of defence attorneys in juvenile
courts, refers to the child saving model, a term made popular again by Platt's(4)) book of that title which explored
the actions and motives of the people responsible for the
first juvenile court act in Chicago in 1898.(41)

THE BALANCE IN JUVENILE JUSTICE

It is my contention of this book that the juvenile justice
system provides a meeting place for the different approaches
of criminal justice, welfare and the community. Here the
child as a threat to society, the child whose potential is
being restricted, and the child who is the victim of the
community, meet in the actual person of an individual
child; here society either manages or fails to achieve a
compromise between the competing viewpoints. The outcome
needs to be a compromise because the juvenile court is

operating in that area between the individual and the other, where to ignore the rights or needs of either side is ultimately to fail. The system has to balance the child's rights against his needs and society's right to protection against its need for individuals who have developed to their full potential.

On another level the juvenile justice system, in providing a meeting place for these different ideas, also provides a meeting place for the mixture of feelings which we all possess. The discussion of the criminal justice, welfare and community approaches has been misleading if it has suggested that it is a matter only of different groups in society selecting and maintaining one approach. The underlying feelings represented in these approaches are to be found inside each man. Within each human being feelings of love and hate, of healing and hurting, of forgiveness and revenge, battle with each other. A desire to hurt and a wish to care coexist, and this is the essential ambivalence of man's nature. Some psychoanalysts consider that the achievement and then the management of these conflicts are the major tasks of maturing. Winnicott(42) wrote of 'the achievement of ambivalence' and regarded it as a desirable attribute because it created the possibility of concern for others. He wrote about individuals, but it is possible that man-made institutions also have to reflect such mixed emotions. If these arguments are right, then those within the juvenile justice system should not manage these conflicting viewpoints by opting for one to the exclusion of the others. Rather it is essential that the system allow for the expression in action of all three approaches, and that it maintain not an equal but a shifting balance in which no aspect ever goes entirely out of sight.

There are many who would not agree with this view of the function which a juvenile justice system should perform. Mead thinks we delude ourselves in even making an attempt at balancing such mixed feelings:(43)

It is quite impossible psychologically to hate the sin and love the sinner. We are very much given to cheating ourselves in this respect. We assume that we can detect, pursue, indict, prosecute, and punish the criminal and still retain toward him the attitude of reinstating him in the community as soon as he indicates a change in social attitude himself, that we can at the same time overwhelm the offender, and comprehend the situation out of which the offense grows. But the two attitudes, that of control of crime by the hostile procedure of the law and that of control through comprehension of social and psychological conditions, cannot

be combined. To understand is to forgive and the
social procedure seems to deny the very responsibility
which the law affirms, and on the other hand, the pursuit by criminal justice inevitably awakens the hostile
attitude in the offender and renders the attitude of
mutual comprehension practically impossible. The social
worker in the court is the sentimentalist, and the legal-
ist in the social settlement in spite of his learned doctrine is the ignoramus.

The report of the Friends Service Committee rejects the
whole attempt at individualising justice and argues for a
return to equal justice in which the punishment fits the
crime and not the criminal. They suggest:(44)

The paradigm of the system . . . is the role of the
parole officer, whose job is simultaneously to help the
parolee under his supervision and to protect society
from that same parolee. The resulting role conflict
of having to serve two masters - the client and the
state - corrodes the mutual trust necessary for therapy
and invites the pollution of service by reducing it to
a manipulative device whereby the officer's control-
police function can be facilitated.

Such writers seem to be considering the approach of criminal justice and welfare at their most extreme and most
conflicting. Nearer the centre, the family seems to provide
a model of concern and control intermingling and coexisting.
Too much is lost by going to the extremes, as Roscoe Pound
suggests:(45)

If we work out a system of making penal treatment fit
the crime, we risk losing sight of the individual delinquent in pursuit of system. If we look only at the
individual delinquent, we risk losing system in pursuit of individual treatment, and lose the objec-
tivity which is demanded when we are constraining the
individual by the force of politically organised society. It comes down to the reconciling of the general security with the individual life, which as I have
said is a fundamental problem of the whole legal order.

Conflicting aims are a reality but, as Fox(46) points out,
they are not necessarily 'a misfortune'. Most social institutions of any importance have multiple aims, and we
do not necessarily consider this a drawback. It may be
enlivening and a point of growth in families, marriages,
schools and universities that they have more than one aim
and that decisions as to priorities are continually necessary. Conflict carries a negative connotation but, when
seen as choices or challenges, such situations may be con-
ducive to freedom and growth. What is important, as Allen
points out, is that the conflict or choices be recognised:(47)

The juvenile court, both in theory and practice, is an
institution of remarkable complexity. It is called
upon to perform a bewildering variety of functions.
On the one hand, it administers what are essentially
welfare functions, such as the exercise of its dependency jurisdiction. On the other hand, it may be required to provide a forum for criminal prosecution, as
in cases of adults alleged to have contributed to the
delinquency of minors. The juvenile court is a court;
but it is also a governmental agency charged with mani-
fold administrative responsibilities and, in some localities, the performance of clinical services. Not
only does the court perform a variety of functions and
assume a variety of roles, it must inevitably express
a wide range of values and aspirations. But functions
conflict and values collide; hence, there must be
some sort of mediation or accommodation of the various
goals and values if the institution is to function at
all. This accommodation and compromise may result from
intelligent deliberation or it may be the product of
caprice and indifference.

The need for intelligent deliberation is the greater
because of the ease with which the welfare approach can
become corrupted in action. Much that has been done in
the name of welfare has been manipulative and punitive,
as the history of juvenile courts in the United States
will show. Juvenile justice has been noticeable for the
gap between its rhetoric and its reality. The rhetoric
tends to be that of welfare, whereas the reality has often
proved to be cruelly punitive and deterrent. Allen points
out:(48)

It is important, first, to recognize that when, in an
authoritative setting, we attempt to do something *for*
a child 'because of what he is and needs', we are also
doing something *to* him. The semantics of 'socialized
justice' are a trap for the unwary. Whatever one's
motivations, however elevated one's objectives, if the
measures taken result in the compulsory loss of the
child's liberty, the involuntary separation of a child
from his family, or even the supervision of a child's
activities by a probation worker, the impact on the
affected individuals is essentially a punitive one.
Good intentions and a flexible vocabulary do not alter
this reality. This is particularly so when, as is often
the case, the institution to which the child is committed is, in fact, a penocustodial establishment.

This quotation suggests not only that ideals can be cur-
rupted in practice, but that what may be seen as helping
by one group may be regarded as punishment by another. If

the aim were only to control or only to care, it might be
possible to ensure that such aims were more frequently
translated into appropriate action. But, even if the aim
is care, the means involve compulsion, and it is this which
tends to corrupt the caring. In such a situation, rights
must be protected in courts and hearings because by protecting rights the rhetoric of welfare is more likely to
be translated into reality. It is also possible that the
aims of criminal justice can only be translated into
action when they are tempered by the compassion of the
welfare approach. Detention centres, which were intended
to provide a short, sharp shock, soon lost their most rigid
and punitive features, and introduced plans for rehabilitation as a result of public criticism of their original
conception. Similarly, in the nineteenth century, juries
refused to convict children, even those who were clearly
guilty, when the punishments for minor crimes were in their
view too harsh. Welfare seasons a criminal justice approach
and criminal justice serves to ensure that the personnel of
the welfare approach do not become corrupted by the power
they have. The community approach serves to check the emphasis on the individual, which can distort both the criminal justice and the welfare approach.

Chapter two

United States: historical background to the juvenile court—before 1900

New ideas, new movements, new countries, all act at first
as if they were superseding history. To have a history,
however, means to be heir to tragic guilt as well as to
past error.(1)

Some twentieth-century writers give the impression that
the idea of a juvenile court was something which, by seren-
dipity or mutation in the minds of lawyers and social reformers, had arisen in Cook County, Illinois, in 1898. This
was far from the case, although there was in the Act(2) of
that date, which established juvenile courts, one new element which was to have an important influence upon future
developments. This was that children who violated the criminal code were to be dealt with, not as criminals by a
criminal court, but as delinquents who were subject to a
court's civil jurisdiction. Apart from this innovation,
the Act created little that was new if one looked at the
United States as a whole. The Illinois Act, and those
which followed it in other States, drew together and applied in one State provisions for the adjudication and
treatment of children which had existed singly in individual States before. These Acts came at the end of a century of developments which had separated children from
criminal and pauper adults at all stages of the judicial
and treatment process in order to prevent their too becoming criminals and paupers.

It is not the purpose of this chapter to give a history
of the treatment of juvenile offenders and destitute children in the United States in the nineteenth century. We
consider some of the ideas, and the institutions to which
they gave rise, only as a basis for understanding what the
juvenile court movement inherited and how its twentieth-
century progress was largely determined by its nineteenth-
century ancestry.

SOCIAL CONDITIONS IN THE NINETEENTH CENTURY

The American colonists had established a system of law
based upon the Common Law system of England. Court systems and the statutes of the different states varied a
little, but their common ancestry was clearly recognis-
able.(3) They had also imported the English Poor Law, which
had originated with the statute of Elizabeth I, and which
placed the control of vagrants and the support of the in-
firm, young or aged poor in the hands of local guardians.
At the beginning of the nineteenth century few special provisions were made for children, either by the criminal laws
of the States or by the Poor Laws. Children over seven
years old who committed crimes were tried in the same courts
and suffered the same punishments as adults, whether the
punishment was imprisonment, the whipping post or the pil-
lory. No doubt judges and juries at times refused to
convict children, especially those just over seven years
old, at which age they were assumed capable of a guilty
mind, but unless the courts took pity in individual cases
there was no general way within the criminal law of dealing with children differently from adults. Similarly with
the Poor Law. Children who were found to be vagrants or
destitute were committed by the guardians to the county
poor houses or farms although unlike adults they were also
boarded out.

Such procedures were tolerable in a stable rural community where crime and pauperism were rare. The nineteenth
century, however, was one in which cities grew at an ever
accelerating speed. The population of New York, Manhattan
and Brooklyn was 87,027 in 1709, 1,350,544 in 1850, and by
1900 was 3,360,397. This increase was typical of the
growth of the eastern cities and Chicago and resulted in
part from the continuous flow of immigrants from Europe.
The immigrants brought social problems in their train, especially when they had no savings to tide them over the
pains of resettlement. Such was frequently the situation
with the Irish immigrants who arrived by the boatload in
the early nineteenth century to escape the conditions of
their own country and to supply the need for labour in the
new world. They had nothing to cushion them against misfortune, and many joined the crowds of poor and desperate
people which were beginning to be a feature of the cities.
These cities faced the problem of adapting a system of local
government and social control based upon a stable rural way
of life, to the new explosive urban situation. City life
created new situations and also the realisation that solutions were urgently required. The growing pressures and
density of city life brought upper- and middle-class people

face to face with the everyday experiences of the poor. It
became impossible to ignore their plight and their threat.
A humanitarian concern for the suffering of the poor linked
itself closely with a fear for the future of self and society, should the poor become desperate enough to revolt.
Pickett, in describing a group of reform-minded Quakers
in New York, at the beginning of the nineteenth century,
says:(4)

> these men, some of New York City's most important citi-
> zens had sensed the existence of a growing body of poor
> people within their city. The flood of idlers had
> swelled to frightening proportions. Discharged soldiers,
> unemployed artisans, rootless immigrants, bewildered
> widows and orphaned children blended into the mass of
> discontented paupers. The presence of so many desper-
> ate men and women, many without a penny in their pock-
> ets, frightened the city's more substantial citizens.

Charles Loring Brace, writing in 1880 and referring to New
York City as it was earlier in the century, says:(5)

> It has been common, since the recent terrible Communis-
> tic outbreak in Paris, to assume that France alone is
> exposed to such horrors; but, in the judgement of one
> who has been familiar with our 'dangerous classes' for
> twenty years, there are just the same explosive social
> elements beneath the surface of New York as of Paris.
>
> There are thousands on thousands in New York who have
> no assignable home, and 'flit' from attic to attic, and
> cellar to cellar; there are other thousands more or
> less connected with criminal enterprises; and still
> other tens of thousands, poor, hardpressed, and depend-
> ing for daily bread on the day's earnings, swarming in
> tenement-houses, who behold the gilded rewards of toil
> all about them, but are never permitted to touch them.
>
> All these great masses of destitute, miserable, and
> criminal persons believe that for ages the rich have had
> all the good things of life, while to them have been
> left the evil things. Capital to them is the tyrant.
>
> Let but Law lift its hand from them for a season, or
> let the civilizing influences of American life fail to
> reach them, and, if the opportunity offered, we should
> see an explosion from this class which might leave this
> city in ashes and blood.

Such conditions spurred the planning and creation of
services which were to transform the towns of the early
nineteenth century into the cities of the twentieth; which
led to the provision of sanitation, housing, education and
care for children and to new forms of local government and
policing. We regard such things as part of a citizen's
rights, but in 1800 they had yet to be created. Thus pro-

visions for children in trouble were part of the development of social services in the widest sense. It was the
growth of towns which drew attention to the needs and the
threat of children and, to a large extent, created these
needs. Individual deviant children have no doubt always
existed, but widespread delinquency and concern about it
accompanies the growth of cities. Juvenile delinquency
and its control was, and still is, essentially an urban
problem.

The next section will consider the institutions which
were created in the United States during the nineteenth
century before turning to the philosophy underlying their
development.

HOUSES OF REFUGE AND REFORMATORIES

At the end of the eighteenth century there were very few
institutions for children in the United States. An orphanage had been founded in New Orleans in 1779 and one in
Charleston in 1790. In 1800 a home was opened in Philadelphia for 'girls who in an unguarded hour have been
robbed of their innocence and sunk into wretchedness and
vice'.(6) It was in the 1820s that a burst of activity
took place in the building of institutions and resulted in
the establishment of homes for the type of children who
today would be the responsibility of juvenile courts. New
York led Boston by one year in being the first city to
establish a separate institution for the care of children
who otherwise would have been sent either to the city's
jails and prisons or to its workhouses. In 1825 the
Society for the Prevention of Juvenile Delinquency opened
the New York House of Refuge in a converted barracks in
Madison Square, bought from the federal administration. The
New York State Legislature authorised the House to take
children who would otherwise have been sentenced to prison,
and a year later, in 1826, they allocated public funds to
the House. Administrative and policy decisions were made
by a committee of the Society, and the House admitted
'vagrant and depraved young people' of both sexes. In
Boston, which already had a home for neglected children,
the city council opened a House of Reformation in 1826 to
take youths convicted of crimes, who formerly had been
sent to the state prison. By the time of Dickens's visit
in 1842 the city had also established a school for potential delinquents, called Boylston School. Dickens compared the residents here with those in the House of Reformation, finding them a 'more chubby full waist coated set
of boys'.(7) Boston had other institutions established by

voluntary groups. Two amalgamated in 1834, to become the
Boston Asylum and Farm School, which admitted minor offenders, potential delinquents and, later in its history, neglected children. In 1842 a Farm School on Thompson Island
in Boston harbour was established for 'boys exposed to
extraordinary temptations and in danger of becoming vicious
and dangerous'.(8) Boston and New York were not the only
cities to start institutions; Philadelphia started a House
of Refuge in 1828 and, by 1850, New Orleans, Cincinnati,
Rochester, Pittsburgh and Baltimore also had Houses of
Refuge.

The impetus for building Houses of Refuge seems to have
died out by the middle of the century and the reform school
movement replaced it. These schools were often based upon
a cottage, or what Wines calls a family system. Unlike the
Houses of Refuge, they were usually in the country. This
siting reflected a belief, which still lingers, that open
spaces and green fields have a healing effect upon troubled
children. In addition the reformatories emphasised work
training and, being in the country, could provide experience of agriculture. This was regarded as particularly
useful, not only as a training but as a preparation for a
future life away from the temptations of cities. E.C. Wines
expressed these ideas, although the following lyrical account comes from his description of an orphanage, not of a
reformatory. The institution he describes is the New Hampshire Orphans Home, which had about forty children in it
and which was started in the farmhouse where Daniel Webster
was born. Since it illustrates many of the ideas of the
time, I quote the description in full:(9)

Mr and Mrs Mack as superintendent and matron have been
in charge from the first, and more competent and devoted
persons it would be difficult to find. Mrs Mack is said
to be to a wonderful degree 'the right woman in the
right place'. All the children call her 'mother', and
she never fails to be in their confidence and love. She
goes to bring the little ones to their orphan home, and
she goes to place them in their new homes when they
leave it. From cutting up and salting meat in the cel-
lar she is called to entertain distinguished visitors
in the drawing-room, and she fills both positions with
equal fitness. She is matron, nurse, book-keeper,
correspondent-general, counsellor, judge, jury, and
executor of discipline, all in one. There is no gap
she cannot fill. Now she cuts the hundred little gar-
ments, now with comb and scissors she goes the round of
little heads (not always a pleasant task with the new-
comers), then she sits darning far into the 'wee short
hours', lest tiny toes be bitten by Jack Frost, and

next day she teaches the boys to sew on buttons. With
opening spring she leads her little flock to the large
garden; how proud they are to carry some implement,
or run back on some errand! They watch Mrs Mack and
her son as they form the beds, plant the seeds, weed,
hoe, etc.

'I can do that', cries one.

'So you can', she replies, 'and each of you shall have
a little plot, use the tools, and play farmer. Here,
divide these seeds between you, and I will buy all you
raise.'

'Can't I have this spot?' asks another.

'Yes'; and the little fellow digs and tugs at the
sod till he builds a turf wall about his 'farm'. 'My
boys are safe for weeks in their gardens', she says. It
is real play and real work as well. When the lettuce,
the quart of beans, the few ears of corn, the melon,
the half-dozen cucumbers come in, she is as pleased and
proud as the boys. 'Now what shall I pay you in? -
money, a knife (that joy of a boy's heart), a book, a
toy, or what? You may choose.'

How wisely is such pay invested! Next time help is
needed on the farm how delightedly the boys enlist in
the hoeing brigade, the corn-club, or in any corps to
do any work that may be pressing! Once it was two
bushels of potato beetles they picked, and saved the
crop. Boys so trained will always love farm-work, and
farm-work is what they most need to learn.

Ah! this is the sort of place needed for the little
waifs of society - the street Arabs - be they orphans,
or simply destitute, neglected wanderers. Begin with
the child, for the man begins in him. It is important
that life starts right. There are thousands of children who live in the streets, orphans tossed about by
the social wave; others who have parents, but parents
who train them to evil. Both these classes are made up
of children that follow the great army of crime - born
for it, brought up for it. All this little world is
borne along by a current that rushes ever towards the
deep sea. We must draw it to the shore. We must
wrest it by force if need be from those who ought to
save it, but who only speed it towards the abyss; from
those who invoke upon its rights only to betray their
duties. We must gather, shelter, elevate, educate
these little ones; and the place of education is the
country, the fields. Make as many tillers of the soil
as you can. Fieldwork is more healthy than shopwork -
to the soul as well as to the body; and the Webster
farm is the right spot for this right work; its moral

associations are inspiring, its rural charms exquisite.
One of the later visits paid to the old homestead by
the illustrious statesman and orator was in the summer
of 1848. Looking out from the eastern window seaward,
he wrote to his son on that occasion. 'This is the most
beautiful place on this earth. Adopting the language
of Alexander Pope when describing his "Boxwood" I say, -
                "Here let me live, here let me die,
                And one small stone tell where I lie."'
    What better place can be found for the boys and girls
gathered there by the loving hand of Christian charity,
and who are
                'To fame and fortune now unknown!'
    Alongside the positive reasons for placing reformatories
in the country, there was also the need to protect the public. The reformatories were probably catering for a more
clearly criminal group of children than were the Houses of
Refuge and had greater need to consider public opinion.
The country had the advantages of isolation and obscurity,
for neither nineteenth- nor twentieth-century citizens welcome offenders as their close neighbours. These political
factors were likely to be important, since reform schools
were usually established by legislative act and were often
run directly by the state department of charities and/or
corrections. This department might be the same as that
responsible for the state prisons and penitentiaries, and
thus reform schools were linked to the penal system. Their
aims, however, were both correctional and educational, as
developments in Indiana reflected.
    Indiana was a State which had not had a House of Refuge
early in the century. In 1855 the legislature authorised
the purchase of land and the seeking of donations for a
House of Refuge, which was contemplated 'not merely as a
place of correction but a reform school where the youth
can receive physical, intellectual and moral training'.(10)
In 1883 the name was changed to Reform School for Boys.
This school was to receive any boy aged over eight and
under sixteen arraigned for violation of a criminal law,
infants whose parents made a complaint that they were
incorrigible or who were vagrants or destitute of a home
or means of making a living and in danger of being brought
up to lead an idle and immoral life. The institutions for
girls in Indiana have a similar history. Originally girls
were admitted to a House of Refuge, but in 1869 the Indiana
Reformatory Institution for Women and Girls(11) was established, with two distinct departments: a prison and a reformatory. Girls under fifteen were sent to the reformatory department for incorrigibility, vagrancy, moral depravity, criminal acts and misdemeanors. In 1889 the name

was changed to Reform School for Girls, although the
grounds for admission of girls remained the same.

In time the types and the numbers of institutions mul-
tiplied. While the legislature established reform schools,
private organisations set up industrial schools catering
for similar, if slightly less criminal, types of children.
By the 1880s New York had thirty-three industrial schools
run by voluntary agencies. The further one moved either
south or west from the coast and the large cities, the
fewer were the residential provisions for children. In
1880 Wines(12) was unable to discover any reformatories
and very few institutions of any kind for children in
Nebraska, Oregon, Nevada, West Virginia, Delaware, Texas,
Louisiana, Florida, South Carolina, Mississippi, Arkansas,
Alabama, Tennessee and Virginia. This confirms the view
that the problems are essentially city problems and that
the States which built reform schools and whose citizens
supported voluntary homes were those with the large towns
in their midst. These States had considerable influence
on each other. Conferences of reform school managers were
held in New York in 1857 and 1859, and from 1874 the yearly
Conference of Charities and Corrections had a section for
reformatories and institutions.

FOSTER HOMES

The aim of the institutions described in the last section
was to separate juvenile from adult offenders and paupers,
but there were other means of achieving this. The nineteenth century saw the growth of an alternative to institutions in the form of foster homes and apprenticeship
schemes. From its first year the New York House of Refuge
placed children out as servants and sent others to families
in the west, after they had spent a period in the House.
This became a regular pattern with most refuges and later
with the reformatories. The institutions varied in their
policies as to where children should be sent. Wines says
many of the children who had passed through the New Hampshire home had been 'provided with permanent Christian
homes, chiefly on the soil of New Hampshire; for the
policy of expatriation to the "great West", or even to
Vermont and Massachusetts, is not popular'.(13) However,
there was little criticism of fostering out itself as a
policy.

Some children were fostered after a period in an institution, but many others were placed direct from their own
families by agencies like the Children's Aid Society and
the New York Juvenile Asylum. When it was founded in 1853

the Children's Aid Society needed to place 207 boys; by
1888 it had already placed 85,890. The director, Charles
L. Brace, described the method of placement to the Conference on Charities in 1876:(14)

> The resident western agent, whose headquarters are at
> Chicago, discovers a farming locality where the assis-
> tance of children is needed. He procures the names of
> a few prominent citizens who will aid in the matter.
> Public notice is given, some weeks beforehand, that a
> company of orphans and homeless children from New York
> will come there on a given day. The farmers gather from
> the country for miles around. The little company of un-
> fortunates, under charge of an experienced agent, are
> billeted around among the families of the village, fed
> and washed, and then appear in the town hall or whatever
> place has been selected for the meeting. Here the agent,
> advised by some of the citizens, forms a committee of
> some of the leading men present. This committee decide
> upon the applications, on consultation of the agent.
> After a few hours' labour, each child is placed in a
> home, and it usually happens, that these homes are the
> best in the country around. The employers agree to send
> the children to school in the winter, and of course to
> treat them kindly. Beyond that, there is no agreement
> and no indentures are made out. The relation is left
> much to the good feeling of both parties.

Miss Davenport Hill quotes the Society's reports on the
results of placements:(15)

> The inspector of the children placed in the far West
> reports that one acute youth invested eleven dollars on
> the 4th of July in an ice-cream and lemonade stand, and
> cleared a net profit of thirty-two dollars, 'besides
> taking the premium in the day's Hoodlum Carnival as a
> hyena ably personated'. Other boys write of 'real and
> personal property', of buying their claims, of losses,
> investments, gains; and the tone is uniformly manly
> and plucky. One young fellow who had done well and
> married, boasts a 'good mother-in-law weighing 200
> pounds', an original way of estimating such a relation.
> He has married, he says, her last girl, and as she is
> so big 'this leaves her in bad shape', and he begs the
> Society to send a girl to help her, promising in return
> kindness and a good home. He asks for inquiries to be
> made for his own mother, from whom he has heard nothing
> since he was twelve. This touching desire to hear of
> long-lost relations reveals itself in many of the let-
> ters, sometimes to lead to cruel disappointment, but now
> and then to be gratified by a happy reunion. One letter
> begins with tender raptures over the coming delight of

finding mother, father and sister after twenty years'
severance. The writer yearns to see them, 'no matter
how poor they are, so they are upright and honest'.
She would fly to them - only business is very brisk
just now; so she contents herself with begging them to
kiss themselves for her. One young man of restless disposition, describing his many wanderings, says 'I don't
like Kansas; it runs to extremes in its weather'. Another writes sadly: 'I haven't got anything except a
good wife and a nice little girl 28 months old. My
moving around so much explains my not having (*sic*). It
is a business (a nursery garden business he had taken
up) that I don't like very well, for I am not naturally
a big talker, but, of course, we can't all have our
likes. I would rather have a business that I can grow
up faster in.'
Other States in the east besides New York developed
Children's Aid and like societies to place deprived and
neglected children in foster homes, as well as to provide
lodging houses and clubs, hostels and homes in the towns
where they were born. By the end of the century a range of
provision existed for children, and in future some children
were to find their way to these establishments through the
juvenile court.

THE PROBATION SYSTEM

Institutions and placements separated troublesome children
from criminal and pauper adults. There also developed
administrative arrangements which the juvenile court was to
adopt, which were essential to the individualisation of justice for children, and which came to be known as the probation system. Probation refers both to a type of sentence
and to an administrative structure. They are not inseparable but are now usually found together, and the term probation covers both aspects. The man credited with founding
this system is John Augustus, who was a shoemaker in Boston.
In 1841, according to his own account, he happened to be in
the Boston court and saw a drunkard who was about to be
locked up because he was unable to pay his fine. John
Augustus asked the court to allow the defendant a short
probation period during which he would be placed in John's
care. The court agreed and fixed a date for the defendant
to re-appear. In the meantime John Augustus helped him to
find work and persuaded him to take the pledge. This was
just the beginning, for John Augustus reports: 'I made up
my mind hereafter (June, 1842) to recognise women's rights
and that the very next woman who applied to me for bail for

her - if I found her a worthy object of aid - I would do it.'(16)

By 1858 John had bailed 1,152 men and boys and 784 women and girls, and after the first two years had extended his help to others besides drunkards. With such a caseload John Augustus found little time for his shoemaking and fell back on his friends for subscriptions to keep his work going. He must have been a fascinating character, full of vitality, fighting corruption and self-interest in the courts with 'that tongue of his which appears to be hung in the middle and oiled at each end'.(17) Like all reformers who treated criminals with humanity and as individuals, he stirred up fear and hatred in the righteous and was accused of creating crime. Despite this, the method he started developed rapidly and became a system instead of a one man crusade. In 1863 the Children's Aid Society was started in Boston and two of its first workers continued John Augustus's work. Rufus R. Cook stood bondsman for children and Miss L.P. Burnham insisted on investigating each child's history and background to determine whether they were suitable cases for reformation.

Massachusetts legislators established probation as a sentence available to all courts. The first probation laws were passed in 1878 and were made mandatory in 1890. The State also developed the administrative aspects of probation. In 1879 the legislature created a State Board of Health, Lunacy and Charity, supported by a State visiting agency. Miss Davenport Hiss described the duties of this agency:(18)

It is the duty of the Head of the Agency, who holds his appointment direct from Government, to attend in person or by deputy whenever a child is brought before the Court. Mr Joseph Sturge, in an instructive and very interesting Memorandum on the Massachusetts Plan, describes the duties performed towards the little ward, which are those of friend and counsel too - of counsel in the best sense, not bent on 'getting off' his client, but, after a full elucidation of all the circumstances, securing for him those conditions which shall enable him to grow up a useful and happy citizen. Sometimes the Agent interposes on behalf of a child before it appears in Court, and by arrangement with its parent or by other means rescues it from a position of danger or misery.

The Act gave the court powers which read much like those later given to juvenile courts. Any judge or magistrate could commit a person under seventeen to the Board of Health, Lunacy and Charity. The Board, acting through their visiting agency, could deal with the child in the following ways:(19)

(1) It may be left, with a warning and under supervision,
with its parent, who is usually fined in a small sum for
costs; but power is retained to remove the child in case
of non-improvement. Thus its continuance at home becomes
a period of wholesome probation to both child and parent.
About four-fifths of the 75 per cent of children committed are thus returned to their parents, and a very small
proportion of these in after years reappear in the Courts
to be more severely dealt with. (2) If removal from the
parent be deemed necessary, the Board can send the child
to the State Primary School, which is not a criminal institution, Magistrates having no power to commit to it;
or (3) to a Reformatory, or (4) even to gaol (but the
latter alternative is rarely resorted to); and thence
to homes when such transference seems desirable. Or
(5) it may be, like the orphan or destitute child, board-
ed-out with payment, or (6) placed out without payment
according to circumstances, very great care being exercised in selecting the homes, whether of employers or
foster-parents. (7) Orphans may be placed on adoption,
but only after trial. (8) The Board can also appoint a
Guardian to a child; the Guardian thenceforth possess-
ing over it, until the age of twenty-one, full parental
power, to the nullifying of the power of its real parents
if it possess them.

A somewhat similar plan is found in the Act establishing the
Board of Children's Guardians established in Indiana in
1889:(20)

All townships of more than 75,000 shall have a Board
composed of 6 persons - 3 of whom shall be women - who
shall have the care and supervision of neglected and
dependent children under 15 years of age. They shall
take such children as are abandoned, neglected, or
cruelly treated by their parents; children begging on
the streets, children of habitually drunk or vicious or
immoral parents, children kept in vicious or immoral
association; children known by their language and their
life to be immoral, vicious or incorrigible; juvenile
delinquents and truants. The Board is to provide a
temporary home for such children or may, with leave of
the Circuit Court, commit them to orphan asylums, the
House of Refuge or Indiana Reformatory for Women and
Girls, or may, under order of the Court, indenture them
as apprentices or have them be adopted, without the consent of parents of said child.

When the Board has reason to believe any of the above
situations exists, it shall file a petition to the Circuit Court and the Court shall issue a writ for custody
of such child and the Board can keep the child in a Home

until the final order of the Court upon the petition.
The child is committed to the custory of the Board if
any of the above situations exists.

By the end of the century the idea of separating children
from adults after a court appearance was well established.
Special forms of treatment existed for children, and the
beginnings of an administrative structure to support the
courts had been made. Other developments took place which
were to be worked out fully in the twentieth century.
There was pressure to separate children from adults at an
earlier stage and to arrange for special sittings of the
courts when children's cases were being considered. In
Massachusetts a law of 1870 required a special session of
the court for hearing cases against juveniles in Suffolk
County, and this was extended to the rest of the State in
1872, with a requirement that the governor should appoint
trial justices for juvenile offenders. In Chicago a provision of 1861 authorised the mayor to appoint a commissioner before whom boys aged six to sixteen could be
brought for petty offences. The commissioner could place
them under supervision or send them to the reform school.
This provision had a short life, as in 1867 the powers conferred on the commissioner were transferred to the regular
judges. In New York in 1892 a new section was added to the
penal code, allowing for separate trial and special dockets
and records for children under sixteen years of age. Rhode
Island required separate trial of juveniles after 1898.

Almost all the features of a juvenile justice system now
existed in some State. What happened in Illinois in 1898
was that all these features were brought together in one
system and applied to one area.

THE INFLUENCE OF CRIMINAL JUSTICE, WELFARE AND COMMUNITY
APPROACHES

This brief account of the developments in social institutions during the nineteenth century provides a backdrop
against which to consider the ideas of the people within
and outside government who sponsored such developments.
The provisions they made for troubled and troublesome
children resulted from the growing influence of a welfare
approach, although a community approach was not entirely
lacking, as the Society for the Prevention of Pauperism
illustrates.

The reformers, prompted by a mixture of fear and concern,
were interested in causes, especially whether poverty and
crime were attributable to individual inadequacy or to
large-scale social and economic factors. Pickett points

out that while some reformers, some of the time, identified structural factors, many, much of the time, 'looked upon social and economic unrest primarily as a crisis brought on by the inherent sinfulness of individual human beings'. (21) It is extremely difficult to hold to a view that individual anti-social behaviour is determined, not by personal psychological factors, but by general sociological influences. Even today it is a view more easily maintained by academics than by those who are trying to deal with individual children who are in conflict with the law. There seem to be two reasons for this: first, the theoretical links between general social conditions and individual behaviour are tenuous. One is required to move from a general to a particular level of thinking, and the intermediate steps are hard to establish. Second, the economic and social problems seem so insoluble to an individual reformer or even to a group, that causes are forgotten and thinking about treatment takes place at the individual level. This occurred amongst the reformers in New York. In 1819 a group of quakers established themselves as the Society for the Prevention of Pauperism. They were centred around John Griscom, who was a school administrator and professor of chemistry, and a retired business man called Thomas Eddy. The latter was well aware of the problems of the poor in the city, as he had played a part in creating a hospital and an insane asylum and in founding the Free School Society. He had also designed, and later administered, New York State's first penitentiary. The new society aimed at conducting 'an operation on the causes of poverty. Whatever contributed to the increase of want and crime they sought to isolate, examine and eliminate'. (22) This proved too great a task, and the move of the group in 1823 to rename themselves the Society for the Reform of Juvenile Delinquents, shows how they found it necessary to concentrate their aims. What they ultimately did was to found the New York House of Refuge, which set the pattern for similar institutions in many other cities. This change from a wide concern with the causes of crime and poverty to a narrow focus upon founding an individual institution, is a process with which we ourselves are familiar. Like these nineteenth-century Quakers, we may see the causes of delinquency as lying in the social, political or economic conditions of the poorer people of our cities. Unwilling or powerless to deal with the root causes, we set up institutions to deal with the results of these conditions. This is not to suggest that remedial action is not required, but that it offers a fall back position when prevention seems impossible. Prevention may be better than cure, but it can also be harder to achieve.

We slip from a community to a welfare approach when faced with demands for action.

The reformers in New York established a special residential facility for certain children. What was later to become a system of juvenile justice, in both Britain and the United States, had its roots in such separate treatment facilities for some children. Separation was thought essential because of contamination. Contamination is one of a number of focal concerns(23) which arise when criminal justice and welfare approaches both exert their influence. It was thought that future crime or pauperism could be prevented if the contamination of the more or less ignorant and innocent by the knowledgeable and vicious were avoided. The method by which children who were potentially delinquent would become paupers and criminals was by being constantly exposed to paupers and criminals. The way to prevent this was to remove them from such contacts and teach them new ways to behave and new values to uphold. Moral education and an ordered and disciplined way of life were thought able to change a child, particularly if offered in an environment away from the child's former home and companions. This led to the removal of children from their own homes, but provided also a powerful argument for special residential provision for children. To remove children from their homes and then immure them with paupers in work farms or with adult criminals in prison, was only a means of ensuring the continuation of the evil which removal was supposed to cure. Concern with the dangers of contamination was widely expressed, and prisons and jails were blamed for creating criminals. We see the idea expressed by Pierce in his history of the New York House of Refuge. Writing in 1869, he quotes the remarks of an English writer, Buxton:(24)

When I first went to Newgate, my attention was directed by my companion to a boy whose apparent innocence and artlessness had attracted his notice. The schoolmaster said he was an example to all the rest; so quiet, so reserved, and so unwilling to have any intercourse with his dissolute companions. At his trial he was acquitted upon evidence which did not leave a shadow of suspicion upon him, but I lately recognised him again in Newgate, but with a very different character. He confessed to me, that, on his release, he had associated with the acquaintances formed in prison. Of his ruin I can feel but little doubt, and as little of the cause of it. He came to Newgate innocent; he left it corrupted.

In the same work is the testimony of a condemned murderer, of Douay, France:

'I await', said he to one who kindly visited him, 'the

hour of execution, and since you are the first person
who had visited me, I will address you with confidence
and conceal from you nothing. I am guilty of the dreadful crime for which I am to suffer, but from infancy my
parents neglected me. I had neither a moral example nor
a religious education. I was abandoned to the violence
of my passions. I fell when young into bad company,
by whom I was corrupted; but it was in prison that I
completed my ruin. Among the persons now in this apart-
ment are several boys, who, with pain I observe are preparing themselves for the further commission of offences,
when the term of their confinement shall expire. I en-
treat you to obtain their removal into a separate ward,
and snatch them from the contagion of such associates.
Believe me, and I speak from bitter experience, you can
confer on those boys no greater favor.'

The same ideas are expressed in the report produced by the
Society for the Prevention of Pauperism on the penitentiary
system in the United States:(25)

A State Prison must necessarily be filled with every
description of offenders, from him who is the least ob-
noxious to the laws, to him who is the most flagrant
aggressor. Felons, according to the ordinary principles
of our nature, will assimilate in moral character by
intercourse; and the standard which will be approached
and adopted, will not be the lowest, but the highest
degree of turpitude. The hardened convict will maintain his abandoned principles, and the novice in guilt
will become his pupil and convert. The greater offender
will not go to the lesser; the tendency is the reverse.
It requires no reflection to perceive, that without
classification, our penitentiaries, instead of preventing crimes, and reforming convicts, directly promote
crimes, and augment the moral baseness of convicts.
They are so many schools of vice - they are so many
seminaries to impart lessons and maxims calculated to
banish legal restraints, moral considerations, pride of
character, and self-regard.

The reformers were aware that there were also risks of
contamination within the institutions they created. They
attempted to deal with this in two ways: by classification
within an institution and by creating different kinds of
institutions. An example of the first is provided by the
House of Refuge in New York, where attempts were made to
classify children on arrival and to prevent the more innocent from mixing with the more corrupted. Wine's(26)
extraordinary survey of the prisons and child-saving institutions of the civilised world, published in 1880,
shows the extent to which alternative types of institutions

had developed. He lists the institutions for each State,
classifying them as reformatory or preventive. Under the
first he includes the reform schools for boys and the reform
and industrial schools for girls. Under preventive institutions he includes orphanages, homes run by religious societies for moral as well as actual orphans, homes for preg-
nant girls and for pre-delinquent youth.

Concern with the idea of contamination reinforced the
belief that, if children were to be saved, they needed a
new environment. Given the conditions in which the poor
lived in the cities, it must have seemed that only by removing children from their homes, their parents and their
friends, could change be achieved. At first the new environment was provided by Houses of Refuge, but later the
belief in the family as the training ground for future
good citizens, led to a greater use of fostering and apprenticeship. C.L. Brace, the director of a large placement
agency, is quoted by Florence Davenport Hill as saying 'The
family is God's reformatory'. This belief was strengthened
by the growing realisation during the century of the disadvantages of institutions. Davenport Hill comments on this:
(27)

> So alive, indeed, have Americans become of late years
> to the evils which arise from the massing together of
> children that they have invented a word to describe its
> effects, and when they speak of a child being 'insti-
> tutionalised' they mean to express that it is mechani-
> cal and helpless from the effect of asylum life.

References to the advantages of the family should not be
taken to mean the natural family. What was normally being
discussed was the advantage of a foster family over that of
an institution. The reformers of the nineteenth century
began with the idea that an institution provided the best
means of preventing children becoming criminals or paupers,
but soon saw the usefulness of foster homes. The next step
to the idea of maintaining children in their own homes was
just being taken when the discovery of battered babies and
abused children highlighted again the problems for some
children of life with their parents.

Another focal concern in juvenile justice is whether
children who commit crimes and those who need care should
be handled together. Most of the Houses of Refuge and
placement agencies took both children who had committed
minor offences and those who were destitute, vagrants and
beggars. They were concerned with preventing children
becoming adult criminals or paupers. To many people, one
fate was as bad as the other. Poverty was shameful because
it was usually seen, not as an outcome of the social and
economic system, but as the result of laziness, lack of

religion and habits of vice and intemperance. The horror
of pauperism, the belief in contamination, and the need for
removal from such influences are expressed in the following
extract from a report of the State Charities Aid Association
of New York in 1873:(28)

It is almost inevitable that a child born a pauper, growing up with paupers, associating solely with them, should
himself become a pauper. It is not an unusual thing to
find three generations of paupers in our County Poor-
houses. But take the child away; remove him from these
evil influences; if diseased, place him in some hospital
home; if well, find a home for him in some kind-hearted
family, and he is saved - saved from what is worse than
death.

Even to people who might not be so appalled by the idea of
pauperism, the need for preventive action was clear, since
paupers were very likely to become criminals. To them there
was nothing strange in dealing with homeless children, who
were begging on the streets, in the same way as they dealt
with children convicted of petty offences, for, as Mary
Carpenter said, 'the neglected child is the material out
of which paupers and criminals are made.'(29) The Houses
of Refuge received both types of child. Their justification was that they were not only dealing with a present
evil, but were preventing a future more serious one. This
is an argument of the welfare approach.

Despite the prevailing horror of pauperism, it would be
inaccurate to think that the nineteenth century made no
distinction between criminal and non-criminal children. At
one extreme were the most serious or persistent offenders
and for them the criminal justice approach prevailed. They
were sent not to reformatories but to prison, for as Fox(30)
points out, the courts retained their power to sentence
children to imprisonment until the passing of the juvenile
court acts. At the other extreme were destitute and abandoned children who would not normally have been sent to
prison but to the workhouse or where one existed to a House
of Refuge. Between these two groups were minor offenders
and wanderers, tramps and beggars. These children might
have gone either to the workhouse or to prison, but as the
century advanced were more and more likely to be sent to
reformatories.

The reformers struggled, as we still do today, with the
criteria for deciding whether or not a child could be helped
and reformed. Whether he was, in Fox's term, a 'salvage-
able offender', a 'proper object'(31) for saving. The criteria were as ill-developed as they are now. Often it seemed that there was really only one ground for the decision,
and this was the child's record. Had he a history of

offences, and how serious were they? Some unstated combination of number, plus seriousness, of past offences would result in the decision that a child was beyond salvation, or - to use the modern term we apply to the same group - was 'a hard core delinquent'. These children remained in the criminal system.

Amongst the ideas which found expression in the separation of children from adults, was a belief in the possibility of accurate prediction and of helpful intervention, intermingled with a hope of saving money. Prevention of future evils implies an ability to predict, and this ability was apparently unquestioned by nineteenth-century reformers. To them it was obvious that children who stole or begged would continue to do so, and that intervention was both necessary and good. 'Only by perseverance' would they 'save numbers of little Devils from becoming big ones'. (32) This certainty seems strange to us in the midst of a period of questioning both of our ability to predict, and, more especially, of our ability to do anything except stigmatise those whom we select for treatment. To judge by their writings, the nineteenth-century reformers were not troubled by such doubts.

We find no such difference between ourselves and our ancestors in looking at the hope that prevention and treatment will ultimately result in a saving of tax dollars. This idea is expressed by the editor of the New York 'Evenine Post' in 1826, and is quoted by Pickett:(33)

> If we can clear our streets of the numberless depraved boys and girls that now infest them and most of whom are frequently tenants of our Bridewell or Penitentiary, a substantial good will be expected and the public relieved of a considerable portion of the taxes raised for these institutions.

IMPLEMENTING A WELFARE APPROACH

It is sometimes hard to distinguish between a welfare and a criminal justice approach in nineteenth-century attitudes to young offenders, because the assumptions in the two systems about how to induce change in human beings were less divergent than they are today. Concern for individuals, and the desire to help them reach their potential, led to the same treatment as did the philosophy of criminal justice. Both approaches shared a belief in man's ability to change on the basis of reason. The divergence in the twentieth century is clearer, because those who support a welfare approach believe that reason is only one of the factors which influence a person to change his behaviour, and that it is less important than sociological influences and internal pressures. However, while the differences between the two approaches in the nineteenth century may be harder for us to see, they were probably clear to contemporaries. In 1825 some of Griscom's views must have seemed as different from the accepted view of the criminal justice system as do the arguments of psychiatrists in our criminal courts today. Pickett writes of Griscom's report to the Society:(34)

An atmosphere of urgency filled the hall as Colden, now president of the Society called the assembly to order. After clearing away a few incidental matters, Colden requested John Griscom to come forward. Grasping his papers firmly, the well-known Griscom began his report.

First, he wanted to clarify the principle of punishment which he felt ought to be endorsed. Heading dead against what he considered to be the predominant view, Griscom declared that the notion of 'revenge' must be totally eliminated. The reformation of the individual must rank equally as high as the protection of society as a whole. Griscom counseled his audience to 'deter others from crime, to prevent the aggressor from the repetition of his offences, and, if possible, to effect the moral reformation of all those who become amenable to the laws'.

In looking back on the progress of the institutions created to implement a welfare approach, what is clear is how difficult it is to put such ideals into practice. It is in institutions for the treatment of juvenile offenders that all too often the worst of the criminal justice philosophy and the worst of the welfare approach combine to make an inhuman warehouse out of a place which is intended to promote growth and individual change. This is clear in the nineteenth century as it is today. All too soon the drive for control, for economy, and for system, corrupted the new Houses of Refuge, as it was later to corrupt the reform schools. In New York the first superintendent, Joseph Curtis, had struggled to put into effect his ideas of running a family type home. He met children on whom kindness and verbal reprimands had no effect, and Pickett reports that he began to lock returned runaways in solitary confinement, sometimes in irons, and to beat those who broke the rules. Even so, he could not prevent children from running away, and this turned the committee of the Society against him. According to his account, he refused to carry out their orders to punish the boys who returned to the House of their own accord, and he resigned. The next superintendent established a system of control, the committee members probably relaxed, but the price paid for

quiet was a rigid routine. They had 'subordinated imagi-
nation to system and got consistent results'.(35)

Mr Curtis was not alone in finding it hard to translate
into everyday living the principles of prevention and education. In Boston, the first superintendent of the House
of Reformation was the Reverend Wells. He initiated a system of self-government, based on the idea that the House was
a small republic, and he seems to have had great success.
His difficulties were not with the boys, but with the city
council, which criticised him for educating the boys rather
than making them productive. Wells was apparently a charis-
matic figure whose optimism and energy created envy. He ignored the ambivalence of ordinary people and lived out a
welfare philosophy, but like others, he found the official
setting of a state institution impossible and left to set
up a school of his own.

In 1825 institutions for young delinquents seemed to
provide a method of rehabilitating and reforming those
children who otherwise were predicted to become paupers
and criminals. Through an institution, society might socialise children into hard-working and law-abiding adults.
Such hopes still infuse the juvenile justice system, although today we are more aware of the problems, and can
agree with Pickett, when he says:(36)

> Perhaps, the idea of the institution has been overworked
> and other economic, social and intellectual systems have
> constantly been underworked. At the outset of the Refuge
> movement in America, Professor John Griscom began the
> work of preventing delinquency by scouring Europe in
> search of an institution which would substitute for what
> he considered to be inadequate parents. In a character-
> istically systematic fashion, however, he sought a scheme
> that could eliminate excessive face-to-face contact.
> Because Johann Pestalozzi based his system on personal
> human interaction instead of a mechanically operated
> scheme, Griscom rejected the old Swiss reformer's ap-
> proach. To Griscom, and to later Americans, despite
> their well-meaning concern, the problem of delinquency
> has meant a search for the most efficient, often imper-
> sonal, and least costly means of disposing of unwanted
> youths.

It is only from the middle of the twentieth century that
society has realised the burden of the inheritance the juvenile justice system carries, and has tried to get away from
the idea of residential institutions: so far without success.

The tension between a criminal justice and a welfare
approach is apparent in other aspects of juvenile justice
development. The development of probation created a system

and a court sentence in which the two philosophies are
welded together. The sanctions of the criminal justice
system are suspended as an ever-present back-drop to the
relationship between officer and client, in which a welfare approach should predominate.

At first sight it might seem that the Boards of Guardians, such as those in Indiana, were concerned with the
welfare of children, and had little connection with a criminal justice approach. A report given by the attorney for
the Board of Children's Guardians in Indianapolis, however,
while commenting on the success of the Board's actions,
also reminds us of their deterrent function, and implies
the need to protect children's rights:(37)

> As to results, it may fairly be said that they have
> been good, else some of the six General Assemblies since
> 1889 would have repealed the act. Boards have been or-
> ganized in four counties. The board of Indianapolis has
> investigated 1,208 cases. The records of its secretary,
> Mrs Julia H. Goodhart, who is the inspiration and main-
> stay of the work, exhibit the alphabetically arranged
> histories of over twenty-five hundred children; and
> all these, it is to be remembered, are in one county.
> The board has lost barely more than a tenth of all the
> cases filed in court. This indicates much as to the
> painstaking care with which the board itself has investi-
> gated every case before ordering prosecution. Latterly
> fewer cases have had to be prosecuted, and this we in-
> terpret to mean that a dread of the Board of Children's
> Guardians has become an efficient deterrent. Indeed, the
> records show 542 children permanently provided for by the
> board during its twelve years without legal process as
> against 459 formally awarded to it by the court.
>
> The critical question is, of course, as to the history
> of the children after they have come into the control
> of the board. The answer is that of all the wards of
> the board, taken though they have been from prostitutes,
> drunkards, thieves, and the like, just eighteen, so far
> as we know have gone to the bad.
>
> Those of us who have been identified with the work
> have become more and more impressed with the idea that
> a board of children's guardians is a frightfully danger-
> ous piece of machinery, and is to be handled only with
> the extremest caution. The danger is in the tendency to
> forget that the work is in no sense charitable. Thou-
> sands of children need charity where only scores need
> separation from their parents. And the important thing -
> always to be remembered - is that no child, howsoever
> unfortunate its condition, should be taken by a board
> of children's guardians unless it is in imminent danger

of becoming a serious menace to society.
This account of the Indiana Board of Guardians draws attention to the question of children's rights, a question on
which the nineteenth century had not been silent.

CHILDREN'S RIGHTS

The idea grew during the century that children were not just
adults in miniature, but were a special class, with particular needs which society had a responsibility to meet.
This resulted in the provision of special institutions for
children. The same ideas were, however, responsible for a
failure to develop safeguards for children's rights. If
people thought about children's rights at all, it must have
seemed obvious that their right to be cared for, fed,
clothed, housed, educated, trained to be self-sufficient,
and taught to serve God, was all important. That children
or their parents might prefer their own poverty-stricken
diseased ignorance, did not even occur to most reformers.
However, there were parents and children who protested.
The Acts which allowed children to be sent to Houses of
Refuge instead of jail, allowed them to be detained for an
indefinite period, ending only with the end of their minority. For many children, a short jail sentence must have
seemed preferable, and parents too became aware that these
commitments infringed their rights. Pickett refers to
parents applying to the New York House of Refuge for the
discharge of their children, and in 1838 an appeal brought
by the father of a child called Mary Ann Crouse, who was
in the Philadelphia House of Refuge, was decided by the
Supreme Court of Pennsylvania. The father argued that the
Acts passed by the Pennsylvania legislature in 1826 and 1835
were unconstitutional. These Acts allowed the managers of
the House of Refuge:(38)

> at their discretion, to receive into their care and
> guardianship, infants, males under the age of twenty-
> one years, and females under the age of eighteen years
> committed to their custody by either of the following
> modes viz. First: Infants committed by an alderman or
> justice of the peace on the complaint and due proof
> made to him by the parent, guardian or next friend of
> such infant, that by reason of incorrigible or vicious
> conduct such infant has rendered his or her control
> beyond the power of such parent, guardian or next friend,
> and made it manifestly requisite that from regard for
> the morals and future welfare of such infant, he or
> she should be placed under the guardianship of the
> managers of the House of Refuge. Second: Infants com-

mitted by the authority aforesaid, where complaint and
due proof have been made that such infant is a proper
subject for the guardianship of the managers of the
House of Refuge, in consequence of vagrancy, or of incorrigible or vicious conduct, and that from the moral
depravity or otherwise of the parent or next friend in
whose custody such infant may be, such parent or next
friend is incapable or unwilling to exercise the proper care and discipline over such incorrigible or vicious infant.   Third: Infants committed by the courts
of this Commonwealth in the mode provided by the act to
which this is a supplement.

The opinion of the court is interesting because it makes
an argument that is to be repeated in later appeals for
the next 130 years. Children have no right to the protection granted in the Bill of Rights to those accused of
crimes because they are being committed, not as criminals,
but for their own welfare, and sent away, not for punishment, but for education and reform. Like many future
judges, the Pennsylvania judges in 1838 did not concern
themselves with the actual conditions in the House of Refuge to which Mary Ann was committed. The stated intentions
of the legislators and managers were sufficient. The judges said:(39)

The House of Refuge is not a prison, but a school, where
reformation, and not punishment, is the end. It may
indeed be used as a prison for juvenile convicts who
would else be committed to a common gaol; and in respect to these, the constitutionality of the act which
incorporated it, stands clear of controversy. . . .

The object of the charity is reformation, by training
its inmaes to industry, by imbuing their minds with principles of morality and religion; by furnishing them with
means to earn a living; and, above all, by separating
them from the corrupting influences of improper associates. To this end may not the natural parents, when
unequal to the task of education, or unworthy of it, be
superseded by the *parens patriae*, or common guardian of
the community? It is to be remembered that the public
has a paramount interest in the virtue and knowledge of
its members, and that of strict right, the business of
education belongs to it. That parents are ordinarily
intrusted with it is because it can seldom be put into
better hands; but where they are incompetent or corrupt, what is there to prevent the public from with-
drawing their faculties, held, as they obviously are,
at its sufference? The right of parental control is a
natural, but not an unalienable one. . . .

As to abridgement of indefeasible rights by confinement of the person, it is not more than what is borne, to a greater or less extent, in every school; and we know of no natural right to exemption from restraints which conduce to an infant's welfare. Nor is there a doubt of the propriety of their application in the particular instance. The infant has been snatched from a course which must have ended in confirmed depravity; and, not only is the restraint of her person lawful, but it would be an act of extreme cruelty to release her from it.

There were few who did not accept these ideas, although later in the century the Illinois Court for a while held the opposite view. A boy called Daniel O'Connell had been sent to the Chicago reform school, without having committed a crime, under the Illinois Acts of 1863 and 1867, which provided that children aged six to sixteen, who were vagrants, destitute of parental care or growing up in mendicancy, ignorance, vice or idleness, could be committed to the school. The court held that Daniel had been imprisoned, and that the laws under which this had occurred were unconstitutional because they were in violation of the Bill of Rights, which declares the inherent and inalienable right of all men to their personal liberty.

In the opinion, the court says:(40)

The bill of rights declares, that 'all men are, by nature, free and independent, and have certain inherent and inalienable rights: among these are life, liberty, and the pursuit of happiness.' This language is not restrictive; it is broad and comprehensive, and declares a grand truth, that 'all men', all people, everywhere, have the inherent and inalienable right to liberty. Shall we say to the children of the State, you shall not enjoy this right - a right independent of all human laws and regulations? It is declared in the constitution; is higher than constitution and law, and should be held forever sacred.

Even criminals can not be convicted and imprisoned without due process of law - without a regular trial, according to the course of the common law. Why should minors be imprisoned for misfortune? Destitution of proper parental care, ignorance, idleness and vice, are misfortune, not crimes.

It can not be said, that in this case, there is no imprisonment. This boy is deprived of a father's care; bereft of home influences; has no freedom of action; is committed for an uncertain time; is branded as a prisoner; made subject to the will of others, and thus feels that he is a slave. Nothing could more contribute to paralyze the youthful energies, crush all noble

aspirations, and unfit him for the duties of manhood.
Other means of a milder character; other influences of
a more kindly nature; other laws less in restraint of
liberty, would better accomplish the reformation of
the depraved, and infringe less upon inalienable rights.

These two cases raise the question of the needs and
rights of children, which is a recurrent theme in the history of the juvenile justice system. In the case of Mary
Ann Crouse, the court denied that she was deprived of liberty to any degree beyond that necessary to meet her needs,
while in People v. Turner, the court found that both needs
and rights would be better served by 'other means of a
milder character'. Neither court faced the problem of
balancing needs against rights. During the years, more
cases were heard, in which the constitutionality of commitment to institutions and of the juvenile court itself was
questioned. The views expressed by the Pennsylvania judges
in 1838 are those of the majority viewpoint until 1967,
when the Supreme Court decision in re Gault(41) used
words reminiscent of those used to free Daniel O'Connell.
In the meantime, however, the Illinois court reversed itself in 1882 in re Alexander Ferrier, when they held the
Industrial School for Girls Act of 1879 to be constitutional. This allowed committal to the school of:(42)

every female infant who begs or receives alms while
actually selling, or pretending to sell any article in
public; or who frequents any street, alley or other
place, for the purpose of begging or receiving alms;
or, who having no permanent place of abode, proper
parental care, or guardianship, or sufficient means of
subsistence, or who for other cause is a wanderer
through streets and alleys and in other public places;
or, who lives with, or frequents the company of, or
consorts with reputed thieves, or other vicious persons;
or is found in a house of ill-fame, or in a poor house.

The judges distinguished this situation from that in People
v. Turner on the debatable grounds that the 1867 law was
nearer to a criminal statute, and that the Chicago reform
school was a place of confinement, and children were sent
there for punishment.

Illinois was not the only state to uphold the constitutionality of such statutes. It was a common trend in most
states. The case of Milwaukee Industrial School v. Milwaukee County shows similar laws being upheld in Wisconsin.(43)

By the end of the century, the general attitude towards
children was reflected by the decisions in the State
Supreme Courts. Children had needs: for care, education
and protection. In providing for such needs, the State

was ensuring to children their rights, as any good parent would do. The frame of reference was that of the family, not the court, and the fact that the needs were enforced by a court, even against the wishes of child and parent, was ignored. Legally, as well as socially, the time was ripe for juvenile courts and the end of criminal charges against children. The welfare approach was in the ascendant.

Chapter three

United States: from the first juvenile court to the present

THE FIRST JUVENILE COURTS

There is some argument whether it was in Illinois or Colorado that all the features of what was to be a juvenile
court were first brought together in one state. Most
writers give the honour to Illinois, although Julia Lathrop,
who had herself been involved in the establishment of the
Cook County Court, avoided the issue later, when she apoke
as first Director of the Federal Children's Bureau, which
was established in 1912.(1)

> 'It is when seven cities claim the honor of being
> Homer's birthplace, that scholars become sure that
> Homer was born in none of them, but rather represents
> a rich and cumulative aggregate of human tradition and
> aspiration.' By these words Julia Lathrop explained,
> in the face of competition for the honor of originating
> the juvenile court idea, its true genesis.

It is, however, the 1898 Act of Illinois which in Section 3
gave the new courts their name.(2)

> In counties having over 500,000 population the judges of
> the circuit court shall, at such times as they shall
> determine, designate one or more of their number whose
> duty it shall be to hear all cases coming under this
> act. A special court room, to be designated as the
> juvenile court room, shall be provided for the hearing
> of such cases, and the findings of the court shall be
> entered in a book or books to be kept for that purpose
> and known as the 'Juvenile Record', and the court may,
> for convenience, be called the 'Juvenile Court'.

This Act was passed as the result of pressure from several
groups in Chicago. These included the Bar, some social
service agencies and a group of women who had organised
themselves as the Women's Club, and had amongst their members a number of forceful articulate personalities, like

53

Jane Adams and Julia Lathrop. The Club had been instrumental in getting women's matrons into the local jails in
1883, and in 1895 had drafted a bill for the establishment
of separate juvenile courts. Attorneys, however, had ad-
vised that such a bill would be unconstitutional, because
it sought to establish new courts. The setting for these
different pressure groups to unite seems to have been provided by the 1898 Illinois State Conference of Charities,
which had as its topic 'The Children of the State'. Dr
Hart, who was superintendent of a private agency, the Illinois Children's Home and Aid Society, urged the promotion
of a juvenile court act. The Chicago Bar Association co-
operated, and Judge Harvey B. Hurd enlarged an existing
five-man committee of lawyers to include representatives
of the social service agencies of the state. Dr Hart
became the committee secretary.

This committee worked fast, and must have had considerable political pull, since in April of the next year the
legislature passed 'An act to regulate the treatment and
control of dependent, neglected and delinquent children'.
(3) The Act required that court hearings concerned with
children were to be separate from those for adults, and
that children were to be detained and treated separately.
The major innovation, however, was that children were no
longer to be charged with criminal offences. As the report
of the Chicago Bar Association said:(4)

> The fundamental idea of the Juvenile Court law is that
> the state must step in and exercise guardianship over a
> child found under such adverse social or individual
> conditions as develop crime . . . it proposes a plan
> whereby he may be treated, not as a criminal, or legally
> charged with a crime, but as a ward of the state, to
> receive practically the care, custody and discipline
> that are accorded the neglected and dependent child,
> and which, as the Act states, 'shall approximate as
> nearly as may be that which should be given by its
> parents.'

Timothy Hurley, writing in 1925, expressed this even more
clearly:(5)

> In the preparation of the bill, great care was taken to
> eliminate in every way the idea of a criminal procedure.
> The law was expressly framed to avoid creating a child
> as a criminal. To this end the proceedings were divested
> of all featured which attach to a criminal proceeding.
> Instead of a complaint or an indictment, a petition was
> suggested; instead of a warrant, a summons. The child
> was not to be arrested, but brought in by the parent or
> guardian, or by a probation officer. The bill expressly
> forbade keeping a child in a jail or enclosure where
> adults were confined.

The idea that offences against the criminal law, when committed by children, were not crimes, was new. It is not
just a logical extension of the belief of the nineteenth-
century reformers that neglected and destitute children
would grow up to be criminals. We have seen how that belief developed, and how the distinction between offenders
and non-offenders was blurred when it came to admitting
children to residential institutions. Julia Lathrop maintained that, before the juvenile courts existed, industrial
schools for dependent children had in fact been receiving
many children whose behaviour had been virtually criminal
and 'whose offences were minimized by the courts in order
to commit to industrial schools and thus save the child
from the sure demoralization of imprisonment'.(6) These,
however, were informal attempts by the courts to avoid the
strict consequences of the law in some instances. The
conclusion to be drawn from such attempts might have been
that what was required was a system in which the disposition of the court could take into account the needs of the
child as well as the legal category into which the offence
was classified. The reformers, however, went farther and
abolished criminal charges against children. Acts, which
if committed by adults would be a crime, when committed by
a child were to be one of several grounds for a finding of
delinquency. That was a major innovation and shifted the
balance in the new juvenile courts towards a welfare approach. In retrospect it seems that the shift may have
been too great because it left children without the protections which accompany a criminal justice approach.

While Chicago was developing its juvenile court under
the pressures of social agencies, influential women and the
local Bar, in Denver, one man, Ben Lindsay, seems to have
exerted a powerful influence towards the creation of a
juvenile court system in Colorado. In his writing, Judge
Lindsay claims to have been the first in the field, because
in 1897 Colorado set up a system of officials who resembled
probation officers, who operated in the schools and were
also teachers and truant officers.(7) Colorado is interesting historically because it attempted to control deviant behaviour through its educational system, and the juvenile
court, which was developed by Judge Lindsay, was seen as
an arm of that system. Judge Lindsay did not hear about
the Illinois court until 1901, and he then visited Chicago
to see it. He commented that he found it far more formal
than his own court. He viewed the juvenile court as extending the moral education provided first by the family
and second by the school. He seems to have had success in
minimising the criminal justice aspect of his court in the
minds of local children. According to his own account:(8)

Many children, perhaps more than half of them in
trouble come to this court of their own volition. This
is particularly true of girls. In a two year period of
over 1000 girls dealt with in Denver's Juvenile Court,
something over 700 came to that court by themselves. . .
people morally sick come along to the court as they
would go along to a doctor's office when physically
ill.
Unfortunately, we do not know if this was how the delinquents themselves viewed the situation, although it is significant if some came voluntarily.

RE-WRITING JUVENILE COURT HISTORY

The forces which brought the juvenile court into being and
which sustain it today, are essentially ambivalent, but
this has only recently been recognised. There was a tendency to view the juvenile court movement through rose-
coloured glasses and attribute to its members only the
highest of humanitarian motives. This version of history
was accepted by the Supreme Court in its opinion in the
Gault decision. The Court suggested that the reformers
brought about a situation where children traded the procedural regularity and harsh punishments of the criminal
justice system for the informal individualised justice of
the juvenile courts. The reformers' motives were of the
highest kind for they were:(9)
appalled by adult procedures and penalties, and by the
fact that children could be given long prison sentences
and mixed in jails with hardened criminals. They were
profoundly convinced that society's duty to the child
could not be confined by the concept of justice alone.
They believed that society's role was not to ascertain
whether the child was 'guilty' or 'innocent', but 'What
is he, how has he become what he is, and what had best
be done in his interest and in the interest of the state
to save him from a downward career.' The child - essentially good, as they saw it - was to be made 'to feel
that he is the object of (the state's) care and solici-
tude', not that he was under arrest or on trial. The
rules of criminal procedure were therefore altogether
inapplicable. The apparent rigidities, technicalities,
and harshness which they observed in both substantive
and procedural criminal law were therefore to be dis-
carded. The idea of crime and punishment was to be
abandoned. The child was to be 'treated' and 'rehabilitated' and the procedures, from apprehension through
institutionalization, were to be 'clinical' rather than
punitive.

We shall consider the many implications of the Gault decision later. Here we are concerned only with the fact that
the Gault decision, which found some of the procedures of
juvenile courts to be unconstitutional, also established
a climate in which a re-appraisal of the birth of the juvenile court became possible. Scholars like Platt,(10)
Lemert,(11) and Fox,(12) in re-writing juvenile court history since Gault, attribute more negative motives to the
reformers. Certainly the reformers were interested in
saving children from contamination by adults, but they were
also concerned that children were committing offences and
getting away without treatment or control. Julia Lathrop,
writing in 1925 of the background of the juvenile court in
Illinois, explained that children over ten who committed
offences were usually tried in the police courts, and the
most common punishment was a fine. When the fine was not
paid the children could be sent to the city prison, but the
justices often 'could neither tolerate sending children
to the Bridewell nor bear to be themselves guilty of the
harsh folly of compelling poverty-stricken parents to pay
fines'.(13) The result was that children were let off, and,
since no records were kept, they could be let off over and
over again. There may have been harshness in the criminal
justice system for some children, and for them there may
also have been procedural protection, but for many the
system did nothing; it neither punished nor treated.
Children were left to their own uncontrolled devices.
     Developing these ideas, Platt suggests that the juvenile
court movement was concerned with the social control of
children whose behaviour threatened middle-class values.
Not only were children who committed offences to come within
the control of the court, and in such a way that the conscience of the judge would no longer be troubled, but other
forms of behaviour were to be controlled.(14)

> The juvenile court movement went far beyond a humani-
> tarian concern for the special treatment of adolescents.
> It brought within the ambit of governmental control a
> set of youthful activities that had been previously
> ignored or handled informally. It was not by accident
> that the behaviour selected for penalizing by the child
> savers - drinking, begging, roaming the streets, fre-
> quenting dance-halls and movies, fightings, sexuality,
> staying out late at night, and incorrigibility - was
> primarily attributable to the children of lower-class
> migrant and immigrant families.

All such behaviour was not proscribed by the original Illinois act, which dealt only with dependent and neglected
children and those who broke the law. However, in 1903,
Illinois added other grounds for jurisdiction such as

incorrigibility and curfew breaking, which are offences
only when committed by children. It may not, however, be
correct to assume that these categories were so new in the
United States as a whole. The Poor Laws and Probate Codes
had provided grounds for state intervention on similar
grounds in the past. We have seen the grounds which allowed
the Children's Guardians in Indiana(15) to take action. In
the nineteenth century, statutes in many states allowed
children, especially girls, to be sent to reform schools
for behaviour which, in later juvenile courts acts, provides
ground for a finding of delinquency. The acts of New York
state of 1886 are typical:(16)

> Whenever any female over the age of 12 years shall be
> brought by the police or shall voluntarily come before
> a committing magistrate in the city of New York, and
> it shall be proved to the satisfaction of such magistrate
> by the confession of such female, or by competent testi-
> mony, that such female (first) is found in a reputed
> house of prostitution or assignation; or is willfully
> disobedient to parent or guardian, and is in danger of
> becoming morally depraved; or (second) is a prostitute,
> or is of intemperate habits and who professes a desire
> to reform and has not been an inmate of the peniten-
> tiary, such magistrate may judge that it is for the wel-
> fare of such female that she be placed in a reformatory,
> and may thereupon commit such female to one of the fol-
> lowing reformatory institutions, viz: The Protestant
> Episcopal House of Mercy, New York, the Roman Catholic
> House of Good Shepherd, foot of 89th Street, or the
> Magdalen Female Benevolent Asylum and Home of Fallen
> Women, which said institutions are hereby severally
> authorized to receive and hold females committed under
> this act.

However, even if such control over children was not new in
1899, Platt's view is helpful in stressing that middle-class
society has an interest in controlling children's behaviour,
not only because of concern for children, but also because
such behaviour is a threat to its own value system.

Fox also suggests that more immediate interests were
served by the 1899 Act, which reinforced the private sectarian interests of those who ran institutions for children.
There had been concern about what actually happened to
children in these institutions, and one group argued that
the State should take over the function of caring for children whose families were unable or unwilling to do so. The
Illinois Act, which confirmed the place of the sectarian
child placement societies and institutions, may have delayed
or even prevented the growth of an adequate State child-
welfare service.

While acknowledging the mixed motives of those who established the juvenile court reformers, it is not necessary
to go to the other extreme and lose sight of their humanitarian concerns and the positive aspects of their work.
Understanding the juvenile court, either historically or
today, requires an attempt to hold a balanced view of conflicting forces. The correcting of what was a distorted
view of history is important, because now we can see that
the problems of balance are not new - they are built into
the system.

Whatever interpretations present-day historians put upon
their behaviour the first juvenile court judges, like Judge
Lindsay in Denver, Judge Mack in Chicago, and Judge Hoffman
in Cincinnati, were fervent believers in the juvenile court.
They believed these new courts would solve the problems of
delinquency. There was nothing modest about their claims
or those of their followers, which illustrate the welfare
approach in an extreme form:(17)

> We have converted the court so far as the law is con-
> cerned into an institution that provides officially or
> unofficially for the treatment of all, adults as well as
> children, afflicted with conduct disorders. The court
> partakes of the nature of a central agency that refers
> cases for diagnosis and treatment to the organization,
> institution, or individual best qualified for the pur-
> pose. The court justifies itself in the pursuance of
> this policy on the ground that the investigations,
> studies and research work of the founders of the juvenile
> courts, and of Healy, Glueck, Salmon, Anderson, Adler,
> White, Hickson, Wooley, and scores of others no less
> noted in this particular field, have brought to light
> a body of scientific knowledge and information which,
> if applied, will relieve mankind of much of its wretch-
> edness and misery, and mark the inauguration of a new
> social order founded on the principles of humanity and
> love rather than that of retribution and hate.

Judge Hoffman further claims that the juvenile court is
'the best plan for the conservation of human life and happiness ever conceived by civilized man'.(18) Judge Miriam
Van Waters, who was referee of the Los Angeles court, writes
of the founders of the juvenile-court movement as toiling to
prepare for 'the building of the Kingdom of childhood on
earth'.(19) Education and science together offered the answer to changing human behaviour, and juvenile courts could
ensure that children found their way to them.

However, the juvenile court was still a court and the presiding official a judge, and it needed legal respectability
as well as education and scientific validity. Perhaps it
was this need which led Judge Lindsay and Judge Mack(20)

to the idea of the judge acting as *parens patriae* (literally parent of the country). This legal doctrine gave the juvenile court a most respectable and ancient ancestry in the court of chancery. Since this doctrine of *parens patriae* recurs throughout discussion of the juvenile court in the United States, we will consider its meaning and origins.

PARENS PATRIAE

The doctrine of *parens patriae* is that the state has an overall parental responsibility towards those of its members who are unable, either temporarily or permanently, to care for and protect themselves. Children, the senile, the retarded and the insane, are the groups to whom this doctrine is usually applied, although it is also used at times to explain the nature of some administrative hearings in connection with parolees.(21) When the condition or behaviour of a member of one of these groups suggests their need for protection, the state intervenes by means of a court hearing and decision. The nature of the court process in such a situation is essentially non-adversary. It is assumed that there is no conflict of interests between the state and the party before the court, since all the state is concerned to do is to see that care is provided for someone who is incapable of providing it for himself. Since there is no conflict of interests, the incapable party requires no procedural protection of the kind secured to defendants in criminal trials. Under the doctrines of *parens patriae* the rules of due process do not apply, because they are unnecessary.

In relation to children, the doctrine has been used to authorise the State's intervention in situations where the parents are not carrying out their responsibilities to their children. We have seen this argument in *ex parte Crouse*. (22) The court held that Mary Ann Crouse had been saved from a course which must have ended in her confirmed depravity, and that, when parents were unable to educate their children, they could be 'superseded by the *parens patriae*, or common guardian of the community'.

Such doctrines were clearly useful and, in part at least, applicable to the new juvenile courts. The early writers claimed that the juvenile courts acquired the duties and responsibilities of *parens patriae* as part of their equitable jurisdiction. This jurisdiction derived from the English Court of Chancery, and for this reason we have to turn to English history to explore the meaning of this claim. This question is discussed in this chapter which is concerned with the juvenile courts of the United States, because only they claim such jurisdiction. The British juvenile courts rely solely upon jurisdiction given by statute.

Amongst the types of jurisdiction which developed in England during the Middle Ages were that of the Common Law and that of Chancery. Both were concerned with the settlement of disputes between contestants, but Chancery Courts developed the use of equitable powers, 'the essential ideas of which are flexibility, guardianship and a balancing of interests in the general welfare, with a view to getting a fairer result than can be obtained by applying the older more rigid legal rules.' (23) In the eighteenth and nineteenth centuries, the Court of Chancery heard a number of cases concerned with the custody and guardianship of children, and it was in these cases that the theory of *parens patriae* was developed. The *Eyre* v. *Shaftesbury*(24) case arose from a dispute between Mr Justice Eyre, who had been appointed guardian to the young Earl of Shaftesbury by his father's will, and the Earl's mother, the Countess of Shaftesbury. Mr Justice Eyre petitioned first for access to the Earl and the power to appoint the boy's servants, and a second time on the grounds that his ward had married without his consent. Counsel for Mr Justice Eyre argued that:

> the care of all infants is lodged in the King as *pater patriae,* and by the King this care is delegated to his court of Chancery . . . the King is bound of common right and by law to defend his subjects, their goods and chattels, lands and tenements and by the law of this realm every loyal subject is taken to be within the King's protection for which reason it is that idiots and lunatics who are incapable to take care of themselves are provided for by the King as *pater patriae,* and there is the same reason to extend this care to infants.

There were some problems to be resolved before the juvenile courts could claim the prerogative of *parens patriae.* It is unclear whether the Court of Chancery acquired jurisdiction because a matter concerned a child who needed protection or because a child was the heir to property. It was suggested in *Eyre* v. *Shaftesbury* that the court was exercising the jurisdiction which formerly belonged to the extinct Court of Wards. This was a feudal court which existed to protect the interest of the feudal lord, ultimately the King, in the lands of his subjects. These lands were held subject to the performance of duties and contribution in kind, and it was necessary for the lord to ensure his rights when the tenant was a minor. If the Chancery jurisdiction over infants derived from the Court of Wards, then it could be exercised only over children with property and was not concerned with the welfare of the child. This issue continued to arise in later cases, and the court distinguished between jurisdictional powers and executive powers.

If anyone will turn his mind attentively to the subject
he must see that this Court does not have the means of
acting except where it has property to act upon. It is
not however from any want of jurisdiction that it does
not act,but from a want of means to exercise its jurisdiction, because the Court cannot take on itself the
maintainence of all the children of the Kingdom. It
can exercise the jurisdiction usefully and practically
only where it has the means of doing so, that is to say,
by its having the means of applying property for the use
and maintenance of the infants.(25)

Thus, for Lord Eldon in 1829, the matter was a practical
not a jurisdictional problem, although counsel in later
cases continued to argue the lack of jurisdiction. In 1847,
in re Spence, a father was attempting to get an order
against his brother-in-law, whom he thought had been instrumental in helping his wife to run away and to stay away,
with the children of the marriage. The counsel for the
mother and brother argued 'that the court had no jurisdiction over infants, distinct from that at common law upon
habeas corpus, unless there was some property to be administered for the infants' benefit'. The Chancellor, however, held that he had:

no doubt about the jurisdiction. The cases in which this
Court interferes on behalf of infants are not confined
to those in which there is property. Courts of law interfere by habeas for the protection of the person of
any body who is suggested to be improperly detained.
This court interferes for the protection of infants by
virtue of the prerogative which belongs to the Crown as
parens patriae, and the exercise of which is delegated
to the Great Seal.(26)

Other cases in which parens patriae is invoked do not raise
the issue of property, although the children concerned seem
in fact to have property, at least in cases heard in the
first half of the century. Another point at issue in the
cases is the reasons which justify a court's intervention
between a father and his children.(27)

The question of property raises some doubts about the
juvenile court's claims to an ancestry in Chancery. There
are other factors which suggest the jurisdiction of the two
Courts is very different. Chancery courts were never concerned with any kind of criminal behaviour, and their jurisdiction was only invoked by people who had or purported to
have a direct familial or legal relationship to the child
in question. If the Court of Chancery had power to deal
with children referred to it by disinterested well-wishers
or law-enforcement agents, this was not a power it used.
The claim is further weakened by the fact that, apart from

Eyre v. *Shaftesbury*, many of the cases which are quoted by
writers on the American juvenile court, occur long after
the Declaration of Independence. It is possible, however,
that these later English cases are cited, either because
their arguments are considered to be sound or because they
are seen as clarifying the powers which had always resided
in Chancery and which were therefore received by the American States.

On the whole it seems likely that early writers, like
Judge Lindsay, were more concerned with acquiring legal
prestige for their juvenile courts than with historical
accuracy. Roscoe Pound suggested that the juvenile court:
(28)

> which is making its way everywhere, is due to the ini-
> tiative of a few definitely known socially minded judges,
> who had the large vision to see what was required and the
> good sense not to be hindered in doing it because there
> had never been such things before. Today we find a le-
> gal basis for it in the jurisdiction of chancery over
> infants. We reconcile it with legal-historical dogmas
> on this basis. But the jurisdiction of equity over in-
> fants was not a factor in creating it. It arose on the
> criminal side of the courts because of the revolt of
> those judges' consciences from legal rules that required
> trial of children over seven as criminals and sentence
> of children over fourteen to penalties provided for
> adult offenders.

If the criminal court was one parent of the juvenile
court, the Poor Laws(29) seem to have at least as good a
claim as Chancery to being the other one. The Poor Laws
combined a concern for the deserving with social control
of vagabonds and rogues, which the juvenile court reflects.
Acknowledging this background gives the court a less illustrious ancestry than that claimed by Judge Lindsay, but
makes clearer the variety of functions it was to perform
for society.

THE DEVELOPMENT OF JUVENILE JUSTICE

Juvenile courts spread rapidly during the first quarter of
the twentieth century. Not only were juvenile court laws
passed in many States, but within each state the areas
covered by the provisions of the acts were extended. Originally juvenile courts were required in only the most populous counties, but they gradually spread to the rural
areas. The form which the system was to take for many
years was established during this period, and the basic
features of a juvenile court became accepted. The most

important differences between the procedure of a juvenile
court and that of an adult court were:(30)

summons instead of warrant; petition on behalf of the
child as opposed to indictment or information; detention separate from adults or in a specialized children's
institution, instead of in jail (or release or bail);
hearing to establish the state's right to intervene on
behalf of the child, as opposed to trial on specific
charge to determine guilt; infrequent use of counsel,
versus usual employment of counsel; infrequent participation of prosecuting attorney, versus invariable pre-
sentation of state's case by prosecutor; private hearing as opposed to public trial; informal hearing, at
which both social and legal data are used and proof is
by preponderance, as opposed to trial under strict rules
of evidence with requirement of proof beyond a reasonable doubt; very infrequent use of jury, as opposed to
right to jury trial; occasional consultation of social
investigation report before hearing, as opposed to use
of investigation report only after establishment of
guilt; disposition aimed at treatment, as opposed to
sentence which not infrequently has a punitive aim; emphasis on need of aid to and guidance of child in contrast with emphasis on protection of society.

The speed with which juvenile court statutes were passed
can be seen from Lou's history published in 1927:(31)
by 1904 the juvenile court was established in ten
states. More than twenty states and the district of
Columbia had somewhat similar institutions within the
first ten years. The system was well and widely established by 1914 when more than thirty states had juvenile court laws. By 1920 all but three states had such
laws. Today every state in the Union save one -
Wyoming - has a probation law for children or applicable to children, and all but two states - Maine and
Wyoming - have juvenile-court laws.

Quoting these figures is misleading unless one realises
that there were great differences between juvenile courts,
and also that, in the United States, the passing of a statute establishing an organisation cannot be taken as an
indication that the organisation exists in fact, or ever
will exist. A clearer picture of the reality is provided
by a report prepared in 1918 by Evelina Belden for the
Children's Bureau. Lou explains that:(32)

Information in that study was secured from 2,034
courts, out of 2,391 addressed, hearing children's
cases. The study shows conclusively that effective
juvenile courts with paid probation staffs were by no
means universally established. It has been pointed

out there that every city having 100,000 or more inhabitants had a court specially organized for children's work, separate hearings for children, regular probation service, and the recording of social information are taken as simple and minimum standards. Specially organized courts were available to 70 per cent of the total population living in cities of 25,000 to 100,000, to 29 per cent of the total population of cities of 5,000 to 25,000, and only 16 per cent of the population of rural communities. About 90 per cent of the courts that hear children's cases were in counties that had no city of more than 25,000 population. Only 321 of 2,034, or 16 per cent of the courts that hear children's cases lived up to the minimum standards defined above. It was estimated that in 1918 approximately 50,000 children's cases out of a total of 175,000 in the United States were brought before courts not adapted to handle children's cases. If we were to add to these minimum standards for a juvenile court the study of the physical and mental as well as the social basis for the behavior problems presented, the number of the specially organized courts would be greatly reduced. In the counties containing no city of more than 5,000 population, only 1 per cent of the courts had facilities for mental examinations; in those with cities of from 5,000 to 25,000, only 7 per cent; in those with cities of from 25,000 to 100,000, only 28 per cent; of the counties with cities over 100,000, 77 per cent had such facilities. But the percentage of all courts hearing children's cases in the United States that had such facilities was only 7 per cent. Only thirteen courts in the United States had clinics working with the court as part of the court machinery. A considerable number of smaller courts reported that hearings were not separate. Thirty-seven courts in eighteen states reported that no effort was made to separate children in jails from adult offenders. Although at that time every state in the Union except one had legislation providing for juvenile probation, less than half the courts having jurisdiction over children's cases - 45 per cent - were known to have had probation service, and in only eight states was there a recognized probation officer for every court. The rural districts were far behind the urban communities. While 66 per cent of the courts in cities of 5,000 to 25,000 had probation service, it was true of only 25 per cent of the courts in districts that were entirely rural. In most courts social records were quite inadequate.

THE GROWTH OF PROBATION

The individualisation of justice for juveniles was in many
ways dependent upon the development of probation services.
In the United States it is scarcely correct to talk about
juvenile courts and probation services as two separate institutions. Probation is an essential part of the juvenile
court, and the procedure of juvenile justice relied, and
still does rely, upon the presence of a probation officer.
In many States the authorisation to employ probation officers, and their job descriptions, are contained in the Act,
which also sets up a juvenile court. For example, it had
been the intention of the reformers in Chicago to include
in the 1898 Act the requirement that the court should
appoint full-time probation officers, paid out of county
funds. In fact, although the act authorised their appointment, no payment was included. Mrs Bowen comments upon the
response of the Women's Juvenile Court Committee to this
omission:(33)

> The law provided for the establishment of a Juvenile
> Court and for the services of probation officers, but it
> made no provision for the salary of these officers nor
> did it provide for a place of detention, although it
> specifically set forth that children were not to be con-
> fined in jails or police stations. The Juvenile Court
> Committee then raised the money for the salaries of the
> probation officers, beginning with five and ending with
> twenty-two. It called an educator of note, Mr Henry
> W. Thurston, to be chief probation officer; it also
> paid an assistant chief probation officer and the sala-
> ries of one or two clerks in the court. During this
> time the probation officers were most carefully selec-
> ted by the Juvenile Court Committee. They met frequent-
> ly with the members of the committee at Hull House and
> we talked to them on their duties. We really knew ab-
> solutely nothing about such duties. There was no lit-
> erature on juvenile courts at that time, nor on pro-
> bation officers, and those of us who had the training
> of these officers had to fall back on our own knowledge
> of human nature and on our best thought as to their
> duties.
>
> I think the first probation officer was Mrs Alzina
> Stevens, perhaps the best example of what a probation
> officer should be. Her great desire was to be of use to
> her fellow-men. Her love of children was great; her
> singleness of purpose and strength of character so re-
> markable that she exerted a great influence over the
> children committed to her charge. I find among some old
> papers the following concerning the duties of probation

officers: 'They must be men and women of many sides,
endowed with the strength of a Samson and the deli-
cacy of an Ariel. They must be tactful, skillful, firm
and patient. They must know how to proceed with wisdom
and intelligence and must be endowed with that rare
virtue - common-sense.' These qualities would seem to
be needed just as much today as they were twenty-five
years ago.

Other States also began with probation officers supplied by
voluntary societies or with volunteers, but by 1922, H.H.
Lou wrote that most probation officers were appointed and
paid by the courts. This meant that probation developed
as a local service for each juvenile court, and that the
probation department was part of the juvenile court system.
It was the administrative arm of the judge, and when probation officers made decisions about children, for example,
in relation to intake, they were exercising an authority
delegated by the judge. Probation offices were, and still
are, usually located in the court house - neither physically nor legally is the probation department separated
from the court.

   Some early juvenile court judges had hoped that they
themselves would establish a personal relationship with
the children referred to the court. They interpreted the
doctrine of *parens patriae* to mean that they should act as
a father to the child. Some judges clung to this belief
and, as late as 1945, Judge Schramm expresses it strongly
in an article whose title suggests this viewpoint, 'A
judge meets the boy and his family'.(34) However, this
had probably become a minority view much earlier in the
century. The opinion of Marjorie Bell gained ground:(35)

   In brief, the success of the juvenile court does not
   depend exclusively, or even primarily, on the kindly
   and understanding interview that a wise and humanitarian judge has with a juvenile delinquent and his
   parents. It depends on the day-to-day treatment carried
   out by various officers and agencies after the judge has
   had his talk. Reorientation of a personality, substi-
   tution of wholesome for morbid attitudes and habits,
   cannot be brought about in a half hour or one hour
   contact which a judge has with a child and his parents.
   It is a long and delicate process, requiring frequent
   adaptation of means to ends, ingenious changes of approach, the mutual cooperation and unflagging interest
   of probation officers, social workers, school teachers,
   parents and companions of the delinquent, and, in a
   certain proportion of cases, psychiatric therapy. Rehabilitation does not occur in the court room; it
   occurs, if at all, in the home, the school, the play-

ground or boys' club, the place of work. Hence it is
futile to look for single nostrums that will 'cure'
delinquency. We are dealing with a complex problem;
the stage on which the drama of personality and un-
wholesome behaviour is enacted is as broad as society
and as deep as human nature.

Bell was expressing an ideal, and it is clear from the report of the Children's Bureau that many juvenile courts
were without probation staff. In those Courts the judge
filled the role of probation officer as well as that of
judge, making decisions about intake and then adjudicating
in those cases which he decided should have a hearing.

As was noted in discussion of the developments in Colorado, it was not clear at first that all states would develop juvenile courts on the Cook County model. Courts
might have grown up in which the links with schools were
of primary importance, and in which probation officers
were employed as part of the educational system. This
was not what took place; juvenile courts grew as independent institutions, providing a focal point through which
delinquent and pre-delinquent children passed for treatment
or referral. There was some opposition to this concentra-
tion in the court of services for delinquents and pre-
delinquents. Thomas Eliot, writing in 1914, makes a plea
for a more community-centred approach to the problems of
delinquents, but he was ahead of his time. He starts his
argument with a statement that 'the world has not been reformed at all'(36) by the juvenile court. Juvenile delinquency, he suggests, is a precipitate of all forms of maladjustment. The juvenile court should not have to fill the
gaps in communities which lacked child-caring agencies to
provide recreation, employment and health care. He considered 'every disposition of the juvenile courts to be an
invasion of penology into the field of social education',
(37) and suggested that the courts should turn over their
probation officers to the school system, because children
should be handled by the community.

By 1922 Eliot was serving as the Chairman of a Committee
of the National Probation Association on the Unofficial
Treatment of Predelinquent Children, and again arguing for
diversion from the court system. Probation officers had
quickly assumed a role in working with children who were
referred to the juvenile court, but who had never been the
subject of an official finding of delinquency. No doubt
they received many referrals from the community, because
other agencies to help children were few and far between.
They became anxious to limit their caseloads and avoid
distributing their efforts so thinly as to have little
effect anywhere. Dr Eliot saw this as another opportunity

for community involvement, and this is what the report
suggests:(38)

Unofficial probation may continue serviceable for many
years to come, but it may also prove possible, and welcome, to turn over an increasing amount of the actual
work, now in this category, to visiting teachers, school
clinics, bureaus, etc., equally or better equipped,
leaving for probation officers the more difficult official cases. In view of the increasingly widespread and
approving interest in such developments among both juvenile court people and school people, your committee suggests that a resolution be considered, directed to the
United States Bureau of Education, to the Department of
Superintendence, National Education Association, to the
Joint Committee on Methods of preventing Delinquency and
to other influential educational bodies, registering the
approval by this organization of the principle of assumption by the educational system, of educational responsibility for the study and treatment of mal-behaviour
problems as primarily educational or reeducational problems, and urging that this be made possible by means of
adequate special equipment and personnel attached to
the educational system, so as to relieve the probation
offices and courts of much extra burden for which they
are not adequately prepared and should not be expected
to assume responsibility; and so as to readjust many
maladjusted children at a much earlier and easier state
of errancy, at a great saving of human misery and social
effort.

Your committee recommends, in the second place, that
probation offices which are handling large numbers of
unofficial cases follow up and study the results of this
policy in individual cases and in the mass, in order that
the standards of judgment and practice may be developed,
and more intelligent recommendations to educational and
social agencies may be made.

Your committee finally recommends that a new standing committee on correlation with educational agencies
be established and that the subject be further studied
and discussed at future meetings.

Again, the idea came too soon. What the NPA were suggesting was to reappear in 1967 in the President's Task Force
Report, under the name of Youth Service Bureau, but Eliot's
report is an early example of the idea that courts are an
inappropriate setting for the management of troubled and
troublesome children.

CONTRIBUTING TO DELINQUENCY

Another development in this early period of thejuvenile
courts was the inclusion in juvenile codes of powers to
deal with adults who contribute to a child's delinquency,
dependency and neglect. In some states this was limited
to jurisdiction over the parents of children, but in others
it referred to any adults. By 1922, forty States had given
their juvenile courts such powers. The rationale seems to
be that children have to appear as witnesses in such cases
and, for them, a juvenile court is a better setting than
an adult criminal court. It is also argued that such cases
involve problems which sooner or later will come to the
juvenile court, and so it is better if they start there.
I have been unable to find any adequate discussion by the
early writers, who seem to regard jurisdiction over those
contributing to delinquency as a logical extension of the
juvenile court's powers. There are, however, arguments
for seeing it as most illogical. The court's jurisdiction
in such cases is clearly criminal, any doubts on that score
having been eliminated in early appeal decisions. This
meant that the juvenile Court, which in all other areas
claimed a non-criminal jurisdiction, in this instance exercised a criminal one. It also seems that, in most instances, there was no need for the new laws, because actions which could be the basis of 'contributing offences'
would have been covered already by sections in the criminal
codes. In fact, in many cases, both juvenile and criminal
courts had jurisdiction. It might be argued that this was
an early attempt at a family focus by the juvenile court,
which was trying to extend to parents some of the welfare
concepts developed in relation to children. However, I can
find little to support this view, except a statement by
Judge Lindsay that he used chancery proceedings for hearing
some charges contributing to delinquency, but had criminal
procedures for use in severe cases.(39) Colorado was the
first State to add contributing clauses to its juvenile
code in 1903 and forty states followed by 1972.

CONSTITUTIONAL QUESTIONS

The early juvenile courts look like a triumph for a welfare
approach to juvenile justice. However, during the first
years there were a number of appeals which raised the question of the constitutionality of these Courts. The appel-
lants argued that children were being committed to State
institutions without due process of law. In particular,
they were deprived of their right to a jury trial. As we

have seen, these were not new arguments, as the earlier
statutes, which allowed magistrates to commit children to
industrial schools, had been subjected to attack on similar
grounds. However, the number of appeals increased with the
passing of the Juvenile Court Acts, and by 1922 a publication of the Children's Bureau lists decisions on appeal
in twenty-two different states. What these decisions have
in common is their finding that juvenile courts when dealing with children were not criminal in nature. From this
they argue that, in a carefully drawn statute, constitutionality is not open to question, even when the act provides none of the safeguards designed to protect the accused in a criminal prosecution. Such protections are unnecessary in actions aimed at meeting the needs of the
child. The opinion in *Cinque* v. *Boyd* in 1923 states the
issue:(40)

> The constitutional objections turn upon whether the Act
> is one for the punishment of crime, and therefore sub-
> ject in its form and in the manner of its administra-
> tion to the constitutional guarantees in various parti-
> culars contained in the Bill of Rights, or whether it
> is concerned with the care and protection which every
> State as *parens patriae* in some measure affords to all
> inhabitants who from personal deficiencies or incapa-
> cities or conditions of life are in some degree abnormal,
> and hence in its scope, intent and method of administra-
> tion is entirely of a civil nature.

The much quoted opinion in an early case *Commonwealth* v.
Fisher gives the prevailing opinion:(41)

> In pressing the objection that the appellant was not
> taken into custody by due process of law, the assumption,
> running through the entire argument of the appellant, is
> continued, that the proceedings of the act of 1903 are
> of a criminal nature for the punishment of offenders
> for crimes committed, and that the appellant was so
> punished. But he was not, and he could not have been
> without due process of law, for the constitutional
> guaranty is that no one charged with a criminal offense
> shall be deprived of life, liberty or property without
> due process of law. To save a child from becoming a
> criminal, or from continuing in a career of crime, to
> end in maturer years in public punishment and disgrace,
> the legislature surely may provide for the salvation of
> such a child, if its parents or guardian be unable or
> unwilling to do so, by bringing it into one of the
> courts of the state without any process at all, for
> the purpose of subjecting it to the state's guardian-
> ship and protection. The natural parent needs no pro-
> cess to temporarily deprive his child of its liberty

by confining it in his own home, to save it and to
shield it from the consequences of persistence in a
career of waywardness, nor is the state, when compelled,
as *parens patriae*, to take the place of the father for
the same purpose, required to adopt any process as a
means of placing its hands upon the child to lead it
into one of its courts. When the child gets there and
the court, with the power to save it, determines on its
salvation, and not its punishment, it is immaterial how
it got there. The act simply provides how children who
ought to be saved may reach the court to be saved. If
experience should show that there ought to be other
ways for it to get there, the legislature can, and un-
doubtedly will, adopt them, and they will never be
regarded as undue processes for depriving a child of its
liberty or property as a penalty for crime committed.
Whether or not the juvenile court was a criminal court
was the central issue in these early appeals, and it was
decided in an absolute way. The idea that a court could
have some criminal aspects and some civil or equitable
ones does not seem to have arisen. Appeal courts are
forced to decide between conflicting parties and to reach
a decision on the issues. They are not an ideal place
for weighing issues and maintaining some balance between
them.

There were only two states which held out against the
trend. In Texas, in 1917, the juvenile court law was
found to be invalid on the ground that it authorised the
court to fix punishment which,(42) by the law which gives
the right to jury trial, must be fixed by the jury. In
Missouri, the 1913 Act was held invalid because it violated that provision of the State Constitution declaring
that 'no person shall be prosecuted criminally for felony
or misdemeanor otherwise than by indictment and information'; and another provision declaring that in criminal
prosecutions the accused shall have the right to appear
and defend, in person or by counsel, 'to demand the nature
and cause of accusation against him' and 'a speedy public
trial by an impartial jury of the county'.(43) But neither
the Supreme Court of Texas nor that of Missouri could hold
out. Both later reversed themselves, and their juvenile
courts were held to be constitutional.

Whether or not the court had criminal jurisdiction was
the major issue, but early appeals also dealt with other
constitutional questions. The constitution of most States
forbade the establishment of new courts, and several early
appeals dealt with the issue of whether or not a juvenile
court was a new court. They held that the acts did not
create a new court, but a division of an existing court, be

it probate, circuit or superior court, which was itself
constitutional. Nor were the acts found to create local
law or to be unconstitutional in that they created special
legislation. Although at the time such acts were passed
they related only to city areas with a certain population
size, they might apply to all counties in the future. Appeal
courts held that the legislature has power to reach out to
densely populated cities, and furnish to a class of children in them the opportunity for reform which is not necessary in other counties, 'where families live far apart and
parental authority is ever present'.(44)

1925 TO 1950 - THE LATENCY PERIOD

By 1925 the major issues seemed settled and the first
exciting years were passed. The next twenty-five years
saw attempts to raise standards in juvenile courts and
probation departments, and to achieve some measure of uniformity across the nation. The Children's Bureau had discovered, in the study undertaken by Miss Belden in 1919,
how wide was the difference between standards in different
areas. In 1923 they published a guide to standards for
Juvenile Courts, which was developed in co-operation with
the National Probation Association. This was followed in
1925 by the first standard Juvenile Court Act; a guide
for States wanting to reform their juvenile codes. This
Act was updated by the National Probation Association,
under its later name of National Probation and Parole
Association, in 1928, 1938, 1943 and 1949. The National
Council of Juvenile Court Judges, founded in 1937, provided another means of achieving common standards. The
period was one of stabilising and organising. Little that
was new was introduced by these standard acts, because the
main lines of development had been set early in the century.
     One important legislative change did occur during the
period, with the establishment of federal juvenile courts.
Previously young people who committed offences which brought
them under the jurisdiction of the federal courts were
either dealt with by those criminal courts or, at the discretion of the federal prosecutor, referred to the state
juvenile court. Not until 1938 were federal courts empowered to sit as juvenile courts themselves.
     With this exception, the important developments of the
period were in social work methods with children rather
than in the legal aspects of the system. Even developments in social work were limited, as the probation departments were not in the forefront of social work. The new
theories of Freud, which revolutionised social work in

psychiatric and private family agencies, had assumed a
very diluted form by the time they reached the juvenile
courts. Probation staff were often untrained, and the new
developments in child study passed them by. Moran, writing
in 1930, comments: 'The staff of probation officers may
not only be inadequate in numbers, but be made up of individuals whose previous experience has been gained as under-
takers, instalment collectors, insurance agents, court
attendants or sign painters'.(45) With such probation officers Chute's words, written in 1949, indicated an aim rather
than a reality: 'Law violators, the anti-social and maladjusted, especially children, should be treated individually through social casework processes for their own protection and that of society, instead of by the punitive and
retaliatory methods of the criminal law'.(46) In some
places some children no doubt received skilled help, but
such writing also served to detract public attention from
the reality of the juvenile courts, and to hide them behind a misty veil of good intentions.

The enthusiasm and reforming zeal had gone. Psychiatry,
and especially child-guidance clinics, assumed the mantle
which juvenile courts had worn earlier. Although the first
child guidance clinics had been set up to provide diagnosis
and treatment for children coming before the juvenile
courts they seem to have distanced themselves from these
courts over the years, and had remarkably little effect
upon courts' structures or procedures or the methods used
by probation staff. Few eminent judges interested themselves in juvenile courts or made their names in those
courts, as had happened in the early years of the century.
Tenney, commenting on this change, says that far from being
famous, 'by mid-century he risked a better than even chance
of being known as a member of what one midwestern judge
described as "the diaper squad".'(47)

Emerson comments on the process in one juvenile court,
suggesting that the court reflected neither a welfare nor
a criminal-justice philosophy:(48)

What began as a radical social experiment has become
routinized and institutionalized. But institutionalization occurs as part of a process whereby the court
adapts itself to its social and organizational environment. . . .

The juvenile court was established at the beginning
of the twentieth century in conjunction with an upper-
class, native American humanitarian and philanthropic
reform movement, and its early judges were drawn from
this tradition. The earlier court staff was also closely
allied with local settlement houses and social agencies
and frequently went on to further careers in profes-

sional social work. Psychologists and psychiatrists
were regularly consulted in court matters. Gradually,
however, all this changed. The court staff increasingly
came to reflect the political power of the city's ethnic
groups. The Irish became prominent, and eventually an
Irish Catholic was appointed to the judgeship that had
come to be regarded by the Yankee Protestants as their
traditional preserve. Concurrently with this development, the professional affiliations of the staff grew
weaker.   This reflected not only the change in training and ethnicity among court staff, but also the increasing professionalization of social work and its
related withdrawal from matters concerning courts and
delinquency. Ties with political, enforcement, and correctional bodies came to be stronger than those with the
world of child welfare.
One way of describing the period from about 1925 to 1950
is to suggest that the juvenile court sank into obscurity
because it no longer provided a focus and a meeting point
for the conflicting approaches of welfare and criminal
justice. The balance had been lost and the welfare approach
had too strong a hold. The vigilance which is part of criminal justice was missing. Issues of control, punishment
and rights are, however, real ones and cannot be ignored
too long. From the late 1940s we can see attention of a
critical kind being focused on the juvenile justice system. The criticisms gained momentum and reached their peak
in the Supreme Court of the United States in the 1960s when,
for the first time, the rights and treatment of juveniles
reached the highest court in the land.

RENEWED CONCERN WITH RIGHTS

A new emphasis began to emerge from the late 1940s. On the
one hand there appeared an inclination to look beyond the
rhetoric and intentions of the juvenile justice system to
the realities of its operation, and on the other there developed a renewed concern with the rights of children. The
question of reality had been amazingly neglected. With the
major exception of the Illinois appeal court in 1970,
when the judges found the Chicago Reform School to be a
place of punishment,(49) the courts and the public managed
to ignore the fact that not only did children who were
sent to reform and industrial schools consider that they
were being punished, but that many of these institutions
were so run that any reasonable person would say they were
punitive. Courts went to extreme lengths to maintain what
was often a fiction. For example, in 1914 the Ohio court

in Leonard v. Licken(50) found that a juvenile's rights
had not been denied, although he had been committed by
a juvenile court to the state reformatory without a jury
trial. They reasoned that, although the reformatory
housed adults and was for them a prison, when a child was
committed there it was only a place of reformation. It
must be admitted that even the Children's Bureau, who were
in the forefront of the movement to socialise juvenile
justice, gave this as an example of a court that had 'gone
too far'. However, there was little opposition to the useful fiction which allowed for the punishment of children
under the guise of reformation and protected the conscience
and the pockets of the tax payers. By the 1950s some realism had emerged. The Gluecks, who were already eminent
criminologists, comment on the myth:(51)

> By a convenient but highly misleading sophistry, it is
> maintained that the child is not charged with a 'crime',
> 'convicted' as a 'criminal', nor 'sentenced to a pun-
> ishment'. Rather, he is merely 'adjudicated' under a
> 'petition' as a 'delinquent', studied to determine how
> he may be 'saved', and then 'treated' in his own best
> interest. The slightest inspection of the character-
> istic methodology and personnel of the children's
> court, the detention facility, or the training school,
> should disillusion any but the most ingenuous about
> these euphemisms. Unfortunately most people never
> scrutinize these facilities critically and are led
> quite readily to confuse what juvenile courts are with
> what interested parties wishfully imagine their be-
> coming.

This realism extended not only to training institutions but
to the effects of a finding of delinquency upon future
prospects. The idea that even a juvenile court appearance
is stigmatising was beginning to develop:(52)

> While the juvenile court law provides that adjudication
> of a minor to be a ward of the court shall not be deemed
> to be a conviction of crime, nevertheless, for all prac-
> tical purposes, this is a legal fiction, presenting a
> challenge to credulity and doing violence to reason.
> Courts cannot and will not shut their eyes and ears to
> everyday contemporary happenings. . . .
>
>   It is common knowledge that such an adjudication when
> based upon a charge of committing an act that amounts to
> a felony, is a blight upon the character of and is a
> serious impediment to the future of such minor. Let
> him attempt to enter the armed services of his country
> or obtain a position of honor and trust and he is im-
> mediately confronted with his juvenile court record.

Despite the promise of confidentiality of juvenile court dockets and records, the exceptions made in the case of persons or agencies deemed to have a legitimate need to inspect are so numerous as to seem as much the rule as the exception.   The Armed Forces, for example, are generally given the right to inquire into delinquency adjudications in the cases of persons being investigated for security clearance, and the more sought-after services erect stringent enlistment barriers to anyone having a juvenile court record.   A study of the New York City Children's Court revealed that representatives of the FBI, the Civil Service, the Army, the Red Cross, the Traveler's Aid Society, various social agencies, the Hack License Bureau, and the Department of Public Welfare had access to the Court's legal records despite the usual statutory provision that 'no adjudication under the provisions of this Act shall operate as a disqualification of any child'.

The rights of children once again become a focus of concern during this period.   Arthur Vanderbilt comments on the need for protection of legal rights in 1953:(53)

In their zeal to care for children neither juvenile judges nor welfare workers can be permitted to violate the Constitution, especially the constitutional provisions as to due process that are involved in moving a child from its home.   The indispensable elements of due process are: first, a tribunal with jurisdiction; second, notice of a hearing to the proper parties; and finally, a fair hearing.   All three must be present if we are to treat the child as an individual human being and not to revert, in spite of good intentions, to the more primitive days when he was treated as a chattel.

Why these issues become important again at this time is difficult to say.   In part, the rising crime rates of the immediate post Second World War years suggested that the juvenile court had failed.   Further rising crime rates seem to have led to a discrediting of a welfare approach and a demand for tougher measures of control and punishment. Emerson's work illustrates just such a shift of opinion in one juvenile court:(54)

earlier beliefs in scientifically based techniques, administered in a spirit of benevolent paternalism, gave way to a more openly moralistic, locally oriented, and 'common-sense' approach.   This shift in orientation can be dramatically illustrated by changes in ideas of the nature of delinquency and the juvenile court.   As the first judge of the court wrote in an early magazine article:

> The Juvenile Court is administered on the assumption
> that the fundamental function of a juvenile court is
> to put each child who comes before it in a normal
> relation to society as promptly and as permanently
> as possible. . . .

But forty years later, the traditional enforcement concern of the criminal law pervaded the testimony of the
immediate predecessor of the current judge before a
United States Senate sub-committee:

> We must educate children to understand that there
> must be respect for authority. We know that you
> cannot have order without law and the respect for
> the law. There is no law without the sanctions
> and penalties for any person who is rash enough to
> offend the law.

Such views can be described as part of a law and order
approach, which is one aspect of a criminal justice philosophy and carries with it the idea of rights and legal
protection for the accused. Another strand in the factors
leading to this change was a developing concern with the
rights of minorities, which included children along with
blacks and, later, women.

What is clear is that once the tide turned, there were
few dissident voices. Tappen, who was one of the first to
raise the issues, puts together the central arguments.
Whatever the intentions, courts must be judged by the facts.
Damaging experiences are not made therapeutic by the good
intentions of the sentencing judge. The child has the
right to protection against dispositions which may determine not only his immediate future but his adult life as
well.(55)

> The attempt to justify certain contemporary experimental
> procedures in children's courts by the concept of 'chan-
> cery' is an irrelevant identification of methods, whether
> the comparison is to ancient chancery, to modern equity,
> or to civil law. The procedures of these courts must
> stand or fall on their own merits in relation to con-
> temporary needs, not on analogies. However, it has
> been popular practice thus to rationalize the abandon-
> ment, partial or complete, of even the most basic con-
> ceptions of due process of law: a specific charge;
> confrontation by one's adverse witnesses; right to
> counsel and appeal; rejection of prejudicial, irrele-
> vant, and hearsay testimony; adjudication only upon
> proof or upon a plea of guilt. The presumption is com-
> monly adopted that since the state has determined to
> protect and save its wards, it will do no injury to
> them through its diverse officials, so that these chil-
> dren need no due process protections against injury.

Several exposures to court; a jail remand of days,
weeks, or even months; and a long period in a correctional school with young thieves, muggers, and mur-
derers - these can do no conceivable harm if the state's
purpose be beneficent and the procedure be 'chancery'.
Children are adjudicated in this way every day without
visible manifestations of due process. They are in-
carcerated. They become adult criminals, too, in thank-
less disregard of the state's good intentions as *parens
patriae*.

These ideas were developed by other lawyers, notably by
the contributors to 'Justice for the Child', published in
1962, which its editor says:(56)

reflects the desire of many that there be renewed attention to what is *just* for children. Discussion of 'problem children' often is cast in terms of 'service' and
'treatment'. Without discrediting the worthiness of
these objectives, the contributors to this book have
emphasized the absolute necessity that just procedures
for judicial intervention into the lives of children be
defined and their existence guaranteed.

While the lawyers were working on the child's rights,
sociologists were developing theories of deviance which
attribute delinquency, not to individual characteristics,
but to the action of society. In 1967 the President's
Task Force on Juvenile Delinquency provided a platform for
the new doctrines. The juvenile court had failed to prevent delinquency and adult crime. This idea, that court
action could prevent children becoming adult recidivists
and paupers, was, as we have seen, important in the nineteenth century. It infused the early juvenile court movement and had been the justification for the court's intervention. The Task Force, however, accepted Tappen's viewpoint:(57)

This point is decisive: social science cannot predict
from a behavior problem to delinquency with any degree
of accuracy. The community may not safely, therefore,
employ the potentially injurous (sic) techniques of court
treatment upon nondelinquents in the hope that here and
there some good may be done. The record of failures in
dealing with delinquents, even first offenders, is far
too bleak to justify courts in experimenting with children who have committed no acts in violation of legislatively established policy. How often delinquents are
manufactured through children's courts there is no way
to tell. But there is no doubt that the courts are
often affirmatively responsible for the delinquent
careers (sic) of individuals upon whom preventive efforts have been practiced. In the 'social surgery' of

juvenile courts, the patient is always left with some
postoperative infection; it may be more serious than
was his disease.

Legislatures and appeal courts began to follow the developments in sociological and legal thought. In 1954 the
United States Children's Bureau published a new 'Standards
for Specialized Courts Dealing with Children', which was
written in co-operation with the National Probation and
Parole Association and the National Council of Juvenile
Court Judges. In commenting on the philosophy of the juvenile courts, this guide suggests:(58)

> the need for a reevaluation of some of the earlier ap-
> proaches and attitudes. The system of handling the prob-
> lems of children must not degenerate 'into a star-
> chamber proceedings with the judge' - or, it might be
> added, the social worker or the psychiatrist - 'impo-
> sing his own particular brand of culture and morals on
> indigent people.' As Roscoe Pound writes, 'The powers
> of the Star Chamber were a trifle in comparison with
> those of our juvenile courts and courts of domestic
> relations. . . . It is well known that too often the
> placing of a child in a home or even in an institution
> is done casually or perfunctorily, or even arbitrarily
> . . . . Even with the most superior personnel, these
> tribunals call for legal checks.

We find the same attention to rights in the Standard
Juvenile Court Act published by the National Probation and
Parole Association in 1959. While suggesting that proceedings should resemble a conference rather than a trial, they
also say:(59)

> Even though the proceedings are universally held to be
> civil in nature, the legal rights of all parties should
> be strictly protected. The judge should explain that
> the child and the parents have a right to counsel,
> that the child will not be required to be a witness
> against himself, that he is entitled to have his own
> witnesses at the hearing, and that confronting witnesses
> may be cross examined.

During the 1950s three states, New York, California and
Illinois, developed new juvenile codes which gave statutory
form to this greater emphasis on rights.

The appeal courts reflect the same trend. There were a
number of appeal decisions, which had the effect of questioning the discretion of the juvenile court. Cases in
North Dakota in 1946(60) and in New York in 1969(61)
reversed committal orders to institutions, partly on the
grounds that such orders had not been arrived at by con-
stitutionally sound procedures. In 1954 the Nebraska Court
questioned legislative intent:(62)

Can it be that the legislature . . . intended to destroy
the traditional and constitutional safeguards of a trial.
Can it be that it intended that trials should be had
without the benefit of testimony of witnesses given
under the sanction of oath or affirmation? Can it be
said that the legislature intended that the liberty
of a child had less sanctity than that of an adult? Even
if it did so intend could that intention be sustained.
We think not.

Reversed.

In 1958 the federal court developed the idea that attempts to classify courts as either criminal or civil
failed to meet the point that due process of the law is
necessary where the law has power to deprive a person of
liberty. The type of jurisdiction is not the relevant
factor.(63)

Ineluctable logic leads to the conclusion that the
constitutional protection against double jeopardy, as
is the case with the right of counsel and the privilege
against self-incrimination, is applicable to all proceedings, irrespective of whether they are denominated
criminal or civil, if the outcome may be deprivation of
liberty of the person. Necessarily, therefore, this is
true of proceedings in the Juvenile Court. Precious
constitutional rights cannot be diminished or whittled
away by the device of changing names of tribunals or
modifying the nomenclature of legal proceedings. The
test must be the nature and the essence of the proceeding rather than its title. If the result may be
a loss of personal liberty, the constitutional safeguards apply.

THE SUPREME COURT DECISIONS

All that was needed now was a decision by the Supreme Court.
Such decisions are binding, not just upon the State from
which the case originates but upon all States. The first
case to reach the Supreme Court was that of Kent v. United
States. This involved the relatively narrow procedural
point as to whether a child was entitled to a hearing on
the question of waiver. Under the laws of the District
of Columbia, a juvenile court might waive to the adult
court without a hearing on the decision to waive. The
Supreme Court considered that the decision whether or not
to waive was vital, since waiver could, and in Kent's
case did, involve the possibility of a death sentence,
which is outside the dispositional powers of a juvenile
court. Apparently some juvenile court judges had been

making a private decision whether or not to waive. Mr
Justice Fortas, delivering the opinion of the court, said:
(64)

> but there is no place in our system of law for reach-
> ing a result of such tremendous consequences without
> ceremony – without hearing, without effective assistance
> of counsel, without a statement of reasons. It is in-
> conceivable that a court of justice dealing with adults,
> with respect to a similar issue, would proceed in this
> manner. It would be extraordinary if society's special
> concern for children, as reflected in the District of
> Columbia's Juvenile Court Act, permitted this proced-
> ure. We hold that it does not. . . .

The opinion hinted at the possibility of more sweeping
decisions, and then drew back.(65) It questioned

> the justifiability of affording a juvenile less pro-
> tection than is accorded to adults suspected of crimi-
> nal offenses, particularly where, as here, there is an
> absence of any indication that the denial of rights
> available to adults was offset, mitigated or explained
> by action of the Government, as *parens patriae*, evi-
> dencing the special solicitude for juveniles commanded
> by the Juvenile Court Act. However, because we remand
> the case on account of the procedural error with respect
> to waiver of jurisdiction, we do not pass upon these
> questions.

There was not long to wait before these wider issues
were raised in *re* Gault. Here the Supreme Court held that
a juvenile who might be sent to a State institution was
entitled to the due process rights of notice of the hearing,
and of the alleged grounds of delinquency, of a warning of
his right to remain silent when being questioned, of counsel at the hearing and of court appointed counsel if he
were unable to afford to retain counsel. The court made
it clear that they were not determining that the juvenile
court had criminal jurisdiction and that due process rights
were therefore involved but were concerned with the safeguards applicable to a juvenile court as such.(66)

> the problem here is to determine what forms of pro-
> cedural protection are necessary to guarantee the fun-
> damental fairness of juvenile proceedings, and not which
> of the procedures now employed in criminal trials should
> be transplanted intact to proceedings in these special-
> ized courts.

The opinion of the court is long, since it includes a review
of the history of the juvenile court and of developments
in modern sociology. Care is taken not to criticise juvenile courts in what might be a destructive way. The following passage is typical:(67)

Further, it is urged that the juvenile benefits from informal proceedings in the court. The early conception
of the Juvenile Court proceeding was one in which a
fatherly judge touched the heart and conscience of the
erring youth by talking over his problems, by paternal
advice and admonition, and in which, in extreme situations, benevolent and wise institutions of the State
provided guidance and help 'to save him from a downward
career'. Then, as now, goodwill and compassion were
admirably prevalent. But recent studies have, with surprising unanimity, entered sharp dissent as to the
validity of this gentle conception. They suggest that
the appearance as well as the actuality of fairness,
impartiality and orderliness - in short, the essentials
of due process - may be a more impressive and more therapeutic attitude so far as the juvenile is concerned. . . .
Mr Justice Black, however, in his concurring but separate
opinion, said: 'This holding strikes a well nigh fatal
blow to much that is unique about the juvenile courts of
the Nation.'

Before shedding any tears for the old status of the juvenile court, it is well to consider the facts which the Gault
case disclosed.(68)

On Monday, June 8, 1964, at about 10 a.m., Gerald Francis
Gault and a friend, Ronald Lewis, were taken into custody
by the Sheriff of Gila County. Gerald was then still
subject to a six months' probation order which had been
entered on February 25, 1964, as a result of his having
been in the company of another boy who had stolen a
wallet from a lady's purse. The police action on June 8
was taken as the result of a verbal complaint by a neigh-
bor of the boys, Mrs Cook, about a telephone call made
to her in which the caller or callers made lewd or inde-
cent remarks. It will suffice for purposes of this
opinion to say that the remarks or questions put to
her were of the irritatingly offensive, adolescent, sex
variety.

   At the time Gerald was picked up, his mother and father were both at work. No notice that Gerald was being
taken into custody was left at the home. No other steps
were taken to advise them that their son had, in effect,
been arrested. Gerald was taken to the Children's
Detention Home. When his mother arrived home at about
6 o'clock, Gerald was not there. Gerald's older brother
was sent to look for him at the trailer home of the
Lewis family. He apparently learned then that Gerald
was in custody. He so informed his mother. The two of
them went to the Detention Home. The deputy probation
officer, Flagg, who was also superintendent of the

Detention Home, told Mrs Gault 'why Jerry was there' and
said that a hearing would be held in Juvenile Court at
3 o'clock the following day, June 9.

Officer Flagg filed a petition with the court on the
hearing day, June 9, 1964. It was not served on the
Gaults. Indeed, none of them saw this petition until
the habeas corpus hearing on August 17, 1964. The petition was entirely formal. It made no reference to
any factual basis for the judicial action which it
initiated. It recited only that 'said minor is under
the age of eighteen years and is in need of the protection of this Honorable Court; (and that) said minor
is a delinquent minor.' It prayed for a hearing and an
order regarding 'the care and custody of said minor'.
Officer Flagg executed a formal affidavit in support of
the petition.

On June 9, Gerald, his mother, his older brother, and
Probation Officers Flagg and Henderson appeared before
the Juvenile Judge in chambers. Gerald's father was not
there. He was at work out of the city. Mrs Cook, the
complainant, was not there. No one was sworn at this
hearing. No transcript or recording was made. No
memorandum or record of the substance of the proceedings was prepared. Our information about the proceedings and the subsequent hearing on June 15, derives
entirely from the testimony of the Juvenile Court Judge,
Mr and Mrs Gault and Officer Flagg at the habeas corpus
proceeding conducted two months later. From this, it
appears that at the June 9 hearing Gerald was questioned
by the judge about the telephone call. There was conflict as to what he said. His mother recalled that
Gerals said he only dialed Mrs Cook's number and handed
the telephone to his friend, Ronald. Officer Flagg recalled that Gerald had admitted making the lewd remarks.
Judge McGhee testified that Gerals 'admitted making one
of these (lewd) statements.' At the conclusion of the
hearing, the judge said he would 'think about it'.
Gerald was taken back to the Detention Home. He was
not sent to his own home with his parents. On June 11
or 12, after having been detained since June 8, Gerald
was released and driven home. There is no explanation
in the record as to why he was kept in the Detention
Home or why he was released. At 5 p.m. on the day of
Gerald's release, Mrs Gault received a note signed by
Officer Flagg. It was on plain paper, not letterhead.
Its entire text was as follows:
    Mrs Gault:
        'Judge McGhee has set Monday June 15, 1964 at
11:00 a.m. as the date and time for further Hearings

on Gerald's delinquency
                    /s/Flagg'

At the appointed time on Monday, June 15, Gerald, his father and mother, Ronald Lewis and his father, and Officers Flagg and Henderson were present before Judge McGhee. Witnesses at the habeas corpus proceeding differed in their recollections of Gerald's testimony at the June 15 hearing. Mr and Mrs Gault recalled that Gerald again testified that he had only dialed the number and that the other boy had made the remarks. Officer Flagg agreed that at this hearing Gerald did not admit making the lewd remarks. But Judge McGhee recalled that 'there was some admission again of some of the lewd statements. He - he didn't admit any of the more serious lewd statements'. Again, the complainant, Mrs Cook, was not present. Mrs Gault asked that Mrs Cook be present 'so she could see which boy that done the talking, the dirty talking over the phone'. The Juvenile Judge said 'she didn't have to be present at that hearing'. The judge did not speak to Mrs Cook or communicate with her at any time. Probation Officer Flagg had talked to her once - over the telephone on June 9.

At this June 15 hearing a 'referral report' made by the probation officers was filed with the court, although not disclosed to Gerald or his parents. This listed the charge as 'Lewd Phone Calls'. At the conclusion of the hearing, the judge committed Gerald as a juvenile delinquent to the State Industrial School 'for the period of his minority (that is, until 21), unless sooner discharged by due process of law'. An order to that effect was entered. It recites that 'after a full hearing and due deliberation the Court finds that said minor is a delinquent child, and that said minor is of the age of 15 years.'

No appeal is permitted by Arizona law in juvenile cases. On August 3, 1964, a petition for a writ of habeas corpus was filed with the Supreme Court of Arizona and referred by it to the Superior Court for hearing.

At the habeas corpus hearing on August 17, Judge McGhee was vigorously cross-examined as to the basis for his actions. He testified that he had taken into account the fact that Gerald was on probation. He was asked 'under what section of . . . the code you found the boy delinquent?'

His answer is set forth in the margin. In substance, he concluded that Gerald came within ARS § 8-201-6(a), which specified that a 'delinquent child' includes one

'who has violated a law of the state or an ordinance or
regulation of a political subdivision thereof'. The
law which Gerald was found to have violated is ARS § 13-
377. This section of the Arizona Criminal Code provides that a person who 'in the presence or hearing of
any woman or child . . . uses vulgar, abusive or obscene
language, is guilty of a misdemeanor . . .' The penalty
specified in the Criminal Code, which would apply to an
adult, is $5 to $50, or imprisonment for not more than
two months. The judge also testified that he acted
under ARS § 8-201-6(d) which includes in the definition
of a 'delinquent child' one who, as the judge phrased
it, is 'habitually involved in immoral matters.'

Asked about the basis for his conclusion that Gerald
was 'habitually involved in immoral matters,' the judge
testified, somewhat vaguely, that two years earlier, on
July 2, 1962, a 'referral' was made concerning Gerald,
'where the boy had stolen a baseball glove from another
boy and lied to the Police Department about it.' The
judge said there was 'no hearing', and 'no accusation'
relating to this incident, 'because of lack of material
foundation.' But it seems to have remained in his mind
as a relevant factor. The judge also testified that
Gerald had admitted making other nuisance phone calls in
the past which, as the judge recalled the boy's testimony,
were 'silly calls, or funny calls, or something like
that.'

Such procedure has little to do with either welfare or criminal justice. Juvenile courts which operated like this
one certainly needed a fatal blow. What is clear is that
if the protections of criminal justice are lost, the welfare approach is likely to become corrupted also.

Gault was a landmark decision and the courts are still
trying to understand its implications. Two later Supreme
Court holdings have clarified it to some extent. In re
Winship(69) the issue raised was the standard of proof required for a finding of delinquency. The standard in criminal trials is beyond reasonable doubt, whereas in civil
proceedings a preponderance of the evidence is sufficient.
The Court held that a juvenile is entitled to proof beyond
a reasonable doubt. Thus far the Supreme Court granted to
juveniles the rights due to an adult in a criminal trial.
McKeiver v. Pennsylvania,(70) however, held that a juvenile
need not be given the choice of trial by jury. Among the
many issues still to be decided are the stage at which procedural protections are to operate. In re Gault dealt only
with the adjudicatory stage of the hearing, and yet the most
vital part, from the child's viewpoint, may be intake, where
it is decided whether he shall come before the court at all,

and the dispositional stage.

Even those parts of the process which have been decided
by the Gault decision require more than a Supreme Court
decision to implement. Studies do suggest that, while many
juvenile courts are a long way from meeting the requirements of in *re* Gault, there is a new emphasis upon procedural rights, and that more attorneys are coming into juvenile courts.

The role confusions the attorneys face will be considered
later but their presence in the courts is likely to focus
attention on the rights of children. What needs to be
guarded against is too violent a swing. Children have
needs as well as rights, and protection of rights may have
no connection at all with meeting needs. The present dis-
illusionment with juvenile courts and the desire to keep
out of them all children who are not seriously delinquent
bodes ill for those who do come to court. No amount of procedural protection can save them if they are to be the
scapegoats for the children who are to be diverted from
the system.

Chapter four

United States: the present juvenile justice system

There is no one juvenile justice system in the United States. Each State and the Federal Government have enacted juvenile codes, and even States with similar laws may organise their courts differently. As Lemert suggests, it is hazardous to generalise:(1)

decisionmaking and judicial outcomes in juvenile courts are phenomena of social organization rather than law *per se*. The variation in such organization is considerable; indeed, this is one of the core difficulties in trying to understand the juvenile court. How to comprehend the protean local adaptations of the many juvenile courts and yet capture those features which make it distinctive as an institution is no mean task....

It is also easy, as Tappen pointed out, to overstate the differences between Criminal and Juvenile Courts:(2)

The wide variety of juvenile courts is matched by the diversity in their mechanics of operation. Unfortunately, in the analysis of their procedures, confusion has come from a common inclination to picture them as uniform throughout the country and to idealize them: to describe optimum practices (or, at least, procedures conceived ideal by the analyst) as though they were characteristic. There has been a tendency to exaggerate the contrasts between juvenile court procedures, pictured in most glowing terms, and those of the criminal court system, viewed in a worst possible and quite inaccurate light. The student should realize that the vast majority of children's courts are distinct from the ordinary court system only in having separate hearings; that in fact their judges and other personnel are engaged in criminal, civil, equity, probate, or other ordinary legal business most of the time....

Such warnings must be kept in mind in attmpting to provide an outline of the juvenile justice system in the United

States which can be used as a basis for comparison with
that of England and Scotland. The Uniform Juvenile Court
Act seems to offer a possible starting point. This was
drafted by the National Conference of Commissioners on
Uniform State Laws in 1968. The Conference was created
partly as a means of achieving some uniformity between the
laws of different States by voluntary processes, in order
to avoid the possibility of uniformity arising out of an
increase in the powers of the Federal Government. The
Commission has drafted Uniform and Model Acts on a number
of topics, and States which plan a change in their statutes are likely to consult the Uniform Act, where one
exists. In their own drafting, the States adapt the uniform acts to their local conditions and priorities, but
such acts are likely to have much in common with acts
similarly drafted in other States. It should be stressed,
however, that the Uniform Juvenile Court Act is
a model of a possible act, rather than a code which anyone actually lives under, so that in some ways we are com-
paring an ideal in the United States with the living law
in England and Scotland. However, the ideal nature of the
Uniform Act may be more apparent than real. It represents
a wide range of interests. In drafting it, the Conference
had the advice and assistance of the US Children's Bureau,
the American Bar Association Committee on Family and Juvenile Law, the National Council of Juvenile Court Judges
and the National Council on Crime and Delinquency. This
last organisation superseded the earlier National Probation and Parole Association, and thus all the groups which
had earlier co-operated in publishing standard Juvenile
Court Acts contributed to this Uniform Act. In its completed form the Act was approved by the American Bar Association. Such wide input and approval suggest that the Act
is neither markedly reactionary nor particularly progressive, since had it been either, it would not have pleased
so many people. In this way it may be comparable to a bill
which becomes law through the British parliamentary process. What makes comparison difficult is that the Uniform Act is a model which the drafters knew would be scru-
tinised again before it actually affected anyone, whereas
an Act of Parliament can have an immediate effect upon the
lives of children, parents and officials. Another difference is that the people who drafted the Uniform Act were
mostly lawyers. Even the National Council of Crime and
Delinquency chose a judge to represent them on the Commission. The discussions preceding the passing of the Social
Work (Scotland) Act, 1968, and the Children and Young Persons Act, 1969, had been stimulated by three White Papers
and were unusually wide. If anything, they may have had

too much social welfare input and too little legal input.
This, however, is indicative of the relative powers of lawyers on the two sides of the Atlantic as well as the movement in the United States away from what the early reformers called 'socialised justice'. (Socialised here has no
political-party connotations, but means concerned with
social and psychological issues.)

The Uniform Act was written in 1968, after the United
States Supreme Court had handed down the decisions in the
Kent(3) and Gault(4) cases. The prefatory note to the Act
says it 'has been drawn with a view to fully meeting the
mandates of these decisions'.(5)

Where they differ from the Uniform Act, reference will
also be made to the United States Children's Bureau publication of 1969; a Legislative Guide for drafting Family
and Juvenile Court Acts, and to the Model Rules for Juvenile Courts, published by the Council of Judges of the
National Council on Crime and Delinquency in 1969. The
legislative guide was 'developed in response to requests
for technical assistance in drafting family and juvenile
court acts and increased interest throughout the country
in juvenile and family acts'.(6) It takes into account
research by the Social and Rehabilitation Service of the
United States Children's Bureau into the State juvenile
justice systems, and also mentions the influence of the
report of the President's Commission on Law Enforcement
and Administration of Justice. This report was critical
of the juvenile justice system, and no doubt the Children's Bureau, which had earlier been a strong supporter of
socialised justice for children, felt the need to issue its
own statement in addition to providing input to the Uniform
Act. The Model Rules are somewhat different since they are
a supplement and not an alternative to a model act. The
compilers suggest they be used together with the Standard
Juvenile and Family Court Act, published by the National
Council of Crime and Delinquency in 1959, and make no mention of the more recent Uniform Act. Rules deal with
practice and procedure and not with substantive law, although the distinction is often difficult to make. In
each State a particular body is empowered to make rules for
the courts. In some it is the Supreme Court of the State
in whom this power is vested, in others a state-wide board
of juvenile court judges has been created to promulgate
rules for juvenile courts, while in some States individual
courts establish their own rules. These rules and the power
to make them are important, because it is often the procedural rules which give reality to the protection of rights.

In outlining the juvenile justice system we shall consider only some of its aspects and provisions. The aim is

not to provide a comprehensive survey, but to offer sufficient material for comparative purposes and as a basis for
the discussion of the underlying approaches. We are omit-
ting, for example, all mention of detention arrangements,
which are an interesting but complicated topic which could
be dealt with independently.

PURPOSES OF THE UNIFORM ACT AND THE LEGISLATIVE GUIDE

Both the Act and the Guide express clearly the dual aims
of the system. It is, so far as possible, to preserve the
family and provide for the care, protection and wholesome
moral, mental and physical development of children, and
to remove from children committing delinquent acts the
taint of criminality and the consequences of criminal behaviour. This is to be done in a way consistent with the
public interest and ensuring to the parties a fair hearing,
in which their constitutional and other legal rights are
recognised and enforced.
     The Guide, in commenting, suggests that the purpose
clause in State Acts often does not include protection of
the public interest nor do the Acts necessarily establish
procedures to ensure due process to children.

THE COURT

There is a commentary to the Act. This suggests jurisdiction be 'vested in the trial court of general jurisdiction
or a branch or division of that court',(7) and the Guide
vests jurisdiction in the 'highest court of general jurisdiction'.(8) The idea behind these clauses is to ensure
to juvenile jurisdiction the advantages of being sited in
the most prestigious court. In the hierarchy of courts in
most States the lowest are those of the justice of the
peace, with a very limited jurisdiction, largely restricted
to minor traffic offences. Next come the police or city
courts, again with a limited jurisdiction. The circuit
and superior courts usually have jurisdiction over all types
of civil and criminal cases, and it is to these courts that
the Act and Guide assign juvenile jurisdiction.
     It is difficult to summarise the actual position in the
fifty-one States because the variations are numerous, not
only between States but within a State, where different
counties may operate different systems. In addition the
names given to courts in different States vary and so do not
provide a basis for comparison. Levin and Sarri,(9) to whom
I am indebted for their survey of juvenile courts, used as

one means of comparison whether or not appeals from a juvenile court were heard in the appellate court or in a higher
trial court. The importance of this distinction is that,
if appeal lies to the appellate court, it rests upon the
trial records, whereas an intermediate trial court would
retry the whole case, despite the fact that it would have
no special knowledge or experience of juvenile problems.
Levin and Sarri found the following distribution in 1974:

Appeals	Nos of States
Taken to a higher court	30
Taken to an appellate court	15
Intrastate variations	5
No provision	1

Another important variation is the amount of time a judge
gives to juvenile court work. When a juvenile court is a
special session of a circuit or superior court, it may be
presided over by a judge who spends most of his time in
the ordinary sessions of that court. When the juvenile
court is a permanent branch or division of the circuit or
superior court, it may have a full-time judge. The latter
situation is usually found in counties with large popula-
tions, although the size varies from a population of 50,000
in Georgia, Nebraska, South Carolina and Washington to one
of 500,000 in Colorado, Maryland, Ohio, Pennsylvania and
Wisconsin.

Amongst the twenty-five States which have the same kind
of juvenile court throughout the State some - Connecticut,
Delaware, Rhode Island and Utah - have a separate State-
wide juvenile court system, funded and administered at the
State level. More usual, however, is a system whereby a
specific level of court is named as the one to handle juvenile cases in each county.

PERSONNEL

Whether juvenile jurisdiction is vested by the State in
circuit court or superior court, in a special juvenile
court, a family court or a probate court, it will be presided over by one person, usually one man, a judge or
referee. Ultimately a judge is always responsible for the
decisions made in the juvenile court, and will be appointed
by the same method as that used to appoint other judges in
the State. In some states judicial appointments are made
by members of an elected board, who appoint judges, subject only to their removal or continuation in office by
public vote. In other States judges are elected in local
political elections every four or six years. In courts
where the judge has juvenile jurisdiction as only one part,

and usually a small part, of his total judicial duties, it
is unlikely that great attention will be paid to the special qualities which the comment on Section 9 of the Uniform Act suggests are required of a judge: 'not only a
knowledge of the law but also a knowledge of behavioral
sciences and a sympathetic understanding of the problems
and needs of children.'

The Act and the Guide both include provision for the
appointment by the judge of referees who substitute for
the judge in conducting juvenile court hearings. The Guide
suggests that the judge should conduct the hearing in all
contested cases or cases where transfer to the adult court
is a possibility, as well as in any case where the party
objects to a hearing by the referee. In cases where a
referee conducts the hearing, he should give written findings and recommendations to the judge and the parties concerned. The judge may order, or the parties within three
days of receiving the written report may ask for, a re-
hearing before the judge. Unless this occurs, the written
disposition becomes the order of the court.

The actual use of referees varies. In some areas a judge
may hand over virtually all of the responsibility for the
juvenile court to a referee and almost never sit himself,
while in others, referees handle only the most routine situations. The idea behind the appointment of referees is to
ease the load on a judge when there is too much work for
one judge but not enough to warrant the appointment of another. In the early days of juvenile courts there were other
reasons for referees, such as providing a woman to hear
girls' cases. Referees then, and even now, are not always
members of the bar, although the Uniform Act suggests that
'in view of Kent and Gault, with their emphasis on the legal
and constitutional rights of the parties, it is believed
important that training in the law should be required.'(10)
The Guide suggests the dangers of another practice, that of
using probation officers as referees, since 'this could
create a conflict of interest in discharging the duties of
a referee in cases where they were active in another capacity. (11)

The other class of personnel whose appointment and duties
are determined by the Act are the probation officers. Here
the Act and the Guide differ. The Act leaves open whether
each court shall appoint and maintain its own probation
service, or whether a state-wide department shall arrange
for each juvenile court to have the services of probation
officers. In comment, the Act sets out the arguments:(12)

A probation service may be established on either a local
or a statewide basis. Competent authorities disagree on
the relative merits of the two alternatives. The

National Council of Juvenile Court Judges favors a local
system stressing the importance of having these services provided by court personnel responsible to and
under the direction of the juvenile court judge since
he is responsible for the successful conduct of the
juvenile program. Proponents of the statewide system
stress the frequent inadequacy of local resources to
provide the needed minimum service required and contend
that better probation service is provided by a state
system, and that the prospect of the judge successfully
achieving the objectives of the court's program is
therefore enhanced.

The Guide, however, states:

The State agency responsible for the administration of
State services for delinquent children, shall establish
a State wide program of probation and other casework
and clinical services to serve the court, the cost
thereof to be paid out of the general revenue funds of
the State.

All employees shall be selected appointed and pro-
moted through a State merit system.

In comment the Guide adds:(13)

It is strongly recommended that probation services be
established on a statewide basis as part of the executive branch of government. Continuity of responsibility and treatment is attained when service and care
for delinquent children are in a single agency. Such
a system also will provide continuity of administration
and will promote a more equitable distribution of services in terms of both quality and quantity, as well as
uniformity of procedure. These characteristics are
presently lacking in most States because the localities
have responsibility for the services and they are often
not in a position to provide them adequately.

Unfortunately the suggestions of the Guide are far from
the reality. Many probation services are local, the power
of appointment resting solely with the judge, who may
know nothing about the qualifications or qualities desirable in a probation officer. At one extreme the judge,
elected himself, may see the job of probation officer as
a patronage position to be filled by one of his political
supporters. At the other are to be found highly trained
and organised probation services, where the relationship
between judge and probation officer is a relationship between professional equals.

The Act and the Guide prescribe the duties of the probation staff in an attempt both to suggest the potential
of a good service and to end the use of probation officers
as general dogs' bodies, additional members of the sheriff's

staff, or substitutes for a prosecutor. The Guide outlines the duties:

(a) For the purpose of carrying out the objectives and provisions of this Act, and subject to the limitations of this Act, probation and social services personnel have the power and duty to:

(1) receive and examine complaints and allegations that a child is neglected, delinquent, or in need of supervision for the purpose of considering the commencement of proceedings under this Act;

(2) make appropriate referrals of cases presented to him as such officer, to other private or public agencies of the community where their assistance appears to be needed or desirable.

(3) make predisposition studies and submit reports and recommendations to the court as required by this Act;

(4) supervise and assist a child placed on probation or under his supervision by order of the court;

(5) provide marital and family counseling;

(6) perform such other functions as are designated by this Act or by rules of court pursuant thereto.

(b) For the purposes of this Act, a probation officer shall have the power to take into custody and place in temporary care a child who is under his supervision as a delinquent or neglected child, or a child in need of supervision when the probation officer has reasonable cause to believe that the child has violated the conditions of his probation or that he may flee from the jurisdiction of the court. A probation officer does not have the powers of a law enforcement officer nor may he sign a petition under this Act with respect to a person who is not on probation or otherwise under his supervision.(14)

JURISDICTION

What is meant by a child and what kinds of behaviour bring a child within the jurisdiction of a juvenile court, are questions which have given rise to considerable dispute. The Uniform Act and the Guide agree that juvenile courts should have original jurisdiction over an individual who is under the age of eighteen years or under the age of twenty-one but has committed an act of delinquency before reaching the age of eighteen years. As Levin and Sarri show in their comparative analysis of juvenile codes, the actual situation is that:

the maximum age for original jurisdiction is 17 years
in 33 states.(15)   In 12 states the maximum age is 16,
(16) and in the remaining (6) states the court can
adjucate only those age 15(17) and under. . . . Three
states (Illinois, Oklahoma and Texas) still set a lower
maximum age for males than for females, but such a distinction has been held unconstitutional by state tribunals.(18)

Once the court has acquired jurisdiction over a juvenile,
the Act in section 36 allows orders of disposition to be
made for periods of up to two years. These may be termi-
nated sooner or, with additional hearings extended for
further two-year periods. All jurisdiction, however, is to
cease when the child becomes twenty-one-years old. In
this respect the Act reflects current State law fairly
closely. Forty-one States give the court continuing jurisdiction over children until they become twenty-one-years
old.(19)

The class of child over whom the juvenile court should
have jurisdiction is defined similarly by the Act and the
Guide, although the Guide uses the term 'persons in need
of supervision' and 'neglected child' to refer to those
children called 'unruly' and 'deprived' in the Act. The
definitions taken from the Act are:(20)

(3)   'delinquent child' means a child who has committed
a delinquent act and is in need of treatment or rehabilitation;

(4)   'unruly child' means a child who:
  (i) while subject to compulsory school attendance
  is habitually and without justification truant from
  school;
  (ii) is habitually disobedient of the reasonable and
  lawful commands of his parent, guardian, or other
  custodian and is ungovernable; [or]
  (iii) has committed an offense applicable only to a
  child; [and]
  (iv) in any of the foregoing is in need of treatment
  or rehabilitation;

(5)   'deprived child' means a child who:
  (i) is without proper parental care or control,
  subsistence, education as required by law, or other
  care or control necessary for his physical, mental
  or emotional health, or morals, and the deprivation
  is not due primarily to the lack of financial means
  of his parents, guardian, or other custodian;
  (ii) has been placed for care or adoption in violation
  of law; [or]
  (iii) has been abandoned by his parents, guardian or
  other custodian; [or]

[(iv) is without a parent, guardian, or legal custodian;]
A delinquent act is earlier defined as 'a crime under the
law', including local ordinances of the State or of another
state or the Federal Government. The definition of delinquency excludes any behaviour covered by section(4) on
the unruly child. It also excludes traffic offences in
general, but allows for the more serious traffic offences,
such as negligent homicide and driving under the influence
of drugs or alcohol, to be included. It is important to
note that a child cannot become subject to the jurisdiction
of the court unless he has behaved in one of the specified
ways *and* is in need of treatment or rehabilitation. How
such need is to be determined is a very difficult question,
but the Act does make it clear that behaviour alone is not
enough to give the court jurisdiction.

The Act sets out the three types of jurisdiction which
have usually been given to juvenile courts: that over
children who are said to have committed offences under
the criminal codes; that over children who are said to
have behaved in ways (such as truanting or being immoral)
which are illegal only for children; and that over depen-
dant or neglected children. In practice, thirty-nine
States categorise those who have committed offences as
delinquents, and the other twelve use terms like 'offenders', 'wards of court' or 'children', which Levin and
Sarri suggest are intended to be less stigmatising than
delinquent.

It is the second grouping - of those who are said to
have behaved in ways forbidden only in children - which
causes the most concern and confusion. The forms of behaviour within this grouping are often referred to as
'status offences', because many of the grounds for jurisdiction refer to the state of being of the child rather
than to specific actions. For example, being 'immoral' or
'incorrigible' or 'in need of supervision' are all terms
included in State codes. The grouping usually also includes some acts such as truancy, curfew breaking and under-
age drinking as well as the status offences. The major controversy is whether children in this grouping should be
classified with children who have broken the law and, more
important, whether courts should be able to send children
in both groups to the same residential institutions.
Twenty-six States classify status offenders and those who
commit acts which in an adult are crimes as delinquents,
and all are subject to the same dispositions. Twenty-five
States have, like the Act, a separate category for status
offenders, although the name given to those in this grouping
varies. Levin and Sarri(21) point out that in these States

'the distinction is generally more than merely semantic'.
Eighteen of the States using a separate category also
place restrictions on the dispositional alternatives available to the juvenile court judge for status offenders, and
four States require separate detention housing. Restrictions on disposition are of two main types:
1 a flat prohibition on housing status offenders and
delinquents together, or
2 a requirement that the judge must first find the child
unamenable to other forms of treatment before committing a status offender to a training school or other correctional facility.

States whose codes have been revised recently show a
definite trend toward division into separate categories.
No special provision for status offenders can be found in
codes predating 1959.

Compared with many State statutes, the Act simplifies
the categories of children who may be subject to juvenile
court jurisdiction and reduces the specific types of behaviour with which it is concerned. In 1954 Sussman(22)
found that fifty-eight different actions were named in
various State codes, and some States still included ana-
chronistic provisions like 'frequenting railroad yards' as
a ground for a finding of delinquency. Attempts to define
jurisdiction highlight the problem of being specific enough
to protect the child's rights and avoiding a charge of being unconstitutionally vague, and yet making the clauses
wide enough to allow the court to meet the needs of children who are acting out against society. In addition, what
society will tolerate as being good or bad in, and for,
children, changes over time, and juvenile codes may lose
touch with public sentiment.

Before leaving the question of jurisdiction, it should
be noted that the Act and the Guide give to the juvenile
court exclusive original jurisdiction over the classes of
child outlined. However in many States the jurisdiction of
the juvenile court over those who commit acts which are
crimes in an adult is limited in various ways. A table
from Levin and Sarri(25) shows the various restrictions:

Limitation	Nos of states
Mandatory transfer for homicide	8
Mandatory transfer for serious offences by juveniles above a certain age	4
Transfer decision not made by juvenile court judge	5
Criminal court has concurrent juris- diction for certain offences	8
Juvenile court has exclusive jurisdiction	28

(nb two states are included in two categories)

WAIVER TO ADULT COURTS

The Act and the Guide deal with the problem of protecting
the public from serious offences by provisions to transfer
or waive some children to the criminal court. A waiver
means that the juvenile court has a hearing to determine
whether the child should be dealt with by the juvenile
court or by the adult criminal court, and the decision is
made in each individual case and not by means of a general
clause in an Act excluding certain types of offence. The
discretion lies with the juvenile court judge, and since
the Kent decision(24) the judge's discretion can be exercised only after a hearing; he cannot make a private decision. Both the Act and the Guide restrict the judge's
power to waive to children over sixteen-years of age and to
cases where there are reasonable grounds to believe that
the child has committed a delinquent act. As in other matters actual practice varies. Although all states except
New York and Vermont have waiver provisions, a minimal age
restriction on waiver exists in thirty-six States and,
where it is included, the actual age varies from thirteen
to sixteen. Later variations in the criteria for waiver
which are written into some juvenile codes will be considered.

THE JUVENILE COURT PROCESS - ENTRY INTO THE SYSTEM

Two procedures are proposed in the Act by which a child can
come to the notice of the juvenile court. The child may be
taken into custory by a law-enforcement officer who, after
deciding whether to hold the child in detention or release
him to his parents, will file a petition to the court.
Alternatively, a petition may be filed by any person who
has knowledge of facts about a child which might make that
child subject to the juvenile court jurisdiction. The
Act allows for any person to file a petition, subject to
authorisation from the court that the petition is in the
best interest of the public and the child.(25) This
authorisation is usually given by a probation officer. The
Guide requires that all petitions, once authorised by the
probation staff, be prepared and counter-signed by the
appropriate prosecuting official.(26) Thus the prosecutor
has the final say in all cases referred for filing by the
probation officer but he also determines whether or not a
petition should be filed in cases where the probation department has ruled against filing, but the complainant asks
for a review by the prosecutor.. This procedure serves several purposes. It reduces the roles the probation officer

is required to play by ensuring the presence of a prosecutor. It also serves as a check on the probation officer's
discretion, and adds weight to the protection of the public
interest in the balance of forces in operation at the entry
to the juvenile court. The Model Rules provide a mid-way
position by allowing a complainant to write to the judge
if the intake unit of the court has refused to authorise
the filing of the petition.

Actual procedures vary greatly, although in all States
entry to the juvenile court system is by arrest or by
petition. The use of administrative screening devices,
particularly for situations where no arrest is involved,
exist in thirty-six,(27) and usually lay down that the purpose is to ensure that the interests of the child and the
public require further action. In fifteen States, where
there is no screening procedure, Lenin and Sarri conclude
that it is 'unclear whether the filing of a complaint neces-
sitates formal court action or whether the court has the
inherent discretion to filter petitions'.(28)

The intake stage of the juvenile court process is a very
important one. About 50 per cent of all referrals to juvenile courts do not result in the filing of a petition. The
Guide gives the probation officer authority to hold conferences with the child and his family and to conduct other
enquiries before filing a petition. The Act allows for
'informal adjustment', subject to certain safeguards, and
authorises the probation officer to give counsel and advice
to the parents and child for a period of up to three months,
instead of filing a petition.(29) The Guide allows for
similar help to be provided by means of a consent degree,
which may be agreed at intake and which can run for a maximum period of six months.(30)

The Act and Guide thus go some way to structure the
jungle of informal handling which is a feature of many juvenile courts. Thirty-four States sanction informal handling
and the trend is towards increasing control of the discretion of judges and probation officers in this area. Not
only are the staff to be sure that the alleged behaviour
would give the court jurisdiction, but often the child and
his parents are required to agree to the facts and to the
informal probation supervision. Even this may give a child
little protection when the alternative is a court hearing
and possible removal from home. A greater protection is
probably provided by clauses which limit the length of informal adjustment, and some States have written this requirement into their juvenile codes. In California the
period is six months, in Illinois and Iowa three, and in
New York, two months. Some States have no time limit and
children may be continued on informal probation for years.

HEARINGS

When a referral of a child leads to a petition, Hearings
are arranged. The Act, the Guide and the Rules are all
explicit about the rights which a child has in a hearing
before a juvenile court. The Act states that a summons
shall be served on the parents, and on the child, if over
fourteen-years of age, at least twenty-four hours before
the Hearing. The summons is to include a copy of the petition, so that the family and child know the allegations before the Hearing. In addition to these rights of notice,
the Act states:(31)

> Except as otherwise provided under this Act a party is
> entitled to representation by legal counsel at all
> stages of any proceedings under this Act and if as a
> needy person he is unable to employ counsel, to have
> the court provide counsel for him. If a party appears
> without counsel the court shall ascertain whether he
> knows of his right thereto and to be provided with
> counsel by the court if he is a needy person. The court
> may continue the proceeding to enable a party to obtain
> counsel and shall provide counsel for an unrepresented
> needy person upon his request. Counsel must be pro-
> vided for a child not represented by his parent, guard-
> ian, or custodian. If the interests of two or more
> parties conflict separate counsel shall be provided for
> each of them.

> A needy person is one who at the time of requesting
> counsel is unable without undue financial hardship to
> provide for full payment of legal counsel and all other
> necessary expenses for representation.

> A party is entitled to the opportunity to introduce
> evidence and otherwise be heard in his own behalf and
> to cross-examine adverse witnesses.

> A child charged with a delinquent act need not be a
> witness against or otherwise incriminate himself. An
> extra-judicial statement, if obtained in the course
> of violation of this Act or which would be constitution-
> ally inadmissible in a criminal proceeding, shall not be
> used against him. Evidence illegally seized or obtained
> shall not be received over objection to establish the
> allegations made against him. A confession validly made
> by child out of court is insufficient to support an ad-
> judication of delinquency unless it is corroborated in
> whole or in part by other evidence.

How far juvenile courts actually meet these due process
standards is hard to determine. It seems likely that many
courts have moved considerably in the direction of protecting rights, especially during the actual hearing, since

Gault. Levin and Sarri's survey supports this view. They
state: 'The right to counsel is now statutorily guaranteed
in all but 11 States.(32) The other Gault requirement has
been enacted in only 15 States,(33) but a denial of these
rights would serve as grounds for reversal of the decicion.'
(34)

The Act and the Guide further require that, when a hearing takes place, it shall be in private and a record shall
be kept. Unless the State statute requires it, there is no
need for a jury, and the Supreme Court in McKeiver v. Pennsylvania has confirmed this view. What does seem to be
necessary is a bifurcated hearing. The first part is an
adjudicatory hearing at which the judge must decide whether
or not the acts alleged as the grounds for delinquency or
unruliness took place, the standard of proof being beyond
a reasonable doubt. Having established this, the court
moves to a second stage, when the decision is whether or
not the child requires treatment or rehabilitation. Finally the court makes a disposition.

The basis for this division is the need to secure the
child's legal rights and ensure a standard of proof beyond
a reasonable doubt of alleged facts, before moving into
the area of the child's needs, where different kinds of
information, including opinions, may be required. In
some courts these two processes are still intermingled
and the judge, who should be deciding on the facts, is
at the same time hearing opinions about the child's emotional state or home background.

DISPOSITION

If the court finds both that the child has behaved in a
delinquent or unruly way and is in need of rehabilitation
and treatment, it may proceed to a disposition best suited
to the child's 'treatment, rehabilitation and welfare'.

The Act empowers the court to select from the following
dispositions for a delinquent or unruly child:(35)

(1) permit the child to remain with his parents,
guardian, or other custodian, subject to conditions
and limitations as the court prescribes, including
supervision as directed by the court for the protection of the child;
(2) subject to conditions and limitations as the court
prescribes transfer temporary legal custody to any of
the following:
(i) any individual who, after study by the probation
officer or other person or agency designated by the
court, is found by the court to be qualified to re-

ceive and care for the child;
(ii) an agency or other private organization licensed
or otherwise authorized by law to receive and provide
care for the child; or
(iii) the Child Welfare Department of the [county]
[state], [or other public agency authorized by law
to receive and provide care for the child];
(iv) an individual in another state with or without
supervision by an appropriate officer; or
(3) without making any of the foregoing orders transfer
custody of the child to the juvenile court of another
state . . . placing the child on probation under the
supervision of the probation officer of the court or the
court of another state or [the Child Welfare Department
operating within the county], under conditions and limitations the court prescribes.
In the case of delinquent children only, the court may make
an order:
placing the child in an institution, camp, or other
facility for delinquent children operated under the
direction of the court [or other local public authority];
or
committing the child to [designate the state department
to which commitments of delinquent children are made or,
if there is no department, the appropriate state institution for delinquent children].

The purpose of these clauses is to ensure that children
who have not broken the criminal laws are not sent to state
institutions for child offenders. The dispositional powers
granted to courts are very wide, and follow the principle
that the juvenile court judge is qualified to make detailed
decisions about the needs of the children brought before
him.

The dispositional clauses of the Guide are similar, and
forbid the placement of a neglected child or a child in
need of supervision in any institution or facility established for the care and rehabilitation of delinquent children. The Guide does allow such a placement for children
in need of supervision who are found to be in such need a
second time.

As we have seen, the length of time for any disposition
made by the juvenile court under the Act is two years or
up to the child's twenty-first birthday, if that is sooner.
The two-year period can be extended, but only after a hearing of which the child and parents have had notice and at
which they have been given an opportunity to speak. The
reason for extension must be that it is necessary for the
treatment or rehabilitation of the child.(36) The model
rules add nothing new to the dispositions available to

juvenile courts. Probation and foster home placements
are statutorily available in all States and, in all States
except Alaska and Arizona, children can be placed in private, residential institutions. In addition twenty-two(37)
States allow judges to fine children or order monetary
restitution, which are powers not included in the Uniform
Act.

   We have already noted that the Act restricts placement
of non-delinquent children in institutions for delinquents,
and that the State codes are beginning to move in this direction. There is also a trend towards limiting the indeterminate nature of dispositions, at least by requirements for
periodic review. The typical pattern, however, is still
for probation, foster placements and committals to institutions to be open-ended.

Chapter five

Britain: the events leading to the 1908 Children Act

In discussing juvenile justice systems it has been assumed that, however they are organised, they include certain features which justify their being considered as distinct from the criminal justice system. For young people below some specified age, hearings are arranged in a setting separated, either spacially or temporarily, from the setting in which adults are tried. Any sentences involving removal from home which are imposed upon young people are served largely in facilities separate from those used for adult offenders. In addition, the system is used to control behaviour in young people which would not be considered criminal in adults and to enforce certain obligations, such as school attendance and obedience to parents, which have no adult parallel. There is another distinguishing factor, although unlike the former features it does not seem to be a necessary one, and that is that juvenile justice systems have, more than adult systems, mixed a welfare philosophy with that of criminal justice. The desire for individualisation and reformation of the child has played an important part in the development of juvenile justice, and in fact is one reason why a separate system arose. Such thinking leads to a search for causes and for treatment methods. There are, for example, many more studies of the causes of juvenile delinquency than of adult criminal behaviour.

Taking separation from adult criminals at trial and during sentence, an expansion of state control over behaviour beyond that which can be called criminal, and a concern with reform as the distinguishing features of a juvenile justice system, the development of these features in Britain will be considered. Again the intention is to look at some major trends, rather than to give a history of juvenile justice in England and Wales and in Scotland. It is hard to find a starting point for these trends, which were

eventually to be crystallised and codified by the Children
Act of 1908. However, in Britain, as in the United States,
the nineteenth century was the time during which the idea
of special treatment for children developed, not only in
the area of law, but in other areas as well. Children
ceased to be seen either as adults in miniature or as the
chattels of their parents, and began to be regarded as
individuals with needs and with rights of their own.

SOCIAL CONDITIONS IN THE EARLY NINETEENTH CENTURY

In discussing the history of the United States, it was noted
that a concern with delinquency was one result of the growth
of towns. In England the towns had a much longer history,
but in the nineteenth century they were growing fast, as
the country changed from a largely agricultural to an industrial society. The existing system of government, however, remained one developed for a stable society rooted
largely in the land. It centred around the parish and the
justice of the peace, and was not designed to control a
dense and more mobile population. Nor was it designed to
meet needs or to improve the quality of life. These were
the tasks facing the citizens of the nineteenth century,
and the reports of their many Select Committees, Royal
Commissions and private charitable conferences show how
they applied their minds to the new problems of their time.
     The social problems in the towns were great. After the
Napoleonic War there was an increase in unemployment and a
series of poor harvests, which must have brought disaster
to many families whose existence in the city slums was mar-
ginal even in good times. Dickens and Mayhew,(1) writing
later in the century, give a picture of what life was like
in London. Their writings exposed the conditions of the
poor to the gaze of many of their contemporaries, who never
took the few steps which would have led them from fashion-
able Oxford Street into what remained of the rookeries.
This was the name given to the maze of alleys and lodging
houses such as Lord Ashley described to the House of Commons in 1848:(2)

> The parlour measures 18 feet by 10. Beds are arranged
> on each side of it, composed of straw, rags and shavings.
> Here are 27 male and female adults, and 31 children,
> with several dogs; in all, 58 human beings in a contrac-
> ted den, from which light and air are systematically
> excluded. It is impossible to convey a just idea of
> their state. The quantities of vermin are amazing. I
> have entered a room, and after a few minutes I have felt
> them dropping on my hat, from the ceiling like peas.

'They may be gathered by handfuls', observed one of the
inmates. 'I could fill a pail in a few minutes. I
have been so tormented with the itch, that on two occa-
sions I filled my pockets with stones, and waited till
a policeman came up, and then broke a lamp, that I might
be sent to prison, and there by cleansed, as is required
before new-comers are admitted.' 'Ah!' said another,
standing by, 'you can get a comfortable snooze and
scrub there.'

Dickens describes a similar area in a short account called
'On Duty with Inspector Field':(3)

Ten, twenty, thirty - who can count them? Men, women,
children, for the most part naked, heaped upon the floor,
like maggots in a cheese! Ho! In that dark corner
yonder! Does anybody lie there? Me, sir, Irish me, a
widder, with six children. And yonder? Me, sir, Irish
me, along with two more Irish boys as is me friends.
And to the right there? Me, sir, and the Murphy fam'ly,
numbering five blessed souls. And what's this, coiling,
now, about my foot? Another Irish me, pitifully in want
of shaving, whom I have awakened from sleep - and across
my other foot lies his wife - and by the shoes of Inspector Field lie their three eldest - and their three youngest are at present squeezed between the open door and
the wall. And why is there no one on that little mat
before the sullen fire? Because O'Donovan, with his
wife and daughter, is not come in from selling lucifers!
Nor on the bit of sacking in the nearest corner? Bad
luck! Because that Irish family is late tonight,
a-cadging in the streets.

It was conditions like these amongst the lower classes,
and particularly the immigrant Irish, in which adults and
children were dying from malnutrition and epidemic dis-
eases, in which crime was endemic, religion almost non-
existant and revolution a possibility, that increased the
motivation for reform. Like their contemporaries in the
United States, middle-class Britons were moved by pity and
fear, by evangelical urges and those of self-interest, to
improve the lot of the masses. The impetus underlying innovations in the treatment of criminal and destitute children came from these ambivalent motives, so that genuine
concern for the welfare of children mingled with a wish to
control them and prevent their developing into adult criminals or paupers.(4) In Britain the same issues concerned
the reformers. How to prevent future evil, how to avoid
contamination of children by corrupt adults, the place of
punishment, and the doctrine of less eligibility, and the
criteria for selection for treatment: all these were crucial issues. It seems that such issues must occur at the

meeting point between a welfare and a criminal justice
approach, because they are another way of stating aspects
of the dilemmas from which these approaches seek an escape.
Concern about such issues and the need to find answers to
the questions they posed influenced the growth of special
social institutions for juvenile justice, whose development in nineteenth-century Britain will now be considered.

THE POOR LAW

In Britain, as in the United States, the pauper and the criminal were often linked in people's minds. It was widely
held that pauperism led to criminality because of the worthless nature of the pauper, although some recognised that
'beggary was the effect of misfortune rather than of
choice; of the want of means rather than the want of
will'.(5) Because of this linking of pauperism and crime,
the juvenile justice system inherited ideas and institutions developed under the aegis of the Poor Law, as well
as those which derived from the criminal justice and penal
system.
     The Poor Law gave legal sanctions to an administrative
system for relieving the destitute, and also included measures for protecting society against vagrants and beggars.
Both aspects of the Poor Law were reflected in the developing juvenile justice system. The juvenile courts were to
acquire jurisdiction over children in need of care and
protection, and the clauses defining this state were first
designed to control beggars. On the other hand, some of
the treatment facilities available to the courts had their
roots in measures developed to relieve pauper children.
It is not necessary to study the nineteenth-century Poor
Law in detail, but just to be aware of general trends.
Early in the century the prevailing idea was that children
should be relieved with their parents, and, despite the
existence of some pauper apprenticeship schemes, little
was done to deal with pauper children as a separate group.
This did not mean that there was no concern about pauper
children for, on the contrary, the 1815 and 1816 reports
of a Select Committee of the House of Commons on Mendicity
in the Metropolis drew attention to the number of beggars
in London who were children. In the second report the
Committee made a plea that Parliament give its attention to
such children 'to prevent their growing up in habits of
vice and idleness destructive to themselves and most highly
dangerous to society'.(6) Parliament, however, did little
except to continue in the 1834 Poor Law Amendment Act the
principle that for relief children should follow their

parents. The new Poor Law Commissioners established by
this Act were not unaware of the needs of children already
in the care of the unions and of those who were also destitute but had not sought, or been brought to, the notice
of the guardians. They were, however, constrained by the
principle of less eligibility. It was this principle which
accounts for the slowness with which children came to be
treated as a separate group from adult paupers, and for
the even longer delay before moves were made by the government, as distinct from voluntary societies, to seek out
children in need of care.

  There were attempts to develop education for pauper
children outside the workhouse in district schools from the
middle of the century, but these barrack-like institutions
were few in number and largely limited to the London area.
They acquired a bad reputation for spreading disease
amongst their child inmates, caused by overcrowded conditions, poor food and lack of fresh air. Gradually they
fell into disrepute, and cottage type homes or boarding-out
began to replace them. It was, however, well into the
twentieth century before even half of the pauper children
in England and Wales who were not in their own homes were
relieved anywhere except in workhouses. The initiative in
the nineteenth century had been taken by voluntary societies such as Dr Barnardo's, whose cottage homes and boarding-out schemes with regular supervision provided a model
for later government child-care practice. Voluntary agencies, however, do not need to consider questions of less
eligibility, because they are free to ration their services
in ways which a universal government service cannot do.

THE CRIMINAL JUSTICE SYSTEM

In criminal justice, as in so many social institutions,
a watershed was reached in the nineteenth century. Collins
points out, in his study of Dickens and crime, that the
system for dealing with criminals when Dickens died in
1870 'was recognisably the one we have inherited; the
system that obtained in his boyhood belongs to another
world, at least as much akin to the sixteenth century as
to the twentieth'.(7) In 1812, when Dickens was born,
there was no separate system of justice for children. They
were brought before the same magistrate or judge as were
adults, sometimes set upon a box or table so that they
could be seen over the rail,(8) and were remanded to the
same prisons as were adult felons, to await their trial.
Once convicted, they were subject to the same sentences,
including death, transportation and imprisonment, as were
adults.

At the end of the eighteenth century the criminal law in
Britain was probably at its most severe, with over two
hundred offences carrying a death sentence. However, the
law was so cruel that the public who made up the juries
refused to enforce it consistently, especially in relation
to children. Not only were many children never charged
with the offences which they committed, but if they did go
to trial, juries would refuse to convict and, in cases
where a conviction was secured, there was always the possibility of a reprieve. Radzinowicz(9) has suggested that
one in seven of the people sentenced to death in the early
years of the nineteenth century was actually hanged, and
for children and young people the likelihood of a death
sentence being carried out was even lower. Knell(10)
found that of 104 children sentenced to death at the Old
Bailey between 1801 and 1836, none was executed. The only
execution that he found to have been carried out was in
1831, when John Andy Aird Bell, aged thirteen, was hanged
after confessing to the murder of a small boy, whom he
robbed and killed in the woods. Despite reports in history books that children were executed for trivial offences, it seems that this was a rare event in the nineteenth century and, in fact, executions may have been rare
in previous centuries also for any offences other than murder, although Pinchbeck and Hewitt quote instances of the
death sentence being carried out on children after the
Gordon riots.(11)

Offences which did not carry a death sentence were usually punished by imprisonment or transportation. As with the
death sentence, so with these sentences, the courts faced a
dilemma where the offender was a child. Neale, writing
of juvenile delinquency in Manchester, explains:(12)

It is a very serious evil that punishments now inflicted
upon juvenile offenders are applicable only to adults
and hardened criminals, the result of which in operation is a compound of extreme barbarity and of dangerous levity; for the magistrate or judge, under these
circumstances, has only the alternative of inflicting
corporal punishment, imprisonment, transportation or
other extreme penalties of the law upon a few, and in
consideration of their severity to suffer the many to
escape, whereby a dangerous impunity is given to crime.

The same concern that punishment was either too harsh or
non-existent was expressed by American writers in Illinois
at the end of the century.

Despite these modifications of the law by practice, it
would be a mistake to assume that early in the nineteenth
century willingness to apply special consideration to
children went very far. Children were imprisoned and were

transported for what would now be considered trivial offences, although they were likely to have committed more
than one of them. Conditions in the prisons and in the
convict hulks were unlikely to lead to reformation, although, for some, the treatment inside such institutions
may have been less harsh than the life they lived outside.

The word children is used to refer to those over the age
of seven. By the nineteenth century the rule that a child
under seven is presumed incapable of committing a crime,
was well established. The occasional references to children aged six-years old in jails and houses of correction
presumably reflects mistakes on the part of either the
magistrates or the authors in assessing the children's
ages. Between seven and fourteen the presumption that a
child was 'destitute of criminal design' could be rebutted
by evidence of guilty knowledge.

Mr Justice Eyre makes the law clear in his instructions
to the jury in *R*. v. *Sidney Smith* in 1845:(13)

where a child is under the age of seven years, the law
presumes him to be incapable of committing a crime;
after the age of fourteen, he is presumed to be responsible for his actions, as entirely as if he were
forty; but between the ages of seven and fourteen, no
presumption of law arises at all, and that which is
termed a malicious intent - a guilty knowledge that he
was doing wrong - must be proved by the evidence, and
cannot be presumed from the mere commission of the act.
You are to determine from a review of the evidence
whether it is satisfactorily proved that at the time
he fired the rick (if you should be of opinion he did
fire it) he had a guilty knowledge that he was committing a crime.

In this case the jury found the young defendant not guilty.
Another jury in an earlier case had found the ten-year-old
defendant not guilty, and the foreman of the jury added
'We do not think that the prisoner had any guilty knowledge'.(14) It is not known how often young people were
found to be without *mens rea*. It may be that such a finding was rare then, as it is in modern juvenile courts,
where the need to prove a guilty mind is largely a formality.

Such was the situation of the criminal justice and penal
system early in the nineteenth century. Different reformers
focused upon different aspects of the system in their attempts to find answers to the problems of contamination and
prevention. Some were particularly interested in developing a separate court for juvenile offenders, others in extending summary justice, and yet others in providing special
institutions for children. All these elements were eventually to form part of a juvenile justice system.

PROBLEMS OF CONTAMINATION

A Separate Court for Juveniles

Difficult as it is to interpret the available evidence, it
does seem that juvenile crime was increasing during the
first half of the century,(15) and certainly people believed that there was an increase. A series of investiga-
tions took place which sought causes and remedies, one of
which was a special form of trial for children. In the
report of the Select Committee on the State of the Police
of the Metropolis, one of a series of Parliamentary committees which led eventually to the establishment of the metropolitan police, the idea of a special jurisdiction over
children is mooted. In 1815 the evidence which the Select
Committee heard included that of Francis Hobler, a magistrate, who argued that there should be a way to deal with
children summarily, and thus avoid committing them to Newgate prison until their trial date.(16)

> I think if the magistrates were entrusted with the sort
> of parental authority to whip them a little and keep
> them upon bread and water and if the child had parents
> which sometimes is not the case to send him back to them
> it would prove highly advantageous; and I can see that
> the magistrate being a gentleman of years and experience
> could not be supposed to be capable of abusing an auth-
> ority of this sort for as men and as parents they must
> feel for the situation of such characters.

He goes on to explain that his plan would reduce contamination:

> Do you not think it would be desirable to give such
> power to magistrates supposing it would be limited to
> those under the age of 14? I should. There are many
> children under that age in London at Bishopsgate Street
> and other places who begin with stealing gingerbread and
> afterwards associating with older thieves committing
> greater offences. When once they have been in the com-
> pany with old thieves there is no hope of them. There
> is not 1 in 100 that is reformed.

The same idea is carried further by Sir John E. Eardley
Wilmot, a Warwickshire magistrate. In letters addressed
to fellow magistrates in 1827 he writes:(17)

> The remedy therefore that I would propose is . . . the
> immediate and summary cognizance of offences committed
> by the youthful depredator; to be heard before an in-
> termediate tribunal where petty offences may be instantly
> proceeded against and punished, without sending the of-
> fender to undergo the stigma and contamination of a
> public prison, the publicity of trial, and all those

evils which infallibly result from early imprisonment.
I would change the law of larceny as affecting offenders
of a certain age, and convert the offence into one of a
minor character, cognizable by two matistrates . . .
and by thus arming the magistracy with the power of
immediate conviction, on sufficient evidence, or on
confession of the parties, I would empower them to
punish the young culprit by whipping, confining him in
an asylum set apart for this purpose, or by discharging him without punishment at all. . . .

When therefore by the loss or neglect of his natural
guardian, the youthful delinquent is thrown upon the
world without any guide to direct or befriend him, instead of being subject to the utmost severity of the law,
he will experience only its protection; and he will
find already appointed as the legal guardians of his
infancy, those who by judicious restraint and by well-
timed instruction will supply the place of his own relatives. It will be an 'act for appointing guardians for
the deserted and friendless', rather than an addition to
our Criminal Code: and instead of being a law of punishment, will be the dispenser of blessings.

At about the same time another Select Committee on the Police asked their witnesses:(18)

Do not you think it might be of advantage if there were
established some tribunal that could almost permanently
sit and which disposed of cases of that kind? The
question refers to cases of simple larceny committed
by young offenders.

In 1840 the same Sir John Eardley Wilmot introduced
into Parliament a bill to establish what would in effect
have been a juvenile court, to which children from seven
to twelve years, charged with minor offences, could be sent
for immediate trial and punishment by the committing magistrate. The aim was to avoid the waiting period between
committal and trial and the contamination that accompanied
this period in prison. It was not a 'bill of punishment',
but would have given to magistrates an authority similar
to that of a:(19)

father over his son - a moral authority, which would
enable them to bring juvenile offenders under a course
of moral training and discipline which should have the
effect of reclaiming them to the paths of honesty and
industry. The bill was a merciful bill, its object
being to provide for those who were without natural
guardians, national parents and guardians, in order to
save them from being sent to gaols to be contaminated
and ruined.

The bill did not become law, although it passed the Commons,

because it was rejected by the Lords. Among the arguments
raised against it was one which recurs throughout the history of juvenile justice, and stems from the criminal justice approach. The bill denied to children the right of
jury trial. General Johnson said:(20)

> there would be no end to juvenile offences, juvenile
> gaols, juvenile courts and all that, without the bene-
> fit to the prisoners of trial by jury. The principle
> of the bill was unconstitutional because it conferred
> a power upon two magistrates to become judge, jury and
> executioner at once.

Extending Summary Jurisdiction

The idea of a special court for young offenders had to
wait, partly because the reformers chose instead to extend
the scope of summary jurisdiction, especially for juveniles.
Various committees considered this question and recommended
minor extensions of the summary powers of magistrates. In
1821(21) and 1829(22) bills were placed before Parliament
to implement such recommendations, but failed to find support and were withdrawn. In 1835 Lord Russell asked the
third Commission on Criminal Law to consider whether:(23)

> it would be advisable to make any distinction in the
> mode of trial between adult and juvenile offenders; and
> if not, whether any class of offenders can be made sub-
> ject to a more summary proceeding than trial by jury?

The Commission were opposed to distinction in the mode of
trial. They considered that it was important that preventive measures should be taken in relation to juvenile offenders, but power to do this lay with the police, and in
any case was part, not of the legal system but of the religious and moral education of the children of the poor. The
commissioners' concern was with the contamination of juveniles while awaiting trial, which they somewhat unrealisti-
cally considered to be a more serious risk than during a
sentence of imprisonment, because pre-trial custody was
'not subject to the salutary discipline applicable to convicted criminals'. To deal with the problem of contamination while awaiting trial, they suggested that summary proceedings should be arranged for minor offenders aged under
fifteen years. In fact it was not until 1847, after yet
another select committee had given cautious approval to
the idea of an extension of summary jurisdiction, that the
first legislative change was made. The Larceny Act empowered justices to deal summarily with offenders under
fourteen who were charged with stealing. In 1850 the age
was raised to sixteen years, but it remained permissive.

In 1879 the Summary Jurisdiction Act gave magistrates greater powers to deal summarily with children under twelve-years old for all indictable offences, and with those under sixteen for larceny and embezzlement.

Alternatives to Remand in Prison

The fear of contamination of children who were awaiting trial in prison led some magistrates to make their own informal arrangements. One told the Committee on Criminal and Destitute Juveniles in 1852:(24)

> for my own guidance I have never ventured to commit a boy under nine years of age. I have, whenever they have been brought before me, always placed them under the care of their parents, if they had parents, or of near relatives if they had them. If they had none, I have sent them to the union.

This reference to the union means the poor law union. These early arrangements were unofficial, but from 1866 magistrates were empowered to send children to the workhouse, instead of to the gaol, to await trial. This power was permissive only, and it was not until the Children Act of 1908 that magistrates were forbidden to commit children to gaol to await trial. Even in 1977, however, certain categories of unruly young people can still be sent to prison on remand, although the government has pledged itself to end this practice.

Separate Residential Institutions for Children

So far we have considered attempts to deal with contamination and corruption of children who were sent to prison to await trial. It was a much greater risk for those who were sentenced to a term of imprisonment, and for the first part of the century there were few alternatives to imprisonment, except transportation, for children who had been convicted. Transportation, which involved long waiting periods in the notorious and overcrowded hulks, was as corrupting as was imprisonment. In the previous century, John Howard had drawn attention to the state of the prisons and, in 1815, another Quaker, Peter Bedford, the Spitalfields philanthropist, was instrumental in founding the Society for Investigating the Causes of the Alarming Increase of Juvenile Delinquency in the Metropolis. Like their fellow Friends in New York, they began their work by making a survey of the background of all boys in the London prisons. From the information they collected, they reported on the causes of

juvenile delinquency and, among many recommendations,
stressed the need for separate prisons for young offenders.
They formed The Society for the Improvement of Prison Discipline and for the Reformation of Juvenile Offenders.

The work of these societies had no immediate practical
effect upon the government, although committees and commissions continued to draw attention to the evils of mixing
adult felons with children. The Select Committee on the
State of the Police of the Metropolis, reporting in 1817,
stated that prisons:(25)

> instead of correcting the criminal delinquent by dis-
> cipline are schools and academies of vice which corrupt
> and vitiate their wretched inmates and throw them back
> upon society confirmed in every bad habit.

In Newgate, where some classification existed, the Committee
still reported that:

> a number of boys are mixed indiscriminately together from
> 8 to 16 or 18 years exhibiting a great variety of charac-
> ter and differing in degrees of guilt the tried and the
> untried and the first offender with the hardened convict.

The report goes on to draw attention to:

> the pleasure older thieves take in corrupting those who
> have just entered into vicious courses, by the detail of
> their exploits, the narrative of hairs breadth escapes,
> the teaching of technical phrases; all of which are a
> great allurement to a youthful mind, being the amusement
> of the idle and the resources of the desperate and serv-
> ing to enliven and dispel the solitude of a prison.

There were two different ideas about the type of provision which should be provided. Some reformers wanted to
see separate prisons for young offenders established by
the government. Others preferred the idea of a special
school or reformatory, after the model of the various institutions run by voluntary groups and organisations. Juvenile prisons were supported by those who believed that
children should be punished, whereas some of those who supported the reformatory movement, like Mary Carpenter, believed in the value of education, a homely atmosphere and
love.

Attempts to establish separate prisons for juveniles
were not successful. In 1823 a hulk had been set aside
for boys, but the evidence which the Select Committee on
the Police of the Metropolis and the Select Committee of
the Lords heard did not suggest that it was either reforming children or protecting them from corruption. In fact
it was suggested that the children existed in fear of the
more powerful boys, who operated a reign of terror.(26)

The next attempt by the government to provide separate
facilities for convicted offenders came in 1838 with the

opening of Parkhurst prison on the Isle of Wight. This
was to house boys awaiting transportation. The preamble
to the Act which established the prison referred to the
reformation of 'young offenders', and it has been said this
was the first time these words were officially used in a
statute. Parkhurst remained a boys' prison for only
twenty-five years, and it is difficult to be certain of
its history. Until recently it was regarded as a place of
repressively harsh discipline, where boys were kept in
irons and watched over by armed guards. This picture was
the one given by Mary Carpenter to the Committee on Criminal and Destitute Juveniles in 1852. She says:(27)

> I cannot say whether there have been any changes in the
> management, but, as far as I have had the means of as-
> certaining, there have been no changes in principle. I
> have even heard of soldiers with loaded guns being
> obliged to watch the boys while they were at work, and
> I know from the authority of residents in the island
> that there is a constant dread of their escaping; that
> many are prevented from going to places of public wor-
> ship on Sunday evening, lest they should find on their
> return these boys secreted in their houses. I therefore
> think that such a system has something radically wrong
> in it. It is to be discovered what it is, but it will
> be seen from what I have said that such is the fact.

Carlebach, however, suggests that Mary Carpenter, whom
he describes as a 'brilliant, volatile, passionate and
arrogant woman'(28) in fact distorted the evidence about
Parkhurst, and gave no credit to the second governor, Cap-
tain Hall, who was an enlightened man. He suggests that
the irons and armed guards were isolated incidents, but
that Mary Carpenter would hear no good of the place, and
influenced not only current thought but also future historians.

Wherever the truth lies, Parkhurst was closed to boys
in 1864, apparently because its own board of governors
turned against it. The direct attempt by the State to provide accommodation for juveniles was not to be part of the
main stream of development for the rest of the century.
This lay with the reformatories.

Several societies were started in the eighteenth century to provide an alternative to prison for selected
children. Particularly influential was the Royal Philanthropic Society, which was originally founded to provide
homes for the children of convicts but which, as Pinchbeck
and Hewitt point out, 'changed from a voluntary organisation with a rather diffuse conception of rescue and reform
of the young to a specialised organisation bent on the rehabilitation of delinquent boys'.(29) The chaplain of the

Society the Reverend Turner, explained its development in
answer to questions put to him by the Committee on Criminal
and Destitute Juveniles in 1852:(30)

How long has that society existed? - More than 60 years;
it was founded in 1788; 64 years ago.

About what number of children, so far as you have
the means of ascertaining, have been under the care of
that society from first to last? - I should think about
2,500; I am not able to give the exact number.

The society did carry on its operations in London?
- It had a large establishment in St. George's Fields,
Southwark, in which there were workshops for shoemaking,
tailoring, ropemaking, and things of that kind. There
it contained three distinct departments; there were
the sons of convicted felons, and criminal boys for reformation in the male school, and girls who were the
daughters of convicts in the female school.

At that time the only establishment of that society
was in London? - Yes; the society was originally founded in Hackney, in small houses. Benevolent people
started a sort of association; they took three or four
cottages in which a dozen boys were collected together,
very much on the principle of the Rauhe Haus, at Hamburgh.
After that, they removed to St. George's Fields, having
a separate establishment in Bermondsey, into which they
took the criminal children received for reformation. They
finally amalgamated that with the establishment in St.
George's Fields; the number there were usually about
110 boys and 30 girls.

When did they cease to occupy those premises in London and remove to Red Hill? - In April 1849, a beginning
was made. The change was carried out in the course of
the year.

After a stay at the School, boys were either apprenticed or
helped to emigrate.

It is interesting to note the reference to the Rauhe Haus
in Germany. This home, one at Mettrai in France, the House
of Refuge in New York and the Royal Philanthropic Society's
home were widely known amongst people interested in institutions for children in both America and Britain. The New
York Quakers had visited the European establishments and
Mary Carpenter, who played an important part in starting
reformatory schools in Britain, visited the United States.
Later the Howard Society used the probation system in Massachusetts as an example in their campaign for a similar
scheme in England. It was a smaller world, in which the
leading reformers knew one another, and where, particularly
amongst the Quakers, religion provided a natural channel of
communication.

The Royal Philanthropic Society's home was only one of
a number of refuges and schools which were in operation
during the 1840s and 1850s. At this time they had no
statutory recognition, and magistrates and judges had to
find ways round the law in order to commit children to them.
In 1851 Mary Carpenter published her first book, 'Reformatory Schools for the Children of the Perishing and Dangerous Classes',(31) and that, together with a conference organised in Bristol by Matthew Davenport Hill, seems to have
crystallised the many individual supporters of reformatories
into a social movement. When the government refused to
introduce legislation on the grounds that there was insufficient interest, pressure from people in the movement led
to the appointment of a Committee to enquire into the Treatment of Criminal and Destitute Juveniles. This Committee
reported in 1853, and in the same year Mary Carpenter(32)
published another book, and a second conference was held.
A bill was introduced into Parliament, and in 1854 the
Youthful Offenders Act became law. It gave courts powers
to commit children to reformatories and provided financial
support for them, on the condition that the reformatories
were approved by government inspectors.
The tension between ideas of welfare and those of criminal justice was apparent in the conflict between the Conference members and the House over the question of punishment. The 1854 Act, as amended, required that a child
must spend fourteen days in prison before going to a reformatory. This is a nice illustration of how the criminal justice approach, which demanded punishment for wrong
doing, was balanced against the child's need for training
and reform. The need for punishment outweighed the risk of
contamination in a fourteen-day period. This power to
imprison first remained with the courts until 1899, although an earlier Act gave a permissive power to commit
children direct to reform schools.
Mary Carpenter was violently and vocally opposed to the
imprisonment clause. She said: 'Love must be the guiding
sentiment of all who attempt to influence and guide these
children.' They must be 'loved for themselves. Love draws
with human cords far stronger than chains of iron'. Mary
Carpenter was also against corporal punishment, and, although her attitude to children was based on religious beliefs which present day workers may not share, many would
accept her ideas about the individual needs of children:
(33)

the children should always be so treated as to excite
and cherish in their minds true self-respect. By this
feeling, we mean a sense of the high duty which each
individual owes to himself as an immortal being, and to

cultivate it in them is peculiarly important. These
children have been hitherto so despised, that they
hardly know whether there is within them anything to be
respected. They therefore feel no respect to others.
Yet let them be treated with respect, with true Christian politeness, and they will give a ready response.
Nor let it be imagined an absurd thing to treat these
poor little dirty children with respect. Their rags
will disappear before those who look at them as young
immortal beings; and so many good and beautiful traits
of character in them will be revealed to those who treat
them with Christian courtesy, that they will learn to
respect them.

Mary Carpenter was more than ahead of her own times; she
was ahead of ours too. She expressed attitudes towards
children which neither she nor many others are able to live
up to. However, although the reality fell short of her
ideal, her knowledge, experience, writing and speaking
contributed to the passing of the 1854 Act and to the
strengthening of the welfare approach. Reformatory schools
increased in number and other statutes gave similar powers
to industrial schools, which were intended for destitute
and abandoned rather than criminal children. Children who
committed only minor offences, or who came to the courts
because of the operation of the Poor Law, rather than by
being charged with criminal offences, were also liable to
be committed to industrial schools.

The 1854 Act and the consolidating Reformatory School
Act of 1866 established a system which was to last in
England until 1969 and which in 1977 still exists in Scotland. Reform and industrial schools changed their names to
approved schools in 1933 and became List D schools in
Scotland in 1970, but their structure changed little. They
continued to take children sent by the courts who had committed offences or who were in need of care, protection
and control. In many instances, until 1970, they were
still run by voluntary bodies, although subject to inspection from the Home Office and eligible for Treasury grants.
This three-part system of local courts, central government
and voluntary bodies was the system established by the 1854
Act. What changed in the late nineteenth century, was the
philosophy of those running the schools. In Mary Carpenter's time the reformatories were opposed to the rule which
made children experience prison before entering the school.
Later conferences of the Reformatory and Refuge Union
fought to maintain this rule when the government wished to
abolish it. From being the most welfare orientated of all
court provisions for children, they later came to be the
closest thing to a penal institution that was available to

the new juvenile courts, and in this position they inevitably came to reflect more of a criminal justice approach.

SEPARATING OFFENDERS FROM NON-OFFENDERS

In considering industrial schools we turn our attention to
another aspect of the juvenile court system: the fact that
it deals with non-offenders as well as with offending children. What was to become the civil side of the British
juvenile courts' jurisdiction can be said to date from the
Industrial Schools Acts of 1854 (which applied to Scotland)
and 1857 (which applied to England and Wales). These and
later consolidating Acts empowered magistrates to commit to
industrial schools vagrant children and young persons,
those said by their parents to be incorrigible, those who
associated with criminals and prostitutes and also children under twelve who were convicted of criminal offences.
These acts incorporated and extended powers previously
contained largely in the Poor Law.

This division between those eligible for reformatories
and those suitable for industrial schools followed the
separation made by Mary Carpenter into the dangerous and
the perishing classes. She wrote:(34)

That part of the community which we are to consider
consists of those who have not yet fallen into actual
crime, but who are almost certain from their ignorance,
destitution, and the circumstances in which they are
growing up, to do so, if a helping hand be not extended
to raise them; - these form the *perishing classes*: -
and of those who have already received the prison brand,
or, if the mark has not been yet visibly set upon them,
are notoriously living by plunder, - who unblushingly
acknowledge that they can gain more for the support of
themselves and their parents by stealing than by working, - whose hand is against every man, for they know
not that any man is their brother; - these form the
dangerous classes.

In these passages Mary Carpenter distinguishes those who
have been caught or who admit to crime from those who have
yet to start on criminal activities. The Reformatory and
Industrial Schools Acts maintained this distinction, although younger children who committed offences were grouped
in Miss Carpenter's perishing class.(35) These Acts marked
the beginning of a discussion which still continues. Should
children who commit offences be distinguished from other
children with problems and, if so, on what basis?

Both sides of the argument were made in the nineteenth
century. The Committee on Criminal and Destitute Juveniles

discussed the topic with the chaplain of the Philanthropic
Society's School(36) and with Mr Adderley.(37)

> Many of the boys of your school ought not to have been
> put in a criminal status from the nature of their crimes,
> and it is a hardship on many of them that they have been
> so put, and most injurious to the interests of the coun-
> try? - There are a few cases of boys who are there, in
> which their offences have been such as sleeping out, or
> hawking without a licence, or trifling things of that
> kind, which hardly seem to be anything more than con-
> ventional offences; but the great mass of them have
> been convicted for dishonesty. If a boy does a crimi-
> nal act, I do not see how I can possibly say he is not
> to be placed in that category.

> Supposing that the Red Hill workhouse school is a
> good one, yet uniting it with Red Hill Reformatory
> would make it a much better school, from having a lar-
> ger number of boys of the same stamp; should you see
> any objection to improving the school by uniting the
> two? - I think you would run the risk of lowering the
> general standard of moral feeling as to crime, and the
> necessary punishment of crime, among the workhouse
> children, if they were to be associated, without any
> restriction, with those who had been sent to prison
> and punished.

> *Mr. Adderley.* Do you see any objection to other
> children being admitted to these schools? - Very great
> indeed.

> On what ground? - On the ground I have already stated:
> I unhesitatingly give my opinion that the project of
> combining penal and pauper schools would be fatal to
> the effect of both. It has already been found impos-
> sible, with the requisite attention to health, to make
> any material distinction in the food, or even the treat-
> ment, of able-bodied paupers in union houses, and crimi-
> nals under imprisonment. The distinction between the
> pauper and criminal boy in the proposed schools would
> be still less; it would provoke most injurious compari-
> sons between both parties.

Miss Carpenter, who did not consider punishment to be the
purpose of these schools, held a different view. In talking of the houses of refuge in the United States, she told
the Committee:(38)

> they make classes in the school, but those classes
> depend not on their previous conduct, but on their pre-
> sent conduct, and that I would strongly advise. I do
> not believe that any real difference can be discovered
> in juvenile criminals, from the circumstance of their
> having been convicted. I would act upon a general

principle, that all in the school are brought for reformation; that they are to be placed in a healthy
atmosphere; that they may begin with a new character,
and that all punishment will be the natural result of
their disobedience and bad conduct.

Mr Adderley and Miss Carpenter were influenced by different approaches to juvenile justice. If one is concerned
with punishment and deterrence, then mixing criminals and
non-criminals is obviously unfair and unwise. If, however,
one is looking at the question within a welfare framework,
then classification should depend upon the type of treatment required to meet the child's needs and not upon past
behaviour.

THE IDEA OF PREVENTION

This has been a recurring theme in juvenile justice. The
mere fact that the system deals with children means that
there is always something worse to be prevented. This
rests on several assumptions: that children have a long
time ahead in which to commit crimes, that they are in a
maleable stage of their lives, and that their actual criminal acts as children are more a nuisance than a threat.
The really serious crimes are those which children may
commit when they become adults. This final assumption is
being subjected to some questioning in the 1970s, but has
been an accepted tenet of thinking on juvenile justice in
the past.

Prevention as an aim is not restricted to children who
have not yet come to the attention of the courts. Obviously disposals such as probation or removal from home have a
preventive aim. However, the idea of prevention at the pre-
court stage has perhaps received most attention, and is
linked with ideas about community responsibility to provide for all children the necessary facilities for physical growth and emotional, educational, social and religious
development.

In line with this approach, Mary Carpenter made it clear
that juveniles will eventually commit offences if society
does not extend a hand 'to raise them'. By the mid-nine-
teenth century, crime and social conditions were firmly
linked together in people's minds. Thus each public health
measure, each act to register common lodging houses or
support education was dealing with the situations which
spawned paupers and criminals. New institutions developed
and some were more directly related to preventing crime and
destitution than others. The ragged schools were directly
involved, being outside the system of justice but clearly

dealing with children who were at risk of becoming criminals
or paupers. They also provided a model for the industrial
schools which developed from them. In England there was
no widespread free education as there was in the parishes
of Scotland. There were schools which had been started by
the Bible Societies from what were originally Sunday
Schools, but, even if the poor could afford the weekly
fees, some children would not go because they were too
ragged and, compared with the children of artisans, were
at a social disadvantage. It was for these children that
the ragged schools were started, first in Portsmouth, next
in London, and then spread to other large towns like Bristol and Manchester. At first they opened for a few hours
a day and advertised themselves as being for children who
did not have the shoes to go to other shcools. They were
staffed originally by volunteers, and must have provided
an education for some of these middle- and upper-class
teachers as well as for the children. Miss Carpenter quotes
an account by one teacher:(39)

I was invited on the 1st of October, 1843, to assist in
establishing a School of the kind, by the City Missionary. It appears that the missionary had given out that
this School was to be opened on the Sunday, for boys who
had no shoes or clothes to go to other schools. About
six or seven of us met in the little room in B———
Street, on the Sunday afternoon, little expecting what
we should have to contend with. We opened our School
this first Sunday afternoon with about twenty lads, from
twelve to twenty years of age; their object, as I after-
wards found, was to have a lark. We attempted to teach
them, but they immediately wished to leave the School;
this we opposed: the boys got resolute, so did some of
the teachers. This very soon broke out into open rebellion, and had the teachers been all as resolute as some
were, we should all have had our heads broken. Some of
the teachers used great violence, and when the boys saw
the blood flowing from one of the boys, in consequence
of one of the teachers holding him so tight by the neck,
I could see and hear that they were urging one another
to the attack. I stood a calm spectator, but I at once
saw the necessity of breaking up the conspiracy by diverting their minds to a new object, and holding out a
prospect of some reward to those who were not so forward in the rebellion; and thus we managed to divide
them. We soon got some of the bigger boys on our side,
and such a scene followed as I shall never forget: some
swearing, some dancing, some whistling, and the teachers
looking some of them as pale as death, and some quite
exhausted: and thus we got over our first afternoon.

Some of the teachers I have never seen since: most of
the boys were reformed. Some short time after this,
one Sunday evening, I was left to manage the School
with one timid little man, when about seventy boys came
in, and literally crammed the place: and seeing no physical force capable of resisting them, they at once put
out the lights, and attempted to carry off every thing
worth a penny in the place, such as the candlesticks,
boys' caps, etc. I at once authorized some of the bigger boys, whom I knew something of, to defend the rights
and property of the School. I set four of the best and
stoutest round the book-desk, which they defended like
men; others I got to help me to clear the room and get
lights, etc., and I found myself at last with sixteen,
who all took part more or less in restoring order, and
who begged of me to let them stay to the prayer meeting which we used to hold every Sunday night after the
School; and it was a sight to see these sixteen boys
on their knees before God, listening silently to the
prayers that were offered up to God for the salvation of
their rebel companions, who had caused so much confusion.
Not that these sixteen were so much better than the rest,
for they were nearly all of the same sort; but the fact
is, that you may always divide the interests of a mob of
poor people, if you know how to go to work.

The ragged schools in England formed unions and gradually
developed a few overnight refuges and, much later, provided
dinners for children. On the whole, however, they did not
provide for children's needs, except their need for education, and the industrial schools grew up to fill the gap
and provide residential care for those whose homes were
unable to support them.

PREVENTION IN SCOTLAND

Although Scotland shared with England a concern about the
spread of pauperism, the measures taken to deal with it
were different, perhaps because education was already available in the parish. The Aberdeen Industrial School, which
became the model for Scotland, was designed primarily to
prevent begging, which was seen as leading to delinquency
and pauperism. Sheriff Watson, in a pamphlet called 'Prevention better than cure', wrote:(40)

A committee appointed by the Commissioners of Supply,
reported in 1840, 'that not less than a thousand persons
were continually wandering about, preying upon the inhabitants; that every part of the country suffered more
or less from these vagrants, but the more remote

districts suffered most; that begging was followed as
a regular profession, and was unfortunately more pro-
fitable than some more creditable pursuits, and that on
every account such a state of things ought not to exist.
Vagrancy is, in every point of view, demoralizing to the
country. It has a bad effect on those who only witness
it, and still worse on those whose trade it is. It is
the immediate cause of a great proportion of the petty
offences committed, and not infrequently leads to the
commission of the most heinous crimes. It has rapidly
increased of late, and, if allowed to go on increasing
for some time longer, will, to all appearance attain
to such a height as to make it extremely difficult to
deal with.'

In 1841, after an unsuccessful attempt to get the children who were begging in the streets to go to school, the
police, magistrates and volunteers co-operated in a new
measure, which Thomson explained to the Committee on Criminal and Destitute Children:(41)

orders were given to the police to lay hold at once of
every little begging boy and girl in the town, and upon
a certain day they were all seized; they were carried
to a place which had been prepared for them as a school,
I may say, forcibly established; 75 were captured.
. . . with regard to the Juvenile School, the first
day, of course, was spent with very great difficulty
with the children. They rebelled exceedingly against
the treatment. They were treated in a manner in which
they had never been treated before; and the only thing
that reconciled them to us was their getting three sub-
stantial meals of food; they had breakfast, dinner, and
supper. They were then informed in the evening that
they might return to school or not next day, according
as they pleased, but that begging would not be suffered.
They were told that if they begged they would be immediately apprehended, and not conveyed to school, but to
prison. They were dismissed with this information, and
the next day the whole of them returned voluntarily,
except three. . . .

Thomson also explained how children were selected, and, in
so doing, shows how difficult it is to set a firm boundary
between children who should be the subject of a welfare approach and those who should be treated according to the
ideas of a criminal justice approach.

What are the conditions of admission into the Industrial
Feeding Schools? - There is no condition whatever but
poverty and destitution, and neglect on the part of the
parent. Criminality is no bar to admission; that is to
say, having committed a petty offence, or even being

known to the police as being in the habit of committing
petty offences, is no bar to admission. But as I will
presently explain to the Committee, we endeavour to get
those children so young that very few can properly be
called criminal; the great majority of the children
have certainly been on the high way of becoming criminals, but can scarcely be said to have actually become
so; of course there are exceptions, but that is the
general rule.

A system of schools in Aberdeen developed from this
first sweeping of the streets. All were open long hours,
from seven or eight in the morning until evening, and on
Sundays as well as weekdays. Unlike the ragged schools
in England, the children were fed, were given some industrial training, and the teachers who looked after them
and taught them were paid. Later the approach was extended
to other categories of children when the Child's Asylum was
started. This:(42)

might justly be called the Juvenile Vagrant and Juvenile
Delinquent Prevention Office - established in December,
1846, for the reception of vagrant and delinquent
youth, brought in by the police. Its committee undertook the delicate and difficult duty of dealing with
these outcasts, sending such of them as were suitable
to the Juvenile School of Industry, and restoring the
others to their parents or the police.

During the first year, the police brought in 95 children
— 56 boys and 39 girls. During the second year they
brought in 46 children — 30 boys and 16 girls. During
the third year they brought in 12 children — 10 boys
and 2 girls. Of these last, 2 went to the House of
Refuge and 10 were delivered to their parents, chiefly
at their own desire.

If the Committee had confined its enquiries to the
quasi-delinquent juvenile, brought up by the police, its
operations would, before this, have been brought to a
close - for it would not have been worth while maintaining a machinery, however simple and unexpensive, for
the mere purpose of sending 2 children to the House of
Refuge, and returning 10 back again to their worthless
parents. But it soon became apparent that, to prevent
juvenile delinquency, it was requisite also to prevent
juvenile vagrancy, by anticipating the necessity of begging, and, therefore, after the first year, the committee
considered the cases of children brought to the Asylum
by destitute parents. During the first year's acting in
this manner, it received applications on behalf of 149
children - 92 boys and 57 girls; second year, 135 children - 103 boys and 32 girls; last year, 112 children —

82 boys and 30 girls — of whom

40 were sent to Boys' School;
45 to Juvenile School;
 2 to House of Refuge;
 4 referred to Inspectors of Poor;
<u>21</u> refused as improper
112

These figures, carelessly read, may excite little
attention, but they are deeply significant. Why, it may
be asked, have the numers of juvenile vagrants, apprehended by the police, diminished from 95 to 12? Have
these functionaries become remiss in their duty, and
allowed the plague spot of society to fester in our
streets, instead of subjecting it by the discipline of
the School. It is thought not, - it is believed that
they have apprehended all the juvenile vagrants they
could catch, and have not willingly allowed a single
juvenile delinquent to escape. It is known that juvenile vagrants are still to be seen; but it is supposed
they are not the children of our native poor, but the
vagrant children of stranger trampers, who, in their
peregrinations, take a few days begging, stealing, and
singing in our streets, and the neglected outcasts of
worthless and abandoned parents who make a profit by
their children's crimes. With these classes, the
Child's Asylum Committee cannot effectually deal. They
require the exercise of a more powerful hand. But their
numbers are comparatively small, and a little more activity on the part of the police, excited by an intelligent and zealous magistracy, might render them considerably smaller. Though the Asylum Committee has not
accomplished everything that could have been wished,
yet, there can be no doubt, that, with the instrumen-
tality of the Industrial Schools, it has effected a
social reformation altogether unexampled.

This account makes the preventive purpose of the schools
clear. The Aberdeen model spread to other Scottish towns.
It is interesting that this model provided day care only.
It was thought best that children should maintain their
links with their parents, not only because this was natural,
but also because the children could carry home to their
parents the religious and moral education they were receiving at school.

In Scotland greater emphasis was placed on the importance
of families and family life. Not only were day industrial
schools developed there, but boarding-out of children was
widely practised. Pauper children from Glasgow and Edinburgh were boarded out with crofter families further north,
a pattern which the voluntary children's societies con-

tinued later. Wines, in his book, 'The State of Prisons
and Child Saving Institutions of the Civilized World',
comments that industrial schools and foster homes 'had
their origin in Scotland where hearts are warm and tender
in spite of frosty climate and rock ribbed soil.'(43) It
may be that economic conditions also influenced these trends.

CONCERN WITH RIGHTS

The question of rights seems to have been even less of an
issue in Britain than it was in the United States, although it was concern about rights which led to the defeat
of Sir John Eardley Wilmot's Bill in the Lords. The 1852
Committee on Criminal and Destitute Children did ask some
of their witnesses about parents' rights. Mr Thomson of
Aberdeen was asked:(44)

> Has it ever occurred that the parents of merely des-
> titute children have expressed any objection to their
> children being mixed up with those who have been guilty
> of petty offences? - It has never occurred, and that is
> a point to which I have given very particular attention.
> It has never occurred in any instance.

Mr Thomson also commented on the question of legality when
describing how the Aberdeen streets were swept of young
beggars:(45)

> Was this done by the authority of the magistrates? -
> Why, it would be difficult to say, because the question
> has often been put to me, whether I had any doubt about
> the legality of the proceedings. I have not the slight-
> est doubt that the proceeding was highly illegal, but at
> the same time it was highly expedient, and it has done
> a great deal of good; but several of the magistrates
> of the town gave their consent and concurrence, and,
> in fact, were managers of the school.

Matthew Davenport Hill, a lawyer and recorder of Birmingham,
in his evidence to the Committee endorses Mr Thomson's
views:(46)

> I am not at all sure whether they do not exercise a
> vigour a little beyond the law for a very good purpose;
> however, nobody objects to it, and its success has been
> very great. . . . Certainly it must be admitted their
> success in diminishing juvenile crime has been aston-
> ishing; it is all but extinguished in the city of
> Aberdeen.

I have been unable to find any records of parents who
attempted to take legal action against the training imposed on their children. Neither in the twentieth nor in
the nineteenth centuries have British people seen the

courts as a ready means of redress in the way the public
of the United States do. In part this is because neither
England nor Scotland have a written constitution against
which to test the validity of statute law.

THE GROWTH OF PROBATION

While industrial schools in Scotland were providing what
we would now call intermediate treatment for children, in
England there were few options open to a court which wanted
to avoid sending a child away from home. Probation did not
develop until the end of the century, but the practice of
Matthew Davenport Hill seems to have been a forerunner of
probation. He described his procedure to the 1852 Committee on Criminal and Destitute Juveniles:(47)

> During my attendance as counsel at the Warwick ses-
> sions I found that the magistrates there were in the
> habit of sending both boys and girls, immediately after
> conviction when they had reason to suppose the prison-
> ers were not hardened, back to their parents or masters
> when they were respectable and when they were willing
> to take care of them. . . . In 1841 I adopted a similar
> practice with this addition that I caused the name of
> the guardian or patron who took the charge of the young
> person to be entered in a book and he signed it as an
> obligation that he would do his best; and I caused the
> police to make enquiry from time to time (at no certain
> intervals in order that their coming might be unexpected
> both by the boy and by his master) as to his treatment
> and as to his conduct.

This practice did not spread, and courts had to choose
between acquittal and some form of residential care until
the Probation of First Offenders Act in 1887 allowed them
to suspend sentence. By this time the Church of England
Temperance Society had started to send missionaries into
the police courts of London. These men were concerned originally with reclaiming people from the evils of drink, but
they quickly developed into general purpose social workers
of the courts. In 1907 the Probation of Offenders Act
brought probation as we know it, involving both the suspen-
sion of a penal sentence and a period under supervision.
The missionaries were there to provide the supervision,
and, when juvenile courts were set up a year later, the
Temperance Societies were able to provide the probation
staff for these new courts.

THE CHILDREN ACT OF 1908

We have traced the development of the various stands which
make up the juvenile justice system and which were brought
together in the Children Act of 1908. It is never easy to
decide why an Act is passed at a particular time, but one
can see some of the forces which influenced the passing of
the Children Act. One was the official position of the Home
Office. The Home Secretary at the time was interested in
the bill, but, in addition, Sir William Harcourt, a former
Home Secretary, had been greatly concerned about children.
In October, 1880, he sent a circular letter to chairmen of
quarter sessions, recorders, stipendaries, magistrates of
metropolitan police courts and borough magistrates. He
asked them to 'consider in what way the law ought to be
amended especially with a view to the prevention of imprisonment of young children whether on remand or after conviction.'(48) The replies contain many different suggestions and reflect a range of criminal justice and welfare
thinking. In general they tend to support an extension of
summary justice for young people, along with an extension
of whipping as a punishment. Here they seem to agree with
Queen Victoria, who, Mrs Cadbury tells us, had been concerned by Sir William's 'undue tenderness to offenders'.
Mrs Cadbury quotes Sir William's letter to the Queen written in 1880:(49)

> Many of these cases were for trifling offences, as, for
> instance, a boy of nine years old for throwing stones,
> several boys of eleven and twelve years for damaging
> grass by running about in the fields; a girl of thir-
> teen for being drunk; several boys of twelve and thir-
> teen for bathing in a canal, and similarly for playing
> at pitch and toss; a boy of nine for stealing scent;
> a boy of thirteen for threatening a woman, three boys of
> eleven for breaking windows; a boy of ten for willfully
> damaging timber. This morning a case is reported of a
> boy of ten years old sentenced to fourteen days' hard
> labour or a fine of £1 15s. 3d., for 'unlawfully throw-
> ing down a boarded fence', and the Governor of Prison
> reports this child as a small, delicate boy who can
> neither read nor write. . . .
> Sir William humbly begs leave to represent to your
> Majesty that protracted imprisonment in such cases has
> an injurious effect both upon the physical and moral
> nature of children of tender years. The child who has
> been guilty only of some mischievous or thoughtless
> prank which does not partake of the real character of
> crime finds himself committed with adult criminals
> guilty of heinous offences to the common gaol. After a

week or a fortnight's imprisonment he comes out of prison tainted in character amongst his former companions,
with a mark of opprobrium set upon him, and he soon
lapses into the criminal class with whom he has been
identified.

That this sort of punishment has not a reformatory,
but a degrading effect, is painfully evident from many
of the cases reported. Most of them are first convictions, but in those where there have been previous im-
prisonments, the child was over and over again brought
up on fresh charges generally exhibiting a progressive
advance in criminal character.

The Queen thereupon sent her approval, and in a private letter written to Harcourt from Balmoral, Sir
Henry Ponsonby wrote:

H.M. was really interested in all you said about the
youthful criminals. She would like to whip them, but
it seems that that cannot be done. What she objected to
was not being forewarned of these numerous remissions.

Outside the Home Office other forces were at work, and
when the bill was going through the House, tribute was paid
to the National Society for the Prevention of Cruelty to
Children for its part in promoting this legislation. The
key figure here was the Reverend Benjamin Waugh, who was
instrumental in founding the London branch of the Society
and later converting it into the National Society. Waugh
had written a book, 'The Gaol Cradle - Who Rocks It?'(50),
in 1872, which had been privately distributed to every
magistrate in England. One chapter of this book is entitled, A New Tribunal - Correction without Ruin, in
which he argues that the state must adopt 'some more fair
and natural mode of procedure'. He claimed that legislative action has two distressful results on the little
street rough. 'It first names him black and then makes
him black.' His writing is somewhat confused, but he
seems to be suggesting a lay tribunal as a remedy:(51)

A New and Distinct Tribunal! This is the best device!
A tribunal of citizens - men and women - superinten-
dents of Sunday Schools, teachers of day schools, if
you will - why not? Citizens whose functions should be
magisterial whose legal qualifications should be their
ability to read the living literature of English children, whose Act of Parliament should be their own moral
instincts, with the discretionary powers of a domes-
tic Habeas corpus and satisfaciendum - above all, who
had committed and had not forgotten the appetitive and
pugnacious follies of youth, and could 'Laugh them o'er
again'.

Although the language is that of the nineteenth century,

the description could apply to the children's panels which
Scotland established almost one-hundred years later.

The juvenile court itself was probably less important to
Waugh than the protections against abuse of children, which
Acts from 1889 onwards had developed and which were collected together in the Children Act. However, Waugh objected to children being ill-treated either by their parents
or by the state *in loco parentis*, and, as Director of the
National Society for the Prevention of Cruelty to Children,
he had behind him a society which had received a Royal
Charter in 1895 and which had considerable support. The
Howard Association, another voluntary society, formed in
1867, also gave its support to the introduction of juvenile
courts although its major interest was in ending imprisonment of children.(52)

THE CONTENT OF THE CHILDREN ACT

Unlike the Illinois Act which ended criminal jurisdiction
over children in the United States, the Children Act included little that was new. It drew together a number of
earlier statutes concerned with the control, treatment,
protection and employment of children, who are those under
fourteen, and of young people, who are those between fourteen and sixteen-years old. It made juvenile courts mandatory, which was an innovation in most areas, although
they had already been established in some towns such as
Birmingham.

The bill passed into law without difficulty, partly no
doubt because the government did not include in it anything
which by 1908 was regarded as particularly controversial.
The Lord Advocate, in introducing the second reading of the
bill in the Commons, said:(53)

There was a time in the history of the House when a
bill of this kind would have been treated as a most revo-
lutionary measure; and half a century ago, if such a
measure had been introduced, it would have been said that
the British constitution was being undermined. Now a
bill of this kind finds itself in smooth waters from
the onset. This measure is not the development of political ideas of one party, but the gradual development
of a quickened sense on the part of the community at
large of the duty it owes to children. . . the object
being to treat these children not by way of punishing
them, which is no remedy, but with a view to their reformation.

The Act established juvenile courts which were to be
special sittings of magistrates' courts(54) and which were

to have criminal and civil jurisdiction. With the exception of murder these courts were to deal with all offences by those aged between seven and sixteen years, unless they were committed jointly with an adult.

The courts were also given jurisdiction over children under fourteen years(55) of age who were apparently in need of care because of the conditions in which they were living. The Act spelt out the grounds, which included being found begging, wandering or destitute, in the care of a criminal or drunken parent, in the company of thieves or prostitutes or with a father who has been convicted of certain sexual offences. Juvenile courts were also given jurisdiction over children who were alleged to be beyond the control of their parents, were failing to attend school or were in the care of the Poor-Law guardian and were considered refractory.

All such children and young people were to be dealt with by the new juvenile courts, from which the public were excluded(56) and which were required to sit at a different time or in a different place from the ordinary sittings of the court. When the court was exercising its criminal jurisdiction, either the child or young person or the court could decide that the case should be transferred to a higher court and decided by a judge and jury. Thus the Act protected the right to jury trial and of referral to a higher court by a juvenile court of cases which were regarded as particularly serious.

The Act dealt with the segregation of children and young people from adults before trial,(57) by requiring that they be kept in special places of detention, unless the police or court certified that they were so unruly or so depraved that they could not safely be contained in a place of detention other than a prison. The responsibility for providing places of detention separate from adult police cells or prisons was placed upon the police outside London and in London upon the County Council.

The Act listed the sentences available to the courts in dealing with offenders as:

    (a) dismissal of the charge;
    (b) discharge on a recognisance;
    (c) discharge to the supervision of a probation officer;
    (d) committal to the care of a relative or other fit person;
    (e) industrial school;
    (f) reformatory school;
    (g) whipping;
    (h) payment of a fine, damages or costs;
    (i) payment of fine; damages or costs by parent or guardian;

(j) security;
(k) place of detention;
(l) imprisonment if over fourteen and with a special
certificate.

In dealing with children found to be in need of care,
the court could require the parents to enter into a recog-
nisance to provide due care, place the child under the
supervision of a probation officer, commit to the care of
a relative or other fit person or commit to an industrial
school.(58)

The Act maintained some difference in the treatment of
offenders and non-offenders by keeping what might be seen
as the more punitive treatments, like whipping, fining and
committal to reformatory schools, only for offenders. It
also finally ended imprisonment as a sentence for children
and greatly reduced the possibilities of imprisonment as
a sentence for young people.

The Act capitalised on the harder-won reforms of earlier
times, but it also decided the direction in which juvenile
justice was to develop for the next seventy or more years.
Before the Act various options were open. Benjamin Waugh
had advocated a lay tribunal,(59) and Judge Lindsey of
Denver, Colorado, claims that Parliament in a resolution
credited much help to the writings and pamphlets issued
from his juvenile court.(60) Judge Lindsey was one of the
most forceful proponents of the idea of the juvenile court
as an extension of the court of chancery. Had his example
been followed, British juvenile courts would not have had
criminal jurisdiction. The 1908 Act decided that juvenile
justice should be dispensed by courts and that these courts
should be a part of the general system of criminal justice,
although they were also to have some civil jurisdiction.
They did not have chancery jurisdiction, which in Britain
had always been restricted to the High Court, but they were
given by statute responsibility for the welfare of juveniles,
as well as for the protection of the community.

Chapter six

England and Wales: the present law

To avoid repetition, the developments between 1908 and 1969 will not be discussed in a separate chapter, as was done for the system in the United States. Instead the present law will be considered, first in England and Wales and then in Scotland, and, in so doing, comment will be made on how the changes since 1908 have come about. The English and Scottish systems will be discussed in the same order as that used in discussing the United States system, by looking first at the intent of the Acts, then at the type of court or hearing which has jurisdiction over juveniles and the people appointed to serve on these courts and hearings. Consideration will then be given to the kinds of children over whom the court or hearing has jurisdiction, and what exceptions there are to this jurisdiction. Finally, the sentence or treatments which are available for children and young people in trouble will be discussed. These subjects form only a part of the areas covered by the Acts, but they are sufficient to indicate the balance between a criminal justice and a welfare philosophy.

Unlike the United States, where many important developments took place outside of the statutes, in Britain the changes that have taken place in the philosophy, organisation and administration of juvenile justice can be traced most readily through the statutes. The major enactments about juvenile justice are to be found in Children Acts or Children and Young Persons Acts, but parts of the relevant law occur in other statutes such as Magistrates Courts Acts and Criminal Justice Acts. Unfortunately there has been no attempt to bring together all the laws relating to children and young people in trouble. Another complication is that, while developments in England and in Scotland took a similar form until the 1960s, the two countries are sometimes covered by one Act and sometimes by separate but similar Acts. The Acts to which most frequent reference will

be made are the Children Act of 1908, which applied to
Britain as a whole, the Children and Young Persons Act of
1933, which applied to England and Wales, the Children and
Young Persons (Scotland) Act, 1937, which applied only to
Scotland, and the Children and Young Persons Act, 1963,
which applied to both countries. After this the laws
separate, and the Children and Young Persons Act, 1969,
applying to England and Wales, has no Scottish counterpart.
The current law for Scotland is to be found in the 1968
Social Work (Scotland) Act, which will be considered later.
This chapter will cover the statute law for Scotland up to
1968.

In the United States the differences between juvenile
courts make generalisations hazardous. To an extent similar differences probably exist in England and Wales, although there are no studies of individual courts which make
these clear. Personal experience and the comments of professionals would suggest that, although all juvenile courts
are subject to the same statute law, there are differences
in the way they interpret and administer this law. There
are also differences in the standards of the probation and
social service departments which serve as the executive arm
of the courts. However, there is probably more uniformity
in English and Welsh juvenile courts than there is between
those of the different States in the United States.

The most recent changes in English juvenile justice were
brought about by the 1969 Children and Young Persons Act
which amended the 1933 Act, which is still referred to as
the principle Act. The 1969 Act had an interesting history.
When it was a bill in Parliament, it was described as 'the
grandchild of one government White Paper and the child of
another'.(1)

Its grandparent, *The Child, the Family and the Young
Offender,* first saw light in August 1965. Its purpose
was 'to invite discussion of possible measures to support the family, forestall and prevent delinquency, and
revise the law and practice relating to young offenders
in England and Wales'. It contained proposals among
other things for establishing 'family councils', for
replacing magistrates by social workers and juvenile
courts by 'family courts', and for setting up a new
kind of court for the trial and treatment of offenders
between the ages of 17 and 21. That White Paper had a
short and troubled life. Magistrates, lawyers, social
workers and men and women of all political persuasions
united to oppose it. Their main ground for doing so
was that the proposals, if adopted, would abrogate the
ancient principle that no subject of the Crown, however
young or undistinguished, may be deprived of his liberty

except by order of a properly constituted court of law.
In face of those criticisms the 1965 White Paper made a
dignified retirement and there was an interval of nearly
three years while its sponsors, the Labour Government,
thought again.

The second White Paper, *Children in Trouble*, was presented to Parliament in April 1968. As was to be expected, it revealed certain family characteristics which
gained it in some quarters a mixed reception. But its
tone was more moderate, the more radical of the earlier
proposals had been dropped, and the undoubted value of
other proposals originally contained in the 1965 White
Paper was no longer obscured by intense controversy.

The procedure which had produced the Act of 1969 was
unusual. The government had issued not one but two White
Papers outlining plans for change. The first Paper(2) took
a radical approach, relying heavily upon ideas first pub-
licised in a report of a Labour Party committee headed by
Lord Longford.(3) This report and the White Paper which
followed it suggested the abolition of juvenile courts and
their replacement by family councils. While this idea
found support amongst many social workers, it was strongly
criticised by magistrates and probation officers. Apparently their criticisms carried weight, as the second White
Paper, 'Children in Trouble',(4) was more traditional and
recommended the continuation of the juvenile court as a
central feature of the system. What the White Papers did
was to ensure wide discussion of the alternative measures.
These discussions reached into the grass roots, and involved the people who were likely to be responsible for
operating whatever system was finally selected. Because of
this extensive input from fields other than law, the
English law may reflect a broader base than the Uniform
Act and model rules of the United States, where the input
seems to have been predominantly legal.

The Act has had a troubled life since it became law. It
was passed while a Labour Government was in power, and
Conservatives in opposition fought against certain aspects
of the bill. In general they were opposed to those clauses
which moved furthest from ideas of criminal justice. By
the time the Act came into force in January 1970, the Conservatives had regained power, and they dealt with their
doubts about the Act by refusing to implement some clauses
and reserving their position on others. They were able to
do this the more easily because many of the clauses in the
Act were to be implemented by the Secretary of State only
when the state of the social services allowed. When the
Labour Party returned to government attitudes towards
young offenders were changing and a financial crisis was

imminent. The opportune time for introducing a juvenile
justice system biased towards a welfare approach had
passed.

THE INTENT OF THE ACTS

The broad intention of the juvenile justice system in
England and Wales remains that expressed in Section 44 of
the Children and Young Persons Act 1933:

Every court in dealing with a child or young person who
is brought before it either as an offender or otherwise,
shall have regard to the welfare of the child or young
person and shall in proper cases take steps for removing
him from undesirable surroundings and for securing that
proper provision is made for his education and training.
Almost identical wording is found in Section 49 of the
Children and Young Persons (Scotland) Act of 1937.

Such provisions were new. The 1908 Act had not spelt
out in this way the principles to be observed by courts
in dealing with children and young persons. However, Mr
Stanley, the Under Secretary of State, had explained the
principles underlying Part IV of that Act, which introduced juvenile courts. The bill, he said, aimed to separate juveniles from adult offenders and to provide for
juveniles 'treatment differentiated to suit their special
needs'. The courts 'should be agencies for the rescue as
well as the punishment of children', and 'commitment of
children to the common gaol is an unsuitable penalty ...
the child is made to feel for the rest of his life that he
is a criminal and belongs to the criminal classes, and at
the same time that vague dread of the unknown penalties of
imprisonment, which is one of the most powerful deterrents
of crime, becomes useless and nugatory'.(5) These remarks
are a good example of the way in which arguments for criminal justice and those for a welfare approach can be used
to support the same measure.

The Lords also combined arguments drawn from the welfare
and criminal justice approaches, but put more emphasis
upon prevention in support of the bill, which it was said
'is conceived not only in a spirit of tenderness and af-
fection for child life but also with a real interest in
the future welfare of the state. These provisions hold out
to us hope for a marked diminution of crime in the future.'
(6) The same view had been put more crudely in the Commons
by an honourable member who reported that he had discussed
the bill with his ghillie. The ghillie had used the illustration of a rabbit warren to express his opinion that 'you
must catch them young and then they will die out'.(7)

There are other clauses of the 1933 and 1937 Acts which
show the gradual shift towards a welfare approach. The
departmental committees(8) which preceded the Acts had reported concern amongst witnesses that children were convicted by juvenile courts. While they agreed that the difference between a conviction and a finding of guilt was
perhaps largely technical, they recommended that the latter
term should replace conviction and that the term sentence
should not be used in relation to juveniles. Instead, the
phrase 'order made upon a finding of guilt' should be used.
These recommendations were enacted in the Children and
Young Persons Acts of 1933 and 1937.(9)

The welfare of the child or young person remains a principle of the present law, but Acts since 1933 have added to
the meaning of welfare the idea of preventing juveniles
appearing in court at all. This found statutory form in
the Children and Young Persons Act of 1963, which stated:
'It shall be the duty of every local authority to make
available such advice and guidance and assistance as may
promote the welfare of children by diminishing the need to
... bring children before a juvenile court'.(10) The 1969
Act continues this trend by requiring consultation between
police and local authority social service departments before a child can be brought to court. There has been delay
in making this consultation mandatory, but the practice has
been adopted in many areas. The original intention of the
Act was to ensure that, if juveniles had to be brought to
court, they should, whenever possible, be brought, not on
a criminal charge, but under the court's civil jurisdiction.
This will be considered further when discussing the extent
of the court's jurisdiction.

THE STRUCTURE AND PERSONNEL OF THE COURTS

Juvenile courts were established in 1908. At that time they
constituted a special sitting of the magistrates court
to hear cases relating to those under sixteen. The juvenile court remains the court in which most troubled and
troublesome juveniles appear, but over the years the courts
have become rather more specialized and more easily distinguished from magistrates courts dealing with adults.
It is part of the lowest level of courts with the most lo-
calised jurisdiction in the English judicial structure,
and, like any other magistrates court, it has both criminal
and civil jurisdiction.

The Children and Young Persons Acts of 1933 and 1937
made it a requirement that a juvenile court should 'sit
either in a different building or room from that in which

sittings of courts other than juvenile courts are held, or
on different days from those on which sittings of such
courts are held'.(11) The separation of adults from juveniles was thus carried a step further, although in 1963 the
law was changed in response to the pressure on court build-
ings, and now a juvenile court may not sit in a room in
which sittings of another court have been or will be held
within an hour of the juvenile court's sitting.(12) The
reasons for this change are administrative and economic, but
the effect is to weaken the welfare approach. Juveniles
are now more likely to mix with adult offenders, not in the
court room itself, but in the corridors and waiting rooms.
Such mixing is unlikely to lead to any direct corruption
of juveniles by adults, although this is possible; much
more damaging may be the effect upon the self image of the
juvenile. If they meet and wait with adult offenders, they
are more likely to begin to see themselves as criminals,
and, according to the labelling theorists, such a change in
self image is a vital step on the road to a delinquent
career.

The juvenile courts are manned by magistrates. The 1908
Act made no provision for the selection of special justices
to sit in juvenile courts, and this came to be regarded as
a weakness. In 1916 the Home Secretary appointed a body
called the Juvenile Organisations Committee to consider the
increase in juvenile delinquency. The Committee was transferred to a Committee of the Board of Education and, when
reporting in 1920, stated:(13)

> The unanimity with which the witnesses, who appeared be-
> fore the Committee, pressed for a more careful selection
> of magistrates to sit in juvenile courts is worthy of
> note. There is no doubt that many children are harshly
> and foolishly treated in the courts because the magis-
> trates sometimes lack experience of the normal boy or
> girl and are consequently incapable of arriving at a
> wise decision as to how best to deal with the young de-
> linquent. Most, if not all of the difficulties exper-
> ienced in juvenile courts centre round this prime need.
> The neglect of the opportunities afforded by the Proba-
> tion of Offenders Act, 1907, for the rehabilitation of
> juvenile offenders without conviction; the loose pro-
> cedure in many so-called 'Children's Courts'; the fail-
> ure to observe the various sections of the Children Act,
> 1908, relating to the conduct of juvenile courts and
> the conditions under which children, and particularly
> girls, are called upon to give evidence; the ignorance
> of Circulars and Instructions issued from the Home Office
> to justices and justices' clerks, are all difficulties
> which would never arise if the magistrate had a sympa-

thetic understanding of child life, and was keen to avail himself of the many facilities for considerate treatment of young people which existing statutes and regulations already place at his disposal. The Committee therefore urge the importance of securing the appointment as magistrates of persons specially experienced in dealing with children, and they are of opinion that women magistrates would be of great service in juvenile courts.

The implication was that, if the welfare of children were to be the concern of the court, then magistrates needed to be specially selected, since those who sat regularly in adult criminal courts were not necessarily qualified to deal with the special situations arising in juvenile courts. The Committee recommended that, in the selection of magistrates, regard should be had to the appointment of those experienced in dealing with children, and that the Lord Chancellor should ask to be furnished 'with evidence as to special qualifications, e.g., teachers, well-known social workers amongst young people, persons recommended by the local Education Authority, local Juvenile Organisations Committee, or other similar body.'(14)

The third report of the Children's Branch of the Home Office, published in 1925, included the results of a survey of juvenile courts in England and Wales, and found it was 'the exception rather than the rule for justices to be specially designated to hear juvenile cases'. From a total of 876 courts only 59 had specially designated justices.(15) The Molony Committee, appointed in 1925 to inquire into the treatment of young offenders, also discussed the selection of magistrates in its report, following which the Home Secretary sent a circular to magistrates, emphasising the importance of having a rota of children's court magistrates with special qualifications. The 1933 Children and Young Persons Act made a special rota of juvenile court magistrates obligatory in England and Wales.

Although it was important to establish the principle that children and young people should appear before specially selected magistrates, it has proved difficult to ensure that these magistrates are in fact particularly well suited to their job. The method by which the juvenile court rota is chosen is by an election amongst the magistrates of each administrative area known as a petty sessional division. Their choice is limited to existing magistrates, and the guide lines on which they operate are necessarily broad. Home Office circulars suggest that those selected should have particular interest or experience with young people, and since 1966 training has been required. Even imposing an age limit on the service of

juvenile court magistrates took a long time. Mr Lunn, MP,
had interrupted the opening speech on the Second Reading of
the 1933 Act to exclaim: 'There ought to be more modern
magistrates. A lot of them are old maids'. Mr Stanley
replied: 'Well, the Hon. Member is no doubt a better judge
of old maids than I am';(16) and an age limit was not introduced until 1936. Elkin states that, before the new
panels were elected in 1936, of approximately 10,000
justices in England and Wales on juvenile court panels,
1,284 were aged between seventy and eighty, and 130 were
over ninety years.(17) Even the present requirement that
they be not over sixty-five-years of age results in many
being the age of the grandparents, rather than of the
parents, of the young people with whom they are concerned.

The great difference in age between magistrates and the
juveniles who appear before them is important. Ideas about
what is tolerable behaviour in young people change over the
generations, and juveniles tend to feel they have a greater
chance of being understood by people near their own age.
Briggs,(18) in his account of his experiences before a
juvenile court, shows how impossible it was for him to
convey how he felt to the court, and anything that in-
creases that difficulty, such as the distance and perhaps
the deafness of old age, lessens the chance of individualising justice.

Apart from attempts to regulate age, the law also refers
to the sex of magistrates. The 1933 Act required that,
where possible, each juvenile court bench should include a
man and a woman magistrate,(19) and the 1926 Juvenile Courts
(Scotland) Act made provision for a woman magistrate to sit
as an assessor in juvenile courts in Scottish burghs where
the presiding magistrate was a man.

Alongside the development of special panels of juvenile
court justices has gone the development of restrictions
upon the numbers of people involved in a juvenile court
hearing. The present size of a juvenile court bench is
three, but although this was the most common number when
the Children's Branch of the Home Office issued one of its
periodic reports in 1925 it was not the number in a majority of courts.

When a large number of magistrates sit, it is clearly
even harder to achieve an atmosphere in which the child and
his parents can understand what is happening and explain
their own views to the bench. This is the aim of a court
concerned with the welfare of children, and restricting
the numbers to three helps to make it nearer a reality.

TABLE 6.1   Table included in the report of the Children's Branch 1925

Number of magistrates present	1	2	3	4	5	6	7	8	9	10
County Boroughs	2	17	36	15	4	2	-	-	-	-
Boroughs	2	14	66	33	23	8	3	2	-	-
Petty Sessional Divisions	2	126	205	169	84	42	13	3	2	3
Total	6	156	307	217	111	52	16	5	2	3

The same applies to the presence of other people in the court. The 1908 Act had intended to allow access only to those involved in the particular case. Juvenile courts never were, as are adult courts, open to the public. However, in 1927 a departmental committee discovered that as many as fifty people were present in some juvenile courts and that twenty was not an unusual number.(21) They recommended that the number of people present be kept as low as possible.

Although juvenile courts have never been open to the public, the press have been allowed to attend. The departmental committee report in 1927 stated that most courts had made informal arrangements with the press that they would not disclose details which would allow a child or young person to be identified. They considered excluding the press entirely, but decided to recommend a statutory ban on the publication of identifying details, to be lifted in individual instances only by order of the Secretary of State. This was enacted in the 1933 and 1937 Acts,(22) and remained unchanged until 1969 when, for England and Wales, publication was forbidden unless the court considered it to be in the interests of a child or young person for the press to give identifying details. The thinking behind this new clause is that in cases where one child or group of children are suspected of acts which in fact were carried out by others, publication may be necessary to serve the welfare of the innocent children or young people. In general, however, those appearing before juvenile courts do not suffer the exposure to the public inflicted on adult offenders, because a concern for their welfare overrides the need to stigmatise and expose them.

Besides the magistrates, the child and his parents, and the press, the other people usually present throughout an English juvenile court hearing are the clerk to the justices, members of the local police, when they are prose-

cuting in a criminal case, and social workers from the probation service and/or the local authority social service
department.

Although some justices may have had a legal training,
this is not required, and the juvenile court is served by
a clerk to the justices. He must have legal training, and
is usually a solicitor with at least five years' practice.
The function of the clerk is twofold: he serves as the administrator of the court and he advises the justices upon
legal questions.

Unlike the Uniform Code in the United States, the laws
establishing the juvenile courts do not themselves set up
a probation service attached to the court, although the
Acts assume that a social service exists and authorises
the probation officer and/or the local authority's social
service department to produce reports.

England has both a probation service and a local authority social service. Scotland now has only a local authority social work service, which includes probation. The
English services are each differently organised and may
cover different geographical areas. A probation service
covers either one large petty sessional division, in cases,
for example, where a borough is a division, or else it
covers a number of divisions which are grouped together to
form a combined probation area. In a large urban area
many probation officers will serve the same court, whereas
in a country district a male and a female officer may each
serve more than one juvenile court and be responsible for
serving a number of different petty sessional divisions.
Probation officers are appointed by a probation committee
composed of justices, but the terms and conditions of work,
including salary scales, are laid down for the whole
country by the Secretary of State. Once officers are appointed and confirmed in that appointment after a proba-
tionary period, they cannot be dismissed except for mis-
conduct, and, if they wish, can serve until they reach
retirement age. The relationship between the juvenile
court bench of justices and the probation staff is a much
less direct one than that between a juvenile court judge
in the United States and his probation department, and
politics play little or no part in the appointment of probation officers in England.

The social service department (or social work department
in Scotland) is one part of the administrative service of
local government and each region or metropolitan area has
its own department. Area offices of the department de-
centralise services and make them more readily available to
the public, but the catchment area of a local office does
not necessarily follow the same boundaries as those of the

petty sessional division. The staff of a local authority
social service department are responsible, through their
director, to the elected councillors. Although the departments have statutory duties in relation to the courts,
their relationship with the court is an indirect one. There
is no hierarchical relationship and they resemble two distinct powers whose relationships may be co-operative or
extremely hostile.

THE JURISDICTION OF THE JUVENILE COURT

The juvenile courts have jurisdiction over children who
are aged under fourteen years and young persons who are
fourteen but under the age of seventeen. The upper age
was raised from sixteen to seventeen by the 1933 and 1937
Acts. Since 1969 a person is held to have attained the
age of seventeen at the beginning of the relevant anni-
versary of his birth and not at the beginning of the day
before, which, in 1918, *Shurey, Savory* v. *Shurey*(23) had
held to be the law unless altered by statute.

CRIMINAL JURISDICTION

The court has both civil and criminal jurisdiction. It
has original criminal jurisdiction over all offences except murder but this jurisdiction is limited by the age of
the accused. If the 1969 Act is ever fully implemented,
no child (i.e. no one under fourteen years) will be subject
to the court's criminal jurisdiction. At common law a
child under seven years is presumed incapable of a criminal offence, and for those under fourteen the prosecution has to prove that they had a guilty mind. The 1933
and 1937 Acts raised the age of criminal responsibility to
eight and the 1963 Act raised it to ten years for children
in England and Wales, although it remained eight years in
Scotland. The 1969 Act did not alter the age of criminal
responsibility, but gave power to the Home Secretary to
raise the age at which a child could be liable to prosecution to twelve and with Parliament's approval ultimately
to fourteen. This power has not been used and it now seems
unlikely that it will be. There is only one exception to
the rule that those under the stated age shall not be
charged with an offence, and that exception relates to
murder. Children over seven will continue to be charged
with murder and will be tried, not by a juvenile court,
but by what were Assizes and are now Crown Courts in
England.

Between the stated age, which is ten, and seventeen, children and young people are subject to the criminal jurisdiction of the juvenile court, although the intention of the Act was to avoid using this jurisdiction wherever possible and to substitute for it the civil jurisdiction invoked by a care proceeding. This intention does not seem to have been implemented in practice.

The criminal jurisdiction of the juvenile court has been reduced slightly since 1908, but this does not mean that the State has surrendered control over children who might formerly have been charged with a criminal offence. Instead the categories of those who are subject to the court's civil jurisdiction have been increased. Had the 1969 Act come fully into force, no one under fourteen years would be charged with an offence except murder, but an offence would be one ground for the finding of a need for care and control. The balance between a criminal justice approach and a welfare approach has shifted gradually during the century, but now seems to have settled at least for a while.

CIVIL JURISDICTION

Care proceedings can be taken in relation to any child or young person from birth to the age of seventeen years. The upper age limit has been seventeen since the 1933 and 1937 Acts, when it was raised from fourteen, which had been the age laid down in the 1908 Act. Under the 1969 Act as amended by the Children Act 1975, a juvenile court may take action in respect of a child or young person when they consider that any of the following conditions is satisfied with respect to him:(24)

(a) His proper development is being avoidably prevented or neglected or his health is being avoidably impaired or neglected or he is being ill-treated; or

(b) it is probable that the condition set out in the preceding paragraph will be satisfied in his case, having regard to the fact that the court or another court has found that that condition is or was satisfied in the case of another child or young person who is or was a member of the household to which he belongs; or

(bb) it is probable that the conditions set out in paragraph (a) of this subsection will be satisfied in his case, having regard to the fact that a person who has been convicted of an offence mentioned in Schedule 1 of the Act of 1933 is, or may become, a member of the same household as the child; or

(c) he is exposed to moral danger; or

(d) he is beyond the control of his parent or guardian; or

(e) he is of compulsory school age within the meaning of the Education Act 1944 and is not receiving efficient full-time education suitable to his age, ability and aptitude; or

(f) he is guilty of an offence, excluding homicide, and that he is in need of care or control which he is unlikely to receive unless the court makes an order under this section in respect of him.

The grounds for what are now called care proceedings have changed during the century, the behaviour which could lead to an industrial school order in 1908 is more specific and more concerned with past acts than that which provides grounds for a care proceeding in 1969. Such a trend marks a movement away from the ideas of criminal justice, in which only proven past actions provide grounds for state intervention, towards a welfare approach which is concerned with states of being.

Alongside this movement was another which restricted the jurisdiction of the courts in civil matters to those situations where intervention was necessary for the welfare of the child or young person concerned. As under the uniform juvenile code of the United States, so under the 1969 Act, English juvenile courts have jurisdiction in civil cases only if certain factual conditions are met *and* if the juvenile requires care and control which cannot be supplied in another way. This was not the case in 1908, when to be found begging, receiving alms or frequenting the company of a reputed thief were sufficient in themselves, if proved, to give the court power to act. Similarly, where a girl was found to be a member of a household in which incest had been committed, the court had power, 'if it seemed expedient', to make an industrial school order. After 1933 in England and Wales and 1937 in Scotland a girl in such circumstances became subject to the court's jursidiction only if she required care or protection, and a child or young person had not only to be in moral danger but to have parents who either did not, or were unfit to, exercise proper care and guardianship. The 1963 Act developed the double proof requirement, giving the court jurisdiction only where the juvenile 'was not receiving such care, protection and guidance as a good parent may reasonably be expected to give'.(25) The section in the 1969 Act 'that he is in need of care or control which he is unlikely to receive unless the court makes an order'(26) is wider and is said to remove the implication of blame from the parents. What is new is that this double proof will be necessary where a child (or a young person brought under this section) is said to be in need of care because he has committed an offence. The offence alone will not be sufficient to give the court power to make an order as is the case with a criminal charge.

REFERRAL TO THE JUVENILE COURT

As the juvenile court has come to be seen as a stigmatising place of last resort, so the statutory hurdles to referral have increased. The underlying idea is to prevent juveniles being referred to the court wherever possible, but the statutory restrictions vary according to whether the juvenile is to be the subject of a criminal charge or a care proceeding. If the relevant sections are implemented a child or young person will be brought before a juvenile court on a criminal charge only when a qualified person lays an information.(27) This effectively restricts prosecution to the police and ends private prosecution. Before an information can be laid, the qualified person must inform the local authority that this action is being considered and must hear any observations the local authority wish to make. The informant must also himself be satisfied that it would 'not be adequate for the case to be dealt with by a parent, teacher or other person or by means of a caution from a constable or through an exercise of powers of a local authority or other body',(28) or by means of a care proceeding. The intention of the Act is clearly to restrict criminal proceedings, but the authority to make the decision rests with the police, despite their duty to inform the local authority. Once the decision is made, the police proceed by summons or by arrest and charge usually followed by release on bail.

The control of referrals of those in need of care has developed over a longer period. At present a child or young person can be brought before a juvenile court for care proceedings by a local authority, a constable or an authorised person.(29) The last means someone authorised by the Secretary of State, and at present the officers of the National Society for the Prevention of Cruelty to Children are so authorised. Before they or a constable can bring a child to court they are required to notify the local authority. The same section of the 1969 Act requires the local authority to cause enquiries to be made when they receive information suggesting that there are grounds for bringing care proceedings in respect of any child or young person in their area. Having investigated them, they have a duty to bring care proceedings in res-

pect of the juvenile unless 'they are satisfied that it is
neither in his interests nor the public interest to do so
or that some other person is about to do so or to charge
him with an offence.(30) This clause ensures that at least
some investigation is undertaken before a decision is made
to take a child to court, and that investigation is made,
not by a person concerned with law enforcement, but by the
social workers of the local authority. They then have an
opportunity to offer voluntary services and casework to
families under the terms of the 1963 Act, which places a
duty on local authorities to prevent children being brought
before the court.

This restriction on those who could initiate care proceedings was not present in the 1908 Act, which stated:
'any person may bring before a petty sessional court any
person apparently under the age of fourteen years'(31) who
appeared to meet the listed conditions. In the 1933 Act
this power was restricted to 'a local authority, constable
or authorised person'.(32) At this time the staff of the
National Society and of the Liverpool Society for the Prevention of Cruelty to Children were authorised by the Secretary of State for this purpose. A similar clause in the
Scottish Act gives these powers to 'any education authority,
constable or authorised person',(33) and here the people
authorised were the staff of the Royal Society for the Prevention of Cruelty to Children.

THE JUVENILE'S RIGHTS

In either a civil or a criminal proceeding the juvenile has
certain rights. The statutes clearly entitle him to notice
of the hearing and to legal aid. Legal aid in a care proceeding takes the form of a legal aid order, granted by the
court as in criminal proceedings, and this saves the delays
which might occur in using the civil forms of legal aid.
The statute also deals with the standard of proof required.
Since juvenile courts have always had criminal jurisdiction,
there has never been a question in England, as there was
in the United States, about juveniles' rights to the protection afforded to adults charged with crimes. The 1969
Act allows for an offence to be the grounds for a civil
proceeding, but it makes clear that where this occurs
the standard of proof must be the same as would have been
required to find the juvenile guilty of an offence,(34)
and that the juvenile is not a competent and compellable
witness, and so cannot be required to incriminate himself.
The juvenile is also protected from being charged at some
future date with an offence that has already served as

part of the grounds for a care proceeding, and has a
right of appeal to the Crown Court against a finding that
the offence condition is satisfied even where the juvenile court decides not to make a care order.

There is one area in which a child or young person, who
is either the subject of care proceedings in which an offence condition is alleged or the subject of criminal proceedings, does not have the rights of an adult in a similar
situation. This is in relation to trial by jury. Neither
children nor young people in England, apart from those
charged with murder, now have a right to jury trial. It
is interesting that this right, which has been gradually
eroded in Britain, is the one which the United States
Supreme Court has not held essential to ensure fairness
in juvenile court hearings. In Britain, the 1908 Act
maintained the right to elect trial by jury for children
and young people facing criminal charges, but the 1933
and 1937 Acts abolished the right for those under fourteen years. The 1927 Departmental Committee, in their
report recommending this change, said that very few children in fact exercised this right. In 1969 the same reason was given for removing entirely from anyone charged
in the juvenile court the right of jury trial. This has
caused concern amongst those who see jury trial as an important protection against arbitrary action and as a
means of ensuring rights. On the other hand, the welfare
of the young person is more fully considered in a juvenile court, which is used to balancing needs and rights,
than in a high court unaccustomed to juveniles, where
great care is taken in reaching a finding of guilt, but
sentencing is often rapid and routine.

The rights of juveniles under the courts' civil jurisdiction are less well protected. Except in relation to an
offence condition, they and their parents are competent
and compellable witnesses, and the standard of proof required is that of a civil situation: the balance of pro-
babilities. This seems illogical. The more serious dispositions, such as removal from home, can be identical
whether the case is civil or criminal. The need to protect rights arises, not from the nature of the complaint,
but from the powers given to a court to intervene and to
change a person's way of life.

TRANSFER TO ADULT COURTS

Like their counterparts in the United States, the English
juvenile courts can, in certain narrowly-defined situations,
transfer a young offender for trial in another court. In

England the transfer is to the Crown Court and can occur
when a young person is charged with certain grave crimes
or when a child and a young person is charged jointly
with an adult with an indictable offence.(35) In neither
situation is the court required to remit for trial. In
the first instance they can do so if they consider that,
should the juvenile be found guilty, it might be desirable
to sentence him to a long term of detention. In the situation of a joint charge they can remit, after considering
the evidence,(36) if the interests of justice require this.
This power to remit has remained unchanged since 1908.

DISPOSITIONAL POWERS

Once the juvenile court has found a juvenile to have committed an offence or to be in need of care and control,
they may discharge the case, make a supervision order or
a guardianship order, or, if they consider that removal
from home is necessary, they can make a care order or a
hospital order. If the child or young person has been
found to have committed an offence, the court may, in addition to the orders already listed, conditionally discharge, fine or order damages and restitution. They may
also make an attendance centre order, or, if the young
person is over fifteen, a detention centre order, or commit to the Crown Court for sentence.
    The way courts have used their powers in relation to
juvenile offenders since the 1969 Act is indicated by
Table 6.2 from the Home Office evidence to the Social
Services and Employment Sub Committee,(37) supplemented by
the 1974(38) and 1975(39) Criminal Statistics. Table 6.3,
also from the Home Office evidence, shows the actions of
courts in care proceedings in 1973.
    The fine balance between criminal justice and welfare
thinking is indicated by the history of dispositional alternatives, and whether or not particular forms of treatment were restricted to those who committed offences. The
1908 Act continued the nineteenth-century practice of
sending older offenders to reformatory schools and younger
offenders and those needing care to industrial schools.
This distribution was never very clear, and it became more
and more blurred by the growth of what Handler calls the
'unified theory of deviance'.(40) This is the belief that
all troubled or troublesome behaviour, but especially such
behaviour in children, is caused by problems in family relationships. The 1927 committee report expressed this
view: 'In many cases the tendency to commit offences is
only an outcome of neglect and there is little room for

discrimination either in the character of the young person
concerned or in the appropriate treatment'.(41) The committee recommended that the difference between industrial
and reformatory schools should be ended, and, after 1933
in England and Wales and 1937 in Scotland, they all came
to be known as Approved Schools. The name came from the
power of the minister or of the Scottish education department to 'approve the school'. The Home Office spokesman,
in explaining the new bill to the Commons, said:(42)

After all, both classes of children, the rejected and
the offenders, have had to suffer a withdrawal of their
liberty, in the one case as a species of punishment, in
the other purely for their own protection. The fact remains that they are both inside and, when they are inside, the object is the same in dealing with them
namely, when they get outside, to give them a good
change of making decent citizens. We have decided to
abolish the distinction between these two types of
schools, and to put them together in future under one
heading of approved schools, to which the distinction
which now exists will no longer apply.

I know that some people feel that it is unwise, and
perhaps unfair, to mix up in the same school those who
are there as punishment for an offence and those who are
merely there for their own protection - that it means
that the poor neglected child is contaminated by the
bad young offender. The fact is that the distinction
between the two is largely accidental. The neglected
child may only just have been lucky enough not to have
been caught in an offence. The character of the child
who has been suffering from a long period of neglect at
home, or a long period of evil surroundings, is much
more likely to have been seriously affected than the
character of the young offender who is perhaps in the
school as the result of one short lapse into crime. We
do not believe that either will suffer from being in the
same school. We shall adopt, instead of the old classification of reformatory and industrial schools, a new
classification - a classification by geographical situation, by religious teaching, by the different opportunities of training different types of people, and, of
course, by age; only to a lesser extent do we take into
account character.

These ideas occur again in the White Papers leading up to
the 1969 Act. The first White Paper carried this view to
its logical but unacceptable conclusion. If it is neglect
and family problems which are the cause both of delinquency
and of a need for care, then a court is an inappropriate
place to deal with such situations, and a family council

TABLE 6.2

All courts	1969	1970	1971	1972	1973	1974	1975
Persons under seventeen found guilty of:							
Indictable offences	72,445	74,307	72,681	75,962	79,138	95,005	93,751
Non-indictable offences (except motoring offences)	20,790	23,609	20,431	19,818	20,597	18,310	17,379
Motoring offences	26,693	26,250	24,951	19,707	18,044	16,980	18,317
	119,928	123,166	118,063	115,487	117,779	130,295	129,447
Absolute discharge	2,789	2,497	2,376	2,361	2,106	2,252	2,597
Recognances	232	221	329	369	379	501	455
Conditional discharge	20,389	20,413	18,838	19,415	20,414	22,400	24,931
Hospital order	54	47	26	18	27	14	15
Restriction order	7	12	6	5	8	9	7
Probation	21,752	21,093	-	-	-	-	-
Supervision	-	-	18,231	17,346	18,152	20,522	18,952
Fine	58,016	60,122	60,182	56,892	55,722	56,850	56,566

Attendance centre	6,173	6,795	6,209	6,785	7,227	8,703	8,388
Detention centre	2,228	2,516	2,475	3,083	3,694	4,451	4,793
Approved school	5,143	5,741	-	-	-	-	-
Fit Person order	1,424	1,716	-	-	-	-	-
Care order	-	-	7,499	7,126	7,602	8,221	7,603
Borstal training	828	1,059	1,159	1,315	1,448	1,645	1,877
Otherwise dealt with	860	934	733	772	1,000	290	603
	119,928	123,166	118,063	115,487	117,779	127,857	126,787

Committed by Magistrates Courts to Crown Courts for
sentence and included in totals at top of table.

	2,438	2,660
	130,285	129,447

TABLE 6.3 Non-criminal proceedings at Magistrates' Courts Care proceedings. Orders made in care proceedings under Section 1 of the Children and Young Persons Act 1969: by type of order, age and sex

Proceedings brought under	Type of order made							
	Total		Recognisance		Supervision		Care	
	M	F	M	F	M	F	M	F
Under 10:								
Children and Young Persons Act 1969								
S.1(2)(a) development neglected, ill-treatment, etc.	622	583	1	–	103	91	518	192
S.1(2)(b) condition (a) met in relation to another member of the household	25	51	–	–	5	20	20	31
S.1(2)(c) exposed to moral danger	19	49	–	–	5	11	14	38
S.1(2)(d) beyond parental control	97	13	–	–	22	2	75	11
S.1(2)(e) not receiving efficient full-time education	103	64	1	1	57	31	45	32
Total	866	760	2	1	192	155	672	604
10 and under 14:								
Children and Young Persons Act 1969								
S.1(2)(a) development neglected, ill-treatment, etc.	97	100	–	–	15	9	82	91
S.1(2)(b) condition (a) met in relation to another member of the household	4	6	–	–	1	1	3	5
S.1(2)(c) exposed to moral danger	17	94	–	–	6	20	11	74
S.1(2)(d) beyond parental control	101	96	–	–	13	15	88	81

S.1(2)(e) not receiving efficient full-time education	483	332	2	1	222	184	259	147
S.1(2)(f) guilty of an offence excluding homicide*	14	2	-	-	-	-	14	2
Total	716	630	2	1	257	229	157	400
14 and under 17 **Children and Young Persons Act 1969**								
S.1(2)(a) development neglected, ill-treatment, etc.	42	74	-	-	-	11	42	63
S.1(2)(b) condition (a) met in relation to another member of the household	2	2	-	-	-	2	2	-
S.1(2)(c) exposed to moral danger	12	234	-	-	2	54	10	180
S.1(2)(d) beyond parental control	111	363	-	-	17	63	94	300
S.1(2)(e) not receiving efficient full-time education	535	581	1	3	283	345	251	233
S.1(2)(f) guilty of an offence excluding homicide*	5	9	-	-	1	4	4	5
Total†	707	1,263	1	3	303	479	403	785
All ages	2,289	2,653	5	5	752	863	1,532	1,790

* This condition can apply only to children and young persons aged 10 and over.
† 13 of the orders were made against persons (11 male and 2 female) who attained the age of 17 before the conclusion of proceedings.

should be created to replace courts. The second White
Paper was less logical but more acceptable, and made use
of similar arguments to those heard in 1927 and 1932.

The 1969 Act, as envisaged by the Labour Government,
would have given further legislative expression to the
idea that the court should meet the needs which underlie
disturbed behaviour. The sections of the Act which were
most vital to this were, however, those which were to come
into force by ministerial order. When the time came to
consider implementation not only the Conservative, but the
subsequent Labour government, held a different ideology
from that held at the time the Act was passed. There had
been a change in the theories held about the causes of delinquency. The unified theory of deviance had lost ground
to a number of other, often conflicting, theories about the
causes of behaviour and the proper treatment of deviance.

In addition to changes in the balance between special
treatments for offenders and treatment shared with non-
offenders, the actual dispositions available to the court
have changed during the twentieth century. From a welfare
viewpoint, the major achievements took place in 1908. The
Act abolished hanging for those under sixteen (the age was
raised to eighteen in 1933 and 1937). It also began the
slow process of restricting the imprisonment of juveniles.
Before 1908 children and young people could be sent to
prison on remand and as a sentence of the court. The 1908
Act made remand to prison for those under sixteen the rare
exception instead of the rule, and required the police to
provide places of detention for those awaiting trial or
on remand from a court. This responsibility was transferred to the local authorities in the 1930s, and remand
homes became part of the system of children's homes and
schools and no longer part of the system of law enforcement. Unruly young people, however, could and still can
be remanded to prison. On 31 March 1976 there were six
boys and two girls held in local prisons on remand, and
the White Paper(43) in which these figures are given
claims these to be average figures. The government have
pledged themselves in principle to end remand to prison
for those under seventeen years. In addition, however,
there were, at the same time, 118 boys and three girls
under seventeen years old being held in remand centres.
These centres were built to house young offenders between
seventeen and twenty-one-years old, are run by the penal
department and, although the White Paper claims that they
are 'in almost all circumstances more suitable for juveniles than the local prisons', this must refer more to the
benefits which result from the limited age range of their
inmates than from their regime or construction which more

closely resembles a prison than even a secure community home.

Another group of young people who spend time in prisons are those who are committed to the Crown Court for consideration of a Borstal sentence. They may wait in prison before the Crown Court sits, and, if sentenced to Borstal, they return to a prison, since all the Borstal allocation units are sited in prisons. The intention of the 1969 Act was to end Borstal as a sentence for those under seventeen years, but this is another clause which has not been implemented, and so juveniles continue to wait in prisons before going to Borstal.

Although the actual numbers of juveniles who experience prison on remand is small compared with the numbers who were sent to prison before 1908, the law has changed very little. The problem of providing secure detention facilities outside the penal system is a difficult one, and progress has been slow. So long as prison and remand centres remain as an alternative, there is little incentive for local authorities to create centres capable of dealing with the small number of very difficult or disturbed juveniles who cannot be contained in the usual way in their own or community homes.

While juveniles can be remanded to prison, they cannot be sentenced to imprisonment. The 1908 Act ended prison sentences for children and penal servitude for those between fourteen and sixteen. The Act also forbade the imprisonment of young people unless they were too unruly or depraved for the alternative sentence of custody in a place of detention for one month. By this time Borstals were available, in addition to reformatory schools, for young offenders who were considered to need a longer period of detention. The situation remained the same after the 1933 and 1937 Acts except that, since a young person was now defined as being under seventeen years, a larger number of juveniles were kept out of prison. In 1948 the Criminal Justice Act removed the power of juvenile courts to imprison anyone aged under fifteen years.(44) Further, before sentencing anyone under twenty-one years to prison, courts were required to consider whether there was no other appropriate method of dealing with the young person. In 1961 the minimum age of imprisonment was raised to seventeen for all courts.(45) This does not mean that there are no young people in prison after sentence. The Home Secretary has power to decide where a child or young person convicted of murder or a young person convicted of certain grave crimes shall be detained. The usual places of detention in the past were approved schools and Borstals until the offender was either discharged or moved on to

an adult prison. Presumably such young offenders now live
in community homes, Borstals or special units, although
the power remains with the Minister to detain them in
prison.

The century has seen the end of whipping as a punishment ordered by the court. Argument had raged around this
subject from early in the nineteenth century. When the
1933 bill was drawn up, it sought to abolish the power
which juvenile courts had to order male children to be
whipped. The Home Secretary drew attention to this as an
important point in the bill. He urged the honourable Members who 'have had experience of whipping and who offer
themselves as shining examples of its effectiveness'(46)
to consider the difference in the setting in which they
were beaten from that in which a child received a court
ordered whipping. His words were in vain, and the Lords
amended the bill to allow whipping to continue. It was
finally abolished by the Criminal Justice Act of 1948.

So far we have considered dispositions which are based
on a criminal justice approach, and which have been abolished or restricted since 1908. We now consider powers
which the court still retains and how these have changed
over time.

The juvenile court shares with other courts of summary
jurisdiction the power to impose fines on those found to
have committed a crime, up to a limit of £10 for a child
and £50 for a young person. The 1908 Act required that when
the fine was imposed on a child, it should be paid by his
parent unless the court were satisfied that the parent had
not contributed to the commission of the offence. A similar order could be imposed on the parents of young people.
A like principle underlies the clause of the 1969 Act which,
while not allowing a fine, does allow an order for damages
to be made when the offence condition in a care proceeding
has been satisfied. These damages are to be paid by a
parent in the case of a child. The idea behind these provisions seems to be to reinforce parental responsibility
for children, which is another of the many aims underlying
the juvenile justice system.

In the United States the development of juvenile courts
was closely linked with the growth of probation, and we
find the same link in Britain. From 1907 the courts had
power to place offenders on probation, and so juvenile
courts from the start had an intermediate form of treatment available to them. Probation under the 1908 Act
could be used for both those who were charged with criminal
offences and some of those juveniles who came under the
court's civil jurisdiction. In 1933 and 1937 this power to
place non-offenders under the supervision of probation

officers was extended by the introduction of supervision
orders. These were similar to a probation order, except
that they were made only in the case of non-offenders and
the supervising officer could be someone other than a probation officer. The supervision order conferred rather
wider powers to bring the child or young person back to
court. Unlike a probation order, it was not necessary to
prove a breach of the order; all the supervisor had to do
was to convince the court that it was in the child's best
interests for the order to be amended. Both supervision
and probation orders could carry conditions, including
conditions that the child or young person should live in
a specified place. This allowed courts to make short term
residential placements. Since the 1969 Act, probation
orders cannot be made in respect of anyone under seventeen years of age in England and Wales. Supervision orders
can be used for both those found in need of care and for
young persons guilty of an offence, and either the local
authority or the probation officer can be named as supervisor for a juvenile aged over thirteen years although the
intention appears to be to phase out probation officers
from work with younger juveniles. Like probation orders
and the former supervision orders, the supervision order
of the 1969 Act runs for a maximum of three years, and
the supervisor has power to require the child or young person to live for a limited period in a particular place or
take part in specified activities. This is a new clause,
giving the supervisor the opportunity to arrange a more
flexible treatment plan for those under his supervision.

Another order which juvenile courts can make, both for
offenders and non-offenders, is a care order, which commits the juvenile to the care of the local authority. Once
in care the local authority social service department decide upon the kind of residence best suited to the child's
needs. This order is a combination of two earlier orders
which no longer exist, an approved school order and a fit
person order. We have already seen how industrial and reformatory schools were combined into a system of approved
schools in 1933 and 1937. Originally courts had the power
to commit direct to an approved school but later they committed to a classifying school, where the final choice of
school for each juvenile was made. Following the 1969 Act,
approved schools became part of the system of community
homes, for which the local authority social service department is responsible. The court can no longer commit
direct to a former approved school but only to the care of
the local authority.

The other component of the care order is the former fit
person order. Up to 1933 the court could commit juveniles

to the care of relatives or friends, and the managers of
industrial schools were empowered to foster children aged
eight to ten years. However, there was no source of
finance for foster parents, and the 1927 committee reported
that these provisions were seldom used. The 1933 Act made
the local authority a fit person to whose care a child or
young person could be committed, and a similar provision in
the 1937 Act named education authorities as fit persons in
Scotland. The effect of these clauses was to provide financial backing for foster parents and to allow those who
were committed to care to be either fostered or placed in
a Children's Home as seemed appropriate to the local authority. Once a fit person order was made, the court had no
authority to decide where a child or young person should
live. Care orders extend this idea. The court decides
whether or not a child or young person should be removed
from their own home, but, having made this decision, the
actual placement of the juvenile is made by the social
service department.

The original intention of the 1969 Act was that juvenile
courts should lose all their powers to decide on particular
forms of residential care and non-residential treatment.
The dispositions of attendance centre, detention centre and
Borstal training were to be phased out from juvenile courts
as intermediate treatment developed. Attendance and detention centres were established after the 1948 Criminal Justice Act, and were to provide an alternative to whipping,
which the Act finally abolished. Juveniles aged between
ten and twenty-one can be ordered to put in a stated number
of hours at an attendance centre, which is open on Satur-
days and often run by the police. The centres vary, but
many have an army-style discipline and make use of drill
and chores as well as teaching crafts and some sports. There
are sixty-three such centres, which are used largely for
younger children, especially those charged with vandalism
and riotous behaviour at football matches. While some centres do offer recreational training, the original purpose
was to punish young hooligans by depriving them of their
leisure.

Detention centres provide, on a residential basis, a
similar type of experience. They were said to offer a
'short, sharp shock' to basically normal adolescents who
had become involved in criminal activities. The 1969 Act
empowered the Secretary of State to close the eighteen
senior and junior detention centres then operating in England and Wales as facilities for intermediate treatment
developed. This was an issue on which the Conservatives
in opposition had reserved their position. By the time
they came to reconsider it when they were in power, the

juvenile court magistrates had begun to make increasingly
heavy use of the five detention centres for those under
seventeen-years old. Instead of closing any centres, the
Home Secretary arranged for an additional centre to be
converted for junior use. Labour ministers who have succeeded him have not reversed these arrangements so there
are now at least 2600 places in junior detention centres,
which is about 600 more than when the Act was passed.

DEVELOPMENTS SINCE 1969

There is a great deal of criticism of the juvenile justice
system in England and Wales from those holding a welfare
approach as well as from those who are closer to a criminal justice approach. Some writers trace the problems to
the piecemeal way in which the Act has been brought into
force.(47) What was intended as a way of providing help
for troubled and troublesome youngsters, has lost its clear
philosophy and is now a jumble of contradictory approaches
which pleases no one. Berlin and Wansell(48) suggest that
social workers saw the Act as giving support to the idea
that offenders need help, not punishment, and as curtail-
ing the power of the magistrates to make detailed decisions about the treatment of children. Such decisions,
according to social workers, should be made by those
professionally trained to understand the special needs of
troubled children. The Act, as it has turned out, is not
based fully upon a welfare approach, and has left the magistrate power to make what social workers regard as punitive orders.
    The magistrates, on the other hand, see the Act as
giving too much power to the executive. One magistrate,
when he resigned, wrote in a letter to 'The Times' that
'the impartial judiciary had been devalued in favour of
the executive'. Magistrates say they sign what amounts to
a blank cheque(49) when they make a care order. Even their
clear intention that the subject of the order should no
longer live at home may be ignored, since the social service department can place a child back home immediately.
This probably does not happen often, but it has considerable impact when it does occur, since it is taken to illustrate the divergence between the sentencing philosophy of
the courts and the thinking of child care specialists.
The magistrates feel powerless to carry out their duty to
protect the public.
    A note from the Magistrates Association to the House of
Commons Expenditure Committee's Social Services Sub-Committee on 13 December 1974, outlined the areas in which the

magistrates experienced particular difficulty. In summing
up their recommendations the Secretary stated:(50)

Fines should be made enforceable. The Juvenile Court
should have power to remand 'in custody' when the local
authority should have a duty to provide secure accommodation. In making a care order the court should have
power to require that the juvenile be sent to an institution. More institutions should be available, and some
reclaimed that were lost when approved schools were
ended. In particular, more secure accommodation should
be provided there. Supervision orders should permit the
court to impose conditions and sanctions for breach. In
short, the law should be tightened up to provide effective powers and facilities for dealing with the minority
of persistent juvenile offenders.

Similar concerns were expressed by many of the individuals
and groups giving evidence to the Expenditure Committee
which began its work on the Children and Young Persons Act
1969 in 1973 and finally reported in July 1975.(51)   The
government replied by means of a White Paper in May 1976
(52) which shows their attempt to placate those wanting
the juvenile courts to be given more powers and yet to prevent the welfare ideals of the 1969 Act from being lost.

The government stated that they shared the general concern about the fact that fines were unenforceable. They
propose giving to the courts the power either to sentence
defaulters to attend an attendance centre, in areas where
one is available, or to require the defaulters' parents to
take responsibility for the payment of the fine. These
suggested powers illustrate the difficulty of mixing criminal justice and welfare approaches since a court may
take action which is not in the interest of an individual
young person in order to ensure that their authority and
that of the law is not flouted.

On the question of residential care the government accepted the need for secure accommodation, not least to end
the practice of sending some young people to prisons and
remand centres. They state that 'it cannot be too strongly
emphasised that it is government policy to phase out the
remand of juveniles to any prison establishments — as soon
as the local authorities bring into use alternative facilities.'(53) They did actually commit themselves to ending
the remand of fourteen-year-old girls to any prison service
establishment as early as possible in 1976.

The need for secure accommodation arises not just from
a wish to keep juveniles out of prisons and remand centres
on remand but because magistrates claim they have no certainty that when they make a care order a juvenile will be
held by the local authority. The juvenile may abscond or

even be living at home and thus creating a danger to the
public. The twelve regional planning committees, set up
by the 1969 Act were required to submit plans to the Minister for accommodation, including secure accommodation, in
their regions. The plans were made slowly and implemented
even more slowly because of the worsening financial situation. The Children Act 1975 gave the government power to
make direct grants to local authorities for the provision
of secure accommodation, and this has no doubt speeded up
some developments. However, it seems unlikely that there
is any immediate hope of local authorities catering for
the four thousand odd juveniles who are remanded to prison
establishments each year, let alone providing adequate
accommodation for those who are committed to care and require a secure environment.

The Expenditure Committee recommended that power should
be given to magistrates to determine where a child or young
person should live after being committed to care. The
government however here followed a welfare approach and
stated that they:(54) 'would be unwilling to contemplate a
procedure which would blur the lines of responsibility between the court and the local authority. A juvenile court
is not, and cannot be, a child welfare department'. They
do go on to suggest that courts should be able, in a minority of cases of special concern, to recommend that the child
be placed in secure accommodation. The decision about placement however will remain wholly within the discretion of the
local authority.

With regard to conditions being imposed in supervision
orders the government intend to seek advice from local authorities and others on the general question of supervision. The
government is obviously attempting to balance the demands
of a criminal justice and a welfare approach and to avoid
taking any strong action to change the 1969 Act.

It has not been just the changes in policy and of underlying ideas which have created difficulties for the Act.
Most unfortunately it came into force on the same day,
1 January 1970, on which the Local Authority Social Services
Act became law. This Act created social service departments in local authorities, and gave to them the powers
and duties formerly handled by the children's departments,
the welfare departments and the social work sections of the
health departments, which dealt with the care of the mentally ill and mentally subnormal. The confusion would have
been great enough if this had just been an administrative
move, but it was much more, because it put into practice
a new generic philosophy. This had two parts, and, although
they do not necessarily have to go together, in many people's
minds they are confused and inseparable. There is the idea

that families who need help should not have to contort
their need to fit the requirements of one or another local
authority department; nor should individual family members have to be involved with different departments. One
door should be provided for those with social and family
problems and, as far as possible, this one door should be
close at hand. Services should be general and decentral-
ised.

It would have been possible simply to develop generic
departments, but the other idea which had gained ground
was that each social worker should also be 'generic'.
No longer would they be specialists in child care or the
blind, but each one would be able to provide a service to
any member of a family in need. Such thinking was based
on the unitary theory of deviance.(52) If all problems had
their roots in family relationships and if the solution lay
in family casework, then the nature of the problem, if not
irrelevant, was at least of secondary importance.

The combination of generic departments with the idea of
generic social workers caused an enormous upheaval, and
it occurred at exactly the time that the 1969 Children and
Young Persons Act came into force. The juvenile court
magistrates' complaints suggest that the expertise of the
former child care officers got lost in the reorganisation,
and they were often faced with social workers who were
young and inexperienced. Social workers with more experience moved quickly into senior positions and were less
often to be seen in the courts.

The situation might have settled down in time if local
government reorganisation had not resulted in another major
administrative upheaval, in April 1974, and if the changes
had not both coincided with and provoked a great increase
in the demands made on the social services. Some of this
increase was created by legislation such as the Chronic
Sick and Disabled Act 1974 and the necessity to provide
facilities for intermediate treatment under the 1969 Children and Young Persons Act.(53) Alongside this were the
effects of the rediscovery of poverty. Local authorities
became more aware of the needs of disadvantaged families,
and members of such families were beginning to feel that
help was a right rather than a charity. The resources to
meet these new demands are not available, and social workers are now caught between the needs of their clients and
a national economic crisis in which capital expenditure has
been restricted and inflation is eating into operating
costs.

It is likely that the 1969 Act, even in its half implemented state, would have worked at least as satisfactorily
as the 1933 Act did eventually, had there been more re-

sources available. The national economic crisis has restricted capital developments and has led to freezing of
social work posts. The Act was designed at a time when the
social services were expanding and the expectations were
that resources of people, skill and accommodation would
continue to grow. Eight years later the situation is one
in which 'no growth' is regarded as a most favourable position and where it is openly acknowledged that many children and young people are getting neither help nor control.
In such a situation it is particularly important that the
welfare approach be given support because lack of resources
leads to feelings of powerlessness and such feelings can
create punitiveness or hopelessness which can lead to a
shift in the balance of the system.

    In dealing with the history of juvenile justice by re-
ference to the statutes, important changes are missed in
the way in which assessment and treatment were carried out,
since these changes were not reflected by legal changes.
During the first part of the twentieth century the developing fields of psychology, social work and psychoanalysis
were influencing juvenile courts, and their influence was
entirely towards a welfare view of the juvenile court.
Freudian psychology opened up the possibility of complex
motivation for anti-social behaviour and made the individualising of justice for children both more possible and
more complicated. Courts came to refer children for psychiatric and psychological reports, and punishment seemed
a less and less appropriate method of dealing with children
who were seen as deprived and disturbed. To a limited
extent, juvenile delinquency was seen as a disease rather
than a wrongful act, and rehabilitation, if not cure, became the aim of the court. Assessment far outstripped
treatment, but there were changes there too. Probation and
child care officers received a more sophisticated training
and support and treatment came to play as important a role
as did control in their relationships with juveniles.

Chapter seven

Scotland: the present law

EVENTS LEADING UP TO THE SOCIAL WORK ACT

Until the Social Work (Scotland) Act, 1968 came into force
the system of juvenile justice in Scotland was, at least
in theory, very similar to that in the rest of the British
Isles. The 1908 Children Act applied on both sides of
the border, but juvenile courts in the form known further
south never came fully into existence in Scotland. In 1928
the Scottish Departmental Committee on Protection and Train-
ing(1) reported that juvenile offenders and those children
who were found begging, wandering abroad, destitute or
otherwise in need of care and training were usually brought
before the sheriff or the burgh courts. The Justice of the
Peace courts were not functioning as juvenile courts in
most areas of Scotland. The Committee recommended that
special Justice of the Peace courts should hear juvenile
cases, and their recommendation was embodied in the 1937
Children and Young Persons (Scotland) Act. This Act provided for justices to select from their own numbers a panel
of justices to serve in juvenile courts in any areas for
which the Secretary of State issued an order. Only four
such areas existed when the Kilbrandon Committee reported
in 1964. These were the counties of Ayr, Fife and Renfrew
and the city of Aberdeen. The Committee estimated that
the distribution of matters concerned with juveniles in the
courts in 1962 was broadly as follows:(2) Sheriff courts
32 per cent; Burgh (police) courts 45 per cent (the
Glasgow police courts accounting for about 33 per cent);
specially constituted Justice of the Peace juvenile courts
16 per cent; other Justice of the Peace courts 7 per cent.
The position was further complicated because not all
courts dealt with both criminal and civil juvenile cases,
and the sheriff courts retained a jurisdiction concurrent
with that of the special Justice of the Peace juvenile

168

courts. Thus a child in one part of Scotland might be
brought before the sheriff or his deputy, either of whom
would be trained lawyers and sitting alone, while another
child in a similar legal and social position would appear
before the local justices, who sat as a bench and were
lay people. Despite these differences, all the courts
administered the same statute law as laid down by the
Children Act 1908, the Children and Young Persons (Scotland) Acts, 1932 and 1937, the Children Act 1948 and the
Children and Young Persons Act 1963. Even where there was
a separate Scottish Act the law was essentially the same
as that contained in the comparable English statutes. It
was not until the report of the Kilbrandon Committee in
1964 that Scotland began to take a separate path.

The Kilbrandon report took the position that the underlying needs of children who appear before juvenile courts
have little to do with the legal categories into which they
are divided. Classifying children and young people into
juvenile offenders, children in need of care or protection, refractory children beyond parental control and persistent truants is a rather meaningless activity. The
Committee found:(3)

The great majority of the witnesses ... agreed, however,
that in terms of the child's actual needs, the legal
distinction between juvenile offenders and children in
need of care or protection was - looking to the underlying realities - very often of little practical significance. At one extreme, there were cases in which
children committed as being in need of care or protection were by reason of background and upbringing suffering from serious emotional disturbance. This found
expression in conduct and behaviour which, while not
resulting in criminal charges, clearly demanded sustained measures of education, training and discipline.
The problems were of a degree and intensity calling for
far more radical measures than in the case of many
minor delinquencies committed by juvenile offenders.
Equally, there were cases in which, where an offence had
been committed by a child, no very drastic steps appeared to be justified on the basis of the offence itself. But these included cases in which, looking to
the whole background, it might be that the child's
quite minor delinquency was simply a symptom of personal
or environmental difficulties, so that, for the prevention of more serious offences and for the future protection of society as much as in the child's own interests, more sustained measures of supervision were
equally called for. From the standpoint of preventive
measures, children in both groups could equally be said

to be in need of special measures of education and
training - 'education' being taken in its widest sense.
The emphasis in these training measures might vary according to the circumstances of the individual case; in
some the protection of the child would be of prime
importance, in others the training regime might place
more emphasis on discipline. Each case had, however,
to be assessed on its merits, and the type of training,
whether stressing the protective aspect, the disci-
plinary, or for that matter the need for special instruction in formal educational subjects on account of
educational backwardness, had no necessary connection
with the legal classification of children as delinquents
or as children in need of care or protection.

The same is true of children brought before the
courts as persistent truants or as beyond parental control. In the experience of the witnesses, persistent
truancy is in many cases a manifestation of emotional
disturbance often attributable to factors in the home
and family background. So also the fact that a child
is so refractory as to be beyond parental control calls
in all cases for careful enquiry into the home and family circumstances and is likely to be attributable to
factors personal to the child or to the parents themselves.

These paragraphs also show the approach which the Committee chose. It is one of social education which involves
strengthening 'those natural influences for good which will
assist the child's development into a mature and useful
member of society' which must in almost all cases mean
working in 'the closest co-operation with the parents'.
These were the two principles on which the Committee built
their innovative proposals. They followed what they described as a preventive rather than a criminal-responsibi-
lity-punishment model, which led them to emphasise the needs
of children and, since families are the best environment
for children, to involve parents in decisions about treatment. The Committee proposed that these principles should
be translated into action through a new social institution
— Juvenile Panel. Juvenile courts would be abolished and,
with them, criminal jurisdiction over children. Any child
whose behaviour indicated that they might require compulsory measures of social education would be brought before
a panel drawn from lay volunteers, who, in discussion with
the family, would decide upon the necessary treatment
methods. If there were any dispute about the behaviour of
the child, the matter would be referred to the sheriff for
an adjudication on the facts. The treatment measures would
be carried out by a social education section in the local

authority departments of education, which would take over the powers and duties of the existing children's departments.

After the publication of the Kilbrandon report, the Secretary of State for Scotland sought advice from individuals and interested organisations. His department set up working groups with the local authority associations and called in a professor of social administration from England and two psychiatric social workers who were teaching at Scottish universities. Not only is the wide discussion and publicity interesting, as we noted with the comparable developments in England, but, compared with America, the choice of advisors is instructive. It is impossible to imagine a similar working group in America where lawyers were not heavily represented; in Britain law and lawyers play a less pervasive role in the consideration of social problems.

The discussion in the Scottish Home and Health Department resulted in the publication in 1966 of a White Paper, 'Social Work and the Community'.(4) This presented proposals 'as a basis for discussion with interested persons and organisations, with a view to comprehensive legislation when opportunity offers'. The White Paper accepted the philosophy of Kilbrandon and its recommendations to abolish juvenile courts and establish children's hearings. Apparently there had been little opposition to this idea, and, since juvenile courts had never developed fully, there was no powerful interest group to protest at their abolition, as there was in England. The White Paper went further than Kilbrandon, however, in its recommendations regarding the organisation of social services. It suggested that a new local government department should be created to co-ordinate all the personal social services, including, but not restricted to, those to which children in trouble might have recourse. Education departments, despite their powerful and respected place in Scottish history were thought to be too narrow to provide a service for all individuals and families with social problems. The White Paper thus proposed a social work department and substituted for the idea of social education the more extensive one of social welfare.

SOCIAL WORK DEPARTMENTS

These proposals found statutory form in the Social Work (Scotland) Act, 1968 and came into force in stages over the next two years. By this Act Scotland acquired a system of juvenile justice which looks basically different

from the one which England has and which Scotland had in
the past. Apart from the discretion reserved to the Lord
Advocate, 'no child shall be prosecuted for any offence'.(5)
This ended the use of a criminal court and of criminal charges and procedures for many children under sixteen.

The new procedure for controlling troublesome behaviour
in children is part of a wide reorganisation of all the personal social services. The Act set up comprehensive social
work departments in local authorities, with powers and responsibilities to provide social services for children, the
aged, the physically and mentally ill and handicapped, the
homeless, those who have personal and family problems and
those who, as adults, break the law or are discharged from
prison. Before 1968 these powers and duties were distributed amongst several departments. The children's department was responsible for the provision of care for children
temporarily or permanently without a home, the welfare department provided services for the homeless, the aged and
the physically handicapped. The health department catered
for the physically sick and the mentally ill and retarded,
while the education department dealt with educational
problems. These were all departments of the local authority. There were also probation departments with a different structure, which dealt with some juvenile offenders
and those in need of care and with adults who were on probation or discharged from prison. Now all these functions
are performed by one department under the management of a
director of social work. These departments are more comprehensive than the equivalent English departments of social service established in 1969, which have not taken over
the probation service or its functions in relation to
adults.

STRUCTURE AND POWERS OF THE CHILDREN'S HEARING

Within the Act establishing this new structure, which aims
to provide a comprehensive cover for families and individuals in need of personal social services, and which is
based on a philosophy of welfare, are provisions for dealing with 'Children in Need of Compulsory Measures of Care'.
The intention of the Act is that, where possible, children
shall be dealt with by voluntary arrangements between social work departments and families. However, if compulsion
is necessary, Part III of the Act establishes children's
hearings, which replace juvenile courts. These hearings
are not courts within the criminal or civil justice system,
because they have no powers to make decisions over contested
facts. Panels of members are established for each local

authority area and the Secretary of State appoints the members and the chairperson from persons whose names are submitted to him by the Children's Panel Advisory Committee. (6) This is another new institution, made up in each case of persons nominated by the local authority and others nominated by the Secretary of State, with the responsibility to advise on suitable persons to fill the local panel. Panel members hold children's hearings in respect of children who may require compulsory measures of care, and a hearing consists of a chairperson and two other panel members; the group must include a man and a woman. The local authority is required to provide accommodation and facilities for these hearings, which must be dissociated from the criminal courts or police stations.

The panels are staffed by an executive officer who is called a reporter and who is appointed by the local authority from a list approved by the Secretary of State, and who can only be removed with the Secretary's consent. Any person who has reason to believe that a child may be in need of compulsory measures of care may give to the reporter what information he has about the child. The reporter is responsible for investigating such information and then making one of the following decisions:(7)

1   that no further action is required;
2   that the local authority be asked to advise, guide and assist the child and his family on a voluntary basis;
3   that the child is in need of compulsory care and that he should be brought to a children's hearing.

Before the reporter can decide to have a hearing, he must believe that one or more of the following conditions may exist in respect of the child, who is defined as a person under sixteen years (or under eighteen years if the subject of a supervision requirement):(8)

(a)   he is beyond the control of his parents; or
(b)   he is falling into bad associations or is exposed to moral danger; or
(c)   lack of parental care is likely to cause him unnecessary suffering or seriously to impair his health or development; or
(d)   any of the offences mentioned in Schedule 1 to the Criminal Procedure (Scotland) Act 1975 has been committed in respect of a child who is a member of the same household; or
(e)   the child is, or is likely to become, a member of the same household as a person who has committed any of the offences mentioned in Schedule 1 of the Criminal Procedure (Scotland) Act 1975; or
(f)   the child, being a female, is a member of the same household as a female in respect of whom an offence

which constitutes the crime of incest has been committed by a member of that household; or
(g) he has failed to attend school regularly without
reasonable excuse; or
(h) he has committed an offence; or
(i) he is a child whose case has been referred to a
children's hearing in pursuance of Part V of this
Act (which refers to children who abscond from
places of safely or from a person or residential
institution where he has been placed under a supervision requirement).
For the purposes of this Part of this section 'care'
includes protection, control, guidance and treatment.

The Lord Advocate still retains power to direct that children who commit offences shall be tried either on indictment
in the High Court or before the sheriff, or summarily before
the sheriff. Those accused of murder are always to be
tried on indictment. From amongst those children referred
to the reporter, the reporter has discretion to decide
whether they shall be brought to a children's hearing. His
discretion is similar to that which the drafters of the 1969
Act had intended should lie with social service departments
in England in respect of children, and to that exercised
for many years by probation officers in the United States.

When the child and his parent appear before the hearing,
the chairperson has a duty 'to explain to the child and
his parents the grounds stated by the reporter for the referral of the case for the purpose of ascertaining whether
these grounds are accepted in whole or in part by the child
and his parents'.(9) If the child and his parents accept
the grounds, the hearing, after further investigation if it
is needed, can discharge the referral or can make what is
called a supervision requirement, which requires the child:
(10)
(a) to submit to supervision in accordance with such
conditions as they may impose; or
(b) to reside in a residential establishment named in
the requirement and to be subject to such conditions
as they may impose.

There are no limits imposed upon the hearing's powers to
write conditions into supervision requirements. The prohibition in the 1937 Act against sending children to approved schools for offences not punishable in an adult by
imprisonment, and the restriction on sending them if they
are under ten-years of age, disappear with respect to the
new residential establishments. Supervision requirements
have no fixed length and, unless discharged earlier, continue until the child becomes eighteen. They must be

reviewed each year, and sooner if a review is asked for by
the child or the local authority. At the review the hearing has the same powers as they had at the original hearing, which means that they can vary a requirement as well
as reducing or discharging it. G.H. Gordon points out: 'It
is thus in theory possible for a child who has been put
under supervision for an offence to be subsequently sent
to a residential establishment for that offence without
the intervention of any fresh ground of referral'.(11)
On the other hand, the Act states that 'the child shall
not continue to be subject to a supervision requirement for
any time longer than is necessary in his interest'.(12)

A social worker from the local authority is the other
person, besides the reporter and panel members, who is always present at a hearing and whose responsibility it is
to provide reports for the hearing and to undertake supervision and arrange residential placements, if these are
required. The powers of the lay members of the panel to
prescribe treatment are wide, and yet other parts of the
act strengthen the social work department and encourage the
development of community and residential treatment in the
light of professional social work assessment of need. The
possibility of conflict here is obvious. Although panels
can only discharge the referral or make a supervision requirement, and thus lose the power of juvenile courts to
impose an absolute discharge, admonition or fine, they have
a wider power to decide on forms of supervision than the
juvenile courts had under the old system of probation,
supervision, fit person and approved school orders.

THE CHILD'S RIGHTS

The children's hearing is governed by the concepts of a
welfare approach, despite the fact that the hearing has
extensive compulsory powers and can remove children from
their homes and keep them away for periods of years. If
the child or his parents dispute the grounds on which referral to the hearing is made, or if it seems to the chairperson that they do not understand the grounds, the case must
be referred to the sheriff for a decision on the facts. In
this hearing before the sheriff, the child and his family
have all the rights which normally accompany a court hearing. When the grounds for referral are that the child has
committed an offence, the sheriff is obliged to 'apply to
the evidence relating to that ground the standard of proof
required in criminal procedure'.(13)

In the hearing itself the rights of the child and his
parents are less protected, because of the assumption that

panel and family are engaged in a co-operative venture to do whatever is in the best interests of the child. The family are allowed to bring with them a person to speak on their behalf, and this person can be a legal representative. Few families make use of this provision and fewer still have a lawyer to represent them. Apart from a requirement that the chairperson shall inform the child and his family of the grounds and establish that they agree to the facts stated, procedure of the hearing varies greatly from one group of three panel members to another. The aim is to have an informal friendly discussion and, with such aims, procedural rules are out of place.

There are, however, rights of appeal. Once the panel have made a supervision requirement, the child or his family or both have three weeks to appeal to the sheriff for a review of the requirement. The sheriff can confirm it, dismiss the referral entirely or require the hearing to arrive at another disposition. Both child and reporter have a right to appeal from the sheriff's decision to the Court of Session by way of stated case on a point of law or in respect of an irregularity in the conduct of the case. No appeal lies where the sole objection to a supervision requirement is that the treatment prescribed is inappropriate for the child.

The Children Act 1975 provides the possibility of protection for a child where the chairperson of a hearing considers there is or may be a conflict of interest between a child and his parents. In such circumstances the chairperson may appoint a person to represent the interests of the child.

DEVELOPMENTS SINCE THE SOCIAL WORK (SCOTLAND) ACT, 1968

The panels started work on 1 April 1971 after a hectic period of selection and training for the new panel members. The general feeling in Scotland seems to be that the hearings are an improvement on what went before and it is only now, six years after the hearings started that general criticisms of the system are becoming frequent. These take a form similar but less vociferous to the criticisms of the Children and Young Person Act 1969 in England. It is said that the panel system has created a vacuum in which the public are not protected from the behaviour of young vandals and hooligans and that the welfare approach which denies the panels the power to punish is inappropriate to such offenders.

These general criticisms mingle with complaints often heard from panel members about the lack of resources available to them. Places in List D schools have been extremely limited and often children whom the panel want to send to such a school waited months or years for a place, committing other offences in the meantime. In some areas of Scotland the panels cannot rely on supervision by social workers and a child who is made the subject of a supervision requirements may barely have been seen by his social worker between a hearing and the review twelve months later. Situations such as this have led to relationships between some panels and some social work departments becoming strained, if not frankly hostile. Social workers see the reports and the supervision required by the panels as yet one more demand which, with depleted staff and increasing pressures, they are unable to meet. Panel members feel helpless when faced with children who need supervision, care and control which they know will not be provided. The lack of resources in terms of staff time and residential places, has upset the delicate balance which the Act aimed to achieve between professionals in social work departments and lay panel members. One of the important parts of the Act was the introduction of a review system which means that panel members actually know what happens to children they have had before them and over whose living situation they are given considerable control. They are therefore fully aware of the shortcomings of the social work departments and are faced with the problem of being held accountable by the community for the behaviour of children but without being able to command the necessary resources.

This situation has had a serious effect upon the morale of panel members and also upon the way in which they personally balance ideas of welfare and criminal justice. Faced with their own powerlessness they are not only demanding increased resources of a welfare kind but some are also asking for powers to fine, order compensation and perhaps community service and to be able to refer to the sheriff court certain older offenders. Such ideas reflect not welfare but criminal justice thinking and provide an example of how powerlessness may lead to punitiveness. Unlike magistrates and judges, panel members are not responsible for protecting the public. Their sole responsibility is the need for care of the child before them, and care is defined to include 'protection, control, guidance and treatment'. Punishment as a means of deterring others had no place in the philosophy of Kilbrandon or the White Paper but it is present now in the minds of some panel members, which suggests the great difficulty which any human who is not a saint may have in holding only a welfare viewpoint.

The present situation is likely to get worse before there

is any chance of improvement because local government reorganisation, which England had already endured, took place
in Scotland in May 1975. Panels have been reorganised on a
regional basis, and social work departments show all the
signs of dislocation and anxiety. One interesting development is that panel members are taking increasing responsibility. In the Grampian region they have started a scheme
to provide volunteers to work with children who appear before the hearing. On a larger scale the three local associations of panel members in Scotland have been able to
come together to form a national association, despite the
suspicion amongst those in other areas that their interests
might be swamped by those of the Strathclyde region. If the
Association can develop a united voice they will be a very
powerful group who could put pressure on central and local
government to provide more resources. Potentially the panel
members are perhaps the only group who have nothing to lose
in protesting for the needs of children in trouble.

Chapter eight

The balance in the statutes

The balance within a juvenile justice system is controlled
by the statutes, by the discretion allowed to those who
operate the system and the resources available to them, and
by the restrictions on referral to the system. This chapter compares the present statutes in the United States,
England and Wales and Scotland.

WHETHER OR NOT TO HAVE A COURT

The statutes settle the major question of whether juvenile
justice is primarily a matter for the courts. In 1927 the
departmental committee in England(1) considered the possibilities of creating tribunals, either under the control
of headmasters, or of the police, to deal with troublesome
children. They rejected these ideas, as they did a court
with jurisdiction similar to the juvenile courts in the
United States, and recommended instead the establishment
of 'courts specially equipped to help rather than punish'.
The question of whether to use a court came up again in
England in 1965 at the time of the White Paper on 'The
Child, the Family and the Young Offender',(2) which recommended the creation of family councils staffed by social
workers to deal with all uncontested matters relating to
juvenile offenders and those in need of care and protection. This idea got an extremely hostile response from
magistrates and probation officers, and was dropped from
later proposals. Juvenile courts were retained by the
1969 Act, and the climate in the mid 1970s is unlikely to
lead to a rejection of the court as the primary decision-
making organ in juvenile justice in England. When alternatives are discussed, they are not now usually welfare
tribunals but fully fledged criminal courts 'with teeth'.

In the United States the same trend is evident. After
having had for years a court which has been to all intents
and purposes a welfare tribunal without the expertise that
this requires, the present trend is to strengthen the
powers of the courts and to give offenders more legal
rights. This, however, relates only to those who commit
what in an adult is a criminal offence. There is also a
movement to remove other kinds of behaviour from the jurisdiction of the court. The Board of Directors of the National Council on Crime and Delinquency(3) advocates 'the removal of "status offences" from the jurisdiction of the
juvenile courts.... Although a matter for community concern,
non-criminal conduct should be referred to social agencies
not to courts of law', where community resources would be
available on a voluntary basis. However, although there
are influential bodies campaigning for such a change, no
state has yet removed control over status offences or incorrigible behaviour from its statute book.

Scotland is the only one of the three countries where
something akin to a welfare tribunal or family council has
been established. Scotland's past history of juvenile
justice made this possible, and the timing of the Kilbrandon report,(4) coming as it did when the belief in a unitary theory of deviance was strongest, and before the fears
of the late 1960s were fully felt, made it a reality. Scotland has not, however, adopted a panel of experts to decide
upon the treatment of children. Panel members are people
with an interest in children, but need have no experience
or training in work with disturbed and delinquent children.
In their composition the panels reflect more a community
than a welfare approach, and certainly panel members feel
themselves to be in some ill-defined but, they claim, important way, representatives of the country.

There are two distinct arguments used for a tribunal
rather than a court deciding on treatment for troublesome
children. One concerns the question of community representation, and particularly the presence on the tribunal
of people who come from, and understand, the social background of the children before them. This is often not the
case with juvenile court judges in the United States or
with English magistrates, and one reason for establishing
children's hearings in Scotland was to bridge the gap,
social, economic and educational, between the child and
the decision makers. In fact this has been achieved to
only a limited extent. The other reason is that courts
which have the responsibility of deciding on guilt or
innocence are not the place for an unhurried discussion,
involving the child and the family, as to the best treatment method. Courts are intimidating places, and the pro-

cedures necessary to protect the rights of the accused
impose barriers to discussion on a basis of shared concern
for the future of a child. One aim of the children's
hearing is to involve the parents in planning for their
own child. Some would take this further and suggest that
courts are forced, traditionally and procedurally, to see
the child as an isolated individual and not as a member of
a group, either a family or a community group. Traditionally the criminal justice system has taken a highly individual view of juveniles. They are usually seen as responsible for their own actions and motivated, if not by
factors within their control, at least by factors within
themselves. Although courts may be heard to exclaim that
it is not the child but the parents who should be brought
before them, this is not to abandon the individual viewpoint, but to extend it back to the parents, who can then
be blamed for their child's behaviour. The welfare and
community view sees children as part of an interacting
family group, and sees families in a similar position
within the community. A person does not determine his
own actions, nor is one person's behaviour seen as the
cause of another's actions, but rather the interaction
between two or more people results in particular forms of
behaviour on the part of each. Parents, by this view, are
not to blame for causing the child's behaviour, but rather
are caught in an interaction which may bring about results
they never consciously intended. This view of families
as people in interaction is commonplace in child guidance
circles, but is relatively unexplored in relation to children's delinquent behaviour. At present courts operate
from an individual viewpoint, and society expects them to
allocate responsibility and apportion blame. The idea of
interaction may find its way into juvenile courts and
hearings, as it is beginning to do in divorce courts with
the concept of non-fault divorce. Courts might then face
the possibility of a family approach to juvenile problems.
To some extent the Scottish panels, and the thinking behind
the English laws which stresses the involvement of the
family, may open the way for such a viewpoint. At the mo-
ment, however, it is directed more towards gaining the family's co-operation than in developing an approach based on
theories of interaction.

THE STATUTES - OVERALL AIM

The general aim of the Social Work (Scotland) Act is the
promotion of social welfare. No separate aims are stated
in relation to the exercise of compulsory powers over chil-

dren. The statutes in the United States and England indicate that the courts are expected to hold a balance between
protecting the public and meeting the needs of the individual child. Section 1 of the Uniform Act states that:
  This Act shall be construed to effectuate the following
  public purposes:
  (1) to provide for the care, protection, and wholesome
  moral, mental and physical development of children
  coming within its provisions;
  (2) consistent with the protection of the public interest, to remove from children committing delinquent
  acts the taint of criminality and the consequences of
  criminal behaviour and to substitute therefore a program of treatment, training and rehabilitation.
In England juvenile courts still operate under the general
directive of the 1933 Children and Young Persons Act that
'every court in dealing with a child or young person who
is brought before it either as an offender or otherwise,
shall have regard to the welfare of the child or young
person'.(4) The 1969 Act has added that a local authority
shall bring care proceedings in respect of a child 'unless
they are satisfied that it is neither in his interest nor
in the public interest to do so'.(5) In the United States
the Uniform Act requires the petition to the juvenile court
to state that 'it is in the best interest of the child and
the public that the proceedings be brought'. The way the
courts balance the protection of the public and assistance
to the individual may vary according to how threatened the
public are by juvenile offences. In the past, juvenile
misbehaviour has not posed too serious a threat to society;
it has traditionally been more a nuisance than a danger,
but this is changing, most rapidly in the United States,
but also in Britain, with the increase in juvenile, inner-
city crime, particularly crimes of violence.
  The statutes give the courts little guidance on where
the emphasis should lie, and read as if the interest of
the child and of the public are the same. In some cases
this may be so, but 'best interest' is a very complicated
concept, with long- and short-term meanings. From the
child's point of view, and often that of his family, his
best interests are served by the court doing as little as
possible and leaving him alone; for although some children
and families may see their own need for help in resolving
personal or family problems or difficulties in school or
with friends, few see being sent away from home as serving
their interests. For society the interests are different
and more ambivalent. On the one hand, a child who grows
up to be a law-abiding, hard-working member of society,
able to raise and support his own children, would seem to

meet society's best interests. On the other hand, the
process of turning a young offender into such a citizen,
even if it is possible, is usually expensive, and society
has been reluctant to deal with the social causes of delinquency or even to fund rehabilitative services. Besides
which, society needs victims. Rules lose their force, and
goodness its virtue, if there are no deviants, and to ignore rule breaking may seem to weaken the rule and, with it,
society's cohesion. These ideas arise both at the point of
intake and at sentencing, particularly when it is decided
to remove a child from home. It is often clear to most
people that what the child before the court needs is either
unattainable or very expensive. The next best thing, if the
aim is to create a law-abiding adult, may be to do nothing,
but this is difficult for society to allow. Frequently
children are sent away from home because the court cannot
allow itself to make yet another supervision or probation
order. The child may not be a danger to society, only a
petty nuisance, so it cannot be claimed that removal pro-
tects the public from serious harm to persons or property.
Nor is there any belief that the alternative living situation will be helpful to the child. But something must be
done or the law will fall into disrepute, and society will
suffer in the end if lawbreakers are not punished.

    Further reading of the statutes of all three countries
supports a welfare approach to juvenile justice. Courts
and hearings are to provide individualised justice and to
assess and meet the needs of each child. In the United
States, since Gault, a child must be found to be in need of
rehabilitation or treatment in addition to proof that he has
behaved in some defined way. In England the Children and
Young Persons Act requires a finding of particular behaviour
and the need 'for care and control which he is unlikely to
receive unless the court makes an order',(6) although this
refers only to those brought under care proceedings. The
dual requirement of behaviour plus need does not relate to
children and young persons charged with a criminal offence.
The Social Work (Scotland) Act does not contain a specific
clause, but the reporter must decide whether a child is in
need of compulsory care or whether his needs can be met by
his parents, with, or without, voluntary help from the
local authority. Such clauses as these in the statutes
suggest an emphasis upon individualised justice. They
imply a need for more than knowledge of a specific act to
decide what a child needs, and involve consideration of the
child's background and potential.

    Once courts enter into such considerations they face the
problem of being seen to be fair both by juveniles themselves and by society at large. The ideas of equal justice

associated with the criminal justice model are always near
the surface. The Parliamentary debates in 1968 on the then
Children and Young Persons Bill illustrate the concern of
society with equal justice.

Alf and Peter, they postulated, both aged 12, stole from
a shop, broke open a gas meter or caused malicious damage. Whatever their offence, it was a combined operation and the boys were caught red-handed. No action was
taken in regard to Alf because there was no evidence, or
insufficient evidence, to satisfy a court that he was
in need of care or control which he was unlikely to
receive unless the court made an order. So nothing at
all was done about Alf who looked upon it as a 'let-
off'. But Peter, because in his case the need for a
court order could be established, was brought before
the magistrates and dealt with and a compensation order
was made against his parents. What, they demanded, would
Peter and his parents think about (to them) an invidious
and inexplicable distinction? Would they accept it phi-
losophically, or would it rankle for years as a dreadful
injustice and so defeat the purpose of any remedial
treatment the court had ordered in Peter's interests?

The danger of this happening provoked Mr. Quintin Hogg
(as he was then), in his Second Reading speech, to the
following: 'If a mere lawyer is allowed to speak, I
would say that some of us care more about justice than
almost anything else in the world, and in that the history of mankind sides with us on the whole. If we choose
to disregard justice in our handling of young people we
shall not achieve the objectives which the Home Secretary
has in mind'.(7)
Presumably, for the former Mr Hogg, the only justice capable
of achievement is equal justice not individual justice.

AGE

Besides the overall aims which the statutes suggest, specific clauses can throw some light upon how the balance between criminal justice and welfare is to be managed. The
regulations about age are one example. A child under
seven is regarded at common law as incapable of having a
guilty mind. British statute law fixed on eight years as
the age of criminal responsibility at which a child could be
prosecuted for a crime, and later raised the age to ten
years in England. The 1969 Act envisaged that it would
ultimately be raised to fourteen, but this is now unlikely.
In Scotland this age is sixteen for those children who come
before a Hearing. Under these ages a child may be found

to be in need of care because he has committed what in an
adult is a crime but he cannot be prosecuted for a crime
per se. Thus, in Britain, the label crime is gradually
being removed from acts committed by children. Since
juvenile courts were established, this has been the position in the United States, where children under the juvenile court upper age limit (which varies between sixteen
and twenty-one years) can be found to be delinquent but
cannot be convicted of a criminal act. The legislatures
of the United States have said that acts committed by
children shall not be classified as crimes, a classification, as we have seen, which belongs to the criminal justice viewpoint. There seem to be some problems with these
statutory decisions since there are some acts, particularly
when committed by older children, which the public regard
as crimes even if the legislature say they are not. Perhaps the central difficulty is where to draw the line,
both in terms of the age of the child and the type of
action. There may be no definable difference between the
situations which could give rise under English law to an
eleven-year-old being found in need of care on the grounds
of having stolen and a thirteen-year-old being found to
have committed the crime of larceny. This is not to imply
that cut-off points are nonsensical, but to suggest that
the need for the system to have some rules about the balance between justice and welfare may involve apparently
ridiculous situations in individual cases.

JUVENILE RECORDS

Besides restrictions upon the age under which a person can
be charged with a crime, the statutes give some protection
against the troublesome behaviour of children being used
later in life as evidence of criminal record. In Britain
the Children and Young Persons Act 1963 states in section
16 that 'in any proceedings for an offence committed or
alleged to have been committed by a person of, or over,
twenty-one, any offence of which he was found guilty while
under fourteen must be disregarded for the purpose of any
evidence relating to his previous convictions. He must
not be asked and, if asked, must not be required to answer
any question relating to such an offence.'(8) A finding of
a need for care presumably will not be included in the record of an adult's previous convictions, since it does not
involve conviction or a finding of guilt. The English law
does not at present provide similar protection to young
people over fourteen who are found guilty of offences, although the Rehabilitation of Offenders Act(9) offers a

means of expurging a minor record for all offenders.

The Uniform Juvenile Court Act of the United States provides in section 57 a potentially more comprehensive, but administratively more cumbersome, procedure for sealing the records of a juvenile. Either on the court's own motion, or on the application of the person formerly adjudicated delinquent or unruly, the court shall hold a hearing. The court is required to notify the prosecuting attorney and any institution or parole board which granted a final discharge to the juvenile and any law enforcement agencies which have records of the juvenile. If the court finds that two years have elapsed since the juvenile's discharge, that he has not been convicted of a felony or a misdemeanour involving moral turpitude nor found delinquent, and that he has been rehabilitated, they shall order the sealing of his records.

Upon the entry of the order the proceeding shall be treated as if it never occurred. All index references shall be deleted and the person, the court, and law enforcement officers and departments shall properly reply that no record exists with respect to the person upon inquiry in any matter. Copies of the order shall be sent to each agency or official therein named. Inspection of the sealed files and records thereafter may be permitted by an order of the court upon petition by the person who is the subject of the records and only by those persons named in the order.

It seems unlikely that such provisions would be used frequently because of their complexity. They are interesting, however, in that they are one of the few ways provided for removing the stigma of a juvenile court history. One of the difficulties of managing a spoiled identity is that, while society has institutionalised entry into the stigmatised roles, it has offered few ceremonial exits. This sealing of records is the nearest equivalent to absolution in the juvenile justice system.

TYPES OF BEHAVIOUR AND THE POSSIBILITIES OF TRANSFER
BETWEEN ADULT AND JUVENILE COURTS

Age is not the only means by which the statutes divide the criminal sheep from the welfare goats. The type of behaviour is also important, and statutes take account of this. All three systems which we have considered exclude from the juvenile courts children who have committed certain types of acts, and therefore place them in the adult criminal justice system. In England children charged with murder and children and young people charged

with murder or with a crime which if committed by an adult
would carry a sentence of fourteen or more years imprisonment, are dealt with by adult criminal courts. The position in Scotland is that there exist side by side two systems of juvenile justice. The one operated by the children's hearings follows the welfare approach, but the other,
which passes largely unnoticed, adheres to the ideas of
criminal justice. The Social Work (Scotland) Act, 1968
states in s. 31 i, 'No child shall be prosecuted for any
offence except on the instructions of the Lord Advocate,
or at his instance'.

In July 1970 the Lord Advocate sent a letter to all procurators fiscal and chief constables, listing the types of
offence which were to be referred to the procurator for
consideration of prosecution. They were:

1 treason, murder, rape, incest and deforcement of mes-
   sengers;
2 culpable homicide, attempted murder, assault to the
   danger of life, attempted rape and attempted incest;
3 offences alleged to have been committed by a child
   whilst acting along with an adult;
4 offences alleged to have been committed by children,
   aged fourteen years or over, which in the event of
   conviction oblige or permit a court order disqualification for driving;
5 offences which in the event of conviction, permit a
   court to order forfeiture of an article and where
   there is an article which should be forfeited;
6 offences alleged to have been committed by children,
   as described in Section 30(1)(b) of the Social Work
   (Scotland) Act;
7 any other offence which in the opinion of the Chief
   Constable is so serious as to warrant the instruction
   of solemn proceedings by the Lord Advocate in the
   public interest.

The result of this letter was that a large number of children, especially those aged fifteen and sixteen, appeared
before the sheriff and occasionally in open court. The
numbers had been increasing and the government took action,
as the Secretary of State for Scotland told the Commons on
30 July 1974:(10)

Section 31 of the 1968 Act provides that no child shall
be prosecuted for any offence except on the instructions
of the Lord Advocate or at his instance. In 1973 court
proceedings were taken against 3,192 children, an increase of a third over the figures for 1972. My Rt Hon.
and learned Friend and I are concerned that court proceedings against children should be taken only in excep-
tional circumstances. He has accordingly decided to

direct procurators fiscal not to commence proceedings
against children under 13 years of age without reference
to the Crown Office for his authority, or against children alleged to have committed offences while acting
along with an adult unless there are circumstances which
make joint prosecution essential.

During 1973, for every three appearances of children before a panel one child was prosecuted in the sheriff court,
because of the way in which the procurators fiscal were exercising their discretion. The Lord Advocate's and the
Secretary of State's cautious direction seems to have been
effective since the ratio in 1974 had dropped to seven to
one. This is important if one is concerned about the welfare of children, not only because greater attention may
be paid to welfare by the panels, but because the dispositional alternatives they have at their disposal differ from
those available to the sheriff, who is subject to the provisions of the Criminal Procedure (Scotland) Act 1975,
which allows him to admonish, discharge absolutely, make a
probation order, impose a fine or a sentence of detention.

The Uniform Juvenile Code in the United States does not
exclude any category of act from the juvenile court jurisdiction except the less-serious traffic offences. This is
not the usual situation, since most States exclude homicide
and others exclude offences commonly regarded as serious,
such as rape, armed robbery, etc., as well as minor traffic offences. It appears that, if the offence is either
particularly shocking to the public or a violation of administrative rules, then the child is viewed as potentially
criminal. Between these two extremes he is a suitable case
for welfare treatment.

So far we have been considering limits on the jurisdiction of the court or hearing, which are either imposed by
statute or subject to the discretion of officials outside
the juvenile justice system itself. Both in the United
States and England there are also means by which the juvenile courts can themselves transfer juveniles to the criminal courts. In the United States this is known as waiver,
and provides a means, in individual cases, for selecting
either a welfare or a criminal justice approach. Under
waiver provisions, a juvenile is brought to a juvenile
court for a hearing to decide whether his case should be
waived to the criminal court or retained in the juvenile
system. Since Kent v. United States, there must be a hearing, and the child is entitled to representation. Some
States restrict the possibility of waiver to children over
a certain age, such as fifteen. The criteria on which a
decision to waive is most frequently made were studied by
the President's Task Force on Juvenile Delinquency. They

found the following factors:(12)
1 Seriousness of the alleged offense
2 Record and history of the juvenile, including prior
   contacts with police, court or other official agencies.
3 Aggressive, violent, premeditated, or willful manner
   by which the offense was committed.
4 Sophistication, maturity, emotional attitude of the
   juvenile.
5 Proximity of juvenile's age to maximum age of juvenile
   court jurisdiction.
6 More appropriate procedures, services and facilities
   available in the adult court for the likelihood of reasonable rehabilitation.
7 The possible need for a longer period of incarcera-
   tion.
8 Evidence apparently sufficient for a grand jury indictment.
9 The juvenile's associates in the alleged offense will
   be charged with a crime in an adult court.
10 Effect of judgement of waiver on public's respect for
   law enforcement and law compliance.
11 Community attitude toward the specific offense.
These are summarised by Schornhorst(13) as 'the four variables of age, seriousness of offense, seriousness of prior
offenses and discouraging treatment prognosis', and show
clearly the interweaving of criminal justice and welfare
ideas.

In England an exception to the jurisdiction of the juvenile court is made which is similar to the waiver provisions under the statutes of the United States, Section 6 of
the Children and Young Persons Act, 1969 states that, where
a person over fourteen years of age and under seventeen is
brought before a court charged with an indictable offence,
punishable by a long period of detention, but for which
the sentence is not fixed by law, and where the court considers that, if found guilty, there should be power to detain him for a long period, the court may commit him for
trial at the Crown Court. This is a situation more like
waiver in the United States before Kent v. United States,
since it appears that the juvenile court is not required to
hold any hearing to consider social and emotional facts
about the young person. It makes the decision on the basis
of the seriousness of the alleged offences, in accordance
with the principles of criminal justice. In fact the decision about trial may make no difference to the place in
which the young person is detained. If the young person
is too young to be sent to Borstal, the Secretary of State,
whose duty it is to name the place where he is to be detained, is likely to name a community home, which would

have been the most likely disposition by the juvenile
court. What can be affected is aftercare, as *R.v. G.*
illustrated. G. had pleaded guilty to eight burglaries
and asked for eighteen similar offences to be taken into
consideration. An order was made under section 53 of the
1933 Act (which allows courts to order those convicted of
certain grave offences to be detained) for his detention
for eighteen months, and he went to a community home. On
appeal it was held that a care order should be substituted,
since the detention order did not provide for after-care
supervision, which was possible under a care order and in
the best interests of the boy.(14)

Unless the 1969 Act is fully implemented and Borstal
restricted to those over seventeen, the British courts have
a power even more like that of waiver, to remit to a higher
court for sentence, following trial in the juvenile court.
This usually means they consider the young person should go
to Borstal, and in effect that he should be transferred to
the criminal justice system, since in Britain Borstals are
part of the penal system, whereas schools for juvenile offenders are not. However, this power to remit is exercised after a hearing in the juvenile court and does not
transfer to the higher court the trial of the case, as waiver does in the United States.

The final exception to juvenile court jurisdiction in
England is provided in the case of a child or young person charged with an indictable offence jointly with 'a person who has attained the age of seventeen and the court
considers it necessary in the interests of justice to commit them both for trial'. No similar exception exists for
those below ten, the age at which they can be criminally
charged, however much the interests of justice may require
it, for there the best interests of the child override the
requirements of equal justice, and in any case such joint
offences are probably rare.

In Scotland the Hearings have no power to transfer children to the Courts, although there is a growing feeling
that such power is necessary. In a document drawn up by
the Social Work Services Group in 1975 to promote discussion
of possible legislative changes in Part III of the Social
Work (Scotland) Act 1968 it is suggested that Hearings
might be given the power to transfer to the Sheriff Court
children over sixteen-years of age. This would correct
the situation which exists at present and which many people
regard as illogical by which someone aged between sixteen
and eighteen, who is already subject to a supervision requirement, can be referred to a Hearing if he commits an
offence whereas another person of the same age who is not
subject to a supervision requirement and may never have been

in trohble before is prosecuted in the Criminal Court.

In England the Criminal Court has power to commit juvenile offenders who appear before them to the juvenile court. Where a child or young person is charged jointly with an adult the magistrates can commit the juvenile to the juvenile court for trial. Except when the charge is murder or one of a number of certain grave crimes which carry sentences of fourteen or more years imprisonment, the adult court must remit a child or young person to the juvenile court for sentence unless the court considers it undesirable to do so.

Similar powers exist in Scotland when a child pleads or is found guilty of an offence by a court, the court may, and must if the child is already the subject of a supervision requirement refer the case to the Hearing for their advice as to treatment. In addition the court may remit to the Hearing for disposal any child who pleads or has been found guilty of an offence, whether or not the court has already sought the advice of the Hearing.

These provisions allow for some flexibility between the adult and the juvenile justice systems. Juvenile courts and Hearings are more likely than adult courts to require social background and school reports and to take into account the demands of a welfare approach that they consider the needs of the child or young person.

CLASSIFICATION OF CHILDREN

Besides allowing for some children to be moved from the juvenile justice system into the adult system, the statutes classify the kinds of behaviour or need in children which make them subject to juvenile court jurisdiction. On both sides of the Atlantic the behaviour which can provide grounds for juvenile court action is very similar. All three countries distinguish in their definitions between children who commit acts which, if committed by an adult, could be crimes; children who behave in ways which are illegal only for children; children who are incorrigible or beyond control; and children who are in physical or moral danger. Only England charges children and young people with crimes. The statutes state what label may be attached by a juvenile court to a child who has been found to fall into one of these categories.

In the United States no child can be found to have committed a crime, and the finding of delinquency has traditionally covered children in the first three groups. Similarly in Scotland, in respect of any child who appears before them a hearing can only decide whether or not the child

is in need of compulsory care. In England children and
young people can be found to be in need of care and control,
but those over ten can be charged with an offence; below
this age only a finding of a need for care is allowed.
The 1969 Act, as originally drawn, would have moved England
closer to the position of Scotland and the United States.
It was intended that the age at which children could be
charged with an offence (except homicide) should ultimately
be raised to fourteen years. However, this seems unlikely
to occur, particularly as a decision to raise the age above
twelve years was made conditional upon a vote in both
Houses and was not to be achieved by ministerial ruling.
This means it would be a public event. The election of
1971, resulted in a Conservative Government implementing
an Act passed when there was a Labour Government and ended
for a time the chance for further movement towards a welfare approach. By the time that a Labour Government was
re-elected, fears of increasing violence in young people
had altered the climate, and the Labour Government no longer
wanted to shift the balance in the juvenile justice system
towards a welfare approach.

THE EFFECTS OF CLASSIFICATION ON DISPOSITION

Classification in itself does not affect the welfare/cri-
minal justice balance, but when it is linked to treatment
choices it becomes important.
     The dispositional powers which do not involve removal
from home will be considered first. In the United States
and the Scottish Hearings these powers are the same, whether or not the child has committed an act which in an
adult is a crime. Courts and hearings can take no action
or can place the child under supervision. The major difference between the two countries - and it is a difference
that is noticeable between England and the United States
also - is that in Britain the courts and hearings are restricted to dispositions laid down by law, whereas in the
United States juvenile courts tend to make any kind of disposition which is not actually forbidden by law. This can
lead to highly imaginative and also very bizarre orders by
juvenile courts. The difference arises from the underlying
belief that the juvenile court in the United States has a
residual parental responsibility for children. British
courts, based as they are on statute and with no claims
to an equitable jurisdiction, take a more restricted view
of their responsibility.
     English juvenile courts, in addition to discharge and

supervision, can, when dealing with those charged with offences, make two other non-custodial orders which are not generally available for children found to be in need of care. They can order payment of a fine, and the 1969 Act allows such an order to be imposed in a care proceeding as well as in a criminal case, when the grounds for the proceeding arise from the commission of an offence. They can also make an attendance centre order which, like a fine, is usually regarded as a sentence based on the ideas of a criminal justice approach.

The Kilbrandon Committee report made two points about the use of fines in juvenile courts. When they are imposed on children, the parents are in fact responsible for payment. The court may suggest that the parents stop their child's pocket money towards meeting the cost of the fine, but they cannot enforce such an arrangement. They add:(15)

the practice of fining parents for their children's misdemeanours seems to be open to serious objection. As a simple expeditious measure not involving continued demands on the parent or intrusion into the home it may be felt to comment itself. In principle, however, it seems to us equally incompatible with what purports to be a system of measures for the education and training of children. Fining of parents is essentially a punitive measure, and, while we certainly do not wish to suggest that punishment as applied to children themselves has never any educational value, the fact is that fining in these circumstances amounts to a vicarious liability on the parents, who are punished (by financial deprivation) for the acts committed by their children. The educational value in relation to the parents, must in the circumstances be highly doubtful; and the argument that the process will indirectly be of educational value to the child we consider to be untenable.

The other point about fining is that of enforcement. It seems plausible to argue that fining young people and children may be compatible with considerations of welfare, but when it comes to removing them from home because they have failed to comply with an order designed, at least in part, to keep them at home, the logic is hard to follow. The 1969 Children and Young Persons Act continues the power to fine but has removed the power to enforce payment by means of detention, and as yet the government have not introduced other means of enforcing fines. The dilemma is important because fines are used extensively by juvenile courts as the figures quoted in chapter six indicate. Roughly one in three of all juveniles found guilty are dealt with by a fine. If they fail to pay their fines, nothing can be done until they become seventeen, when they can be sentenced to detention. However, the idea of enforcement perhaps long after the event is repugnant to ideas both of welfare and of criminal justice, so that few non-paid fines are enforced. It would be unfortunate, especially for a community approach, if other types of order came to replace fining, since the replacements would in most cases be more stigmatising and labelling than a fine. If courts have to make orders, fines have advantages. They are the usual way of dealing with traffic offenders and such offences carry little stigma. They are quickly over and need not involve any continuing relationship with a social worker, so that the dangers of labelling do not arise. Nor does paying a fine add any new status, like that of probation, to a person. People are not known as finees.

In turning to orders which involve removing children from home, it seems that all three countries are struggling with the question whether children who commit offences and those who need care should be housed together. Roughly, those who argue for separation follow a criminal justice viewpoint and those who say allocation should depend upon a child's needs, and not on the behaviour which brought him to court, are following a welfare approach. In the United States there has traditionally been no separation, but the Uniform Juvenile Code differentiates between children who are offenders and those who are not and uses the term delinquent only for offenders. It then forbids the placement of unruly children (the non-offender group) in state institutions for delinquent children. This is the outcome of several lines of thought. With the Gault hearing the United States woke up to the deficiencies of many state institutions for children and recognised that, while they may be rehabilitative in theory, in practice they are often retributive. Places which claim to reform children are run as junior prisons which punish and degrade their inmates and which seem to encourage rather than reduce anti-social behaviour. The gap between rhetoric and reality was acknowledged:(17)

> The disciplinary or punishment barracks - sometimes
> these veritable cell blocks were more forbidding than
> adult prisons - were known officially as 'adjustment
> cottages' or 'lost privilege cottages'. Guards were
> 'supervisors'. Employees who were often little more
> than caretakers and custodians were called 'cottage
> parents'. Whips, paddles, blackjacks and straps were
> 'tools of control'. Isolation cells were 'meditation
> rooms' .... Catchwords of the trade - 'individualiza-
> tion of treatment', 'rehabilitating the maladjusted' -
> rolled easily off the tongues of many institutional

officials who not only didn't put these principles
into practice but didn't even understand their meaning.
Strangely, the response was not an all-out attempt to alter
the institutions or to provide alternative facilities. It
has instead taken the form of ensuring that children shall
not be sent to such damaging places without full protection
of their rights at the juvenile court hearing. It was in
Kent v. United States that this point was first publicly
raised when they questioned:(18)

> the justifiability of affording a juvenile less protec-
> tion than is accorded to adults suspected of criminal
> offences, particularly where, as here, there is an ab-
> sence of any indication that the denial of rights avail-
> able to adults was offset, mitigated or explained by
> action of the Government as *parens patriae*, evidencing
> the special solicitude for juveniles commanded by the
> Juvenile Court Act.

Apparently, it does not matter that children are confined
in juvenile prisons so long as their rights were protected.
In arguments like this the welfare viewpoint has been almost completely submerged by criminal justice thinking.

Other arguments seem to have a similar theoretical base.
It is suggested that children who 'have not even broken
the law' should not be confined in such places. Senator
Birch Bayh(19) stated in 1972 that 'more than half the
children now held in detention centers, training schools
and other correctional institutions have never been charged
with the equivalent of an adult crime', while Sarri(20)
maintained that for girls the percentage is 75. The logic
behind these statements is not easy to follow. Birch says:
'Children whose delinquent behaviour stems from emotional
problems and family environments must not be co-mingled
with juveniles who have committed crimes'. He does not
state the cause of criminal acts, but we can only assume
it is not to be found in the emotional disturbances of
individuals or families. This seems to leave the possibility that criminal acts are caused by social factors such
as poverty, ghettos and so on or by individual wilful wick-
edness. The latter fits the argument better, since it goes
on to suggest that the punishment should fit the crime,
and that prisons - even juvenile ones - are for criminals,
and to send non-offenders there is unfair. It is not only
unfair, it is dangerous, since these institutions are
schools for crime. Children are contaminated by close contacts with other more-hardened and vicious children who
will be forming the future hard core of recidivists. It
is never clear in the writing how it is decided who is
vicious, but it is assumed that viciousness lies in vicious
acts, since non-offenders and those who commit only the

equivalent of minor offences, are not vicious although they may become so by close contact in a juvenile institution.

It is easy to criticise the simplified criteria developed by politicians, but the problems of contamination and of stigma are very difficult ones. When children live together as inmates in the kinds of institutions usually provided, it is unfortunately true that peer relationships are likely to be far more important than inmate/staff relationships. What is not so obvious is whether the children who provide the bad influence on others can be so easily identified as being those who committed serious criminal acts. Even if this is correct, and in fact we do not know this, it does not follow that the solution is to remove the non-offender children. A better solution might be to provide adequate funding for juvenile facilities and break the large institutions into small group facilities where an inmate counter culture is less likely to develop. This would be to follow a welfare approach. The Uniform Act, however, separates offenders and non-offenders and, in so doing, espouses a criminal justice viewpoint. Here, in effect it says, the treatment of the child shall depend upon the nature of his acts and not upon an assessment of his needs.

Besides contaminating children, institutions also label and stigmatise them. The question of stigma arises at all stages of contact between a child and a juvenile court, and the further into the system a child goes the greater the problem for him and for society of managing a spoiled identity. The history of the juvenile courts shows how difficult it is to avoid stigma.

The early juvenile courts were clear that they were saving children from the stigma of the criminal courts. Frederick Wines, speaking to the Illinois Conference of Charities in 1899, said:(21)

We make criminals out of children who are not criminals by treating them as if they were criminals. That ought to be stopped. What we should have, in our system of criminal jurisprudence, is an entirely separate system of courts for children, in large cities, who commit offenses which would be criminal in adults. We ought to have a 'children's court' in Chicago, and we ought to have a 'children's judge' who should attend to no other business. We want some place of detention for those children other than a prison.... No child ought to be tried unless he has a friend in court to look after his real interests. There should be someone there who has the confidence of the judge, and who can say to the court, 'Will you allow me to make an investigation of this case? Will you allow me to make a suggestion to the court?'

Today juvenile courts themselves have come to be regarded
as having a stigmatising effect upon children who appear in
them. We shall look later at attempts to deal with this
problem by diverting children from the system entirely. Now
our concern is with those who do enter the system and require a placement away from home. In the United States originally, one reason for treating children who committed offences in the same way as those who truanted or were incorrigible was to save children from the stigma of having been
charged with an offence.

The United States view is that this has failed. In England the sponsors of the 1969 Act hoped that, by giving the
decision about placement not to the courts but to the child-
care agencies, the stigma on children committed by the
courts would be reduced and their needs more nearly met.
Before the new Act, juvenile courts in Britain could make
two major kinds of order which would result in children or
young people being removed from their own homes. They could
be made both for those charged with an offence and for those
found to be in need of care or protection. The court could
make a 'fit person' order which resulted in the child being
received into the care of the local authority children's department. This department then provided the type of care
most appropriate to the child's needs, which was usually
either a small group home or a private foster home. The
children's department was also responsible for children who
had not come via the courts but whose parents had requested
temporary or permanent care for them. These children and
those committed by the courts were frequently housed together in residential homes or schools. The second order
the court could make was an approved school order. Approved
Schools were only for children committed by the courts, and
were the successors of reformatories and industrial schools.
Some were run by local authorities and others by private
bodies but all had to be approved by the Secretary of State
— hence their name, Approved Schools.

The 1969 Children and Young Persons Act has abolished
Approved Schools, and the new local government departments
of social service in England and Wales guided by the Regional Planning Committees, are charged with the development of a system of community homes. The juvenile courts
can now make only a care order in respect of a child or
young person who, they consider, should live away from
home. The social workers of the local authority then decide which of their community or private homes is most
suitable for the child. All children from the courts can
(at least in theory) be housed with other children whom
the authority has in their care, and there will be no facilities, with the exception of a few regional secure establishments maintained only for children from the courts.

Many of the children whom the local authorities have in
their care have not been received via the courts. The
hope is that the children who do come into care by a court
order will lose any stigma they may have by being part of
a larger group of children who are seen by society as unfortunate but not wicked, as needing not punishment but
care.

Had the Act been fully implemented, the policy would
have been unequivocally that of a welfare approach. But
it has not been and juvenile courts retain powers which
were to have been removed from them. Thus detention
centres remain a possible placement for those over fourteen
years, and the decision to commit to them is made, not by
social workers, but by the court itself. There is little
doubt that detention centres conform to a criminal justice
approach. Their aim is to expose the juvenile to 'a short
sharp shock' and place young people in rigid regimented
centres where they are subjected to army-type discipline.
Cavanagh said of them: 'Possibly the outstanding feature
of these centres is that their intention is primarily deterrent and no one is there except as a punishment'.(22)
Interestingly, they also provide an example of how the two
approaches we are considering can never be entirely separated. The explicitly primitive aims of detention centres
provoked considerable public criticism and staff at detention centres found themselves unable to act just as gaolers
to young people. Rehabilitative ideals began to creep in.
Visiting detention centres regularly, I noticed the staff
would refer to the old days when the discipline was really
severe and go on to explain how they now took a personal
interest in the boys and made close relationships with
some of them, who came back to visit after their release.
This impression is confirmed by Cavanagh: 'The detention
centres for their part are tending to move away from their
rather repellent and unconstructively punitive regime.'(23)
However, they are still far from conforming to a welfare
approach.

The power to commit those aged fifteen and sixteen to
Borstal training also remains, although the stated intention had been to raise the age to seventeen years as soon
as local authorities had had an opportunity to develop
intermediate forms of treatment. Both detention centres
and Borstals are run in Britain by the prison department
of the central government. They are thus a part of the
penal system, and their organisation and practice is much
closer to that of a prison than to that of a home for disturbed children.

The future of both institutions is now under consideration. The Advisory Council on the Penal System,(24) in a

report on young adult offenders, suggested that detention centres, Borstals and young prisoners' institutions should be abolished as distinct institutions. Instead, a regional system of custodial care for young offenders should be developed, and all sentences should be served partly in custody and partly in the community under a custody order. The report, which refers only to those between seventeen and twenty-one and to England, illustrates the shifting balance of welfare and criminal justice thinking. Originally Borstals were established to train young offenders, and because they offered training, not punishment, courts were justified in making a three-year Borstal sentence on those who, had they been sent to prison, would have merited a shorter period in custody. The report rejects this justification but takes an interesting mid-way position by suggesting custody orders which combine the punishment and deterrence of a period in custody with the rehabilitation offered by a period of supervision in the community. The report and discussions following it may influence the future of juvenile courts particularly in relation to offenders of fifteen and sixteen years of age. The Council's report could be used to argue for juvenile courts having power to make custody orders in cases where they can now make detention centre orders or remit for a sentence of Borstal training. This might combat the juvenile court magistrates' feeling of powerlessness but would also move the juvenile court nearer to the penal system and so away from a welfare approach.

In relation to residential provision Scotland again differs from England. Before the 1968 Act approved schools took both those charged with an offence and those in need of care. Unlike England, when Scotland moved to a unified social work service, the approved schools remained independent and were not incorporated into the system of homes run by social work departments. They changed only in name, acquiring the extraordinary name of List D schools. Establishments on this list, which was drawn up by the Social Work Services Group of the Scottish Education Department, are for children committed by the children's hearings and the courts. The allocation of children to the schools is made by civil servants, although eventually both the allocation and the running of the schools will be the responsibility of local government in each of the seven new regions. Whether the local government department concerned will be social work or education is, at the time of writing, still undecided and hotly contested. The indications are that the social work department will acquire this responsibility. Unlike the community homes south of the border, List D schools seldom take children who have come into the care of local authorities by means other than the order of a hearing. List D schools thus resemble Approved Schools more closely than do community homes. Despite the fact that Scotland has moved further away from a criminal justice approach, special institutions are reserved for those who need compulsory care. This may illustrate the fact that a shift towards a welfare approach in one aspect of the system is compensated for by maintaining the ideas of criminal justice in another area.

Thus in Britain it is still an open question whether or not the deprived and the depraved should be housed in the same institutions. In the United States the trend seems clearer. It is more widely accepted that the failure to distinguish between offenders and non-offenders has resulted in stigma attaching to both, rather than reducing the stigma on the offenders. For many people the answer to this problem is obvious. The two groups must be separated and only children who have committed offences – the delinquent children of the Uniform Code – shall be sent to state institutions. These institutions are often the responsibility of the State Department of Corrections, which is also responsible for the prisons and reformatories in the state. To send a child to such an institution is to set him firmly in the criminal justice system. The price which is to be paid for separating the two types of children is not always spelt out, but, to those who hold a welfare approach, it seems to be that one group of children, those who commit offences (or at any rate serious offences) shall be left to carry the stigma in order to free the non-offender children. Perhaps this is a good choice, but it should be made in the knowledge that it may be creating a class of scapegoats.

PUNISHMENT

We have moved from a consideration of the types of children over whom the juvenile court can have jurisdiction to the court's dispositional powers, since the classification of children seems to gain meaning largely from differences in disposition. While considering dispositional powers, we should consider the question of punishment.

Punishment is difficult to define since it has different meanings from different viewpoints. Whether an experience is punishing will depend upon the intent of the initiator, the feelings of the recipient and the social norms of the culture in which they are operating. We have all experienced a feeling of being punished when none was intended and of intending to punish another, only to find they were

unaware of what we were doing. It is also possible for
society to regard as punishing an interaction which neither
of the actors feels to be so. These are subjective views
of punishment, and they need to be kept in mind while considering the place of punishment in a welfare and a criminal justice approach. If punishment has a place in a welfare philosophy, and this is doubtful, it is limited to
situations where it is considered to be for the good of
the child and to be a means of bringing about his rehabilitation. It can never be used to deter others from similar behaviour. The fact that, according to this approach,
rehabilitation can only take place with the co-operation of
the child and cannot ultimately be imposed upon him, sets
strict limits on the use of punishment, because it is more
likely to create resentment and hostility than co-operation.
There can be no place within a welfare approach for juvenile court actions where the sole purpose is to deter offenders. There may, however, be a place for actions the
court intends that the child shall feel as punishing. For
example, it may be necessary to create some anxiety in
some children as the basis for working with them towards
a change in their situation or attitude. No one is going
to change unless they feel some discomfort in their present
situation, and punishment may appear to be the only
way to create such discomfort. Another situation in which
the court may want a child to feel punished may arise with
what is probably a rather rare group of children. There
are some who appear to be driven by intense unconscious
guilt which can only be relieved by punishment. Their anti-
social acts are means of getting punishment. For such
children punishment will be no long term solution to their
problem, but may be necessary to ease their anxiety sufficiently to begin some psychotherapeutic treatment. Too
high a level of anxiety is as incapacitating as too low
a level for the purpose of bringing about change. Such
children are rare and seriously disturbed, but many normal children may be better able to start afresh after un-
dergoing something which they regard as punishing but also
fair.

While intentional punishment may have a small part in
welfare philosophy, sentences which, at least for a time,
feel punitive to the child but are not intended to be so,
will frequently be found. Children removed from home find
this a punitive experience, although the intention of the
court may be to provide them with better care and understanding than their home can offer. Children, even in the
most progressive and enlightened group homes, are likely
to feel thay have been 'put away', although their perceptions may change over time. Unfortunately, we know far too

little about how children view the treatment which the
courts order for them. As with many social services and
other aspects of the criminal justice system, we seldom
ask the recipients of the juvenile justice system what it
means to them.

If punishment in a welfare philosophy is for the good of
the child, it serves other functions in criminal justice
systems; it can be retributive and aimed at general deterrence. Juvenile courts and hearings get caught between
the two systems in the way they use the possibility of removal from home. When no removal is actually being considered, judges, magistrates, panel members, lawyers and
social workers use future removal as a threat. Children
are told that, if they appear again, the judge or magistrate
will not be able to be so lenient with them. When the court
or hearing actually has to take the step of sending a child
away, it may change its attitude and talk of the advantages to the child which will come from this change. The
problem is that many children (and adults) have some control
over their behaviour, and the threat of future sanctions
can serve to reinforce that control. On the other hand,
where this reinforcement fails or is insufficient, it has
created a situation where the next step in the juvenile justice system has become a negative one from the start, not
only in the eyes of the child but in the opinion of the
court as well.

It will be clear now that it is almost impossible to
look at the sentencing alternatives made available by the
statutes to juvenile courts and determine whether and in
what way they are punitive. State institutions, community
homes and probation supervision may be punitive because the
court intends the sentence to be so or because the child
feels it to be so or because the actual conditions in the
home or of the supervision would be held to be punitive by
society, whatever the expressed intent of the people involved.

We have probably become more aware of the problem of
understanding the effects of official actions on juveniles
in the past ten years. This arises in part from an increased interest in interaction in all human relationships.
The largely individual psychology of Freud and his early
followers gave way to an emphasis upon interpersonal processes. Theories about groups were advanced which looked,
not at individuals, but at group processes in which individuals were at one and the same time instigators and res-
pondents. There is now some movement away from this focus
upon interaction because existential ideas and theories
like those in Gestalt therapy, have re-emphasised the psychology of the individual. However, this latest trend has

had little influence yet upon thinking about delinquency. There the ideas of interaction are still important, and are supported by developments in sociology which emphasise, not the individual characteristics of delinquents but society's actions towards him. This way of thinking in psychology and sociology has helped to develop a holistic view more in accord with reality. It has also helped us to lift the distorting veil of good intention from our institutions and see them as they are. Goffman's essay on total institutions was influential in exposing the processes that operate in institutions.(25) What his work and other studies of prisons and mental hospitals have shown is not only that staff, like other humans, can be, and often are, cruel and sadistic, but that total institutions seem to take on a life of their own. When people live together in large numbers, where they are grouped into staff and inmates and each group has a different status, certain dehumanising patterns tend to develop. These run counter to the welfare ideals which the institution may be planning to promote. We are beginning to understand the processes which operate between intention and action. We also know a good deal about how to mitigate and overcome these forces, but the methods are expensive. The most certain way to avoid institutionalisation is to keep all groups of people down to a size in which everyone can have face to face relationships with everyone else. Such treatment programmes can only be established by societies which have dealt with their own ambivalence and will pay the price of a welfare philosophy.

INDETERMINATE SENTENCES

While considering dispositions, we should also consider the question of fixed and indeterminate sentences. It is sometimes held that an indeterminate sentence is more closely associated with the idea of rehabilitation than is a fixed sentence. In the former, the people responsible for treatment can decide when the delinquent has been re-habilitated and is ready to be released from supervision or returned to the community. The latter smacks of 'doing time' and of serving out a sentence to satisfy the need of society for revenge and retribution. Traditionally, juve-niles who were removed from home, on both sides of the At-lantic, had a maximum period set by the court, but the parole board, local authority or approved school managers could release the child earlier. With probation orders the two countries had different procedures. Probation in the United States is not usually for a fixed term, whereas

in Britain a probation or supervision order has always been
for a term, fixed by the court, of one, two or three years.
This continues in England. In Scotland, however, a 'supervision requirement shall cease to have effect in respect
of a child when he attains the age of eighteen years' and
'no child shall continue to be subject to supervision requirement for any time longer than is necessary in his
interest'. The decisions about the length of the requirement are made by the panel members at a review hearing.
It may be argued that in this respect Scotland and the United
States follow a welfare philosophy. However, this again
illustrates the problem of deciding how to interpret particular requirements. There is a school of thought in
social work and psychotherapy which holds that clients can
make better use of treatment when the length of that treatment is known in advance. The client is then able to work
on his problems with a deadline in mind, whereas in treatment with no fixed end there is less pressure to work. It
is most unlikely, however, that the time limit on English
probation and supervision orders was continued in the 1969
Act on the basis of such thinking. More likely it was
designed to protect offenders from the potential injustice
of indeterminate sentences.

PROCEDURAL RIGHTS

The State statutes and recent holdings of the United States
Supreme Court make certain statements about procedure which
can be interpreted as emphasising the criminal justice
aspect of the courts. These statements are concerned with
the rights of children, and rights, as we have seen, belong
to a criminal justice system and are less relevant to welfare, although not contradictory to it. In all three
countries an adult criminal defendant is entitled to certain protections before and during his trial. In the United
States these arise from the rights granted in the Constitution to trial according to 'due process of law'. By interpretation, 'due process' has come to include the right to
a hearing, to a notice of that hearing, the right to remain
silent under questioning, to representation in court, to a
decision based on evidence beyond a reasonable doubt, and
to a jury trial. What has happened in the United States is
that the Supreme Court has held that the clause in the
Constitution, which guarantees to all men trial by due process of law, includes within its scope children who are in
situations which may result in their being deprived of their
liberty. At present children have all the due process
rights of adults facing a criminal charge, except the right

to a jury trial. From our point of view the importance of
this trend is that due process rights for adults attach to
criminal proceedings. They cannot be claimed in civil
proceedings, and an emphasis on rights in the juvenile
court seems to support a criminal justice viewpoint. The
trend is sometimes referred to as 'criminalising the juvenile court', and it certainly is a marked change of emphasis from the pre-Gault days, when the judge was not a
judge but a wise father, and procedureal protections were
as unnecessary as they are between benevolent father and
erring son.

The trend in Britain is in the opposite direction. Juvenile courts were never, as in the United States, new types
of courts operating on a principle of fatherly concern, but
clearly had both criminal and civil jurisdiction. When being tried for a criminal offence a child is entitled to the
same protection as an adult offender, with the exception of
trial by jury. The 1969 Act reduces the criminal jurisdiction of the court, but at the same time gives children
the legal protection they would have had in criminal hearings, when they are brought as in need of care or control
on the grounds that they have committed an offence. Section
33 states 'the same proof shall be required to substantiate
or refute an allegation that the offence condition is satisfied in consequence of an offence as is required to warrant
a finding of guilty or, as the case may be, of not guilty
of the offence'. In addition to stipulating the standard
of evidence, the Act ensures that the same offence cannot
provide an offence condition more than once, nor can it be
used after the statutory period of limitation has run.

Similar protection is included in Scottish law. Where
a child contests the facts which result in his being brought
to a juvenile panel, the Sheriff is asked to settle the
question. The Sheriff holds a hearing in chambers, at
which the child is entitled to representation and where, if
the 'ground for referral of the case is the condition referred in Section 32(2)(9) (i.e., he has committed an offence) of this Act, the Sheriff in hearing the application
shall apply to the evidence relating to that ground the
standard of proof required in criminal procedure'.

Unlike the United States holdings, which assure procedural rights to all children liable to be deprived of their
liberty, in England and Scotland the statutes do not define
the legal rights of children brought to court as in need of
care and control where the ground is not that they have
committed an offence. This seems likely to cause problems
in the future, since the disposition of children does not
vary according to the grounds of referral. In England,
children in respect of whom an offence condition is proved,

and those who are found in need of care on other grounds,
can be removed from their homes for indefinite periods of
time and kept in institutions whose rehabilitative capa-
cities are at least questionable. Perhaps the next few
years in Britain may see an increasing concern with procedural rights for all children in need of care and control,
and particularly for those who have not committed an offence. The intention of the present laws was to end the
categorising of children according to their behaviour and
open up greater possibilities of handling them according
to their needs. The half-implemented current Act shows how
far society is prepared to go along this path. It produces
a position which to many will seem anomalous, whereby children who commit offences get greater protection than those
who do not, while both face the same risks of removal from
home.

Legal rights are useless to people who do not know they
have them, and this is the position of many children and
parents caught up in the juvenile justice system. The
courts in the United States have gone much further than
those in Britain to ensure that children know their rights
and that, when they waive them, they do so with understanding. Since Gault, all children in the United States
in juvenile courts must be told what rights they have and
be informed that they may be represented, if they wish.
Should their parents be unable to afford a lawyer, the
court is required to appoint one. In England, legal aid is
available to those who ask for it, but there is no obligation upon the court to offer it, and many unrepresented
children and young people are found to have committed offences which the prosecution could never have proved, and
on which a defence lawyer could have obtained a not guilty
verdict. The situation is even more perilous from a rights
viewpoint in Scotland. The hearing is only allowed to continue if the child admits the acts which provide ground for
its jurisdiction. This admission can be complicated by
questions of intent, of which an unrepresented child, even
with parental help, would be unaware. From a welfare viewpoint such considerations are unimportant, because the purpose of the hearing is to meet the needs of the child, and
the exact grounds for referral may be unimportant.

The Children Act, 1975 had introduced a new form of protection for children and young persons, designed not to
ensure their legal rights vis a vis the court or hearing,
but to protect their interests in situations of possible
conflict between them and their parents. In England and
Wales,(26) in certain defined situations which include care
proceedings and the discharge of supervision and care orders, the court may, if it appears there is or may be con-

flict between the interests of the child or young person
and those of his parent or guardian, order that the parent
or guardian is not to be treated as representing the child
or young person. Having made such an order the court is
then required to appoint a guardian ad litem unless this is
unnecessary for safeguarding the interests of the child or
young person. They may also order that legal aid be given
to the parent or guardian.

In Scotland in any proceedings before a children's hearing or in cases referred or appealed to the sheriff the
chairman or the sheriff:(27)

shall consider whether it is necessary for the purpose
of safeguarding the interests of the child in the proceedings, because there is or may be conflict, on any
matter relevant to the proceedings, between the interests of the child and those of his parents, to appoint
a person to act for that purpose.

These parts of the Act were to be brought into effect by
the appropriate ministers when the necessary provisions had
been made by the local authorities. The ministers have
responsibility also for naming the type of people who may
be appointed to act for the child, which in effect means
whether they are to be social workers or lawyers. Obviously
this decision will affect the balance between a welfare and
a criminal justice approach in the juvenile courts and
hearings.

These clauses were included in an Act which is largely
concerned with adoption and the implementation of the ideas
of the Houghton Committee(28) because of the public and
Parliamentary concern which followed the report of the inquiry into the death of Maria Colwell(29) and which happened to co-incide with and revitalise, discussions about the
Houghton Report. One reading of the events leading up to
the death of Maria, who was under the supervision of the
local authority, is that the juvenile court which revoked
the fit person order in respect of Maria were not aware of
all the facts, or at least that all the possible implications of these facts were not spelt out to them. The reason for this may have been that the social worker was concerned not just with Maria, but also with her mother who
was applying for revocation and whose husband was eventually to kill Maria. This meant that the social worker
was in a conflict of interest situation and a demand arose
for someone to represent the interests of the child in
situations where what has come to be called a 'tug of
love' situation might exist between children and parents
and perhaps foster parents.

The Act acknowledges the possibility of conflict within
families and strengthens the rights of a child as distinct

from those of his parents. While it is clear that it is
the child's interests which are to be protected and this is
in line with a welfare approach, the method adopted, which
is that of advocacy seems to suggest criminal justice
thinking. Much will depend upon how the Act is implemented,
upon who are appointed to safeguard the interest of children, how they develop their case and how much weight the
court or hearing give to their representations.

Chapter nine

The people who run the juvenile justice system

Historical and sociological factors provide a background, and statutes and rules the general framework, within which the juvenile justice system operates. The way it actually operates in relation to a particular child is determined by the behaviour of the people in the system. The system balances criminal justice and welfare approaches so nicely, that the measure of each which a child receives is often decided by individuals.

For the juvenile justice system to function, certain tasks have to be carried out and decisions made, which involve the exercise of discretion. It must be decided whether a child shall enter the system and then whether the facts of the child's background and behaviour are such as to justify the use of compulsory powers. In order that this decision can be made, the facts which are thought to provide grounds for the exercise of compulsion must be stated, and the child and his family must be allowed to give their point of view, either personally or through a representative. If it is decided that grounds exist for the use of compulsory powers, a decision has to be made as to the way these powers shall be used, and for this additional information about the social background is required.

Another way of expressing this is to say that certain roles have to be filled in order that the system may operate. These roles are those of gate keeper, prosecutor, defender, social worker, judge and sentencer. It is confusing that some of the words used to describe these roles are either usually associated with members of the legal profession or, in the case of social work, involve the same word as that used for members of a particular occupational group. Here, however, I am using them to describe roles,(1) that is, particular sets of activities and decisions. In the juvenile court system the role of defender may be filled by a person who is by profession a lawyer or

a social worker or who is serving as a magistrate; the
role of social worker by a person who is a lawyer and who
may also occupy the role of judge, as well as by a person
employed as a social worker. These roles are important in
the exploration of discretion because each role structures,
to some extent, the behaviour of the person who fills it:
roles partly consist of shared expectations of behaviour.
Some of the roles in juvenile justice are more clearly defined than others. Some, such as those of prosecutor,
defender, judge and sentencer, are found in criminal as
well as juvenile justice systems and have therefore acquired clarity in the course of a long history. The role
of judge carries an expectation of impartiality and of
being open to influence from both sides of the argument.
The same people in other situations might fail to consider
the approach, be it that of welfare, community or criminal justice with which they have least sympathy, but
when magistrate, judge or Sheriff is acting in the role of
judge, the role itself influences them towards open-mind-
edness. Similarly, the role of sentencer requires consideration of the needs of the public and of the offender,
while prosecutors or defenders are expected to show their
case to its best advantage, but without misleading the court
by distorting or concealing the facts. A prosecutor is expected to be particularly concerned with the protection of
the public, while the defender serves his client to the
best of his ability to ensure the outcome the client wants.
The roles of gate keeper and social worker are less well
defined; they are still in the process of formation. It
seems that a gate keeper is expected to consider many of
the same factors as a jury or sentencer and to balance individual and community concerns. The role of social worker
seems to require a consideration of the child's social and
emotional needs, and to free the person in the role from
a particular concern with the protection of society or the
rights of the child.
    People enacting roles in a system are partly excused
from the expectation that their behaviour shall reflect personal values, because the values associated with the correct
balance in the total system, which is maintained by the expected performance in roles, is of more importance than are
individual values. This is clearest in the role of defender
in a criminal justice system. A defender is expected to
represent people whom he may think are guilty and whose behaviour he may deplore because of the need in the system as
a whole to provide a fair trial. In the juvenile justice
system the roles are less clear but, as they develop, they
determine to some extent how a person will behave in his
role and how he will use his discretion.

In any system it is the interaction between people in roles which ensures that the system fulfils its function. There have been few studies of juvenile justice systems which show how people in various roles interact with each other. Such studies are best carried out amongst groups of people who work together over time and whose interactions become relatively fixed. Emerson(2) and Platt(3) have studied individual juvenile courts in the United States, and their works show how the performances of people in roles dovetail to produce a court with a particular balance between the welfare and criminal justice approach. Platt shows how the public defender in a Chicago juvenile court modified his role as advocate to fit in with the court's welfare approach and, in so doing, ensured not justice for his clients but a smoothly-run court which got through its heavy load of cases without straining the personal relationships of the people who ran the system.

These group pressures probably operate in any juvenile justice situation, although where, as in most courts and hearings, a new combination of people gather on each occasion, the interaction is more difficult to see.

Although group interaction and roles serve to structure the way discretion is used, there is still need to posit an individual component which determines in part the way the discretion is exercised or a role is performed. This individual component is probably the result of personal background, attitudes and professional training. Training also tends to strengthen those values and beliefs which initially led an individual to seek a particular training.

The people who fill particular roles in the juvenile justice system vary not only between the three countries with which we are concerned, but also between different courts and hearings in the same country. The roles are, however, allocated amongst four groups of people; three of these, lawyers, social workers and police, are groups with functions outside juvenile justice who are recognised as professional groups by society, have special training and are paid. The fourth group cannot be defined in the same way, since what its members share is their role in making decisions on the facts and as to treatment in the juvenile justice system. They may be members of a professional group but, with the exception of sheriffs and juvenile court judges, need not be. They come into the juvenile justice system not because work in the system is part of their wider function in society, but in order to make impartial decisions. In the United States, juvenile court judges are paid as are sheriffs in Scotland, but magistrates and panel members are not. These latter groups have a brief training for their role in the juvenile justice system. Judges and sheriffs usually have no special preparation for their role beyond that which a legal training may be thought to provide.

We will now consider the training of police, lawyers and social workers, and then the roles assigned to them and the other decision makers in the juvenile justice system, and how what is known about their background may affect the ways in which they exercise their discretion.

THE POLICE

The police force in England and Scotland is the organisation responsible for the prevention of crime, for law enforcement and keeping the peace. It is organised on a local basis, but the tendency has been for smaller units to unite, so that the police force does not necessarily serve the same geographical area as do other organisations with a local basis, like the courts and the local authorities.

Police are trained on entry to the force in District Training Centres in England and at the Police College in Scotland. Training is organised by the police themselves, and initial training concentrates upon general police work, with emphasis upon law enforcement and police procedures. Specialised training is provided on an in-service basis and, in England, includes year-long courses at the Police College in Hampshire, where staff are selected for a range of special courses. Those concerned with management include some teaching about the social sciences. The Scottish police college also provides management courses of three or six months' duration for sergeants and higher-ranking officers. While some of the ideas of a welfare approach have always been held by police officers, and are now given a limited place in advanced training, the overriding approach is that of law enforcement, which in Britain and the United States is a part of the criminal justice approach. Even police officers directly involved with juveniles have no specific training for this work, although they are probably more influenced by ideas of welfare than are their colleagues in other branches of the force.

Two patterns have developed in police work with juveniles in England. Since 1948, when the Liverpool police first developed the scheme, police juvenile liaison schemes have been established in various forces. These schemes provide police supervision for a year or more of children and young people who admit to having committed offences. Before deciding upon this measure, police visit the child's home, and supervision only takes place where child and parents agree and where a court appearance is considered unnecessary. These schemes have always been subject to much controversy, and not all forces operate one. Social workers have been particularly suspicious of police doing what they consider to be a social work job. In England, although some juvenile liaison schemes continue, Watson suggests that since the 1969 Act came into force:(4)

It is now recognised that the responsibility for super- vision is officially that of the local authority's social service department and that the role of the po- lice should be confined to affording that department the closest possible co-operation.

The trend since the 1969 Act has, Watson claims, been in the development of police juvenile bureaux. The staff of these bureaux receive reports on all the juvenile offen- ders in their area and investigate by home visits, as well as by consultation with social service and education de- partments. On the basis of this information, the inspector makes a decision whether to prosecute or, if not, whether to caution the child or young person.

Scotland, too, developed police liaison schemes, the earliest being started in Greenock in 1956, and in fact their numbers are increasing, with twelve of the twenty forces now operating such a scheme. However, Mack and Ritchie(5) suggest that the number of children subject to police supervision is not increasing at a proportionate rate, and that the major increase in police/child inter- action since the 1968 Act came into force has been in police warning. From the point of view of police attitudes, the most important development in Scotland has been that of Community Involvement Branches which, among their many tasks in relation to police/community relations, deal with all reports on young offenders and handle the contacts with reporters and social workers. Community Involvement Branches are based on the idea 'that crime prevention is not a purely technical matter, not a branch of criminalis- tics; it is a way of working which envisages as the first principle of police work the securing of the respect, trust and co-operation of the public, and particularly of the local community'.(6)

Mack suggests that officers in a Community Involvement Branch come to have a less purely law and order attitude to young offenders than that held by their colleagues, whose work seldom brings them into contact with the mis- erable reality of the lives of many young offenders or the welfare approach of the social workers. What he says pro- bably also applies to the juvenile bureaux and liaison scheme staff in England. Within their own organisation

these officers may represent something nearer to a welfare
approach than is usual amongst police officers, and may
perhaps in time influence their own organisations. By
what special training they may have, by their daily exposure to children's needs as well as their misdeeds, and by
their group ethos, these particular police are likely to be
influenced by a welfare and community approach when exercising their discretion.

Bruce and Spencer,(7) however, while praising the police
for the way in which they have co-operated with the Hearing
system, suggest that those police whom they interviewed in
their survey of how the panel system was working 'remained
unshaken in their belief in the greater effectiveness of
the courts'. The author's view is that 'it is the preser-
vation of a dual system which has undermined police confidence in the hearings'.

It is more difficult to describe law enforcement in the
United States because it is a function distributed between
a number of different forces, some operating in the same
locality. The sheriff may be responsible for the same area
as the city police, and there may be a State-wide police
force as well. In addition, there are federal law enforcement agents responsible to the Federal Bureau of Investigation. All these forces may at times be involved with juveniles. There is great variety in the training or lack of
training which exist in these many different forces. In
general, the amount of in-service training provided and the
educational qualifications required for entry increase as
one moves from the local to the nationally organised forces.
Many local police chiefs and their staff are political
appointees and, as such, they change when the party in
power changes. Anyone is eligible for appointment to
these local positions, whereas State and Federal officers
are required to pass examinations before they can be
appointed, and rank and file jobs in these organisations
are held on merit, not by political appointment.

By British standards, the police of the United States
are untouched by the ideas of a welfare approach and follow a tough law-enforcement line, which accords with some
aspects of a criminal justice approach.

THE LAWYERS

In the United States admission to the bar is essential
before anyone can practise as a lawyer. In most States
admission is open to graduates who obtain the required
grades from an accredited law school, who meet some routine
requirements as to honesty and sanity, and who pass the bar

examinations of the State in which they wish to practise.
The first step in this process is entry to a law school,
which is itself highly competitive. In the United States
law is a postgraduate subject and, although there are
law schools outside the universities, the best known and
most prestigious are attached to State and private universities. Law students are almost all selected on the basis
of written applications, and the decisive factors in selection are undergraduate grade point averages and, for the
many schools which make use of this, the Law School Aptitude Test Score. This test is administered nationally by
a commercial firm and claims to predict a student's ability to make use of legal training. Selection is thus based
on evidence of intellectual ability as demonstrated by
grades and LSAT scores; personal suitability is not considered. The emphasis is upon rationality, and this emphasis is continued in the law school curriculum. Students, particularly in their first year, are frequently
taught by what is called the Socratic method, in which the
instructor carries on a dialogue with an individual student picked from the usually large class group. The dialogue relates to material in the casebook for the course,
which the student will supposedly have studied in preparation for the class. This method of teaching develops an
ability to 'think on one's feet' in a competitive and often
hostile atmosphere. It is an excellent way to learn how to
isolate the issues in a tense situation and to think rationally about them. The personal cost for many students
is high, since the system ignores individuals and their
feelings, and creates highly competitive relations between
student and student, and emphasises the distance between
students and faculty. Law schools give little help to
students in how to apply their legal knowledge or their
ability to 'think like a lawyer' to practice which involves
working with people as well as with issues. It seems likely that those who are exposed to such a training may tend
to discount the emotional component in themselves and others
and to exercise their discretion on the basis of a view of
man as a rational being. Thus, lawyers are socialised in
law school into this aspect of a criminal justice approach.
In addition, for many students training also includes a
strong emphasis upon rights, because one of the few things
law school faculty members seem to share is a kind of
liberalism which values civil liberties highly and which
influences their teaching.
   Neither the legal profession nor legal education holds
such an elite position in Britain. Future solicitors in
England and Scotland now usually take an undergraduate
law degree at a university and then spend a period as an

articled clerk in a solicitor's office.   In England they
take the examination of the Law Society before qualifying.
Some non-graduates and graduates with degrees in subjects
other than law take courses organised by the Law Society
before and alongside their time as a clerk.   Passing the
Law Society examinations seems to demand a good memory
rather than a capacity to struggle with the issues, but
for those who are articled to a responsible firm, training
on the job can be of a high standard.

British law students are even less likely than are students in the United States to have any formal teaching in
the behavioural sciences or on ways of communicating with
people.   This is a great disadvantage, since for many
lawyers law will have been the only subject of their higher education, and their only exposure to the humanities or
the social sciences will have been at school.   Nor will they
have had any training in how to work with people.   The
Ormrod report comments on this aspect of legal education:
(8)

> The successful handling of fact requires another skill
> which has not yet received the attention which it de-
> serves from lawyers.   In the vast majority of cases the
> facts will have to be obtained from the client and other
> people.   The ability to understand and handle people,
> and to perceive the implications of what is said or not
> said, and of attitudes, demeanour, or even gestures is,
> therefore, an important aspect of the practitioner's
> professional skill.   Much is known about interviewing
> techniques in other professions, but in the legal pro-
> fession it still depends upon intuition and experience.

Like lawyers in the United States, those in Britain are
likely by their training to concentrate upon general external facts when exercising their discretion, and to pay
but limited attention to individual emotional differences.

THE SOCIAL WORKERS

Social work is not restricted to those who have undertaken
a training, and many people employed in the United States
as probation officers and in Britain as local authority
social workers have not had any training.   We shall, therefore, be describing training which only a proportion of workers have received, although the ideas and values emphasised in training have, particularly in Britain, an influence upon all social work staff and not just upon the
graduates of the training courses.

In the United States, training for social work has, until
recently, been almost exclusively at a postgraduate level,

with admission dependent upon undergraduate grades. Schools
of social work were formerly distinguished by the method
they taught, be it casework, groupwork or community work,
but now schools are more likely to offer courses in all
three methods, although students may put a major emphasis
upon one of them. Of the three methods, casework has had
the greatest influence, not only upon probation and corrections, but upon all aspects of social work. It emphasises
the uniqueness of an individual, and is concerned with that
individual's perceptions and attitudes towards outside
events. The facts of a person's feelings are regarded as
at least as important as other kinds of more readily established fact. Casework has relied heavily upon psychological, especially psychoanalytic, theories and these are still
of major importance, although sociological theories are
coming to play a more important part in social work teaching. The emphasis upon social background and labelling
processes may lead to a new brand of social workers who
are less influenced by consideration of personal attitudes
when exercising discretion. It is difficult to predict how
training affects social workers in a court setting, because
schools of social work have done little to develop teaching
related to the particular tasks of probation officers who
provide treatment within a compulsory framework and for whom
social control is an important function. Social work training focuses upon individual needs and social problems. It
has been slow to develop teaching about law, although the
welfare rights movement has forced upon social work educators the realisation that their students must be taught to
consider rights as well as needs.

In Britain, social work training takes a variety of
forms, all of which lead to the same basic Certificate of
Qualification in Social Work (CQSW). This is awarded by
the Central Council for Education and Training in Social
Work to students who satisfactorily complete, at college or
university, courses which have been approved by the Council.
These courses include one- and two-year postgraduate courses
for people with relevant or non-relevant first degrees,
four-year degree courses which combine a social science
degree with professional training, and courses for non-
graduates, including some specially designed for mature
entrants and for those without the usual educational certi-
ficates. The aim is to attract as wide as possible a range
of people into social work, and to provide training suited
both to those accustomed to academic types of education and
to those whose experience has been of a more practical kind.
Competition for places on social work courses is said to
be intense, and a great deal of time is spent in selection.
Most courses state that they are looking for people with an

adequate intellectual capacity, but, more importantly, with
concern for people and a motivation to help. Selection is
usually by means of personal interviews, although some recent research questions the validity of this, suggesting
that selection can equally well be made on the basis of the
fairly extensive written material provided by most applicants.(9)

Traditionally, social work training in Britain has meant
casework training. Recently, some group work and community
work has been included in some courses, but a recent survey
showed that casework is still the method to which most emphasis is given in training.(10) Also, like schools of social work in the United States, little attention has been
given to teaching about law. In a survey(11) of courses
conducted by the Central Council in 1974, it was discovered
that, of ninety-six courses, ninety taught law, but on
only fifty-six was it taught as a separate subject, and
there the time allocated ranged from two to one-hundred
hours per year. This survey was part of a Council curriculum study on legal studies which has been one influence
in moving social work training away from its exclusive concern with the welfare approach. The so-called re-discovery
of poverty and the growing belief that it is caused by
structural factors, rather than personal inadequacy, has
led to considerable criticism of social workers for trying
to change clients' attitudes, when what was required was a
change in society. Increasingly, the sociology taught to
social-work students is that of the interactionist school
and leads to a community rather than a welfare approach.
In Britain, as in the United States, the welfare rights
movement has alerted social workers to clients' rights as
well as to their needs - the latter having been the traditional emphasis in social work training. Nevertheless,
however training may change in the future, at present most
social-work students on most courses are taught mainly
those theories which support a welfare approach, and it is
this approach which influences them in the use of their
professional discretion.

In writing about social work training, it has appeared
that, whatever their future job, all social workers train
alongside each other on generic courses leading to a CQSW.
This is true for Scotland. In England, however, the juvenile courts are served both by local authority social
workers who, if qualified, will have had a generic training, and by probation officers. Probation officers may
have trained on generic courses, but may still train on
courses which take only probation students. It might be
thought that such courses would train their students more
in accordance with the ideas of a criminal justice approach,

and less exclusively in those of a welfare approach, than
do generic courses. Strangely, this is not the case. Probation officers in England have always seen themselves as
part of the profession of social work, and, at one time,
as the best-trained part of that profession, with particular claims to the use of intensive casework methods. In
fact, far from leading the way in balancing a welfare and
a criminal justice approach, probation training can be
accused of being slower than other courses to see the
drawbacks of too exclusive a reliance upon welfare thinking.

Professional training is only one influence upon people.
Their background and the role they occupy are probably at
least equally important, so we will turn now to the roles
in the juvenile justice system, and to what is known of the
background and behaviour of those who fill them.

THE DECISION MAKERS: JUDGES, MAGISTRATES AND PANEL MEMBERS

Judges

In juvenile courts in the United States, it is the judge
who decides whether or not the facts give grounds for a
finding of delinquency and, if so, what the disposition
shall be. In many courts the judge is also involved in the
earlier but equally crucial decision whether or not a petition shall be filed and the child therefore brought to
court, instead of being dealt with informally by the probation officer or referred to another social agency.
Judges are clearly the single most important person in a
juvenile court in the United States, so the way they use
their discretion has a powerful influence on the balance
between a welfare and criminal justice approach. Unfortunately, we know little of the characteristics of judges
of any kind, and even less of juvenile court judges. In
the more populous counties, juvenile court judges are chosen for that purpose, and they work full time in the juvenile court. In other counties, the juvenile court work
is but a part, and often an insignificant part, of their
more important and prestigious job as circuit or district
court judge. This means that juvenile court judges outside the large cities are not appointed because of special
skills in relation to difficult children, but for the usual
mixture of professional and political skills for which men
win election to judgeships. In thirty-eight States,(12)
juvenile court judges are elected, in some States by popular vote, for periods of four or six years. The trend,
however, is towards the Missouri plan by which judges are
appointed in the first instance by a State-wide panel.

After they have been in office for a period, the public
have the opportunity, by means of a vote, to say whether
or not they should be confirmed in their appointment. If
they are confirmed, they serve until retirement, and are
thus removed from the political pressures which influence
judges who face regular re-election. This scheme would
seem to avoid some of the disadvantages of election, while
still leaving the public a say in the appointment of
judges. The judge influences his court not only directly, but also indirectly, since the judges often appoint
their own probation officers. The temptation is great for
elected judges to appoint party members who have been good
at campaigning - a quality not necessarily related to
skill in assessing and working with difficult children.

In twelve States juvenile court judges are appointed;
(13) by the Governor in nine States, by the President in
the District of Columbia, by the public welfare commission
in Utah, and by the presiding superior court judge in each
judicial district in Alaska.

Typically, judges are men, and in forty-one States they
must be attorneys. In a further five they must be a lawyer or have had previous judicial experience. Only five
States make no requirements beyond the necessity of the
judge being a 'man of upright character'. In addition to
legal requirements, in some States, like Delaware, a juvenile court judge must be 'knowledgeable about family and
child problems'.(14)

In many instances, the decision whether a child shall be
brought to a juvenile court and what the disposition shall
be are made, not by a juvenile court judge, but by a referee. Levin and Sarri point out the significance of this.
(15) While New York City has twenty-four juvenile court
judges, Los Angeles has only one judge, with twenty-four
referees. Consequently, information about the qualifications, methods of selection, and procedures followed by
referees takes on considerable importance in California. In
other States probation officers have the responsibility of
deciding whether a child is brought to court. For example,
in Connecticut, 90 per cent of all juvenile cases are
handled by an informal adjustment procedure that allows a
juvenile to be placed on probation without a judicial hearing. In this system, where the judge plays a decidedly
reduced role, the qualifications and supervision of probation officers assume greater importance.

Despite the significance of referees and probation officers in the juvenile justice system, few States have rules
governing their selection and conduct. In many States
the judge was wide discretion in selecting referees and
probation officers, and in delegating to them the perfor-

mance of judicial functions.

Twenty-eight States have statutory provisions for referees.(16) Of these, nine require a referee to have a law degree, although many referees in other States are also attorneys. Decisions by referees are not usually final in law, although probably in practice few juveniles or their families make use of their right of appeal to the judge, and where there is a requirement for a judicial review, it can be either a reality or a rubber stamp.

There is an amazing lack of any research findings on the social and educational background of juvenile court judges and referees. A study in 1962(17) of juvenile court judges is now out of date, and was based on a low return of questionnaires from 500 of a possible 3,000 juvenile court judges. It must thus be regarded with caution. The replies suggested that 96 per cent were male, the average age was fifty-three, 93 per cent were married and under 19 per cent divorced. The findings were summarised in two statements about the judges:

> They have more family and marital stability and have experience in the parental role and more commitments to social and middle class norms than the country as a whole and are a group of elected public servants with a background emphasizing public service as an antecedent to the judicial office.

Ninety per cent had been trained as lawyers. Forty-five per cent were elected; 22 per cent appointed and 33 per cent had an interim appointment and a subsequent election.

While juvenile court judges have not been selected for much research, sociologists and political scientists have, since Pritchett's(18) study of the Roosevelt Supreme Court in 1948 paid increasing attention to appeal courts and in particular to the United States Supreme Court. Using either a stimuli-organism-response model(19) or a systems approach the studies have concentrated on two areas: the relationship between the background characteristics of judges and their attitudes and the relationship between their attitudes and their decisions as shown in their votes in non-unanimous cases.

The studies attempting to relate background to attitude are somewhat contradictory. An early(20) study suggested that the more a State Supreme Court judge was tied by his background to the Southern States the more likely he was to have an anti-black attitude. The background attributes related to attitudes here were being a protestant, having held a State office before becoming a judge and being a Democrat. In a later study S. Nagel(21) has found that a conservative approach to criminal cases (i.e. supporting the State against the defendant) is associated with mem-

bership of the American Bar Association, having had a
former job as a prosecutor and being a protestant. Another study(22) however, also of Federal district court
judges, found no connection between background and attitudes as demonstrated by voting in non-unanimous cases.

More work has been done on the relationship of attitudes
to decision making. Pritchett(23) found what he described
as conservative and liberal blocks amongst Supreme Court
judges as revealed by their votes in non-unanimous decisions. Schubert, who developed Pritchett's work, explains
the meanings of these terms:(24)

> political liberalism is the belief in and the support
> of civil rights and liberties; political conservatism
> is the upholding of law and order and the defense of
> the status quo - no matter what may be the pattern of
> accepted values that the status quo happens to repre-
> sent. Social liberalism advocates egalitarianism in
> regard to political representation, citizenship, and
> ethnic status; social conservatism opposes equality
> of access to the polity, to the economy, and to so-
> ciety. Economic liberalism is the belief in and the
> support of a more equal distribution of wealth, goods,
> and services; the economic conservative defends pri-
> vate enterprise, vested interests, and broad differen-
> tials in wealth and income between laborers and the
> owners of property.

Researchers since Pritchett have found three groupings on
the Supreme Court, liberals, economic conservatives and
those politically conservative.(25) This three-fold division is confirmed by Snyder(26) who approached the Supreme
Court from the base of small group theory and found a
liberal, a conservative and what she called a pivotal
clique.

Interesting as these studies are, they are confined to
a small part of the influences acting upon the judges of a
very special kind of court, where no litigants ever appear
in person and where the great emphasis is placed upon verbal reasoning and legal argument.

Hogarth's(27) study of Ontario magistrates (who were
similar to British stipendary magistrates) comes nearer
both to dealing with an every day judicial situation and
to taking into account more of the variables which may
affect judicial decision making. This sophisticated study
cannot be summarised in a few words but the core of his
findings is to be found in the title of his book 'Sentencing as a Human Process' for 'sentencing is not a rational mechanical process. It is a human process and is
subject to all the frailties of the human mind'. Magistrates, he suggests, have attitudes which are linked to

their backgrounds and which predispose them to respond in
particular ways to certain crimes but their actual behaviour depends upon how they define the social and legal
constraints in the situation and their capacity - which
varies - to perceive and use complex information. Like all
humans they also tend to interpret cases, law, and others'
expectations in ways which help to minimise inconsistency
and thus protect their self concepts from threatening influences.

Another study has considered the behaviour of one man
judges in draft-evasion cases. Cook(28) suggested that it
was necessary to consider four factors which may affect
the decisions of these judges: attribute both ascribed and
achieved, reference groups, judicial role definitions and
values and attitudes. Some such factors are necessary to
explain between 15 and 40 per cent of the amount of variation between sentences, precedent and public opinion accounting for the remainder. No one has applied these findings to juvenile courts, but one might expect the factors
to account for a larger percentage of the variation there.
Public opinion is usually relatively unimportant in juvenile courts, where the restrictions on identifying juveniles tend to minimise the interest of the press. Precedent also plays only a small part because there are few
appeals in juvenile cases, and precedent is largely created
by appeal decisions.

Since most judges are lawyers, another way of discover-
ing their social and educational background is to explore
what is known about lawyers. What few studies there are of
the legal profession have not considered lawyers' backgrounds. The exception is 'Lawyers in the Making', a
study undertaken in 1961 of intending law students, which
concluded that 'in comparison with non lawyers, students
endorsing law as a career were significantly higher in
social status'.(29) The latter was measured by the occupation of the head of the student's household, parental educational levels and parental income. Law attracted a dis-
proportionate number of talented students from the June
1961 graduating class. This was not surprising since the
factors which predict academic success - female sex, high-
status families, Jewishness, and residence in a large city
also, with the exception of the sex factor predicted the
choice of law as a career. The most important single pre-
dictor, however, was having a lawyer father. This study
is out of date and changes in admission policies, particularly positive discrimination towards black and women
students, may have altered the profile of a typical entrant
to law. My own impression based on a small study of students entering a mid-west law school in 1970 and 1971 and

using Warkov's questionnaire is that while the situation
is no longer so clear cut as it was in 1961 the social
status of law students remains high. It is certain that
lawyers who become juvenile court judges are likely to have
come from more affluent families and to have had more academic success than the children who appear before them.

Within the legal profession however, juvenile court
judges do not rank highly, for neither financially nor
intellectually does the juvenile court compare with Wall
Street and the Supreme Court. There have been but few
nationally known juvenile court judges, and these were
mostly in office in the early years of the century, when
they were building a new institution. Even then, however,
their enthusiasm was more apparent than were their legal
and intellectual skills, and this is probably still true
today. In part the law schools are to blame. It is only
recently that juvenile court law has entered the curriculum
of law schools, and only as an elective course. Until the
Gault case in 1967, few law teachers would have thought of
offering such courses.

It is difficult to relate our scrappy knowledge about
who juvenile court judges are to the way in which they
might use their discretion. The fact that they sit alone
is likely to increase the influence of whatever are the
factors which affect decision making. Cook, in describing
judges in draft-evasion cases, says: 'The predictable product of normless and unsupervised decision making by judges
with weak communication links is extreme variation along
the continuum of choice'.(30) Juvenile court judges are
in such a position. They are caught between the norms of
a criminal justice, welfare and community approach, and
they sit alone. Referees may or may not be so free. For
some the supervision by the juvenile court judge may be a
reality and, if so, some similarity will develop in the
decisions and dispositions of the referees subject to the
supervision of one judge.

Magistrates

If our knowledge of juvenile court judges is limited, so
also is our knowledge of English magistrates. A group with
a long history, they have been used by kings and govern-
ments for the management of local law, order and administration. They are appointed for life to each commission of
the peace by the Lord Chancellor, on the recommendations
of the Lord Lieutenant of the county. There used to be
considerable public uncertainty about how a person came to
be suggested for consideration as a magistrate. Now the

situation has been clarified in a government publication,
'Justices of the Peace: How they are appointed: What they
do'. Justices are appointed by the Lord Chancellor or the
Chancellor of the Duchy of Lancaster, acting mostly on the advice of Advisory Committees which cover non-metropolitan
counties and districts of such counties. The membership of
these committees is said to be drawn from all sections of
the local community, but to avoid members being subjected to
undesirable influences their names are not usually made
public. Any one can put forward a name, including their own,
as a possible magistrate but nominations from recognised organisations may, according to the Magistrates Association,
(32) carry more weight. Some Advisory Committees are making
public announcements at the time of the year when they are
open to accept nominations, in order to secure more openness rather than to attract additional names, of which they
have more than enough. Any British subject is eligible to
serve as a justice, but as the Magistrates Association point
out the following will not be appointed:

1 a person over 60 years of age;
2 a person convicted of certain offences, or subject
   to certain Court orders;
3 an undischarged bankrupt;
4 a person whose sight or hearing is impaired, or who
   by reason of infirmity cannot carry out all the duties
   of a justice;
5 a serving member of Her Majesty's Forces; a member of
   the Police;
6 close relations of a person who is already a Justice
   on the same bench.

They go on to comment that political views are neither a
qualification nor a disqualification for appointment as a
Justice of the Peace. The Lord Chancellor when making
appointments does enquire about political affiliations,
but only to make sure that no Bench becomes unduly over-
weighted in favour of any one political party; nor should
it be over-weighted by any other sectional interest.

Juvenile court magistrates are elected for a three-year
period from their own number by the total group of magistrates forming the Commission of the Peace in a petty sessional division. Those so elected then choose their own
chairman. As we have seen, there are some rather vague
requirements that too many juvenile court magistrates
should not be of grandparent age, and should have some particular experience or knowledge of children. Whether or
not they have this, we do not know, although there is a
feeling that teachers are prominently - perhaps too prominently - represented.

The major source of information about magistrates is

Hood's(33) study undertaken in 1966 when, as part of his
research into the sentencing of motoring offences, he collected information about 500 magistrates in three areas
covering sixteen counties. This included their age, educational background, occupation, political affiliations,
newspaper reading habits. He found the youngest was
twenty-nine and the oldest seventy-four but three-quarters
were over fifty and one-third had retired. One-quarter
had been at elementary school, leaving at fourteen, one-
third at public schools and 35 per cent had been in full
time higher education. They were more likely than the
general population to be party members and when asked how
they would vote 50 per cent said Conservative, 10 per cent
Liberal and 33 per cent Labour. Three-quarters read the
'Guardian', 'The Times' or 'Telegraph'.

Hood also administered personality tests and found that
as a group magistrates were stable introverts, which means
they tend to be thoughtful, controlled and reliable.

Hood's study supports the widely-held view that magistrates tend to over-represent the professions and older
people, and to include few working-class and working people. The Royal Commission on the Justices of the Peace
(34) in 1948 found that 67 per cent were professionals,
employers or self-employed, 13 per cent were salaried and
15 per cent wage-earners. Hood compared these 1947 figures
with his own collected in 1966. A third source is provided by a study in 1974 of magistrates sitting in the Crown
Courts in the Oxford and Midlands circuit.(35) Although
the three sources are not strictly comparable they do still
suggest that the occupational background of magistrates has
changed little over the past twenty-seven years except that
there has been an increase in the number of professional
people on the commission.

TABLE 9.1 Occupational background of magistrates
(percentages)

Royal Commission 1947		Hood's study 1966-7	Hawker's study 1974	
Without gainful occupation	3.5	0.8	Unknown	4.3
Professional	21.3	30.8		41.9
Employers, managers	30.0	21.8		24.3
In business on own account	16.5	14.6	Sales	6.4
Salaried	13.7	11.4	Clerical	5.7
Wage earners	15.0	15.9	Manual	8.8
			Service	1.5
Farmers	-	4.3	Agricul-tural	7.1

Since juvenile court magistrates (except in London) are drawn from magistrates and not from the general population, they are likely to show the same characteristics. However, juvenile court panels almost certainly include more women proportionately than does the full Commission which in 1975 contained on the active list 12,946 men and 6,508 women. A higher ratio would be necessary to meet the legal requirement that there be one woman amongst the three magistrates comprising each juvenile court bench. How juvenile court magistrates use their discretion in sentencing and how this relates to their personal characteristics we do not know since the only studies are now out of date.(36)

Unlike juvenile court judges in the United States, magistrates are not required to be legally trained, and few of them are in fact lawyers. They are assisted in court by the Clerk to the Justices, who is a lawyer of at least five years' standing. His role is to advise the magistrates on the law, but not on the decisions they make. This is a nice distinction and it works with different degrees of success in different juvenile courts. There have been no studies of the interaction of clerks and magistrates in juvenile courts, so it is difficult to comment upon the clerk's part in the magistrates' decision making. What the clerk's presence should ensure is that the magistrates keep within the law, and his being part of the court allows magistrates to bring to the court room experience of many kinds, other than those provided by a legal education.

There have been continuous complaints about magistrates in general and juvenile court magistrates in particular. They are based on one major ground: that magistrates by their age, education, social background and life experience are out of touch with the children and young people appearing before them, and are ill-equipped to make decisions as to the best treatment for them. We do know that finding younger magistrates is difficult. The survey reported in the fifth report of the Children's Branch in 1938(37) found that the greatest number of juvenile court magistrates were to be found in the sixty to sixty-nine age brackets, 2,013 men and 637 women, whereas only 591 men and 174 women were aged under fifty. Again in 1967 the command paper on the Training of Justices of the Peace reported:(38) 'It is extremely difficult to find men and women between the ages of 30 and 45 who can spare enough time'. This paper however does not say what attempts had been made, and one is left with the suspicion that the problem might lie in the image of a magistrate held by the Lord Chancellor, or by those who recommend to him, rather than

in a lack of potential candidates. Mentioning thirty as
if it were the lower age limit adds substance to this suspicion.

Hawker's(39) study showed the following age structure in
1974 but his study included all magistrates in a Midlands
area and not only those on the juvenile court panel.

Age group	% of magistrates
- 34	1.2
35 - 39	4.0
40 - 44	10.1
45 - 49	18.0
50 - 54	20.1
55 - 59	17.4
60 - 64	14.0
65 - 69	10.8
70	1.0
No answer	3.4

Age, however, is not the only barrier. Social class and
lack of knowledge are others, and the latter has been
tackled to some extent since the introduction in 1967
of required training for juvenile court magistrates. Up
to this time only a few Magistrate Courts Committees had
been administering special training schemes for their
juvenile court magistrates, despite encouragement from the
Royal Commission in 1948 and the publication of a model
scheme by the Lord Chancellor's office in 1958. The 1967
command paper outlined a syllabus for juvenile court justices which included observation in juvenile courts,
visits to institutions and special instruction. It was
designed to enable justices to:(40)

1   understand the place of the Juvenile Court in the judi-
    cial system and certain special aspects of procedure
    in Juvenile Courts;
2   appreciate the social and educational background of
    juveniles before the Court;
3   know the services available to them, particularly the
    educational, medical and psychiatric services;
4   learn the various courses which may be taken in deal-
    ing with juveniles who are brought before the Court,
    whether as offenders or in need of care and protec-
    tion or control, so that they understand the nature
    and purpose of the sentences which they impose, and
    the other methods of treatment which they may use,
    and their effect.

Such a method of training, which consists essentially
of socialisation into the existing practices of the juvenile court and of the treatment institutions serving the
court, is likely to reinforce the status quo. It may thus

add to the conservative force which juvenile court magistrates already, by their age and their background, bring
to decision making. This is perhaps particularly unfortunate, because magistrates are dealing at times with
care and protection situations in which the norms change
rapidly from one generation to another. A good many cases
magistrates hear may concern adolescent sexual behaviour,
in which the norms have certainly changed out of all recognition since most people who serve as magistrates were
themselves adolescent.

Unlike judges in the United States, English juvenile
court magistrates do not sit alone. The rules require
that three justices sit together and that one of them be a
woman. Such a combination should prevent the more bizarre
behaviour which may result from single-person decisions.
It may also tend to keep decisions within the middle range
and so cut out the original as well as those on the lunatic
fringe.

It is very difficult to remove a magistrate from office.
Since 1941, the Lord Chancellor can move to the supple-
mental list any justice who, through age or infirmity, is
unfit to carry on. However, this is less likely to apply
to juvenile court magistrates, who must cease to serve on
the juvenile panel when they become sixty-five years old.
The fact that they have to be re-elected to the panel every
three years also provides some protection for the juvenile
panel from the most prejudiced or inept magistrates.

Sheriffs and panel members

In Scotland, the decision as to whether a situation giving
jurisdiction exists and the decision as to disposition,
which are taken by the same people in the United States
and England, are split. When there is a dispute as to the
grounds for a hearing, the matter is referred to the
sheriff. The panel members make only the decision as to
disposition.

Sheriffs are judges, appointed by the Secretary of
State on behalf of the Queen. Their courts deal with both
civil and criminal matters, and before 1970, in many parts
of Scotland, they dealt with all juveniles. They are all
lawyers and they sit alone. In these ways they resemble
judges in the United States, but their prestige is greater
and they probably come from a narrower social and educational grouping. Scotland's total population is only
5,211,700, and each professional group tends to be close-
knit and its individual members well-known to each other.
In cases referred by the panel for decision on the facts,

the sheriff's discretion is limited. All he is asked to
do is to decide on the facts, and the decision as to guilt
or innocence - with which this decision is comparable - is
highly structured by precedent and legal rules. In this
area, the sheriff's more personal views and values have
little influence. However, the sheriff also deals with a
number of children who enter the hearing system only at
his discretion, for, as we saw earlier, Scotland has a
dual system of juvenile justice. When a child who is not
subject to a supervision requirement is charged with an
offence in the sheriff or High Court, and pleads or is
found guilty, the sheriff can make an order for disposition in accordance with the Criminal Procedure (Scotland)
Act, 1975. On the other hand, he can, if he wishes, remit
the case to the reporter for disposal by the hearing, or
may request the advice of the hearing as to the treatment
of the child. In the latter case the sheriff is under no
obligation to accept the advice he is given. Where a child
is already subject to a supervision requirement, the sheriff must seek the hearing's advice and can then either remit the case to the hearing or deal with it himself. The
sheriff thus has a wide range of choice in dealing with
those juveniles charged before him, and as yet we know
little about the criteria on which sheriffs exercise their
discretion. They are required to consider the welfare of
the child, but the very fact that they are dealing with the
case suggests that the Lord Advocate and his staff consider
that this particular child must be dealt with, not by a
hearing whose sole responsibility is the child's welfare,
but by a court where the protection of the public and the
demands of deterrence are important considerations.

The number of children who become subject to the courts
is considerable. In 1974, 2,900(41) children were proceeded against in courts, 31,524(42) referrals were made
to reporters and thus the children who were the subject
of these referrals did not enter the criminal justice system. 11,466 children were dealt with by police warnings
or liaison schemes. Of the 2,900 charged, 1,392 were
referred to a hearing for advice and of these 212 were remitted to a hearing for disposal. In addition 208 were
remitted from the courts to a hearing without a previous
referral for advice. The figures available for 1975 show
that 2,262 children were proceeded against in courts.

Children's panel members are a new group on the juvenile justice scene. They were conceived by the Kilbrandon Committee(43) as the people who would translate into
practice the ideas of social education on which the report
was based. The White Paper, Social Work and the Community,(44) while spelling out the task of panel members

also exposed difficulties inherent in the idea of finding
people who both represented - in some symbolic and experi-
ential way - the community from which troubled children
were likely to come, and at the same time were individually
suitable for the task. The task, it must be remembered,
was to implement an approach in which the needs of the
child were to be the only consideration. Retribution and
general deterrence were to have no place in this new system. Mapstone points out the difficulty:(45)

It seems clear that the values implicit in Kilbrandon,
the White Paper and the Social Work (Scotland) Act
are most likely to be held by professional people,
least likely to be common in those working class neigh-
bourhoods from which children coming before the Hearings
are likely to be drawn. As comparative studies of child
rearing and language use have shown, the very process
of discussing reasons for, and results of, behaviour is
typical of white-collar families, unfamiliar in the
homes of manual workers. Similarly the different social groups have dissimilar views of interpersonal problems; the concept of considered treatment as opposed
to repressive, short-term control measures is likely
to find a more ready acceptance among middle-class
workers and their wives. If, as Smith and May suggest,
the concept of 'community involvement' might be taken
to imply a system of justice reflecting the neighbourhood values and standards, then these would probably
be retributive in character; more likely perhaps to
result in the kind of direct action towards deviants
taken by dwellers in the Bogside than the treatment-
based measures of the Social Work (Scotland) Act.

Studies of panel members suggest that the selectors
concentrate on personal suitability and, only in making
up the final panel when they were choosing from amongst
a small group considered personally suitable, do they consider the structure of the panel as a whole and its need
to involve and represent the community.(46) Personal suitability seems to have included a capacity to understand
written reports, to be able to talk in group situations,
and the acceptance of an approach to problem solving which
involves reflection on causes and on the meaning of behaviour. Taken together, the studies of panel membership
suggest that there is a higher representation of people
from social class I and II than in the general population
and an over-representation from areas within cities with
a high status residentially. Of the first 1,200 panel
members 50 per cent were graduates of colleges and universities and 15 per cent manual workers. Housewives and
teachers form the main occupational groups, and while men

and women are fairly equally represented, the younger and
the older age groups are not as fully represented on the
panel as in the general population. Despite what must be
seen as failures if community representation is considered
important, the panels certainly contain a wider cross-
section of society than was present amongst the sheriffs
and justices who operated Scotland's old juvenile justice
system. In particular, they are free from any close relationships with the legal profession.

The methods of recruitment of panel members were designed to attract people from all walks of life, and this
is the continuing aim whenever more panel members are
needed. Advertisements are put in local papers, and this
appears to be the most successful recruiting method. Few
people came forward as a result of radio or television advertisements, but a significant group came as a result of
personal approaches, and there is some evidence to suggest
that this method was particularly important in gaining
working-class recruits. However, the recruitment is biased
towards middle age and middle-income groups, and the bias
is in those who offer themselves as recruits, and is not
created by the selection from amongst recruits. It seems
that the panel membership reflects the background typical
of those who volunteer for public service in Britain. It
may be that the factors which make them volunteer, which
are likely to include a feeling of confidence and of having something to offer to other people, are less prevalent
amongst adults in areas from which most children come who
appear before panels.

Panel members are selected from recruits by the CPAC by
means of individual and group interviews. Each of the original CPAC areas had slightly different methods of selection, and the new regional CPAC also vary in the methods
they use. However, it seems they are continuing to use as
criteria for selection the personal attitudes similar to
those outlined by Clarke, when he was discussing selection
in Moray and Nairn prior to regionalisation. These criteria were:(47)

1 Freedom from unreasonable prejudice and bias.
2 Ability and willingness to consider and evaluate
   reports.
3 Ability to appreciate or to learn to appreciate other
   people's problems.
4 Ability to manage the responsibilities of a panel
   member without undue stress.
5 Ability to discuss issues and to give their own
   opinion simply.

Once selected, new members are required to undergo
training, which is currently the responsibility of the

Social Work Services Group who have arranged for it to be
organised under the auspices of Glasgow, Edinburgh, Dundee
and Aberdeen universities. Training involves sitting in
on hearings, and also lectures and discussions on the legal
aspects of the system, the resources available in the form
of supervision, intermediate treatment, residential homes
and schools, communication and interviewing and some aspects of child development. It is very hard to know what
people who are selected for their 'layness', and as volunteers, should be given as training. Clearly they should
not be turned into either lawyers or social workers. One
theory is that the emphasis should be on enabling panel
members to form pressure groups to demand resources for
children in trouble and to educate the local community
about children's problems. This would be in line with the
community approach. Another group emphasises the need for
panel members to learn how to talk with children and parents, and to have some awareness of their own biases
about children, parents and child-rearing practices. This
approach reflects welfare thinking.

Panel members are appointed by the Secretary of State
on the recommendation of the local Children's Panel Advisory Committee for a three-year period. They can then
be re-appointed on the recommendation of the panel chairman. At the time of writing the Secretary of State has
not decided whether panel members can be re-appointed
without limit of terms, but there is some pressure on him
to limit re-appointments to two, so that no panel member
serves for more than nine consecutive years. The second
round of appointments and re-appointments is now over, but
it is too soon to say whether the new panels reflect different background characteristics. There have been suggestions that Glasgow, which was less-fully studied than
other areas, has managed to achieve a wider class and age
distribution. The fact that panel chairmen recommend members for re-appointment may result in the panels coming to
value the status quo. Certainly, there was considerable
anxiety amongst existing Grampian panel members that new
members might not accept 'the philosophy of the panel',
by which they meant the interpretation of the Kilbrandon
report and the Social Work (Scotland) Act, which they had
come to share.

Like English juvenile court justices, panel members sit
in threes, but the same members will not necessarily sit
together at all frequently. In cities, where Hearings are
held regularly, the rota system results in panel members
sitting in different combinations and with a different
member as Hearing chairman. In rural areas Hearings are
infrequent and so, although the panel is small, its members

may not meet often. The result of this may be that panel
members usually work in a new situation so far as their
colleagues are concerned. According to group studies, it
seems likely that the newness of the Hearing group will
affect the way members use their discretion. They are
unlikely to get themselves built into roles in the three-
some and thus liable always to behave in a particular way.
On the other hand, new groups are extremely threatening
and uncomfortable, and this may make people either more
than usually careful in the exercise of their discretion
or more than usually wild. The threat of the situation
is increased by the fact that most discussion about the
final decision as to what to do with the child takes place
in the open. Unlike magistrates in juvenile courts, panel
members seldom retire to consider their decision; they
arrive at it in open discussion with the child, the family
and the social worker.

THE GATE KEEPERS - REPORTERS, SOCIAL WORKERS, PROBATION
OFFICERS AND POLICE

We have been considering the people who make decisions
about the facts and the disposition in juvenile justice.
It can be argued that the much more important decision
rests with those who decide which children shall be chan-
nelled into the system in the first place. In many instances, particularly where an offence may be involved,
this decision is made in two stages. First, the police
will decide whether to caution or warn the child themselves, or perhaps to refer him or her to the police liaison scheme. If they decide that something more is required,
they then refer the child on to the other gate keepers. The
process differs in each of the three countries.

In Scotland, if a child has committed an offence, he is
first considered by the police, and they decide whether to
deal with him themselves or whether to refer him to the
official gate keeper of the Hearing system, the reporter.
This is a new position created by the Social Work (Scotland)
Act. All children who are considered by anyone to be in
need of compulsory measures of care are referred to the reporter. There is no other way into the system, and the reporter has absolute discretion to decide whether or not
compulsory measures may be necessary.

Reporters are appointed by the local authority, but
cannot be dismissed by them, and are thus free to make
decisions about children without fear of control from the
body which appointed them. There have been few guidelines
as to the sort of people reporters should be, apart from

the requirement that they should have some legal knowledge.
There are twelve regional reporters, forty-nine full time
deputes and assistants and twelve part time. The background qualifications of the regional reporters in 1975
were:

Legal	4
Social Work	4
Minister of Religion	1
Police	2
Prison Service	1

At present there is no training for reporters beyond short
induction courses and brief in-service courses, which aim
to develop the social-work knowledge of legally-qualified
reporters and the legal knowledge of those with a social-
work background. This situation is likely to change. In
July 1975, in the case of *Kennedy* v. *O'Donnell*,(48) the
Court of Session held that reporters who did not possess a
practising certificate from the Law Society of Scotland
had no right of audience in the High Court or the Sheriff
Court. Of the sixty-one reporters, a maximum of sixteen
had such a certificate and, as a result of the decision,
only these reporters could in future present the facts of
a case to the sheriff, where these were in dispute, or
appear in appeals. The Association of Reporters began to
press for amending legislation to include reporters amongst
those given right of audience. They also emphasised the
training needs of their members and their concern to establish appropriate standards of pleading. By a fortunate chance these events coincided with the final stages
of the Children Act becoming law and in November 1975 a
clause was inserted which gave to reporters with one year's
experience the right of audience.(49) The Act also included a clause by which the Secretary of State undertook to
develop qualifying courses for reporters which would meet
the approval of the Lord Advocate.

At the time of writing, discussions have started in the
Advisory Council on Social Work about the nature of this
training. It seems generally agreed that reporters are
required to straddle criminal justice and welfare approaches. They need an understanding of criminal law,
criminal procedure and the rules of evidence to carry out
the very small part of their job which relates to court
practice, but they also need a general understanding of
legal rights to ensure fairness in the hearings. On the
welfare side, their function is to consider the needs of
the child, and this requires an understanding of social
and emotional situations as they affect and are affected
by young people. In addition, reporters need to be able
to run a complex administration which depends upon the

goodwill and commitment of volunteers. These discussions
about training for reporters offer a very interesting example of an attempt to integrate the criminal justice and
the welfare approach, with a slight acknowledgment of the
existence of a community approach as well.

Before leaving the gate keeper in Scotland, it should
be noted that access to the other part of Scotland's juvenile justice system is through the regular channels of
criminal justice. In 1970 the Lord Advocate instructed
chief constables that certain kinds of criminal cases involving juveniles were to be reported to the procurator
fiscal who was then to decide whether to refer the case to
the reporter or to institute proceedings. Later the Lord
Advocate restricted the discretion of the fiscal by stating that no child under thirteen should be charged without
reference to the Crown Office and that where a child was
involved in an offence jointly with an adult the child
should be charged only where this was essential. Procurators fiscal are all legally trained and are appointed
by the Lord Advocate on a full-time basis, except in some
rural areas. Although the Lord Advocate, the Solicitor
General and the six Crown counsel normally change with a
change of government, the procurators fiscal do not.

Much of what has been said about the implications of a
legal education for judges in the United States applies to
procurators fiscal, except that in Scotland they are even
less likely than in the United States to have any teaching
about human relationships and juvenile delinquency. They
are likely to approach decisions about whether to prosecute juveniles in the same way as they approach decisions
about prosecution of adults, which, as we will see in
chapter ten are based upon a criminal justice approach.

The gate keepers in the English system are much less-
clearly defined than they are in Scotland, partly because
the Children and Young Persons Act, 1969 has not been fully
implemented. Both the police and the local authority
social workers may be involved in decisions as to whether
a child or young person is to be brought to court. In
England the police are both law enforcement officers and
prosecutors, an unfortunate dual role which they are not
called upon to occupy in Scotland or the United States.
The 1969 Act recognised this dual role in attempting to
establish consultation between police and social service
departments over the decision to refer to a juvenile court.
The structure provides the possibility for a meeting between those who hold a criminal justice and those who hold
a welfare approach. Unlike the systems in Scotland or the
United States, the English system, as envisaged in the 1969
Act, is more openly a compromise. It does not require one

person to balance the diverse approaches and make an individual decision.

We have already looked at how training may influence the use of discretion by the police, and we will consider the training and background characteristics of social workers and probation officers in connection with their other roles in the juvenile justice system. Before leaving the gate keepers, we should consider who has this role in the United States' system. Although there is variation between States, broadly speaking juveniles reach the court in two ways. Either as the result of a petition made or approved by the probation officer, acting on the delegated authority of the judge, or by arrest by the police or probation officer. Increasingly arrest is sanctioned either by a court order or a Hearing, although these usually take place after the child has been placed in detention. Fifteen states have no requirement that there be either a Hearing or a court order, and here the decision to arrest and detain, and later bring to an adjudication, rests with the peace officers, be they police or probation staff.

PROVIDING INFORMATION FOR AND INFLUENCING THE DECISION MAKERS

We have been considering the people in the juvenile justice system who are involved in three decisions: the decision to put a child or young person into the system, the decision as to the accuracy of the facts which are the reason for the child's appearance and the decision as to what to do with the child. These decisions involve the exercise of discretion since they are not controlled by rules. The system also allows for other people to attempt to influence the decision makers, and for information on which they can base their decisions to be made available to them. There can be no clear division between influencing and providing information in the juvenile justice system. They are activities along a continuum, and, although the emphasis in the role of defender or prosecutor may be to influence and the emphasis in the role of the person who makes the social enquiries to provide information, each role also carries some latitude to influence and some duty to inform the decision makers.

In the juvenile justice system in all three countries, someone presents the facts which they believe give the decision makers jurisdiction. In Scottish hearings this person is the reporter, who must explain to the hearing the grounds for thinking that the child is in need of compul-

sory measures of care. In the Sheriff Courts it is the
procurator fiscal. In England the facts are presented
either by the police, by a solicitor briefed by the police
or may, in care proceedings be presented by a social worker. In juvenile courts in the United States the probation
officer is the most likely person to be found presenting
the petition that the child be adjudicated delinquent, but
increasingly this role is being taken by the public prosecutor. When this occurs, the gate keeper and the person
who presents the facts to the decision makers are not the
same, since the prosecutor or district attorney is unlikely
to have made the decision to present a petition. He is
usually called in after the probation officer or the judge
has made the decision that a particular child shall be the
subject of a petition.

This entry of the prosecutor on the juvenile justice
scene in the United States is a direct result of the appearance in juvenile courts of more defence council. So long
as children went undefended, probation officers or the
judge himself could take the role of prosecutor, defender
and information provider. Once a defence lawyer appeared,
the system became lopsided and prosecutors began to come in
to ensure that the facts were fully presented.

A survey in 1973 of sixty-eight large city juvenile
courts in the United States showed that in sixty-four a
lawyer made regular appearances as prosecutor or state representative.(50) This is an increase from 1963 when
Skoler and Tenney, in a similar survey, found that the
State was represented on a regular basis in only about 15
per cent of metropolitan courts.(51) This illustrates a
shift towards a criminal justice model, and this is inten-
sified because of the way the prosecutor is likely to play
his role. Prosecutors are part of the criminal justice
system. They are lawyers who are elected locally, and who
often regard their position as a stepping-stone to judicial office. Traditionally and personally, they are under
more pressure than are procurators fiscal, perhaps even
than are the English police, to win the cases they prosecute. They tend to put the protection and satisfaction of
the public before the individual needs of offenders. In
moving into juvenile courts they are likely to be influenced by their traditional role in adult criminal courts.
Their new role in juvenile courts has been little explored,
but Feldman, in an article about the prosecutor's special
task in juvenile delinquency proceedings, seems to suggest
that the prosecutor should support the treatment orientation of the juvenile court 'except when public safety requires institutionalisation'.(52) This avoids the question
which is how to decide when it is necessary for public

safety. The likelihood is that the role and professional
training of the prosecutor may make him consider this a
necessity in situations which to a social worker would
appear to involve minimal risk.

The prosecutor has appeared, it seems, to balance the
defence counsel, another newcomer to juvenile justice. In
Scotland and England lawyers seldom appear to represent
children, but since Gault they are increasingly to be seen
in the juvenile courts of the United States. In the survey
conducted by the Centre for Judicial Studies(53) in 1973,
in 62 per cent of the cities involved, more than 75 per
cent of juveniles involved in delinquency cases based upon
a felony or serious crime, were represented by counsel.
The problem lawyers are facing in this new role illustrates
on an individual level the problems which face the system
in maintaining a balance between the welfare and the criminal justice model. Unlike the role of fact finder or
decision maker, the role of prosecutor and defender in
juvenile justice is in the process of being defined. The
role is as yet unsupported by established norms, and so
leaves more scope for individually inspired role performances. The question for the defence attorney, which has
been discussed in a host of law journal articles in the
United States in recent years, is whether he shall defend
his client as he would an adult client in a criminal court,
or whether the fact that juvenile courts are concerned with
children's needs somehow changes his role, if not into an
ally of the court, at least into an interpreter to the
child of the court's policy. Treadwell poses the questions:(54)

> Thus it is that the attorney who approaches the juve-
> nile court with substantial information in hand is
> nevertheless confronted with the basic problem of ap-
> pearing in that court; namely, is he an advocate, in
> the traditional legal sense of the term, defending in
> every available, ethical way, the rights of his
> juvenile client? Or is he a legal officer doing
> social work - a socio-legal worker so to speak, striv-
> ing to conciliate conflicting parties in a manner that
> will serve the ultimate 'best interests' of the juve-
> nile? Or is his responsibility some kind of an amal-
> gamation of the two roles, so that he is at times an
> unrelenting legal advocate for his client, and at other
> times a willing social disciplinarian of the youth?

Defending a child as you would an adult means getting
and using every technical point to avoid a finding of delinquency, including perhaps the very dubious methods, from
a welfare viewpoint, of plea bargaining and playing for delay. If an adjudication of delinquency is made, the

defence attorney then views the dispositional alternative
as a tariff system, and makes every effort to pay the lowest price. Unless the child wants to leave home, the defence attorney will oppose all residential solutions, even
if the child's home is unsuitable in every imaginable
way. To do otherwise is unethical according to a comment
in 'Trial':(55)

> If a juvenile does not desire incarceration in a reform
> school, he has a right to a lawyer who will defend him
> vigourously and to the best of his ability - one who
> will consider it his obligation to prevent that result
> if possible.
>
> A lawyer who would fail to do that because he feels
> that his client might benefit from a court-imposed
> treatment program is behaving unethically.

In practice, few defence attorneys, especially when they
are appointed or are public defenders, adopt such a role.
Their position in the court system and their particular
training make such a clear-cut position unlikely.

Platt(56) has explored the way the public defender
operates in one large city court. He tends to select some
children as good, and with them he plays the classic defender role. In order to do this and remain part of the
court system, he compromises other children. Some he considers bad, and so in their case he allows the system to
take its course. The basis on which these decisions as
to goodness or badness are made are necessarily superfi-
cial. Lawyers are not trained in either sociology or psychology, and their assessment is strongly influenced by
external facts and first impressions. Another reason why
lawyers find it hard to take an uncompromising defence line
in the juvenile court is that they are adults, and it is
very difficult for adults in our western society to believe
that children might know what they want and should be allowed to act on this belief. Lawyers may have particular
difficulty here, as they tend to have, or acquire in training, a marked respect for established authority.

We have considered laymen and lawyers and the various
roles they carry within juvenile justice. We now turn to
social workers and probation officers. Both terms are
necessary and for two reasons. The simple reason is that
in Scotland probation officers no longer exist. Their
functions and many of them in person have been incorporated
into local authority social work departments. No separate
probation department exists in Scotland. The other reason
is that the term probation officer at least raises the
possibility that the officer operates from a value base
different from that generally accepted by social workers.
This is particularly the case in the United States, where

many probation officers consider themselves a part of the corrections system rather than a part of the profession of social work.

The role of English probation officer may also be ambiguous. Carlen, in a study of a London magistrate's court, comments on the:(57)

ambivalence of the probation officer concerning the nature of their relationship to the court. Who is their client? Is it the court or is it the defendant? If the client is the court then how does the probation officer stand in relation to the court? Is he by definition an agent of social control or is he a professional offering his services to the court?

There is no general British research into the social and educational backgrounds of social workers, so we cannot know the personal factors which might influence their use of discretion. What they are required to do is to provide information about the child's emotional and social background, the locality he comes from and the school he attends, to help those who decide whether the child shall enter the system and what treatment, if any, he shall receive. This is always the role of the social worker, but they may also, in the United States and England, actually fill the role of gate keeper; they may be required to act as the State's representative in presenting the reasons why compulsory powers should be exercised, and they may take upon themselves the role of defender. The social worker performs any of these tasks in the knowledge that he or she may, once the hearing is finished, have an ongoing relationship with the child and his family.

We know very little of how social workers and probation officers use their discretion in performing these tasks. What we do know suggests that they are little concerned about clients' rights. Recent research(58) into the making of reports for the courts by English probation officers suggests that they value highly, far too highly, one might suggest, their own assessments of individuals, and also what these individuals tell them. They seem to pay little attention to factual information, such as previous offences, or even the details of the current offence. It seems as if professional social workers have difficulty in reconciling their role of providing information for the court with their possible future role of supervisor to a probationer. Their behaviour may be functional for building a working relationship, but it is disfunctional in giving the court accurate information on which to reach a decision. If this is the situation with English probation officers in adult courts, who at least acknowledge their position as officers of the court, it is most likely that

social workers from local authority departments serving
juvenile courts and children's hearings may show similar
tendencies. Social workers share with all other members
of the juvenile court system the problem of managing the
conflicts between welfare and justice approaches within
themselves in such a way that they can perform their roles
in the system. Hardiker's(59) study of a small group of
probation officers showed how they did this in practice.
She was interested in whether probation officers held a
treatment ideology (as defined by May, see p. 12) both in
theory and in their practice as shown in the recommendations in their social enquiry reports. She concluded that
whatever the probation officers said in theory, in practice they all held a treatment ideology in some cases.
Their ideology seemed to be a result of the interpretation they put upon the offence. If they saw it as a cry
for help their recommendation seemed to imply a treatment
ideology whereas if they saw the offence as a prank it
would not. When the offender had a serious criminal history and a stressful social background probation officers
were likely to show the influence of a treatment ideology
in their recommendations. There is, however, some doubt
whether this was cause or effect although Hardiker argues
it was probably the latter. She also found that probation
officers were more likely to hold a treatment ideology
towards adults than towards juveniles.

Many people working as probation officers in the United
States see themselves as part of corrections, and carry
out their job as if it were simply to be an agent of the
court and a representative of society. Many probation officers have had no training and are appointed by the judge,
who is himself untrained in social work. Their allegiance
is to the judge, and they have no outside professional body
to serve as a reference point. Professional social work
in the United States still tends to ignore probation as
part of its arena, and, as a result, probation officers
become bureaucrats of the courts, carrying out the wishes
of the judge. This is Emerson's view:(60)

The probation officer's primary responsibility, however,
is to the judge and not to the public or any outside
agency. Hence it is generally more important for him
to consider how the judge will react to a recommendation or to a report on how he has handled a case than
it is for him to worry about what the public might say.

This attempt to link what is known about background and
training of police, lawyers and social workers with their
use of discretion is extremely unsatisfactory for two
reasons. There is an almost total lack of research into
background characteristics, and very few studies of the

sociology and philosophy of these occupational and professional groups. Added to this is the difficulty that we
do not know, except in a general commonsense way, how these
factors may relate to the use of discretion in particular
roles.

However, the United States research on judicial decision
making does provide some theoretical models which may be
useful in conceptualising the use of discretion in the
juvenile justice system. Figure 1 which is based on a
figure of Sheldon's (61) offers a way of thinking about how
magistrates or panel members reach decisions.

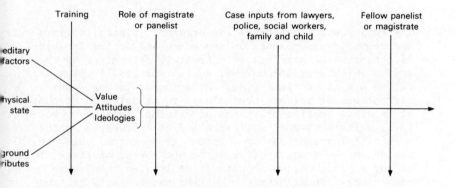

Figure 1   Factors shaping the decisions of Magistrates
or Panel Members.

Chapter ten

Recognising and controlling discretion

The relative influences of the criminal justice, welfare
and community approaches on procedure and action in juvenile courts and hearings is ultimately determined by the
way in which decision makers, social workers, lawyers and
police use their discretion. My argument is that considerations of welfare need always to be balanced by those
of criminal justice and those of criminal justice by welfare, while both must influence and be influenced by the
possibilities inherent in a community approach. History
has shown the dangers of ignoring one aspect of these competing approaches, which paradoxically also compliment
each other. In all three countries there exists the possibility of a swing towards repressive and punitive measures in response to the increasing violence and serious
crime amongst young people. This seems particularly likely in Britain where, because of the economic situation, resources for a welfare approach are in short supply, and
the magistrates and panel members feel powerless. In such
a situation shifts may take place in the balance of the
system which are not the result of any conscious policy
but can arise in two circumstances. They can occur because of a failure to recognise that there are different
approaches to juvenile justice and that the system is required to balance these and, in order to do so, has to ensure that each approach is represented in a court or a
hearing. Shifts may also occur because individuals may
not use their discretion consistently, or the use of discretion by individuals may change as one generation of
social workers and lawyers succeeds another. Such changes
may go unnoticed if the influence of discretion in the
system is not first acknowledged and then controlled.

ENSURING DIFFERENT APPROACHES

Everyone in the juvenile justice system has constantly to
balance within themselves the demands of the criminal justice, welfare and community approaches, but this does not
preclude the need for clarity about the primary responsibility carried by various actors. Someone must accept and
be accepted as having primary responsibility for putting
before the court or hearing the facts which suggest that
compulsory care may be required. Someone must put, and be
expected to put, the view of the child and his family, and
ensure that his rights are protected. Someone must give the
court information about the child's social, emotional and
community situation. The person in each role will be influenced by their own balancing of the different approaches,
but it is also clear that some roles involve a primary responsibility which is likely to affect whatever may be the
personal balance of the holder. The person giving the facts,
be he prosecutor, reporter or social worker, should be seen
as having a primary responsibility to show the interest of
the state which requires compulsory action. He may also
give information about a child's needs, or ensure that his
rights be protected, but these are secondary activities.
Similarly, the person to take the role of defence counsel,
be he lawyer or social worker, should be clearly responsible for stating the child's view and his wishes about
treatment, and for making sure that the emphasis upon welfare does not lead to a denial of rights or a failure to
acknowledge that the situation is one of compulsion. The
person in the social work role may add to the factual situation a comment on the dangers to the public, or may make
sure that families understand what rights they have, but
his primary responsibility is to give the court or hearing
information about the child's social and emotional needs.
Only the decision makers, the judges, magistrates and panel
members, do not have a bias towards a particular approach
built into their role, since their function is to balance
the various and, at times, conflicting demands of child,
family and society in the short and in the long term.
    If the people in the juvenile justice system are to be
clear about their primary responsibilities, some job descriptions or guide lines may be necessary. Leaving it to tradition,
personal inclination of the changes of professional education
seems to provide inadequate protection for the important social
values embedded in the different approaches. The guide lines
for the prosecutors in the Boston juvenile court, developed by the Center for Judicial Studies, (1) provide an
example of an attempt to acknowledge and clarify the responsibilities of the prosecutor, and, since such examples

are rare, they are quoted in full. They also illustrate
how guide lines serve not only to clarify roles, but also
to structure the discretion in the role, a point to which
we shall return later.

PROSECUTION GUIDELINES FOR BOSTON JUVENILE COURT

A. General principles for juvenile prosecution

   1.1. The prosecutor is an *advocate* of the State's interest
        in juvenile court. The 'State's interest' is com-
        plex and multivalued, and may vary with the type
        of proceeding and the nature of the particular case.
        Foremost, it includes: (a) protection of the commu-
        nity from the danger of harmful conduct by the res-
        traint and rehabilitation of juvenile offenders;
        and (b) concern, shared by all juvenile justice sys-
        tem personnel, as *parens patriae*, with promotion of
        the best interests of juveniles.
   1.2. To the extent that the State's interest in community
        protection may conflict with its interest as *parens
        patriae* in promoting the well-being of a particular
        child, the prosecutor will be required to balance the
        interests based upon the nature and facts of the par-
        ticular case. For example, to the extent that in-
        terests have to be balanced in given cases, the
        balance might be struck in favor of community pro-
        tection when the juvenile presents a substantial
        threat to community security but of promoting the
        well being of a child for most other types of sit-
        uations.
   1.3. In his role as *advocate*, the prosecutor has respon-
        sibility to ensure adequate preparation and presen-
        tation of the State's case, from the stage of police
        investigation through post-disposition proceedings.
        He is also committed generally to the advancement
        of legitimate law enforcement and child welfare
        goals by the participation of his office, together
        with other agencies such as the public defender's
        office, in drafting court rules and legislation, in
        appellate litigation, and in other activities which
        shape development of the law.
   1.4. Commitment to the rehabilitative philosophy of the
        juvenile court bars the use of certain penal objec-
        tives to achieve community security and protection.
        Retribution, for example, is not a proper goal of
        juvenile court prosecution.
   1.5. Since unnecessary exposure to juvenile court pro-

ceedings and to formal labeling and treatment in the
juvenile court process is often counter-productive
for many juveniles, the prosecutor's duty to promote
both the community's long-term security and the best
interest of particular juveniles requires him to
encourage and stimulate early diversion of cases
from the court and to strive for imposing the least
restrictive alternative available in dealing with a
juvenile throughout the juvenile justice process. It
also requires that a prosecutor proceed only on legally sufficient complaints or petitions even though
a juvenile may require treatment or other types of
assistance. Responsibility in this area is exercised by such means as issuing enforcement guidelines to the police, screening out deficient, insufficient, or trivial complaints, and actively en-
couraging and participating in efforts to refer juveniles to other agencies or reach agreement on other
acceptable dispositions in cases where court handling is not the best means for either protecting
the community or helping the juvenile.

1.6. The prosecutor shares the responsibility with other
juvenile court personnel to ensure that rehabilitative measures undertaken as alternatives to court
handling or pursuant to court-ordered disposition
are actually carried out, and that facilities and
services for treatment and detention meet proper
standards of quality.

1.7. The prosecutor has a duty to *seek justice* in juvenile
court by insisting upon fair and lawful procedures.
This entails the responsibility to ensure, for example, that baseless prosecutions are not brought,
that all juveniles receive fair and equal treatment,
that liberal discovery of the State's case is available to defense counsel, that exculpatory evidence
is made available to the defense, and that exces-
sively harsh dispositions are not sought. It also
entails the responsibility to oversee police inves-
tigative behavior to ensure its compliance with the
law.

The guide goes on to list a number of specific guidelines,
which include:

Court intake The prosecutor, in conjunction with probation staff, has an important role at court intake to
ensure that cases inappropriate for judicial handling,
and only such cases, are dismissed or diverted. Prior
to the filing of any complaint with the court the prosecutor should review the case to assess its merits.

He also has the primary responsibility to initiate proceedings to transfer cases for criminal trial.

Diversion of cases before adjudication   In suitable
instances the prosecutor should encourage the use of
consent decrees to avoid adjudication in cases in which
a complaint has been filed.

Preparation of cases for trial   The prosecutor has primary responsibility for preparing cases for trial,
including the selection, interviewing and summoning of
witnesses, and the conduct of further investigation
when necessary.

Disposition   If there is a finding of delinquency or
waywardness, the prosecutor should ensure that a fair
disposition hearing is held, and that appropriate recommendations for disposition are presented to the court.
In appropriate cases, he should make a recommendation as
to disposition based upon his own knowledge of the case.
The objective of the recommendation should be to secure
not the most severe disposition in each case, but one
entailing the minimum restriction on the child calculated to prevent further delinquency or waywardness.
To this end, the prosecutor should consult with probation staff and, if requested by counsel for the child,
should disclose the disposition recommendation he proposes to make to the court and the reasons therefor.

Personnel and training   Juvenile Court Prosecutors
should be members of the Bar. They should have demonstrated legal ability in the field of juvenile or criminal justice, demonstrated interest in the problems
of juvenile delinquency and a commitment to non-punitive responses to those problems.
   In addition to lawyers, the Office of Prosecution
should include adequate numbers of trained social workers, criminal investigators, and para-professionals in
law and social work.

These guide lines suggest that the prosecutor be asked
to balance the demands of a criminal justice and a welfare
approach in himself and in his own office. Where interests
conflict, however, his first responsibility is to protect
the community. By making this clear, the guide lines avoid
the danger that the prosecutor may usurp the role of the
judge, whose ultimate task is to balance conflicting interests.
   While clarifying roles is necessary, the present reality

is that some people are required to perform several different tasks in one hearing. Social workers may combine
the roles of prosecutor and defence counsel with their
special responsibility to provide information about the
child's needs. Magistrates and judges may act as defenders or prosecutors in an attempt to maintain a balance in
the hearing. Situations such as these create a conflict of
interest which it is exceedingly difficult for an individual to manage without damage to one or other side. Even
more vital, it is hard for the child or for society to
believe that their interests are protected when the same
person is asked to represent them both. Such a position
may be tenable in a voluntary situation, where the only
outcome can be one reached by agreement. This, however, is
not the situation in a juvenile court or hearing, which is
taking place for the very reason that compulsion may be
required. A similar danger that some interests are ignored
arises when one function is omitted from the proceedings;
when, for example, there is no one to protect the child's
rights or to make clear to the decision makers what are
his needs. Here the problem is not just to clarify roles,
but to find people to carry them.

To maintain the balance all three functions must be performed and, if the possibility of conflict of interest is
taken seriously, any court or hearing must have the assistance of three different persons, one to give the facts,
one to protect the child's rights, and one to provide information about his needs. In the United States there has
been a move since Gault to introduce more lawyers into
juvenile courts to undertake the tasks of presenting the
facts and defending the child. Lawyers first began appearing for the defence, and this as we have seen, led to a
recognition of the need for legal prosecutors. In many
instances these lawyers are law students operating under
the supervision of a member of the bar, since most states
allow senior law students to practise under supervision.
In Britain neither lawyers nor law students have moved
into juvenile courts or hearings and there is little evidence of any anxiety about the quality of prosecution or of
defence in juvenile justice. The exception is the concern amongst reporters in Scotland, since the decision in
Kennedy v. *O'Donnell* to develop training to ensure an adequate standard of pleading in the higher courts.

In Britain discussion about representation has centred
on the question of how to ensure that children are protected in situations where their interests and those
of their parents may conflict and where the social worker
involved may get caught between the child and parents'
needs and fail to be clear about the child's needs. Such

a situation arose in the Maria Colwell(2) case and in another tragedy to a child, this time in Scotland, called Richard Clark.(3) The Children Act(4) of 1975 has therefore provided that where there is or may be a conflict of interest between parents and a child in care proceedings, or any proceedings before a children's Hearing, the court or chairman may appoint a person to represent the interests of the child. The intention is that this person should be an experienced social worker who has no responsibility to any local authority concerned with the child or to the parents of the child.

This may be a partial solution in certain kinds of juvenile court cases, but there are some difficulties which need to be acknowledged. One is the ability of the social worker to play the role of advocate. As we have seen, social workers have little legal training, and they are taught more about how to operate in consensus situations than they are about advocacy. On the other hand, the role of advocate contains within it certain assumptions about the importance of rights, and social workers taking on such a role may be able to develop the behaviour appropriate to it. There is also a change in social work training, and some more recently trained workers may be better equipped to manage an adversarial role than were their predecessors, whose training was geared to therapy rather than advocacy.

The discussion in Britain about advocates in adoption and care cases has obscured the more general and less spectacular problem of how the rights of other children who appear before courts and hearings are to be protected, when the threat to their interests lies not with their parents but with the court and Hearing. While it might be possible to extend the use of special social workers as advocates, the social services are seriously overburdened, and it would be hard to argue that this work should take precedence over, for example, supervising children and supporting the elderly.

Similar arguments will no doubt be advanced if it is suggested that lawyers be asked to fill this role, and lawyers are not only as scarce as social workers but tend to be more expensive. Despite this, there is a need for more lawyers to acquire an understanding of juvenile justice, and perhaps for law students in universities to have supervised practice, as do their colleagues in the United States. The impact of lawyers in the juvenile justice system would extend beyond the case in which they were actually appearing and influence the attitudes of decision makers, police and social workers to their own use of discretion. Few social workers will at first welcome lawyers

into juvenile justice, because it is claimed they slow
down the proceedings and introduce irrelevant technicalities, formalise procedure and create an adversary situation.
They also question social workers and often dispute their
judgements as to what the child may need. Paulsen describes the situation:(5)

> few in the probation staff will take kindly to the
> challenge put by lawyers to a probation officer's re-
> commendations regarding the disposition of an adjudi-
> cated delinquent. The questions asked by advocates
> seem like an attack on the officer's professional
> qualifications and his integrity. The staff is likely
> to view lawyers as interlopers, as persons who will
> destroy a possible relationship between the probation
> officer and the respondent, or as misguided amateurs
> interfering with the benefits which can be derived
> from a court acting upon expert information.

This is a natural response from those who do not appreciate
the need to balance welfare with justice, and who tend to
ignore the compulsory nature of courts and hearings. However, experience may convince social workers of the ultimate value to their clients of what Paulsen calls 'constant
searching and creative questioning'.

If any advance is to be made, it seems that no one
solution will be adequate. More social work advocates and
more lawyers will both help, but there is also room for
volunteers. The Scottish hearing allows for a friend to
accompany the child and family, and this friend could be
a volunteer trained to protect the rights of children at
hearings. A similar idea is being developed by a community
worker in Aberdeen(6) in relation to appeals to the Supplementary Benefits Tribunal. He is hoping to train a number
of volunteers to act as advocates for claimants, and a
similar procedure could be used in children's hearings
which, of the three systems we have considered, pay the
least attention to the protection of rights.

CONTROLLING DISCRETION

Acknowledging the particular responsibility in various
roles and ensuring that these roles are filled are means
of allowing both the criminal justice and the welfare
approach to influence a court or hearing. This can also
be achieved by controls on the discretion given to those
who provide the influence and fill the roles. This is
particularly necessary in juvenile justice because it is
not open to the public. The purpose of closed hearings is
to facilitate the welfare approach to children, but it has

also closed the system to what is the most effective means
of recognising and checking discretion-openness. Davis(7)
quotes an 1827 opinion to make this point: 'Without publicity all other checks are insufficient; in comparison of
publicity all other checks are of small account.' This is
perhaps an overly pessimistic view since, even without
openness, acknowledging the existence of discretion allows
for the problems connected with it to be explored. As
Davis also points out:(8)

> discretionary power can be either too broad or too
> narrow. When it is too broad, justice may suffer from
> arbitrariness or inequality. When it is too narrow,
> justice may suffer from insufficient individualizing.

It is the width of discretion in juvenile justice which
causes concern and which requires recognition and structure, but to argue for recognition and control is not to
argue for the end of discretion. Indeed, as Stevenson,(9)
quoting Tillich, points out, the only way to balance the
tension between: 'creative and proportional justice; the
former concerned with the unique needs of individuals, the
latter with ideas of equity ... fair shares for all' is by
the exercise of discretion. Creative and proportional justice are respectively aspects of a welfare and a criminal
justice approach. Without discretion we would have not a
balance of different approaches but a mere wooden uniformity.(10) Perhaps it is this fear of uniformity which
makes people suspicious and hostile at any suggestion that
discretion be recognised and controlled, because it is
assumed that this is the first step towards abolishing
discretion. Control, however, does not mean abolition of
discretion itself, but only an end to the more negative
features sometimes associated with discretion, such as
secrecy and arbitrariness. The unacceptable aspects of
discretion are much easier to see when it is exercised by
other people than when it is exercised by oneself or a
member of one's own working or professional group. Part
of the problem of recognising discretion is that what we
regard as discretion in another, we tend to call professional judgement in ourselves, and the idea of controlling
professional judgement smacks of bureaucracy.

This is unfortunate, particularly perhaps for the clients
of professionals, who lose the protection and respect for
their independence which is provided by control of discretion. Discretion at its best is only the exercise of judgment based on knowledge and experience. Controls need only
serve to spell out what factors should be taken into account in exercising judgment. Ultimately the best check
upon the arbitrary or unbalanced exercise of discretion
is honesty and self-awareness in the decision makers, but

these are hard virtues to achieve. Good intentions need to be supported by an open acknowledgment of the discretionary nature of professional judgment and by controls.

Davis(11) has suggested that discretion can be controlled in three ways: by limiting, by structuring and by checking. To illustrate these ideas, we shall consider how discretion in the juvenile justice system is, or could be, limited, structured and controlled at the crucial point of entry to the system. We will then consider the control of social work discretion, since social workers are in touch with the system throughout and, as a professional group, have paid even less attention than have lawyers, and a great deal less attention than have police, to the question of control of discretion. For social workers there is also the question of how discretion can be controlled within the overriding values of a welfare approach and avoid becoming either legalistic or bureaucratic.

What Davis calls limiting is concerned with setting the outer boundaries to discretion, both the areas in which it may operate and the people who can exercise it. Limiting is typically brought about by statutes and statutory rules, but can also be created by administrative rule making, which offers a more local and flexible way to limit discretion. We have seen how statutes limit the type of children who may become subject to the juvenile justice process, and the adults who may bring them before a court or a hearing.

The second method of control which Davis describes is structuring, which is concerned not with who exercises discretion or the areas to which it can relate, but to how it is exercised. Davis says:(12)

> The seven instruments that are most useful in the structuring of discretionary power are open plans, open policy statements, open rules, open findings, open reasons, open precedents, and fair and informal procedure. The reason for repeating the word 'open' is a powerful one: openness is the natural enemy of arbitrariness and a natural ally in the fight against injustice.

This statement makes clear that there are two parts to structuring discretion. One is that plans be made and reasons for decisions established, and the other is that such plans and reasons be made public, certainly to the people concerned and preferably more widely.

The final form of control is checking, either by means of judicial checks which are provided by appeals procedures or administrative checks. The latter take two forms. The work of ground level staff can be subject to checks by senior staff, but alternatively or in addition,

the people affected by the decisions may have access to
senior officials when they dislike the decision of a staff
member.

In each of the three countries we are considering, the
decision that a child shall come to a court or a hearing
may be made by one of several different people, or may
require independent decisions by, for example, the police
and a probation officer. We know more about the way a
child who commits an offence gets to a court or a hearing
than we do about the process for a neglected child or one
in need of care and control. The reason for this is that
children who commit offences are usually subject to police
decisions, while social workers tend to make decisions
about children thought to be in need of care and protection. In general the more hierarchically organised police
forces have developed controls on their own discretion
whereas the social workers have not.

Individual police in the United States and Britain may
warn a child whom they see committing some minor offence,
and there is no study which shows how frequently this
occurs. What we are concerned with, however, is the more
formal situation, where a child or young person arrives
at the police station and the police have to decide whether to warn or caution him or to refer him on towards a
court or hearing. We know that in all three countries
about half the children who appear at the station house
are not referred on to court; which means that the
police alone, by means of their discretion, are dealing
with as many children as is the whole juvenile justice
system.

The number of different police forces in the United
States makes it difficult to make general statements
about the way they structure their discretion in relation
to the decision that a child shall enter the juvenile
justice system. In Britain, however, the pattern is somewhat clearer. A child or young person may originally come
to the notice of any member of the police force, but the
decision to caution or proceed to court is limited to
senior officers, in particular those attached to the juvenile bureaux in England or the Community Involvement Branch
in Scotland. The discretion of these officers is also
limited by statutes and rules, which specify that certain
types of offence either fall outside the jurisdiction of
the juvenile court or, in Scotland, must be reported to
the procurator fiscal for consideration for prosecution.
However, these rules do not apply in most cases and in
relation to the majority the discretion of the officers
concerned is statutorily unlimited. It is, however, becoming more and more clearly regulated as each force de-

velops criteria for warning or cautioning. Various forces
and various writers include slightly different criteria,
but Watson, writing of England, suggests that, despite
local variations, most forces will caution only if:(13)

1   the juvenile freely admits having committed the
    offence;
2   his parents are content with his admission, agree to
    his being cautioned and appear likely to be co-opera-
    tive;
3   enquiries have revealed no grave social or psycho-
    logical problem in the offender's background;
4   the complainant is willing to leave the way in which
    the boy or girl shall be dealt with to the discre-
    tion of the police.

Becke(14) adds to this a requirement that the offence must
be fully capable of proof in court, if need be, and that
when two or more children are concerned together in one
offence, they will be dealt with in the same way. Ritchie
and Mack,(15) in their study of police warnings in Scotland, suggest that being a first offender and being involved in very minor offences are likely to lead to a
warning rather than referral to the reporter.

These criteria are interesting because of the way in
which they balance criminal justice and welfare thinking.
From a welfare viewpoint, the views of the complainant
and the need for equal treatment of co-accused are irrelevant considerations. On the other hand, consultation with
social work, social service and education departments,
which is necessary to meet criteria 3, is not part of a
criminal justice approach.

While the police are certainly structuring their discretion, it is not so clear that they do this openly, if
being open means taking action to make criteria public
rather than simply not keeping it secret.

The final control of discretion is checking. Administrative checks are a feature of police organisation and,
in the rare event of parents complaining about a police
decision to refer to the court, a senior police officer
would hear their complaint and check the decision. Ag-
grieved parents, however, have no means of judicial appeal,
since this police discretion is part of the decision to
prosecute, and this decision is not subject to any judicial control in either Britain or the United States.

In England the police decision to charge a child or
young person is the final step in their entry to the
juvenile justice system. In Scotland the police decide
not on referral to the hearing but on referral to the
reporter, except in those cases which they are required
to refer to the procurator fiscal. At present the

reporters' powers are an example of almost uncontrolled
discretion. They are not limited, they are not openly
structured, and they are not subject to checks. Structuring is probably developing. Reporters have no formally
agreed or published criteria as to how to decide whether
a child requires compulsory measures of care, but in discussions with reporters one gets the impression that they
are beginning to share the following criteria:(16)
1 whether the facts of the situation can be proved;
2 the seriousness of the offence;
3 whether the child has committed other offences in
   the past;
4 the state of children's behaviour in the particular
   district;
5 the needs of the child for emotional, physical and dis-
   ciplinary care;
6 the capacity of the family to provide the care needed.
These criteria are remarkably similar to those used, for
example, in considering waiver of a child from a juvenile
court to an adult court in the United States. Given the
need for a juvenile justice system to contain both criminal justice and welfare approaches, this list is not surprising. It is surprising, however, when one remembers
that the panel system in Scotland was not designed to
accommodate a criminal justice approach. One might argue
that what the list makes clear is that, whatever the philosophy of Kilbrandon, the panel system in its operation has
taken on the task of balancing criminal justice, community
and welfare approaches. It is not concerned only with the
child's welfare, because, if it were, the seriousness
of the offence and the state of children's behaviour in
the neighbourhood could have no influence on the decision
about a need for compulsory care.

Before regionalisation in May 1975, the reporters' decisions were not often subject to administrative checking.
However, there are now only twelve reporters instead of
forty-three in Scotland, and each reporter has a staff.
In such a situation administrative checking and informal
comparison is likely to occur because reporters will wish
to develop a similar policy over their entire region. It
seems unlikely that the child or parents concerned will
ever have much freedom to challenge the reporter's decision, although, once they get to a hearing, they and the
panel members are told by the reporter his reasons for considering that the child requires compulsory measures of
care.

For some children in Scotland the decision about their
entry to the juvenile justice system is made not by the
reporter but by the procurator fiscal. Again there are no

published criteria by which the fiscals decide, although, in discussions with them, they say that they consider whether or not the child's welfare will be served best by a court or a hearing, and whether the public will be adequately protected by the measures available to the hearings. Procurators fiscal are, of course, accustomed to making decisions as to the prosecution of adults, and here the tests to be applied are well established, and set out by Renton and Brown:(17)

1   Whether the facts disclosed in the information constitute either a crime according to the common law of Scotland or contravention of an Act of Parliament which extends to that country.
2   Whether there is sufficient evidence in support of these facts to justify the institution of criminal proceedings.
3   Whether the act or omission charged is of sufficient importance to be made the subject of a criminal prosecution.
4   Whether there is any reason to suspect that the information is inspired by malice or ill-will on the part of the informant towards the person charged.
5   Whether there is sufficient excuse for the conduct of the accused person to warrant the abandonment of proceedings against him.
6   Whether the case is more suitable for trial in the civil court in respect that the facts raise a question of civil rights.

An interesting example of limiting and checking discretion is provided by the decision of the Lord Advocate, announced by the Secretary of State for Scotland in July 1974. He directed procurators fiscal not to begin proceedings 'against children under 13 without his prior authority, or against children alleged to have committed offences while acting along with an adult unless there were circumstances which made a joint prosecution essential'. (18) The concern behind this directive was that the fiscals, by their use of discretion, were introducing a criminal justice approach for too many children.

We now turn to social workers, and, as in the rest of this chapter, the term covers probation officers in the United States and England as well as welfare and child agency workers in the United States and local authority workers in Britain.

These social workers have three major functions in relation to juvenile justice. They may decide that a child should be brought to court, or they may provide social enquiry reports for those who make this decision and for those who decide on the form of compulsory treatment required. They also carry out the treatment, either by order of a court or a hearing or by voluntary agreement with the child and family concerned. The first two functions require the collection of information and a judgment based on the analysis of this information. The third requires not one informed recommendation, but the development of a plan and involvement of the family and child concerned in its formulation and implementation. The major complaint against social workers is not that they abuse their discretion, and thus reduce the freedom of children and families, although this is sometimes alleged, particularly in the United States, but that they lack either the skill or the time to exercise their discretion. Reports are often said to be of poor quality or never to materialise, and supervision can be perfunctory or even non-existent. How then can families and children receive the help which good social work can provide, and the public the protection which it offers? How can the standard of work which many able social workers achieve become more often the general standard of social service to courts and hearings and to troubled and troublesome children? Much of the answer lies in the area of resources, training and general social policy, but a small part may lie in the control of discretion.

Limiting discretion is already achieved in some areas of Britain by departmental rules that only certain social work staff can take the decision that a child be taken to court, or that only certain staff may sign reports for courts. Limiting in this way raises the question of specialisation. Social service and social work departments have reached the point at which they are prepared to consider some functional specialism, and no longer regard this as violating the principle of a generic department. Even if one is convinced of the value of a generic department and of a broad based initial training for social workers, it has been disastrous, particularly for the clients of social workers, that specialisation was virtually allowed to die, and that by 1975 no post-qualifying training had developed to encourage greater knowledge in particular areas of work. The climate seems right for change now, and it is accepted that generic departments need not mean that every worker within the department must be able to work with every kind of person and in relation to the whole range of social problems. Some specialism amongst workers is now beginning to develop. It would certainly meet the criticisms of some magistrates and panel members if the responsibility for providing information for police, reporters, magistrates and panels, were limited to social workers with some combination of training, experience and

special interest.(19) Similar limits could be imposed
upon those who carry out the supervision of children and
young people. This limiting can be done, as it is in the
Highlands region of Scotland, by having a regional team who
undertake work in relation to the children's hearings, composed of staff drawn from the geographically-based teams,
who have special skills or interest in this type of work.
Alternatively, limiting could be achieved by means of authorisation of individual social workers within a department,
as is done in England in relation to authorisation under
the Mental Health Act.

In the United States probation officers are normally
attached to the juvenile court, and they are always specialists. The danger for them is that they become too much
a part of the court and too little a part of the wider
profession of social work. Limiting of discretion does
not seem to offer a solution to this problem, which needs
to be tackled at the levels of training and professional
organisation.

Another form of limiting operates in England, and
should perhaps be more openly acknowledged. It seems that
in many instances social service departments ignore noti-
fications from police about children they are considering
for prosecution, unless they are already known to them.
While this may be justifiable in view of the demands on
social workers, it certainly prevents the influence of
the welfare approach operating fully in the decision about
entry to the system. A similar kind of limit operates in
Scotland. It was apparently the intention of the Act
that some children who were referred by the police to the
reporter should be referred by him, not to the hearing,
but to the social work department for voluntary supervision. This does occur with some cases in some areas, but
Mack's study suggests that many children so referred get
no supervision, because the social workers have decided
that they are not able to undertake this work when other
work has a higher priority. Both these situations are
examples of limits to the use of discretion which have not
been acknowledged sufficiently to allow their implications
to be explored.

Turning to the structuring of discretion, the earlier
discussion of how the police have developed criteria for
making decisions about entry to the juvenile justice system suggests ways in which criteria might also be developed by social workers. In fact when enquiries are made
either for the police or reporter or for the court or hearing, most social workers have in their mind, and may have
in their hand in the shape of a form, certain topics which
they wish to explore. What Perry's(20) research shows is

that the information about these traditional topics is usually obtained only from the child or family. There is room for more attention to be paid to information from other sources, such as police and schools, if the social worker is really to provide a social background report and not just an account of an interview with the family concerned. This tendency to rely heavily on information from the client and on impressions gained from the interview, arises from the role confusion of the social worker, who tends to see himself as building for a possible future relationship rather than acquiring information on which to make a decision or assist others in making it. There is no simple answer because the social worker has to do both, and because forming a relationship is more attractive to many social workers than collecting information for a body of whom they may at most, only grudgingly approve. In such a situation there is a particular need for clear and agreed guide lines to structure the collection of information.

Guide lines for collecting information are only one half of structuring. The other half is the need for openness. Clients need to be shown the guide lines and to have the reasons for questions explained to them. It is an excellent check upon the unwarranted use of discretion to have to explain to a client the reasons for the questions one asks. In Britain, but not in the United States, social workers as a rule show the reports they write for courts and hearings to the families concerned and discuss any recommendations with them. In the United States probation officers argue that, if they were to show reports to offenders, many sources of information, such as neighbours, would be closed to them, that they might damage their chances of establishing a relationship with the offender, and that the hearing would be unduly prolonged while the defence questioned the report and called witnesses to rebut it. To date, the Supreme Court has upheld the practice that reports are not made available to the accused, and, unless and until practice in the criminal courts changes, it is unlikely to change in juvenile courts. Despite the arguments put forward, failure to show people reports about themselves, which can affect them as seriously as can court and hearing reports, seems to deny both the emphasis upon rights inherent in the criminal justice approach, and the importance of involving the client in his own treatment, emphasised by the welfare approach. It also allows unchecked discretion to social workers and creates a situation in which inaccurate or biased reporting is not corrected.

While social workers in Britain usually show parents

court and hearing reports, they less frequently share with
them reports made at the intake stage. When these reports
lead to voluntary supervision, there is a particular need
for structure. The rights of the child and family are un-
protected in this situation, and many families probably
accept voluntary supervision, or informal probation, as it
is called in the United States, simply to avoid the supposedly worse fate of a court or hearing. In the United
States some probation officers have developed consent decrees to structure this situation. These spell out what
the probation officer is offering and what the child and
his family undertake on their side, and will include the
length of time the contact will continue. For example,
such a decree might state that the probation officer had
decided not to proceed to a hearing in respect of a particular episode of truancy. He would visit the family for
a group session on a particular evening each week for the
next six weeks, would introduce the child concerned to an
after school club, and arrange remedial reading classes.
On their side the family would agree to attend the family
sessions, and the child would try the club at least twice
and attend the reading class for eight weeks.

In British terminology such an agreement would be more
likely to be called a contract than a consent decree, but
it would serve the same purpose of making the obligations
clear on both sides, and of giving the family and child
some opportunity to understand what voluntary supervision
is and whether it was in the event, actually provided.

This kind of openness is probably even more desirable
when a court has made a treatment order than with voluntary supervision. What little we know about children's
perception of treatment tends to support the view that they
see any court ordered treatment as punishment, have little
idea what being on probation or under supervision means,
and certainly do not see it as a situation in which they
can make demands upon the probation officer or social
worker. Few probation or social work departments lay down
minimum requirements as to frequency of contact between the
social worker and the child. In Britain there is now some
pressure, following the events leading up to Maria Colwell's
death, to introduce minimum visiting requirements. It
seems likely that in many instances in Britain at the present the public are not getting the protection, nor the
children the welfare support which adequate supervision
can provide, and since there are no accepted guide lines
as to what adequate supervision is, the public cannot develop a case for a right to protection, nor clients one for
a right to treatment.

This use of guide lines as a basis for demands from

public and clients brings us to the last of Davis's methods
for controlling discretion, which is checking. Checks on
the discretion, particularly of the decision makers, are
built into the juvenile justice system in the form of
appeals to higher courts but what is often lacking are administrative checks. These can take two forms. The discretion of ground-level staff can be subject to checking by
senior staff. This is to be found some of the time in some
probation departments in the United States and England and
in some local authority social work departments. The tendency, however, is for the social worker to decide which
parts of his work he will show to his senior, and here
supervision is concerned more with the personal development of the social worker than with protecting clients from
the arbitrary operation of discretion. Alternatively, the
entire workload of each social worker may be subject to
scrutiny by his senior at stated intervals. What is less
common is regular checking of particular types of work,
such as court reports or supervision interviews.

The other type of checking is that open to clients, and
this is very rare in social work. Few clients complain
about their social worker to senior officers in the social
work and probation department or to councillors. Even in
the United States, where making complaints against officials is far more common than in Britain, few probationers
complain to the chief probation officer or the judge. This
reluctance is regrettable, since administrative appeal is
a useful way to structure discretion.

What is clear from the discussion of controlling discretion is that it is not easy, and that the methods of
control are not alternatives, but need to be used together.
Hill, in discussing discretion in supplementary benefits,
suggests that:(21)

> If each of these so-called checks on discretion can be
> found operating together they may contribute to provi-
> ding some safeguards to the individual who is subject
> to such decisions. Rules confine the scope of discre-
> tion, appeals and complaints secure the maximum scrutiny
> of decisions, and the presence of explicit professional
> standards, even if these are not always adhered to, pro-
> vide some basis either for checking individual deviant
> officials or, if the standards are unacceptable, attack-
> ing the whole system.

Above all, what is necessary in social workers is an attitude of mind which recognises discretion where it exists
and sees the benefit for clients in some limiting, structuring and control.

Chapter eleven

Continuing concerns and new forms of intervention

The community approach has had less influence upon the
structure and procedure of the juvenile justice system
than has the criminal justice or welfare approach. This
may be because it is a relatively new approach. In Britain and the United States it was certainly recognised in
the nineteenth century that the environment within which a
young person grew up could lead him into criminal behaviour and that, once he was branded a criminal, particularly by a prison sentence, it was difficult for him to
lose the label and to re-establish himself as an honest
citizen. Nineteenth-century authors were aware of the
connection between labelling and subsequent criminal behaviour, but this led them more often to a welfare than to
a community approach, because they emphasised the unique
personal elements of the situation. They were concerned
with whether a young offender had sufficient will power
and faith to overcome the disadvantages of his background,
convictions and prison sentence. Twentieth-century developments in the sociology of deviance and interactionist
theory have emphasised society's part in these processes,
and it is this which justifies the inclusion of the community approach as separate from the welfare approach.
Denying that delinquents differ from non-delinquents
either in their personal attributes, social class or sub-
cultural membership, the interactionists suggest that they
suffer rather from contingencies, they are the ones who
have been processed by the juvenile justice system.
    Another reason why the community approach seems to have
had little influence upon the juvenile justice system may
lie in the failure of the interactionists to follow through
the implications of their theory. While deviance theory
denies that socio-economic factors are a cause of delinquency, it recognises that those selected for processing
are usually socially disadvantaged. They tend to be poor,

to come from inner city areas of inadequate and crowded
housing and poor schooling, and to have little power to
influence their own lives. It is also suggested that they
may hold different values from those held by the middle-
class members of society who have the power to impose delinquent labels. Some of these ideas mean that what is
necessary is to change the structure of society and that
attempts to change the juvenile justice system are meaningless efforts to tinker with a corrupt capitalist institution. This, however, is not where interactionist theory
usually leads its adherents. As Gouldner points out, in
discussing Becker's argument, it:(1)

> is essentially a critique of the caretaking organi-
> sations, and in particular of the low level officialdom
> that manages them. It is not a critique of the social
> institutions that engenders suffering or of the high
> level officialdom that shapes the character of care-
> taking establishments.

Gouldner was writing of the United States in 1968 but his
comments apply equally to Britain at that time. More
recent studies make the political context more explicit.
Carlen(2) examining a magistrates' court and Bankowski and
Mungham(3) in their book 'Images of Law' show the behaviour of police, lawyers and social workers not as the
result of malice but as the inevitable outcome of the place
of law in a capitalist society. Law, they suggest, is designed to protect the property holders and to continue the
domination of one group in society over the rest. To do
this it is essential that people must be kept in ignorance
of the fact that law is not something given and natural
but something which arises from a particular society and
which can be changed once people believe they have the
power to change it. Courts provide the opportunity for
reinforcing the given nature of the law. This becomes
obvious if one approaches a court hearing as if it might
fit the frameworks offered by a degradation ceremony, a
drama, game or conspiracy. The police, lawyers and social
workers then become the staff of these performances and
their readiness to be involved can be explained by their
need to protect their social relationships and their live-
lihoods. Professionals are a necessary feature of a capitalist society because they reinforce and service the
myth that most people are incapable and powerless to organise their own lives. Courts provide a forum for a de-
monstration of the need for professionals. As Bankowski
and Mungham put it:(4)

> Law is the celebration of the professional mode; the
> institution of a society 'fit for experts to live in',
> a society where people are dehumanised by being denied

the capacity to determine self-consciously their own
lives.

While Bankowski and Mungham seem to base their work largely on their own observations, Parker's study of adolescent
and young adults in a deprived area of Liverpool lends
support to this view of the courts. Parker's study is
important because it is that rare thing, a study of the
defendant's viewpoint. These young men were clear that
'the law's on the law's fuckin' side' and that the court-
room is 'a put up job, a "show" more concerned with bringing you down and punishing than with implementing fairness
and justice.'(5)

These remarks I think referred to an adult court but
despite the attempts at informality in juvenile justice it
could be argued the principles apply there too. In fact,
the underlying purpose of protecting capitalist values
which these writers see as the function of courts might
be particularly evident in relation to status offences in
the United States and a need for care and protection in
Britain. One of the problems in such situations is to
decide how far a child needs protection against potentially
damaging home situations (and child abuse cases suggest
this can be a tragic reality) and how far courts and hearings are imposing middle-class standards of child care
upon powerless working-class parents. It is not necessary
to accept, as some workers do, that all decisions are an
attempt to maintain the domination of the powerful, in
order to be concerned that this may sometimes be the case.

Such questions currently concern social workers more
than lawyers because, while as Bankowski and Mungham suggest legal training is creating 'technicians for capitalist
society',(6) the theories of the interactionists, at least
in their early form, are widely taught(7) to British social
work students. It has certainly helped them to see their
clients within a political and social context, and has corrected the earlier heavy reliance upon psychological
theories of human behaviour. The price for this wider
perspective, however, is an undermining of the confidence
of social workers in their ability to help. This has resulted in part from the persistent emphasis of interactionist theory upon the negative aspects of social workers' social control functions and the implicit rejection of the
possibility that a treatment ideology might have not just
one but a range of outcomes. This idea is criticised by
Hardiker who makes a plea for empirical studies to test
out the reality of ideologies in action. Her own study of
probation officers' ideologies in fact suggests that a
treatment orientation is not just a euphemism for social
control but when expressed in a social enquiry report

could also be an 'organisational procedure by which probation officers could represent an offender in court so
that where appropriate a recommendation might be made
which would provide him with access to important resources
given the stresses in his life.'(8)

Another development from interactionist theory is what
Horowitz and Liebowitz(9) describe as the disappearance of
the line separating social deviance from political dissent.
Cohen(10) discusses an aspect of this trend, which he suggests is particularly noticeable amongst those sociologists in Britain who are associated with the National De-
viancy Conference. This is the romanticising of deviance
and the attempt to find, amongst groups of deviants, a new
political militancy and consciousness. These ideas have
had but small influence on criminal justice practice, and
virtually no influence upon juvenile justice, where little
attempt has been made to find signs of militancy and class
consciousness amongst juvenile offenders.

Interactionist theory and the community approach which
it informs have contributed to the general failure of confidence and questioning of authority which characterises
the management of social problems in the 1970s and which
leaves a necessary but uncomfortable vacuum. These attitudes are to be found amongst those involved in the juvenile justice systems although here they have had little
influence upon procedure and practice. Some idea that the
middle class has different values and therefore cannot communicate with delinquents, has combined with a belief in
participation to encourage the involvement of delinquents
in solving the problems of delinquency, as well as to attempt to engage volunteers from the same economic and social backgrounds as delinquents.

New careers projects are an example of engaging former
delinquents in work with social problem groups. Growing
out of the ideas underlying the war on want in the United
States, and in particular from some aspects of the mobili-
sation for youth programme, schemes have developed for
using former Chicago probationers as case aids and prisoners
from San Quentin as social change agents. The closest that
such schemes have come to the juvenile age group is the
project run by the National Association for the Care and
Resettlement of Offenders in Bristol. This offers training
for the social services as an alternative to a Borstal sentence for a small and carefully selected group of young
men. Their own life experience and social background are
said to make them able to communicate with the poor and the
deprived in a way which is difficult for people who have
undertaken a professional training which has either confirmed, or moved them into, a middle-class view of the
world.

The Children's Panels in Scotland provide an example of an attempt to include in the juvenile justice system people whose own background was similar to that of the children coming before them. As we have seen, this has not been particularly successful.(11) A similar hope underlies the emphasis upon the use of volunteers, who have been rediscovered during the 1960s and 1970s in both Britain and the United States. They are only slowly becoming part of the juvenile justice systems; strangely, they have been used to greater extent with former prisoners than with juveniles, at least in England. In the United States Big Brother and Big Sister schemes are beginning to flourish. Federal funding has been used to appoint local directors to recruit volunteer 'brothers' and 'sisters' and to match them with needy and delinquent children in the locality. While relationships between delinquents and volunteers may avoid some of the problems of the difference in power between a social worker and a client, they seldom avoid the difficulties of communication said to arise from differences in social and economic background. Neither in Britain nor in the United States has it proved easy to recruit volunteers from the areas from which the delinquents come. Volunteers tend to be both more stable economically and better educated than are the people they befriend.

The major contribution of the community approach, however, has been to make clear that any compulsory treatment of juveniles run a serious risk of stigmatising them and leaving them not cured, but with a spoiled identity. Intervention led not to an end but to what has been called an amplification of deviance. Interestingly, this general idea is now being questioned. Parker, as a result of his study of boys from a deprived area of Liverpool, concludes:(12)

> The fact of social control is always problematic; it may deter some, it may also propel others into action to change the nature of controls or it may engender self-conceptions in those affected by social control in such a way that amplification does in fact occur.

but in his group of young adults: 'amplification of deviance in relation to taking on of a soiled or spoiled identity was negligible.'(13)

In the United States Gibbs(14) found a tendency, as compared with a non-detained control group, towards a delinquent self-image amongst boys detained by the police. However, after the same group had appeared before a probation officer and a juvenile court their delinquent self-image was less pronounced than it had been after detention.

However, whether the ideas of stigma and amplification are correct or not, they have had a powerful influence

upon the juvenile justice system. They have led to screening processes to avoid any child unnecessarily entering the
juvenile justice system and to an added emphasis on prevention. As we saw in the historical survey, prevention
itself is nothing new. Much nineteenth-century policy
towards young offenders was justified by the belief that
present treatment prevented future criminality or pauperism. What happened over the years is that the stage at
which prevention is seen as necessary is pushed back. Reform schools and refuges prevented (it was hoped) adult
recidivism by separating children from the corrupting influence of adult criminals after sentence; later juvenile
courts separated them at the trial stage. Now juvenile
courts are themselves seen as the first step in a deviant
career, and young people must be prevented from ever entering the juvenile justice system. This is thinking
typical of the 1960s and in the United States and Britain
led to two new institutions: Youth Service Bureau and
Intermediate Treatment. We will describe these and then
consider how each balance community, criminal justice and
welfare approaches in the management of certain crucial
issues which are central to juvenile justice in our societies.

YOUTH SERVICE BUREAU

This name first appears in the report of the President's
(15) task force in 1967, a report which was strongly influenced by the thinking of the interactionists, whom we
have seen contribute to the community approach. It is
still hard to describe what a Youth Service Bureau is,
despite the fact that a study in 1973 found over 200
organisations in the United States which claimed to be
Bureaux.(16) The Youth Service Bureau may still be best
described in Rosenheim's(17) phrase, 'a concept in search
of a definition'. Norman(18) suggests that:
      the Youth Service Bureau is a non-coercive independent
      public agency established to divert children and youths
      from the justice system by 1) mobilising community
      resources to solve youth problems, 2) strengthening
      existing youth resources and developing new ones, and
      3) promoting programs to remedy delinquency breeding
      conditions.
      The Youth Service Bureaux have been established in a
variety of different ways. The most usual has been for a
new local or State government agency to be established,
funded partly by federal funds and partly by a matching
local contribution from charitable and tax sources. Over

time the federal funds are planned to decrease as the local funding builds up. In some areas an existing agency may add a Youth Service Bureau to its functions. Despite the strong recommendations in the President's commissions' report, there is no way of introducing Youth Service Bureaux by Federal law. They have developed where there has been local initiative, which usually arises from the combination of a wish to draw federal money into the area and a concern about local failure to co-ordinate resources for delinquents.

In 1973 the Youth Authority of California examined 200 organisations which claimed to be Youth Service Bureaux, and selected for study fifty-five which met the criteria that they

1 aimed to divert juveniles from the juvenile justice system and to prevent delinquency developing;
2 had as their target population youth aged 10 to 18 years who were likely to get involved in the juvenile justice system; and
3 had a variety of services available which included direct counselling, referral and cultural enrichment.

Earlier thinking had suggested that Youth Service Bureaux should work at three levels, that of direct service provision, that of referral and advocacy and that of community change agent. The California survey suggested that Youth Service Bureaux have been most active, and probably most successful, in direct service provision, which is more frequent than is referral. Three-quarters of the Youth Service Bureaux studied gave individual counselling, and the report makes clear that they are able at times to do this in a way existing agencies could or would not. They may make use of out-reach workers, hot lines and store front walk-in type offices located in the areas frequented by local youth. They may employ young people similar in age and social background to the youth they hope to serve, and the emphasis is upon practical and legal advice rather than psychotherapeutic relationships. Some Youth Service Bureaux provide other services, such as temporary accommodation, legal advocacy and community discussions with police and educators. Typically they are small agencies with five or six staff, offering help to about 350 young people each year. Young people reach the Bureaux in a variety of ways. Some are referred by schools or other community agencies, and others come via the police, probation officers or courts. Some have not been in any official trouble, and others may have been referred to the probation officers as alleged delinquents or may have been the subject of a formal court hearing.

Some Bureaux were established more to ensure the avail-

ability and co-ordination of local services on behalf of
delinquent and pre-delinquent youth than to provide direct
service. In Bloomington, Indiana, one group of citizens
was particularly anxious not to antagonise existing social
service agencies and yet was aware that the criticism of
the President's task force, that existing agencies were
failing delinquent youth, was justified in the locality.
To deal with the situation, it was decided that the Youth
Service Bureau should have no service function, but would
refer all young people who needed medical, psychiatric,
counselling or educational services to existing agencies.
The staff of the Youth Service Bureau were to act as
agents and, if necessary, advocates for young people to
see that they got the services which were readily available
to more privileged youngsters. They would go out and find
youths as well as meeting those who came into their office.
They were to follow up referrals to ensure that they had
'taken', and were empowered to use funds to buy services for
youth when they were unable to persuade a local agency to
give them. The Bureau was established on these principles,
but its development was marred by staff problems and an
inclination on the part of the out-reach workers to undertake counselling themselves rather than to refer youth to
other agencies, which they regarded as professional in the
negative sense of restrictive and inaccessible. This history illustrates the comment in the California survey that
Youth Service Bureaux programmes are the staff and particularly the directors.
     The third area of operation for Youth Service Bureaux,
and the one which shows the clearest influence of the community approach, is in changing the attitudes of the local
population towards young offenders. It is suggested that
the local community is responsible for the delinquent behaviour of its young people in two ways. It may show
little tolerance for the behaviour of young people and so
define as delinquent what might equally well be seen as
normal adolescent behaviour. Then, once having defined
certain ways of behaving as deviant, the community contributes to labelling certain young people as deviant because
of this behaviour, and so contributes to a process which
leads, via the juvenile court, to state schools and perhaps
adult recidivism. Youth Service Bureaux hope to increase
the tolerance of adult communities to the behaviour of
young people. There is little to show that they are doing
this, apart from the development of volunteers from local
communities whom the Bureaux recruit to work with young
people who are, or may be, at risk.

INTERMEDIATE TREATMENT

Before discussing Youth Service Bureaux further it is necessary to consider the British scene, where similar developments are taking place, albeit on a slightly different
theoretical base. The British equivalent of the Youth Service Bureau is Intermediate Treatment, although many of the
activities now covered by that term existed before the
White Paper(19) and the 1969 Act gave a name to the idea.
     Child care and probation officers traditionally provided
support and counselling to children who seemed likely to
get into trouble, in the hope of preventing a court appearance. Juvenile courts in Britain were never seen as a
gateway to service as were the early courts in the United
States, and social workers seldom believed that a court
appearance was desirable. They had no statutory right to
offer preventive help to families, although such work was
so frequently undertaken by probation officers that it had
a place in their statistical returns. In 1963, however,
the Children and Young Persons Act placed a duty on local
authorities to provide services, including, where necessary, cash payments to prevent children from being brought
before a juvenile court. The thinking behind this Act
shows the influence not only of those theories of deviance
which were so important in the United States, but also of
a set of ideas commonly held by British social workers,
which Handler(20) calls the unified theory of deviance.
According to this theory, all troubled and troublesome
behaviour, be it stealing, immorality, being beyond control or truancy, springs from failures in family relationships, and it is chance whether a child ends up in care,
before a court or in a child guidance clinic. Courts, however, involve stigma and, since delinquency is another form
of disturbance and deprivation, there is no need to stigmatise children by referral to the court, when the problem can be dealt with informally.
     The 1969 Act took the process a step further in England
by making clear that children were to be brought to court
only when they could not be helped by other means. For
those who were brought before a court the Act introduced
the possibility of new kinds of requirements within supervision orders. The overall name for the range of activities covered by such requirements is Intermediate Treatment, although this name is not found in the Act. A Department of Health and Social Security document, published
in 1973, described Intermediate Treatment thus:(21)
     a. It is a form of treatment for children and young
        persons who have been found to be in need of care or
        control by a juvenile court.

b. It is a form of treatment which can only be provided by a requirement which is added to a supervision order.

c. It is 'intermediate' in its nature between other measures which either place a child in the care of the local authority or leave him in the care of his parents.

d. It is a form of treatment which, within the conditions of the order made by a juvenile court, may be exercised at the discretion of the supervisor. He will have a range of facilities at his disposal, both residential and non-residential, set out under a scheme prepared by the Children's Regional Planning Committee.

e. As a form of treatment it is intended to enable a child or young person to develop new and beneficial attitudes and activities which may be continued after his supervision order has ended and by so doing help him to develop generally and avoid further trouble.

f. The range of facilities available for intermediate treatment in the main will be those which are already being, or may be, used by other children and young persons who are not subject to supervision orders. These facilities are those which fall into categories approved by the Secretary of State for the purpose of intermediate treatment.

Unlike Youth Service Bureaux, which depend upon local initiative, every area of England and Wales is required to provide Intermediate Treatment. For this purpose, Children's Regional Planning Committees were established by the 1969 Act in the twelve regions into which England and Wales were divided. The Planning Committees are made up of members nominated from local authority councillors. These members always form a majority, but the Committee also have powers to co-opt members. The Department of Health and Social Security Guide 1972(22) suggested that juvenile court magistrates and probation officers would be particularly suitable people for co-option, since they are involved in making supervision orders and in carrying out the supervision. Among other duties, these committees were required to undertake a survey of potential Intermediate Treatment facilities and then to develop a plan for their region. When the Secretary of State received a plan, he announced the date on which supervision requirements could be made in the region. This meant that Intermediate Treatment could not be ordered by the court until there were local facilities in the area and that Intermediate Treatment became available at different times in different regions. It is now available in some form all over England and Wales and magistrates can include in a supervision order a requirement that the child or young person spends(23)

1   up to 90 days in a residential establishment, starting
    in the first year of the supervision order, or

2   that he attends a place or participates in activities
    on not more than 30 days in each year of the super-
    vision order.

The court decides whether one or both these requirements
should be included in an order, but the social worker or
probation officer decides, within the limits, where and
for how long the child shall attend or participate.

So far we have considered England and Wales. The idea
of Intermediate Treatment has moved north and is being incorporated into the Children's Hearing System. The Social
Work (Scotland) Act provides the necessary statutory basis,
since panels can specify the nature of supervision requirements, and can therefore require children to take part in
the Intermediate Treatment which exists in their areas.

The aims of Intermediate Treatment are confusing.
Roberts and Davies explain that:

through the use of positive, non-punitive and individually enriching experiences society will be provided
with not only a more humane mode of confronting deprivation and disadvantage but also a more efficient and
effective means of changing delinquent behaviour and
controlling juvenile crime and deviance.

They suggest that Intermediate Treatment is intended to
provide:(24)

facilities or opportunities in 3 major areas.

   i. A preventive measure.
      It was intended to prevent at-risk youngsters
      from committing crimes and thereby being drawn
      into the juvenile court process, and to prevent
      early offenders from becoming recidivists and
      being absorbed into the community home system.

  ii. Leisure alternatives and new horizons.
      It was intended to provide a means of access to
      new interests and activities either of a kind not
      readily available to youngsters or which were not
      being fully or properly utilised by them.

 iii. It was intended that through activities or ex-
      periences of a rewarding, enriching and enjoyable
      kind the youngsters would be provided with a self-
      fulfilling and self-enhancing conception of them-
      selves. It was seen as an opportunity for personal
      growth and learning within a range of settings, in-
      cluding groups of youngsters, other than in the
      traditional one-to-one social work contact or
      family visit.

It seems likely that these aims may not always be compatible and that the provision of interesting leisure activities may not prove to be a means of controlling delinquency, however desirable for other reasons.

The facilities which regions have developed for Intermediate Treatment have been subject to a great deal of criticism. The then Secretary of State for Social Services, Sir Keith Joseph, in an introduction to 'Intermediate Treatment', wrote 'This booklet develops a new approach to helping children in trouble'.(25) It is this claim to newness which may account for the feeling of disappointment and déjà vu that accompanies reading of the accounts and, more particularly, of the regional plans for Intermediate Treatment. The plans, following closely a sample printed by the Department of Health and Social Security in their Guide, consist largely of lists of youth organisations in the area. They do not suggest that a range of different types of Intermediate Treatment are becoming available to meet the needs of many kinds of children in trouble.

There has been no research yet published on Intermediate Treatment requirements in supervision orders, so it is impossible to tell whether children and young people who appear before the courts are being ordered to join youth organisations and, if so, with what success. What is described in the literature is not the use of existing services for youth, but special projects set up by or within social service and probation departments. Many authorities have appointed Intermediate Treatment officers to expand, co-ordinate and publicise Intermediate Treatment to their staff. Sometimes before their appointment and sometimes at their instigation some special Intermediate Treatment projects have developed. They are usually concerned to meet the thirty-day requirement and typically take the form of one or two evening meetings per week over a period of three or six months, with a short residential period or periods in addition, provided for small groups of between six and ten children, staffed at the ratio of about one adult to three children. Besides these on-going programmes, there is a growth of short courses or camps which provide a residential experience for children or young people. For example, the broadsheet 'Super-Vision', issued by the Intermediate Treatment office for Devon in May 1975, lists ten forthcoming events to which social workers might send children. Typical of these are a week's course on drama, writing and poetry for fourteen-fifteen-year-olds, one on sailing, camping and elementary navigation for the same age group, a camp in which groups can be 'self-programming', and another consisting of various outdoor activities for eleven-fifteen-year-old boys.

When considering the effectiveness of Intermediate

Treatment, one needs to distinguish its varying aims. If
it is to alter children's anti-social behaviour, Roberts
and Davies(26) suggest that there is no evidence from the
Wythenshawe project they describe, or from any other, to
suggest that it 'was able to significantly influence the
immediate behaviour of the youngsters who attended it'.
What this project and many others clearly do is to give a
small number of children an enjoyable experience and to
introduce some to new pursuits and skills. If the aim is
to give to deprived and disadvantaged children some of the
opportunities for widening their horizons, which are the
usual lot of middle-class children, then Intermediate
Treatment may be having some success, although Naftali(27)
points out that, when young people are introduced during
Intermediate Treatment to activities which they will not be
able to continue, the experience may be depriving rather
than compensating. If Intermediate Treatment is a means
of breaking down the barriers between troubled people and
social workers, here again it may have some success. While
not all Intermediate Treatment involves the supervising
social worker as well as the child or young person on
supervision, there has been a trend towards supervisors
being involved, and contact developed during activities
and outside pursuits has led to increased understanding
between children and supervisors.

For those who hold the community approach, Intermediate
Treatment offers an opportunity to overcome the stigma involved in labelling, and at the same time encourages young
people to take control of their own lives and contribute
to helping their peers. Paley and Thorpe(28) suggest
that Intermediate Treatment should be seen as 'a style of
working not a piece of legislation', and go on to explain
that the style should be group work:

Our resources should be focused on the delinquent
group, its attitudes, norms and relationships. Techniques must be found for 'group intervention' and
'group learning' - an attempt to diminish the importance of delinquent norms and replace them with more acceptable ones. There should be opportunities for young
people to experience success in other than delinquent
terms, and to renew their confidence in handling larger
non-delinquent group situations like schools and youth
clubs. In the case of the isolated individual, confidence in any kind of group situation may have to be
renewed. There should also be an attempt to overcome
the delinquents' attitudes towards external agencies,
such as social workers, teachers and police, and to
help them develop better relationships with adults
generally and these adults in particular. This latter

task spans two headings: it is both the provision of
opportunities for new relationships with adults, and
the promotion of attitudes within the group which will
combat its norm structure.
This discussion of Youth Service Bureaux and Intermediate
Treatment shows how the concerns of the criminal justice,
welfare and community approaches create and then influence
new forms of intervention in juvenile justice. This leads
to a number of recurring themes and questions, to which we
will now turn.

The Youth Service Bureaux and Intermediate Treatment
are new institutions, and yet they raise again all the
dilemmas which continually confront a juvenile justice
system which attempts to embody the different, and sometimes conflicting approaches of criminal justice, welfare
and community. A number of phrases, such as 'lesser eligibility', 'when is a crime not a crime?', 'the deprived
and the depraved' and 'contamination', exemplify the
dilemmas. These dilemmas worried earlier reformers and,
by examining how they appear in relation to Youth Service
Bureaux and Intermediate Treatment, their present and
continuing nature will become apparent.

'Lesser eligibility' was a concept which disturbed nineteenth-century writers, who feared that parents might encourage their children to steal to ensure for them the
comfort of a refuge or reformatory. The same argument is
raised about Intermediate Treatment, which has been called
'holidays for hooligans'. Mr Smith, Dorset Intermediate
Treatment officer, reported that:(29)

Generally one hears the view expressed by magistrates
that to be sent to an outward bound or sail training
ship after committing an offence, is likely to be seen
as a reward by the youngster and encourage his peer
group to get into trouble so that they can enjoy the
same experience. . . . In another juvenile court the
chairman . . . sees Intermediate Treatment as a privilege which the youngster has to prove he deserves.

There are two major issues which underlie the magistrates' comments, one concerned with the causes of anti-
social behaviour in children and the other with its appropriate treatment. The issue about causes hinges on the
question 'When is a crime not a crime?' It is clear that
to hold to the pre-nineteenth century view that an act
which is a crime when committed by an adult is also a
crime when committed by a child, creates certain difficulties. These difficulties became apparent as society accepted that a child was not just a small adult, but that
children differed from adults in being more impetuous, less
responsible, more innocent and more maleable. The so-called

crimes of children may possibly spring from those very
attributes which define them as children, and, if this is
the case, it seems unnatural and unjust to call these acts
crimes or to think of children as criminal.

The tendency to think of children's anti-social behaviour as not the same as adult criminal behaviour has been
strengthened by a general belief that children's behaviour
was usually more an irritation than a danger. This belief is now much less widely held. A slightly different
and largely unexplored reason for separating adult and juvenile behaviour is put forward by Mays,(30) who suggest that
the nature of the anti-social acts of juveniles differs
from those of adults, not necessarily in seriousness but
certainly in kind.

Other ideas have contributed to our doubts about what
is a crime. The so-called unitary theory of deviance,
which was particularly popular in Britain during the 1950s
and 1960s, suggested that what some may call criminal acts
of children are but one symptom of a disturbed family. Such
disturbance might equally well be shown by maladjustment
or mental disorder in the child. While this theory is now
less widely accepted, it has been replaced by another
theory, that of labelling, which equally questions the meaning of calling children's behaviour criminal. This theory
suggests that children, whose behaviour is so labelled, are
selected from many who commit similar acts, which are either
not noticed or are defined in some other way. This theory,
like the unitary theory of deviance, has implications for
treatment as well as explaining causation, for it suggests
that by labelling children as criminals, society stigma-
tises them and so makes the prevention of future anti-
social behaviour more difficult.

The difficulty with all these ideas, which come from the
welfare and community approach, is that there is a widely
held view in western society that certain acts are crimes.
They do not lose this quality because a legislature states
that when carried out by a person of a particular age they
are not crimes, but grounds for a finding of delinquency or
a need for care. Most people use the ideas from the different approaches on a sliding scale, so that acts become
crimes when they are committed by older rather than younger
children, and as the act itself moves from being trivial to
being serious, either in terms of violence to people or
of damage to property. Because most people differ as to
the point at which they will describe an action by a child
as a crime, the definition is inevitably open to continuous debate.

The other idea which most people hold is that some part
of their own and other people's behaviour is the result of

conscious choice and, more importantly for theories about treatment, that this choice can be influenced by rewarding some and punishing other behaviour. Again, people vary greatly in how much and what kind of behaviour they believe to be subject to such controls and influences. The magistrates quoted earlier clearly consider that the youngsters before them could control their behaviour and should not be rewarded for failing to do so. Evidence of the impact of heavy sentencing upon the incidence of adult crimes does suggest that, if the aim is to prevent further similar behaviour, then deterrence may be given too small a place in juvenile justice. But this, of course, raises the question whether the system is pursuing this relatively simple aim or whether it is concerned with meeting the social and emotional needs of children or with changing community attitudes.

These same questions have been posed in the debates about the deprived and depraved which, as Mays explained, when discussing the Children and Young Persons Act, 1969: (31)

> centres around the provision of community homes for children who have broken the law or committed acts which as adults would have brought them into a court, where they would live together with children who have not broken the law. The issue is a genuine one, however bedevilled by partisan viewpoints and special pleading. The fact that at present we send both delinquents and non-delinquents to approved schools should not affect judgement as to the wisdom or desirability of such a policy. Do delinquents contaminate non-delinquents? Are children who steal really to be thought of as deprived? If so, why does one deprived child steal and another merely run away from home or truant from school?

The same questions are of concern in the United States, where, as we have seen, considerable pressure is being exerted to prevent these children who commit acts which, when committed by adults, are crimes, from being mixed in institutions with truants, neglected children and those beyond the control of their parents.

We have already dealt with the question of causes and whether delinquent and non-delinquent behaviour may have similar causes. Because there is no single answer, the debate is likely to continue, and in any individual instance we will need to consider the importance of a number of different influences. It seems extremely unlikely that one theory will ever provide an explanation of all troubled and troublesome behaviour in children. The question, however, raises the issue of contamination. This has had a

long history. It was clearly stated in the case of Milwaukee Industrial School and the Supervisors of Milwaukee
County in 1876:(32)

> It was strongly objected to the statute, that it au-
> thorizes the same disposition of children destitute
> by misfortune, and of children convicted of crime; com-
> mitting them alike to these schools, during minority,
> there to associate together.

It is not only in residential provision that contamination
is feared, although the risk is clearly greater because the
exposure is also greater. Andrews(33) quotes an example
of a tenants' association which succeeded in closing down
a club designed in part for Intermediate Treatment because
the members did not want their children to mix with delinquents. The idea is not as straightforward as it may appear. We know very little about how children influence
each other, and even the notion of prisonisation,(34)
which has influenced theories about peer group pressures
in institutions, is now being questioned. What we need to
know is which way the influence is most likely to operate,
for it is also widely held that delinquent youngsters can
adopt more law-abiding norms if their peer group is a non-
delinquent one. Both Youth Service Bureaux and Intermediate Treatment thinking stresses the need for children at
risk or who have been before a court to become involved in
youth organisations and recreational activities with
children who have not been, and are unlikely to be, in
trouble. Roberts and Davies,(35) while not addressing
themselves to the subject of contamination, argue that
Intermediate Treatment should not be a means of mixing
delinquents and non-delinquents or of providing imaginative facilities for youngsters. They argue that 'the
Social Services departments, the Probation Service and
perhaps even the schools also carry a major responsibility in social control'. The responsibility of Intermediate Treatment programmes 'is to contain and control
the behaviour of youngsters placed under their care by
the courts'. Roberts and Davies consider that delinquents
should be as eligible as any other youth for programmes of
activity, but that Intermediate Treatment should be concerned with their delinquent behaviour and include options,
'some of which will be unmistakably controlling in their
ethos or even mildly punitive'.

Contamination is concerned not only with catching or
copying criminal behaviour, but also with non-delinquents
coming to share the stigma, and hence the spoiled identity
which attaches to delinquents. In the United States,
where traditionally few distinctions have been made between law violators and other children in trouble, the

current concern is that those who do not break the law are
stigmatised because the juvenile court is seen by the public as a place for law breakers.(36)

> the failure to differentiate between neglected and de-
> linquent children supports a popular confusion of the
> two groups. 'The public', a California report states,
> 'primarily identified juvenile courts with delinquents
> and consequently assumes that all juvenile court wards
> are delinquent.' Since fifty per cent of the Califor-
> nian probation department caseload are neglected and
> dependent, this unwarranted taint attaches to a large
> proportion of children brought to court.

Intermediate Treatment and Youth Service Bureaux run
the same risk of being seen as institutions for law breakers. At the present time they are not seen as stigmatising
agencies, but the evidence from history is clear: each
time an institution is set up to deal with troublesome
children so as to avoid the stigma attached to the existing procedure, the new institution itself becomes stigmatising in time. Perhaps this is inevitable where compulsion is involved.

COMPULSORY TREATMENT

If stigma arises not so much from the nature of a child's
behaviour but from the fact that compulsion is involved,
then it may be important how children reach Youth Service
Bureaux and Intermediate Treatment. The President's commission was unclear about coercion to attend Youth Service
Bureaux. 'It is essential', they said:(37)

> that acceptance of Youth Service Bureaux service be
> voluntary. Otherwise the dangers and disadvantages of
> coercive power would merely be transferred from the
> juvenile court to it. Nevertheless, it may be neces-
> sary to vest the Youth Service Bureau with authority to
> refer to the court . . . those with whom it cannot deal
> effectively.

Even if one can determine what that passage means, it is
difficult to discover what is happening in practice. Juveniles are being referred to Youth Service Bureaux by
schools, police and probation officers. In some areas referral to a Youth Service Bureau is an alternative to a
court appearance and, once referred, the possibility of a
petition on the same grounds as gave rise to the referral
is ruled out whether or not the referral succeeds. In
others, the police or the court have a period of time in
which to decide on their action after the initial referral
None of the reports I have seen indicate what happens if a

child becomes involved with a Youth Service Bureau and later breaks away against the wishes of the staff. It is unlikely that the staff would take any official action, although in any future allegations of delinquency, 'failure' to obtain help from a Youth Service Bureau might be part of the information on which a need for treatment might be founded.

With Intermediate Treatment the situation is apparently clearer. Intermediate Treatment is compulsory and follows an Intermediate Treatment order in England or a condition in a supervision requirement in Scotland. Other children may share the same facilities, but they need not attend, whereas the child subject to an Intermediate Treatment order is required to do so. However, the juvenile court has little or no power to enforce an Intermediate Treatment order, since they cannot make a care order solely on the grounds that a child or young person has failed to keep to the requirements of an Intermediate Treatment order. This seems logical, since one aim of Intermediate Treatment is to avoid making care orders, but it leaves the court and supervisors with no means of enforcing a compulsory order. In Scotland a hearing can review a supervision requirement at the instigation of the supervisor and legally could make a requirement of residential care when a child fails to attend an Intermediate Treatment facility. It seems unlikely that they would use this power unless there were other reasons for removing a child from home.

The question of compulsion raises the question of rights. Youth Service Bureaux and Intermediate Treatment are obviously concerned with children's needs, and yet they involve compulsion and possibly stigma, and we should heed Justice Brandeis' words: 'Experience should teach us to be most on our guard to protect liberty when the Government purposes are beneficent',(38) and more recently Allen gave a similar warning:(39)

above all, we cannot afford to be lured into the belief that good intentions are a sufficient substitute for procedural fairness. Indeed, it may almost be true that the naive man of good intentions is more dangerous in this area than the knave, for the latter at least may be constrained by the consciousness of guilt.

These considerations bring us face to face again with the different ideas behind the juvenile court system. The more either the child's needs or the child's rights are pushed to their logical conclusion, the more they seem to be in conflict. The British juvenile courts have traditionally, in comparison with their counterparts in the United States, paid great attention to children's rights. It is said that this made it difficult for them to 'deal with an offender's

social needs'. It was especially difficult if the court
felt it had to follow the tariff tradition of criminal
courts that there should be a relationship between the seriousness of the event which brought the offender to court
and the sentence he received.

In the United States, where juvenile courts were established to meet children's needs, it is the failure to protect their rights which has caused concern. This failure
has been particularly important because of the misleading
rhetoric which described what were virtually prisons as
places for meeting social and emotional needs.

Whatever the solution may be, it is not to push the
claims of either side to their logical, but often unreasonable, conclusions. Larson suggests the dangers of extending the focus on rights which:(40)

> if carried to an illogical conclusion, might suggest to
> the uninformed (or those devotees favoring a more legal-
> istic court) that protection of rights will solve the
> behavioral problem. . . . This kind of thinking . . .
> is a fraud on the child and the public. It neither af-
> fords the public protection it can rightfully expect nor
> does it assure development of the child to the measure
> of his potential.

The answer seems to lie in a continuous debate in which
those involved in the juvenile justice system recognise
and balance the competing and important demands of the
criminal justice, welfare and community approaches. Some
way too must be found to include in the debate the children and families who come before courts and hearings.
Their viewpoints have been virtually ignored in this book,
not because I do not consider their ideas important, but
because they have not been collected. Including their
viewpoints will complicate the debate yet further but will
bring it nearer to reality, for the real world within which
the juvenile justice system operates is complex, confused,
contradictory, changing and rich. Only our perceptions,
restricted as they are by our values, can make this real
world simple or offer one approach as the answer to its
many different human situations.

References

CHAPTER 1   JUVENILE JUSTICE SYSTEMS

1 See for example, 'The Report of the President's Commission on Law Enforcement and Administration of Justice (1967)';   in re Gault, 387 US 1 (1967);   M.G. Paulsen, Juvenile Courts and the Legacy of 1967, 'Indiana Law Journal', 43, 1968, p. 523;   S. Coxe, Lawyers in the Juvenile Court, 'Crime and Delinquency', 13, 1967, p. 488;   D.L. Bazelon, Beyond Control of the Juvenile Court, 'Juvenile Court Judges Journal', 20, 1969, p. 91.
2 See for example, 'The Child, the Family and the Young Offender', Cmnd 2742 (1965);   'Children in Trouble', Cmnd 3601 (1968);   'Social Work and the Community', Cmnd 3065 (1967).
3 Social Work (Scotland) Act 1968, c. 49.
4 Children and Young Persons Act 1969, c. 54.
5 Social Work (Scotland) Act 1968, sec. 33(i).
6 M.G. Paulsen, The Child, the Court and the Commission', 'Juvenile Court Judges Journal', 18, 1967, p. 83.
7 In re Gault, supra note 1 at footnote 21.   See for example, Shears, Legal Problems peculiar to Children's Courts, 'American Bar Association Journal', 48, 1962, p. 719.   (The basic right of a juvenile is not to liberty, but to custody.   He has the right to have someone to take care of him, and if his parents do not afford him this custodial privilege the law must do so.).   Ex parte Crouse, 4 Whart. 9 11 (Sup. Ct. Pa. 1839).   Petition of Ferrier, 103 Ill. 367, 371-3 (1883).
8 For Britain, see 8 Edw. 7 c. 67 (1908) Children Act, Sec. 58 (i).   For US see for example, Revised laws of Illinois, 1879;   Industrial School for Girls Act.
9 To avoid repetition, the term 'offender', when applied to children, will mean children who are brought before

a court as a result of an act which, if committed by an adult, would constitute a crime. 'Non-offenders' will mean all other children brought to juvenile courts, either for behaviour such as truancy or curfew-breaking, which is illegal only in children, or for being incorrigible or in physical or moral danger. The terms 'children' and a 'child' will be used to include children and young people, except where the law in England creates a separate category of 'young people'.

10   See for example, Indiana Senate Enrolled Act, No. 90, Sec. 4 (2) d. In Indiana Juvenile Code, Burns 9-3204 ((10) 'Being under the age of thirteen years (13) is habitually present upon any street, highway, park, public building or other public place between the hours of 10.01 p.m. and 5.00 a.m. unless he is accompanied or supervised by his parent or legal guardian or other responsible companion.').

11   See for example, Indiana Juvenile Code, Burns 9-3204 ((14) 'Uses intoxicating liquor as a beverage.').

12   Local authorities may assume parental rights over children in their care. For England the authority lies in Sec. 2 of the Children Act (1948) and for Scotland in Sec. 16 of the Social Work Act (Scotland). The grounds for assuming rights have been extended for both countries by the Children Act (1975).

13   G.H. Mead, The Psychology of Punitive Justice, 'American Journal of Sociology', 23, 1918, p. 577.

14   R. Pound, 'Social Control through Law', p. 121.

15   F.J. Ludwig, 'Youth and the Law', p. 26.

16   M. Rosenheim, 'Justice for the Child'.

17   V.W. Stapleton and L.E. Teitelbaum, 'In Defense of Youth', p. 98.

18   Ibid.

19   G. Hazard, Limitations in the Uses of Behavioral Sciences in the Law, 'Case Western Reserve Law Review', 19, 1967, p. 71.

20   H.A. Davidson, That Other Helping Profession, 'American Journal of Psychiatry', 122, 1965, p. 691.

21   P.P. Tamilia, Neglect Proceedings and the Conflict between Law and Social Work,'Duquesne Law Review', 9, 1971, p. 579.

22   D. May, Delinquency Control and the Treatment Model, 'British Journal of Criminology', 11, 1971, p. 361.

23   H.H. Lou, 'Juvenile Courts in the United States', p. 51.

24   Report of the Chicago Bar Association, 1899.

25   M. Rosenheim, op.cit., p. 84.

26   H.H. Lou, op.cit., p. 179.

27   A. Thompson, 'Punishment and Prevention', pp. 178-9.

28 R.A. Cloward and L.E. Ohlin, 'Delinquency and Opportunity'.
29 A.K. Cohen, 'Delinquent Boys'.
30 K.A. Menninger, 'The Crime of Punishment', pp. 154 and 196.
31 E. Lemert, 'Instead of Court', p. 7.
32 Ibid., p. 95.
33 W.B. Miller, Ideology and Criminal Justice Policy, 'Journal of Criminal Law and Criminology', 64 (2), 1973.
34 G. Smith, Social Policy and Professional Identity: the Case of Children's Panels, unpublished paper, 1975.
35 E.M. Schur, 'Radical Intervention', p. 21.
36 Ibid., p. 22.
37 See the writings of R. Hood, e.g. Some fundamental dilemmas of the English Parole system, in D.A. Thomas (ed.) 'Parole'.
38 D. May, op.cit., p. 359.
39 F.A. Allen, 'The Borderland of Criminal Justice'.
40 A.M. Platt, 'The Child Savers'.
41 Laws of Illinois, 1898.
42 D.W. Winnicott, 'The Maturational Processes and the Facilitating Environment', p. 75.
43 Mead, op.cit., p. 577.
44 Society of Friends, American Friends Service Committee, 'The Struggle for Justice', p. 27.

CHAPTER 2 UNITED STATES: HISTORICAL BACKGROUND TO THE JUVENILE COURT

1 E. Erikson, 'Insight and Responsibility'.
2 Laws of Illinois, 1898.
3 Louisiana was an exception since its laws were based on the civil law system of France.
4 R.S. Pickett, 'House of Refuge', p. 26.
5 C.L. Brace, 'The Dangerous Classes of New York'.
6 Quoted by N.G. Teeters, Institutional Treatment of Juvenile Delinquents, 'Nebraska Law Review', 29, 1949, p. 579.
7 C. Dickens, 'American Notes', p. 66, quoted by Pickett, op.cit., p. 97.
8 N.G. Teeters, op.cit., p. 581.
9 E.C. Wines, 'The State of Prisons and Child Saving Institutions of the Civilized World'.
10 Indiana Acts of 1855, ch. 93, p. 191. Although called a House of Refuge, it has many of the attributes of a reform school, being established by statute, outside the city and run on a cottage system.

11 Indiana Acts of 1869, ch. 305, p. 61.
12 E.C. Wines, op.cit., p. 143.
13 Ibid.
14 C.L. Brace, 'Proceedings of the Conference of Boards of Public Charities', p. 138.
15 F. Davenport Hill, 'Children of the State', p. 220.
16 'A Report of the Labors of John Augustus', p. 11.
17 B. Fenner, 'Raising the Veil'.
18 Davenport Hill, op.cit., p. 225.
19 Ibid., p. 226.
20 Indiana Acts of 1889, ch. 125, p. 261.
21 Pickett, op.cit., p. 4.
22 Ibid., p. 26.
23 The idea of a focal concern is developed by D.S. Whittaker and D. Liebermann in 'Psychotherapy Through the Group Process'. They suggest that in a therapy group the members begin to talk about matters important to them as individuals until some topic is found which represents an area of shared concern. The group will then develop discussion around this focal concern, taking up a number of different themes associated with it. Focal concerns are necessarily limited in number and tend to recur, since they represent basic human dilemmas. This idea seems a useful way of expressing the shared and recurring concerns of those people who are, or were in the past, involved with juvenile justice.
24 B.K. Pierce, 'A Half Century with Juvenile Delinquents: or the New York House of Refuge and its Times', p. 23.
25 Society for the Prevention of Pauperism in the City of New York, Report on the Penitentiary System of the United States (1822), quoted by S.J. Fox, 'Modern Juvenile Court Justice', p. 16.
26 Wines, op.cit.
27 Davenport Hill, op.cit., p. 222.
28 'Report of the State Charities Aid Association' (1873), quoted by Davenport Hill, op.cit., p. 216.
29 M. Carpenter, 'Juvenile Delinquents, their Conditions and Treatment'.
30 Fox, op.cit., p. 18.
31 Ibid.
32 Pickett, op.cit., p. 82.
33 Ibid., p. 92.
34 Ibid., p. 46.
35 Ibid., p. 92.
36 Ibid., p. 186.
37 Evans Woollen, The Indiana Board of Children's Guardians Act, 'Twenty-eighth National Conference of Charities and Corrections'.

38   *Ex parte* Crouse, 4 Whart. 9 Pa. 1839.
39   Ibid., p. 12.
40   The People v. Turner, 55 Ill. 280, 1870.
41   In re Gault, 387, US 1, 1967.
42   In re Alexander Ferrier 103, Ill. 367, 1882.
43   Milwaukee Industrial School v. Milwaukee County, 40 Wsc., 328, 1876.

CHAPTER 3   UNITED STATES: FROM THE FIRST JUVENILE COURT TO THE PRESENT

1   Quoted by M. Rosenheim, ed., in 'Justice for the Child', p. 1.
2   Acts of Illinois, 1898, sec. 3.
3   Ibid.
4   Report of the Chicago Bar Association, 1899.
5   T.D. Hurley, Origin of the Illinois Juvenile Court Law, 'The Child, the Clinic and the Court', p. 327.
6   J.C. Lathrop, The Background of the Juvenile Court in Illinois, 'The Child, the Clinic and the Court', *supra,* p. 290.
7   B.B. Lindsay, Colorado's Contribution to the Juvenile Court, 'The Child, the Clinic and the Court', *supra,* p. 274.
8   Ibid., p. 285.
9   In re Gault, 387, US, 15, 1967.
10   A.M. Platt, 'The Child Savers'.
11   E.M. Lemert, 'Instead of Court'.
12   S.J. Fox, 'Modern Juvenile Justice'.
13   Lathrop, op.cit., p. 291.
14   Platt, op.cit., p. 139.
15   See chapter two, p. 47.
16   New York, Laws of 1886, ch. 353, sec. 1466.
17   C.W. Hoffman, Organization of Family Courts, 'The Child, the Clinic and the Court', *supra,* p. 258.
18   Ibid., p. 266.
19   M. Van Waters, The Juvenile Court from the Child's Viewpoint, 'The Child, the Clinic and the Court', *supra,* pp. 276 and 310.
20   See for example Judge Lindsay's and Judge Mack's articles in 'The Child, the Clinic and the Court', *supra,* pp. 276 and 310.
21   One of the theories of parole hearings is that there is no conflict between prisoner and Board, since both are concerned to decide whether or not parole is in the prisoner's best interests. This is carrying the doctrine to absurd lengths, since most Parole Boards have a statutory duty to protect the public.

22   *Ex parte* Crouse, 44 Whart. 11 Pa. 18-39. Quoted in
      chapter two, p.48.
23   F.B. Sussman, 'Law of Juvenile Delinquency', p. 15.
24   *Eyre* v. *Shaftesbury,* 2 P. Wmsn. 103, 24 Eng. Rep.
      Reprints 659 1722.
25   *Wellesley* v. *Beaufort*, 2 Russ. 1, 38 Eng. Rep. Reprints
      236 1829.
26   In *re* Spence, 2 Ph. 247, 41 Eng. Rep. Reprints 937
      1847.
27   The question of what constitutes grounds for interfer-
      ing with a father's rights over his children occurs in
      several cases during the nineteenth century. In 1817
      the poet Shelley, who was an avowed atheist and who was
      living with a woman to whom he was not married, de-
      manded the return of his children from his deceased
      wife's parents. The grandparents petitioned on behalf
      of the children, and the Lord Chancellor states:
      > This is a case in which, as the matter appears to
      > me, the father's principles cannot be misunderstood,
      > in which his conduct, which I cannot but consider as
      > highly immoral, has been established in proof, and
      > established as to the effect of those principles:
      > conduct nevertheless, which he represents to him-
      > self and others, not as conduct to be considered as
      > immoral, but to be recommended and observed in prac-
      > tice, and as worthy of approbation.
      >
      > I consider this, therefore, as a case in which
      > the father has demonstrated that he must, and does
      > deem it to be matter of duty which his principles
      > impose upon him, to recommend to those whose opin-
      > ions and habits he may take upon himself to form,
      > that conduct in some of the most important rela-
      > tions of life, as moral and virtuous, which the law
      > calls upon me to consider as immoral and vicious -
      > conduct which the law animadverts upon as inconsis-
      > tent with the duties of persons in such relations
      > of life, and which it considers as injuriously af-
      > fecting both the interests of such persons and those
      > of the community.
      >
      > I cannot, therefore, think that I should be justi-
      > fied in delivering over these children for their edu-
      > cation exclusively, to what is called the care to
      > which Mr. S. wished it to be intrusted. 3/9.
      >
      > (*Shelley* v. *Westbrooke*, 37 Eng. Rep. Reprints 850
      > 1817.)
      Similar behaviour on the part of Mr Wellesley caused
      Lord Eldon to decide that his children should remain
      with their maternal aunts. The Vice-Chancellor could
      not allow the infant daughter, Victoria, to join her

father in a house where he was co-habiting with a Mrs
Bligh. The effect of Mrs Bligh's influence was apparently likely to be less damaging to Victoria's
brothers, but, in Lord Eldon's opinion, it was not in
the interests of the children that they should be separated. An interesting example of judicial concern for
sibling relationships. (*Wellesley* v. *Beaufort*, 2 Russ.
1, 38 Eng. Rep. Reprints 236 1829.)
    Later cases continue the attempt to define what is
in the interests of a child, and several deal with the
question of religious education. The father has a
right to bring up his children in the religion of his
choice, and the court 'never does interfere between a
father and his children unless there be abandonment
of the parental duty and that may be considered to
take place when the father brings them up irreligiously'.
(In *re* Agar Ellis (10 Ch. 49 1878)). This was said in
1878, but by the 1890s the court is looking at the
child's welfare in a wider context. In *R*. v. *Gyngall*
(2 Q.B. 232 1893) and in *re* McGrath (1 Ch. 143 1893)
the court declines to interfere with guardianship
arrangements, even where there is some doubt whether
the religion of the guardians is that which the parent
desired.

28 R. Pound, 'Interpretations of Legal History'.
29 This idea is developed by D. Rendleman, *Parens Patriae:
    From Chancery to Juvenile Court*, 'South Carolina Law
    Review', 23, 1972, p. 205.
30 H.A. Bloch and F.T. Flynn, 'Delinquency: The Juvenile
    Offender in America Today'.
31 H.H. Lou, 'Juvenile Courts in the United States', p. 24.
32 Ibid., p. 28.
33 J.T. Bowen, The Early Days of the Juvenile Court, 'The
    Child, the Clinic and the Court', *supra*, p. 298.
34 G.L. Schram, The Judge Meets the Boy and His Family,
    'National Probation Association Yearbook, 1945', p. 182.
35 M. Bell, 'Coping with Crime'.
36 T.D. Eliot, 'The Juvenile Court and the Community', p. 3.
37 Ibid., p. 148.
38 Quoted by E.F. Waite in The Outlook for the Juvenile
    Court, 'Annals of the American Academy', 105, 1923,
    p. 229.
39 Lindsay, op.cit., p. 280.
40 Cinque v. Boyd, 99 Conn. 74 1923.
41 Commonwealth v. Fisher, 213 Pa. 53 1905.
42 *Ex parte* Pruitt, 82 Tex. Cr. Rep. 394 1917.
43 State v. Tincher, 258 Mo. 1 1914.
44 *Ex parte* Loving, 178 Mo. 194 1903.
45 F.A. Moran, New Light on the Juvenile Court and Proba-

tion, 'National Probation Association Yearbook, 1930', p. 73.

46 C. Chute, Juvenile Court in Retrospect, 'Federal Probation', XIII,(1949) p.3.

47 C.W. Tenney, The Utopian World of the Juvenile Court, 'Annals of the American Academy', 383, 1969, p. 101.

48 R.M. Emerson, 'Judging Delinquents', p. 77.

49 The People ex rel v. Turner, 55 Ill. 280 1870.

50 Leonard v. Licken, 3 Ohio App 379 1914.

51 S. Glueck, 'The Problem of Delinquency', p. 297.

52 Ibid., pp. 488-9.

53 Quoted by W.H. Sheridan in 'Standards for Juvenile and Family Courts', p. 7.

54 Emerson, op.cit., p. 78.

55 P. Tappen, 'Juvenile Delinquency', p. 204.

56 Rosenheim, op.cit., p. ix.

57 Tappen, op.cit., p. 201.

58 Children's Bureau, US Department of Health, Education and Welfare, 'Standards for Specialized Courts Dealing with Children'.

59 National Council on Crime and Delinquency, 'Standard Juvenile Court Act'.

60 State v. Myers, 22 NW 2nd 199 1946.

61 In re Smith, 92 NYS 2nd 529 1949.

62 In re Mantell, 62 NW 2nd 308 1954.

63 US v. Dickerson, 168 F. Supp. 901 1958.

64 Kent v. US, 383 US 554 1966.

65 Ibid., p. 551.

66 In re Gault, 387 US 1 1967.

67 Ibid., p. 25.

68 Ibid., pp. 4-9.

69 In re Winship, 387 US 358.

70 McKeiver v. Pennsylvania, 402 US 528.

CHAPTER 4   UNITED STATES: THE PRESENT JUVENILE JUSTICE SYSTEM

1 E.M. Lemert, 'Instead of Court'.

2 P. Tappen, 'Juvenile Delinquency', p. 179.

3 Kent v. US, 383 US 556 1966.

4 In re Gault, 387 US 1 1967.

5 National Conference of Commissioners on Uniform State Laws, 'Uniform Juvenile Court Act', p. 4, 1968. The Uniform Juvenile Court Act is referred to as the Uniform Act hereafter.

6 W.H. Sheridan, 'Legislative Guide for Drafting Family and Juvenile Court Acts', hereafter referred to as the Guide.

7   Uniform Act, Comment, p. 7.
8   Guide, p. 6.
9   M.M. Levin and R.C. Sarri, 'Juvenile Delinquency: a
    Comparative Analysis of Legal Codes in the United
    States', p. 38.
10 Uniform Act, Comment, p. 11.
11 Guide, p. 7.
12 Uniform Act, p. 9.
13 Guide, p. 8.
14 Ibid., p. 9.
15 Alaska, Ariz., Ark., Calif., Colo., Del., DC, Hawaii,
    Ida., Ind., Iowa, Kans., Ky, Minn., Miss., Mont., Neb.,
    Nev., NJ, N. Mex., N. Dak., Ohio, Ore., Pa., RI, S. Dak.,
    Tenn., Utah, Va., Wash., W. Va., Wis., Wyo.
16 Fla., Ga., Ill., La., Me., Md., Mass., Mich., Mo., NH,
    SC, Tex.
17 Ala., Conn., NY, NC, Okla., Vt.
18 Levin and Sarri, op.cit., p. 13.
19 Ala., Alaska, Ariz., Ark., Calif., Colo., Del., DC,
    Fla., Ga., Hawaii, Ida., Ill., Ind., Iowa, Kans., Ky,
    La., Md., Mass., Minn., Mo., Nev., NH, N. Mex., NC,
    N. Dak., Ohio, Okla., Ore., Pa., RI, S. Dak., Tenn.,
    Tex., Utah, Vt, Va., Wash., W. Va., Wis.
20 Uniform Act, pp. 6-7.
21 Levin and Sarri, op.cit., p. 12.
22 F.B. Sussman, 'Law of Juvenile Delinquency'.
23 Levin and Sarri, op.cit., p. 17.
24 Kent v. US, 383 US 554 1966.
25 Uniform Act, sec. 19.
26 Guide, p. 14.
27 Ala., Alaska, Calif., Colo., Conn., DC, Fla., Ga.,
    Hawaii, Ida., Ind., Iowa, Kans., Ky, La., Me., Md.,
    Mich., Minn., Miss., Mo., Mont., Nev., N. Med., NC,
    N. Dak., Okla., Ore., RI, SC, S. Dak., Tex., Utah, Vt,
    Wash., Wis.
28 Levin and Sarri, op.cit., p. 27.
29 Uniform Act, sec. 10.
30 Guide, p. 35.
31 Uniform Act, secs 26 and 27.
32 Ala., Del., Ky, La., Mass., NH, NJ, N. Mex., Pa.,
    Wash., Wis.
33 Calif., Conn., DC, Ga., Hawaii, Ill., NY, NC, N. Dak.,
    Ohio, Okla., SC, Tenn., Vt, Wyo.
34 Levin and Sarri, op.cit., p. 51.
35 Uniform Act, secs 30 and 31.
36 Uniform Act, sec. 36.
37 Ark., Calif., Colo., Del., DC, Ky, Me., Md., Mass.,
    Minn., Neb., N. Mex., NY, Ohio, Ore., Pa., S. Dak.,
    Tenn., Utah, Va., Wis., Wyo.

CHAPTER 5   BRITAIN: THE EVENTS LEADING TO THE 1908
CHILDREN ACT

1   H. Mayhew, 'London Labour and the London Poor'.
2   Lord Ashley's Speech to the House of Commons 1848.
    Quoted by T. Begg, 'An Inquiry into the Extent and
    Causes of Juvenile Depravity'.
3   C. Dickens, 'Reprinted Pieces'.
4   Pauperism in the nineteenth century meant more than
    poverty. It meant both being poor and making demands
    upon others for support, and was often attributed to
    personal weakness and failure. All the present day
    hatred which is directed at those thought to be scroung-
    ers on supplementary benefits, was felt towards paupers
    in the nineteenth century. There was great concern
    that children brought up in contact with paupers would
    grow to be paupers. In our day the culture of poverty
    and the circle of deprivation theory carry some of this
    fear, but with less intensity and blame than was attached
    to the reproduction of pauperism.
5   The Select Committee on the State of Mendicity in the
    Metropolis, Minutes of Evidence. Parliamentary Papers
    1814-15, 111, p. 29. Quoted by Pinchbeck and Hewitt,
    'Children in English Society', p. 498.
6   Ibid., p. 499.
7   P. Collins, 'Dickens and Crime', p. 3.
8   A. McNeel-Caird, 'The Cry of the Children', pp. 14-15.
    'A creature', he says, 'six or seven years old, was re-
    cently brought up for housebreaking. Its age mani-
    festly put punishment out of the question, and the
    only practical resource left to the administrators of
    the law, under the guidance of the highest authorities,
    was a solemn reprimand from the judge, - a measure
    whose propriety no one will dispute. Behold, then, the
    majesty of offended justice adequately personified on
    the bench, and surrounded by all the circumstantials
    which are calculated to affect the imagination, - the
    grave deportment of a public prosecutor, armed with
    authority to denounce or to spare, and then most fitly
    exercising his office of forbearance, - the anxious
    countenances of the bar, stirred by unwonted feelings,
    - the attendant lictors ready to execute the behest of
    the law, the crowded spectators eager to catch a glimpse
    of the prisoner: - and thus, - "parturiunt montes,"
    turn to the greater depredator who has put all in
    action, elevated on a table to bring him into view,
    answering to his name with infantine pipe, on being
    prompted, - and studying with intense satisfaction the
    dress in which he has been equipped for the occasion.

With this hopeful subject the judge had to deal; and
after feeling his way with all the tact and patience
for which he is distinguished, and anxious to test the
little culprit's ideas of a court of judicature, he
put the question, "Do you know that I am a judge?" The
shrill, simple, Scottish answer, "What's that?" electri-
fied the court, upset its gravity, and showed all too
clearly the hopelessness of dealing effectually with
such a creature in the imposing forms of law. But it
was not all a mockery: for thus was tried and found
wanting the society of which that child was an outcast,
and there was written in the record of a higher tribunal, "Inasmuch as ye did it not to one, the least of
these my brethren, ye did it not to me!"'

9 L. Radzinowicz, 'History of English Criminal Law'.
10 B.E.F. Knell, Capital punishment, its administration in
relation to juvenile offenders, 'British Journal of
Delinquency', 5, 1968, p. 198.
11 Pinchbeck and Hewitt, op.cit., p. 352.
12 W. Neale, 'Juvenile Delinquency in Manchester', p. 40.
13 R. v. Sidney Smith, 1 Cox 260 1845.
14 R. v. Elizabeth Owen, 4 Card P 236 1830.
15 For discussion of the trends in crime in the nineteenth century, see J. Tobias, 'Crime and Industrial
Society in the Nineteenth Century'.
16 'Report from the Select Committee on the State of the
Police of the Metropolis', 1815.
17 Sir John Eardley Wilmot, 'A Letter to the Magistrates
of England', p. 15.
18 'Report of the Select Committee on the State of the
Police of the Metropolis', P.P. 1828. vi. i.
19 Quoted by W.B. Sanders, Some Early Beginnings of the
Children's Court Movement in England, 'National Probation Association Yearbook', 39, 1945, p. 67.
20 Ibid., p. 68.
21 A Bill for the Punishment, Correction and Reform of
Young Persons charged with privately stealing from
Houses or the Person in Certain Cases.
22 A Bill to Extend the Power of Summary Conviction of
Juvenile Offenders.
23 '3rd Report of the Commissioners on Criminal Law',
Brt. Sess. Pap., 1837 (79) xxxi, p. i.
24 T. Paynter in Evidence to the Select Committee on
Criminal and Destitute Juveniles, 1852, p. 83, para.
1714.
25 'Report of the 2nd Select Committee on the State of
the Police of the Metropolis', 1817.
26 Quoted by Pinchbeck and Hewitt, op.cit., pp. 448, 452.
27 Miss M. Carpenter in evidence to the Select Committee

28   J. Carlebach, 'Caring for Children in Trouble', p. 40.
29   Pinchbeck and Hewitt, op.cit., p. 429.
30   The Reverend Turner in evidence to the Select Committee on Criminal and Destitute Juveniles, p. 22, paras 221-5.
31   M. Carpenter, 'Reformatory Schools for the Children of the Perishing and Dangerous Classes'.
32   M. Carpenter, 'Juvenile Delinquents, their Condition and Treatment'.
33   M. Carpenter, 'Reformatory Schools', p. 83.
34   Ibid., p. 2.
35   Ibid.
36   The Reverend S. Turner in evidence to the Select Committee on Criminal and Destitute Juveniles 1852, p. 31, para. 355.
37   Ibid., Mr Adderley in evidence, p. 16, para. 188.
38   Ibid., Miss Carpenter in evidence, p. 110, para. 888.
39   M. Carpenter, 'Reformatory Schools', p. 131.
40   Quoted by M. Carpenter in 'Reformatory Schools', p. 226.
41   A. Thomson in evidence to the Select Committee on Criminal and Destitute Juveniles, p. 288, paras 3034-9.
42   Quoted by M. Carpenter in 'Reformatory Schools', p. 232.
43   E.C. Wines, 'The State of Prisons and Child Caring Institutions of the Civilised World', p. 233.
44   A. Thomson in evidence to the Select Committee on Criminal and Destitute Juveniles, p. 300, para. 3163.
45   Ibid., p. 288.
46   Ibid., M. Davenport Hill in evidence, p. 33, para. 380.
47   Ibid.
48   Sir William Harcourt, letter to chairmen of quarter sessions, recorders, stipendaries, magistrates, etc.
49   G.S. Cadbury, 'Young Offenders, Yesterday and Today', p. 68.
50   B. Waugh, 'The Gaol Cradle - Who Rocks It?'
51   Ibid., p. 64.
52   'Annual Reports of the Howard Association', 1872-1901 and 1907-9.
53   Hansard Parliamentary Debates, 4th series, 1908 (186) p. 1251.
54   Children Act 1908, 8 Edw. 7 c. 67.
55   Ibid., sec. 58.
56   Ibid., sec. 11.
57   Ibid., sec. 107.
58   Ibid., secs 18, 21, 58, 59, 60.
59   B. Waugh, op.cit.
60   'The Child, the Clinic and the Court'. I have been unable to find the Parliamentary resolution to which Judge Lindsey refers.

CHAPTER 6   ENGLAND AND WALES: THE PRESENT LAW

1   J. Watson, 'The Juvenile Court 1970 Onwards', p. ix.
2   HMSO, 'The Child, the Family and the Young Offender',
    Cmnd 2742, 1965.
3   'Crime a Challenge to Us All'.
4   HMSO, 'Children in Trouble', Cmnd 3601, 1968.
5   Hansard Parliamentary Debates, 4th series, 1908 (183)
    p. 1437.
6   Ibid. (195) p. 227.
7   Ibid (186) p. 1259.
8   HMSO, 'Report of the Departmental Committee on the Treat-
    ment of Young Offenders', Cmnd 2831, 1927.
    HMSO Edinburgh, 'Protection and Training. Report of
    the Departmental Committee', 1928.
9   Children and Young Persons Act 1933, 23 Geo. 5, ch. 12.
    Children and Young Persons (Scotland) Act 1937, 1 Edw.
    8 and 1 Geo. 6, ch. 37.
10 Children and Young Persons Act 1963, ch. 37, sec. 1.
11 Children and Young Persons Act (1933), sec. 47; (1937),
    sec. 52.
12 Children and Young Persons Act 1963, sec. 17 (2).
13 'Report by the Juvenile Organisations Committee of the
    Board of Education on Juvenile Delinquency', 1920,
    p. 36.
14 Ibid., p. 36.
15 '3rd Report of the Work of the Children's Branch',
    1925, p. 7.
16 Hansard Parliamentary Debates, 5th series, 1932 (261)
    p. 1172.
17 W.A. Elkin, 'English Juvenile Courts'.
18 I.G. Briggs, 'Reformatory Reform', p. 109.
19 2nd Schedule. Children and Young Persons Act, 1933.
20 '3rd Report the Work of the Children's Branch', op.
    cit., p. 8.
21 Ibid.
22 Children and Young Persons Act (1933), sec. 49;
    (1937), sec. 46.
23 Shurey, Savory v. Shurey, 1 Ch. 263 1918.
24 Children and Young Persons Act 1969, ch. 54, sec. 1.
25 Children and Young Persons Act 1963, sec. 2 (1) a.
26 Children and Young Persons Act 1969, sec. 1.
27 Ibid., sec. 5 (1).
28 Ibid., sec. 5 (2).
29 Ibid., sec. 1.
30 Ibid., sec. 2 (2).
31 Children Act 1908, 8 Edw. 7, ch. 67, sec. 58.
32 Children and Young Persons Act 1933, sec. 62.
33 Children and Young Persons (Scotland) Act 1937, sec. 66.

34 Children and Young Persons Act 1969, sec. 3 (3).
35 Ibid., sec. 6.
36 Ibid., sec. 7.
37 Eleventh Report from the Expenditure Committee, Session 1973-4, 1974, 1974-5, House of Commons 534, i and ii, pp. 75 and 76, 1974-5.
38 Criminal Statistics Cmnd 6168, 1974.
39 Criminal Statistics Cmnd 6566, 1975.
40 J. Handler, 'The Coercive Social Worker'.
41 HMSO, 'Report of the Departmental Committee on the Treatment of Young Offenders', op.cit., p. 71.
42 Hansard Parliamentary Debates, 5th series, 1932 (261) p. 1179.
43 Children and Young Persons Act 1969, Cmnd 6494, 1976.
44 Criminal Justice Act 1948,   11 and 12 Geo. 6, ch. 58, sec. 17.
45 Criminal Justice Act 1961, 9 and 10 Eliz. 2, ch. 39, sec. 2.
46 Hansard Parliamentary Debates, 5th series (261), p. 1171.
47 See for example, B. Harris, Children's Act in Trouble, 'Criminal Law Review', 1972, p. 670.
48 M. Berlin and G. Wansell, 'Caught in the Act'.
49 Ibid., p. 81.
50 The Magistrates' Association, 52nd Annual Report, 'The Working of the Children and Young Persons Act 1969'.
51 Eleventh Report of the Expenditure Committee.
52 Children and Young Persons Act 1969.
53 Ibid., p. 6.
54 Ibid., p. 8.

CHAPTER 7   SCOTLAND: THE PRESENT LAW

1 HMSO, 'Report of the Departmental Committee on Training and Protection', 1928.
2 HMSO, 'Report of the Committee on Children and Young Persons', Scotland   (Kilbrandon Report), 1964, Cmnd 2306, para. 45.
3 Ibid., paras 13 and 14.
4 HMSO, 'Social Work and the Community', 1966, Cmnd 3065.
5 Social Work (Scotland) Act, 1968, ch. 49, as amended by the Criminal Procedure (Scotland) Act 1975 and the Children Act 1975, sec. 31 (1).
6 Ibid., sec. 32.
7 Ibid., sec. 39.
8 Ibid., sec. 32 (2).
9 Ibid., sec. 42.
10 Ibid., sec. 44.

11 G.H. Gordon, Social Work (Scotland) Bill 1968, 'Scots Law Times', 3 May 1968, p. 68.
12 Social Work (Scotland) Act 1968, sec. 47.
13 Ibid., sec. 42 (6).
14 Children Act 1975, ch. 72, sec. 66.

CHAPTER 8   THE BALANCE IN THE STATUTES

1 HMSO, 'Report of the Departmental Committee on the Care and Treatment of Young Offenders', Cmnd 2831, 1927.
2 HMSO, 'The Child, the Family and the Young Offender', Cmnd 2742, 1965.
3 HMSO, 'Report of the Committee on Children and Young Persons, Scotland' (Kilbrandon Report), Cmnd 2306, 1964.
4 Children and Young Persons Act 1933, 23 Geo. 5, ch. 12, sec. 44.
5 Children and Young Persons Act 1969, ch. 54, sec. 2 (2).
6 Ibid., sec. 1 (4).
7 J. Watson, 'The Juvenile Court 1970 Onwards', p. 11.
8 Children and Young Persons Act 1963, ch. 37, sec. 16.
9 Rehabilitation of Offenders Act 1974, ch. 53.
10 Hansard Parliamentary Reports, 5th series, 1974, 878, col. 166.
11 HMSO, 'Criminal Statistics (Scotland)', Cmnd 5464, Edinburgh, 1972, Cmnd 5640, Edinburgh, 1973, Cmnd 6081, Edinburgh, 1974.
12 'The Report of the President's Commission on Law Enforcement and the Administration of Justice. The Challenge of Crime in a Free Society', Appendix B, table 5.
13 T. Schornhorst, The Waiver of Juvenile Court Jurisdiction: Kent revisited, 'Indiana Law Journal', 43, 1968, p. 583.
14 R. v. G., 'The Times', 21 September 1971.
15 Kilbrandon Report, supra ref. 3.
16 HMSO, 'Criminal Statistics England and Wales', Cmnd 6168, 1974.
17 Quoted by S.J. Fox from A. Deutsch, Our Neglected Children in Juvenile Justice Reform, 'Stanford Law Review', 22, 1970, p. 1233.
18 Kent v. US, 383 US, 554, 1966.
19 B. Bayh, Ten Building Blocks, 'Trial', October 1971.
20 R.C. Sarri, The Rehabilitation Failure, 'Trial', October 1971.
21 Quoted by A. Platt from E.C. Wines, Proceedings of the Illinois Conference of Charities, p. 310, 1898 in 'The Child Savers', p. 132.

22   W. Cavenagh, 'Juvenile Courts, the Child and the Law', p. 112.
23   Ibid., p. 114.
24   HMSO, Report of the Advisory Council on the Penal System, 'Young Adult Offenders'.
25   E. Goffman, 'Asylums'.
26   Children Act 1975, ch. 72, secs 64 and 65.
27   Ibid., sec. 66.
28   HMSO, 'Report of the Departmental Committee on the Adoption of Children', Cmnd 5107, 1972.
29   HMSO, 'Report of the Committee of Enquiry into the Care and Supervision Provided in Relation to Maria Colwell.

CHAPTER 9   THE PEOPLE WHO RUN THE JUVENILE JUSTICE SYSTEM

1   See E. Goffman, 'Encounters', p. 75, for a discussion of the strict meaning of role and role performance.
2   R. Emerson, 'Judging Delinquents'.
3   A. Platt, 'The Child Savers'.
4   J. Watson, 'The Modern Juvenile Court', p. 81.
5   M. Ritchie and J. Mack, 'Police Warnings'.
6   Ibid., p. 72.
7   N. Bruce and J. Spence, 'Face to Face with Families'.
8   'Report of the Committee on Legal Education' (Ormrod Report), para. 92.
9   J. Ellis, Selecting Students for Social Work Training, 'British Journal of Social Work' 5 (2), 1975, p. 137.
10   P. Parsloe, et al., Social Work as Taught, 'New Society', 4 March 1976.
11   Central Council for Education and Training in Social Work, 'Legal Studies in Social Work Education', paper no. 4, 1974.
12   M. Levin and R. Sarri, 'Juvenile Delinquency: a Comparative Analysis of Legal Codes in the United States', p. 44.
13   Ibid., p. 43.
14   Ibid.
15   Ibid., p. 45.
16   Ibid., p. 46.
17   D. Skolen and C.W. Tenney, A Survey of Juvenile Court Judges, 'Journal of Family Law', 4, 1964, p. 77.
18   C.H. Pritchett, 'The Roosevelt Court: A Study in Judicial Politics and Values 1937-47'.
19   C.H. Sheldon in 'The American Judicial Process', sets out seven different theoretical models of the judicial process used by political scientists. Of these the decision-making model based on S-O-R, and the systems

model have been most used although some interesting research has been done using a small group model.

20 K. Vines, Federal District Court Judges and Race Re-
    lations in the South, 'Journal of Public Law', 26,
    1964, p. 338.

21 S. Nagel, Political Party Affiliations and Judges
    Decisions, 'American Political Science Review, 55,
    1965, p. 843.

22 K. Dolbeere, The Federal District Courts and Urban
    Public Policy, in J. Grossman and J. Tanenhaus eds,
    'Frontiers of Judicial Research'.

23 Pritchett, op.cit.

24 G. Schubert, 'Judicial Policy Making', p. 61.

25 See for example, G. Schubert, 'The Judicial Mind Re-
    visited'.

26 E. Snyder, The Supreme Court as a Small Group, 'Social
    Forces', 36, 1958, p. 232.

27 J. Hogarth, 'Sentencing as a Human Process', p. 356.

28 B. Cook, Sentencing Behavior of Federal Judges, 'Cin-
    cinnati Law Review', 42, 1973, p. 4.

29 S. Markov and J. Zelan, 'Lawyers in the Making', p. 2.

30 Cook, op.cit., p. 598.

31 'Justices of the Peace: How they are appointed: What
    they do', Central Office of Information.

32 'Speakers Notes No. 3', Magistrates Association, 1975.

33 R. Hood, 'Sentencing the Motoring Offender'.

34 'Royal Commission on the Justices of the Peace', Cmnd
    7463.

35 G. Hawker, 'Magistrates in the Crown Courts'.

36 See for example, M. Gunhut, 'Juvenile Offenders before
    the Court', and H. Mannheim et al., Magisterial Policy
    in the London Juvenile Courts, 'British Journal of
    Delinquency', 8 (13), 1957, p. 119.

37 '5th Report of the Children's Branch'.

38 'The Training of Justices of the Peace in England and
    Wales', Cmnd 2856.

39 Hawker, op.cit.

40 'The Training of Justices of the Peace in England and
    Wales', op.cit., p. 5.

41 'Criminal Statistics in Scotland 1974, Cmnd 6081.

42 'Scottish Social Work Statistics 1974'.

43 'Report of the Committee on Children and Young Persons
    (Scotland)', Cmnd 2306.

44 'Social Work and the Community', Cmnd 3065, HMSO, 1966.

45 E. Mapston, The Selection of the Children's Panel for
    the County of Fife, 'British Journal of Social Work',
    vol. 2, 1972, pp. 445-80.

46 G. Smith and D. May, The Appointment of the Aberdeen
    Children's Panel, 'British Journal of Social Work',
    1 (1), 1971, pp. 5-27.

47   D. Clark, 'Personality Characteristics of Applicants
     and Members of Children's Panels'.
48   *Kennedy* v. *O'Donnell*, 1975, SLT 235.
49   The Reporters (Conduct of Proceedings before the
     Sheriff (Scotland) Regulations), Local Government
     Scotland 1975 No. 2251 (S.285).
50   M. Finkelstein et al., 'Prosecution in the Juvenile
     Court'.
51   Skoler and Tenney, op.cit., p. 83.
52   M. Feldman, The Prosecutor's Special Role in the Juve-
     nile Court, 'Illinois Bar Journal', 1970.
53   Finkelstein, op.cit.
54   W. Treadwell, The Lawyer in Juvenile Court Dispositional
     Proceedings, 'Juvenile Court Judges Journal', 16, 1965,
     p. 109.
55   Juveniles and Justice, 'Trial', September/October,
     1971, p. 31.
56   A. Platt, op.cit., p. 169.
57   P. Carter, 'Magistrates' Justice'.
58   F. Perry, 'Information for the Court'.
59   P. Hardiker, Social Work Ideologies in the Probation
     Service, 'British Journal of Social Work', 7, 1977.
60   R. Emerson, 'Judging Delinquents', p. 129.
61   Sheldon, op.cit., p. 27.

CHAPTER 10   RECOGNISING AND CONTROLLING DISCRETION

1   M. Finkelstein, et al., 'Prosecution in the Juvenile
    Courts'.
2   HMSO, 'Report of the Committee to enquire into the Care
    and Supervision provided in relation to Maria Colwell'.
3   HMSO, 'Report of the Committee of Inquiry into the
    consideration given and steps taken towards securing
    the welfare of Richard Clark by Perth Town Council and
    other bodies or persons concerned'.
4   Children Act 1975, ch. 72, secs 64-6. To be brought
    into force by order of the appropriate ministers.
5   T. Paulsen, Juvenile Courts, 'Indiana Law Journal',
    43, 1969, p. 540.
6   Personal communication from Mr W. Forrest, Community
    Worker at St Katherine's Centre, Aberdeen.
7   K.C. Davis, 'Discretionary Justice', p. 52.
8   Ibid., p. 112.
9   O. Stevenson, 'Claimant or Client', p. 48.
10 Davis, op.cit., p. 112.
11 Ibid., p. 98.
12 Ibid.
13 J.A. Watson and P. Austin, 'The Modern Juvenile Court',
    p. 80.

14 S. Becke, et al., 'Children still in Trouble', p. 6.
15 M. Ritchie and J.A. Mack, 'Police Warnings'.
16 Personal communications from discussions with reporters during in-service training.
17 R. Renton and H. Brown, 'Criminal Procedure according
to the Law of Scotland'.
18 HMSO, 'Social Work in Scotland 1974', Cmnd 6153, p. 13.
19 For example, in the Lothian region of Scotland social
work assistants are specifically barred from under-
taking work in connection with the Hearings.
20 F. Perry, 'Information for the Court'.
21 M. Hill, 'The Sociology of Public Administration',
p. 85.

CHAPTER 11   CONTINUING CONCERNS AND NEW FORMS OF
INTERVENTION

1 A. Gouldner, 'For Sociology', p. 41.
2 P. Carlen, 'Magistrates Justice'.
3 Z. Bankowski and G. Mungham, 'Images of Law'.
4 Ibid., p. 28.
5 H. Parker, 'View from the Boys', p. 172.
6 Bankowski and Mungham, op.cit., p. 6.
7 Current research studies undertaken by Oxford and
Aberdeen Universities into social work education,
support this generalisation.
8 P. Hardiker, Social Work Ideologies in the Probation
Service, 'British Journal of Social Work', 7, 1977.
9 I.L. Horowitz and M. Liebowitz, Social Deviance and
Political Marginality, 'Social Problems', 15, 1968,
p. 283.
10 L. Cohen in M. Brake and M. Bailey, 'Radical Social
Work'.
11 See chapter nine, p.231 .
12 Parker, op.cit., p. 156.
13 Ibid., p. 189.
14 L. Gibbs, The Effects of Juvenile Legal Procedures on
Juvenile Offenders' Self Attitudes, 'Journal of Research in Crime and Delinquency', p. 51.
15 'The Challenge of Crime in a Free Society', report of
the President's Commission on Law Enforcement and the
Administration of Justice.
16 Youth Development and Delinquency Prevention Administration, 'The Challenge of Youth Service Bureau'.
17 M. Rosenheim, Youth Service Bureau - a concept in
search of a definition, 'Juvenile Court Judges Journal',
20 (2), 1969.
18 S. Norman, 'Youth Service Bureau'.

19 HMSO, 'Children in Trouble', Cmnd 3601.
20 J. Handler, 'The Coercive Social Worker'.
21 HMSO, 'Intermediate Treatment Project', p. 10.
22 Ibid.
23 Children and Young Persons Act 1969, sec. 12.
24 C. Roberts and M. Davies, 'The Wythenshawe Inter-
    mediate Treatment Project'. Mimeograph from Depart-
    ment of Social Administration, Manchester University,
    1974.
25 HMSO, 'Intermediate Treatment', op.cit., p. 5.
26 Roberts and Davies, op.cit., p. 6.
27 I. Naftali, 'Issues raised through the Youth Develop-
    ment Project'.
28 J. Paley and D. Thorpe, 'Children, Handle with Care'.
29 Report of a Conference held in October 1974.
30 J.B. Mays, 'Crime and its Treatment'.
31 Ibid., p. 87.
32 Milwaukee Industrial School v. Supervisors of Milwaukee
    County, 40 Wisc. 328 1976.
33 C. Andrews, Intermediate Treatment, 'Social Service
    News', July 1971.
34 P. Morris and M. Beverley, 'On License', p. 70.
35 Roberts and Davies, op.cit.
36 M. Rosenheim ed., 'Justice for the Child', p. 46.
37 'Crime in a Free Society', Report of the President's
    Commission on Law Enforcement and the Administration
    of Justice, US Government Printing Office, Washington,
    1967.
38 Olmstead v. US, 277 US 438 1928. (Justice Brandeis
    in a dissenting opinion.)
39 F. Allen, 'The Borderline of Criminal Justice', p. 24.
40 J.F. Larsen, Identifying Court Needs, 'Juvenile Court
    Judges Journal', 20, 1969, p. 91.

Bibliography

OFFICIAL PUBLICATIONS AND REPORTS

Britain

Second report of the Select Committee on the State of
Police of the Metropolis, 1817.
Third report of the Committee on the State of Police of
the Metropolis, 1818.
Report of the Committee on the Criminal Laws, 1819.
Report of the Select Committee on the State of Prisons in
Scotland, 1826.
Report of the Select Committee on the Police of the Metro-
polis, 1828.
Third report of the Commissioners on Criminal Laws, 1837.
Report from the Select Committee on the Education of the
Poorer Classes, 1838.
Report from the Select Committee on Criminal and Desti-
tute Juveniles, 1852.
Report of the Commissioners on Reformatory and Industrial
Schools, 1884.
Report of the Departmental Committee on Reformatory and
Industrial Schools, Cmnd 8204, HMSO, 1896.
Report of the Juvenile Organisations Committee, Board of
Education, 1920.
Third report of the Work of the Children's Branch, Home
Office, 1925.
Report of the Departmental Committee on the Care and Treat-
ment of Young Offenders (Molony), Cmnd 2831, HMSO, 1927.
Protection and Training. Report of the Departmental Com-
mittee on Young Offenders (Morton), HMSO, Edinburgh, 1928.
Fifth report of the Work of the Children's Branch, Home
Office, 1938.
Hereford Juvenile Court Enquiry, Report of the Tribunal,
House of Commons 579, HMSO, 1943.

Report of the Committee on Homeless Children (Clyde), Cmnd 6911, HMSO, Edinburgh, 1945.

Report of the Committee on the Care of Children (Curtis), Cmnd 6922, HMSO, 1946.

Report of the Committee on Children and Young Persons (Ingleby), Cmnd 1191, HMSO, 1960.

The Probation Service in Scotland, Scottish Home and Health Department, HMSO, Edinburgh, 1961.

Report of the Departmental Committee on the Probation Service (Manson), Cmnd 1650, HMSO, 1962.

Second report of the Departmental Committee on the Probation Service, Cmnd 1800, HMSO, 1962.

Report of the Committee on Children and Young Persons (Scotland) (Kilbrandon), Cmnd 2306, HMSO, Edinburgh, 1964.

The Child, the Family and the Young Offender, Cmnd 2742, HMSO, 1965.

The Training of the Justices of the Peace in England and Wales, Cmnd 2856, HMSO, 1967.

Social Work and the Community, Cmnd 3065, HMSO, Edinburgh, 1966.

Children in Trouble, Cmnd 3601, HMSO, 1968.

Report of the Work of the Probation and After Care Service 1966-8, Cmnd 4233, HMSO, 1969.

Part I of the Children and Young Persons Act 1969, Home Office, HMSO, 1970.

Report of the Committee on Legal Education (Ormrod), Cmnd 4595, HMSO, 1971.

Justices of the Peace: how they are appointed: what they do, Central Office of Information, 1972.

Report of the Committee into the work and pay of probation officers and social workers (Butterworth), Cmnd 5076, HMSO, 1972.

Report of the Departmental Committee on the Adoption of Children (Houghton), Cmnd 5107, HMSO, 1972.

Report of the Departmental Committee on Social Service in Courts of Summary Jurisdiction, Cmnd 5122, HMSO, 1972.

Intermediate Treatment Project, Department of Health and Social Security, Development Group Report, HMSO, 1973.

Social Work in Scotland in 1972, Cmnd 5337, HMSO, Edinburgh, 1973.

Criminal Statistics, England and Wales 1972, Cmnd 5402, HMSO, 1973.

Criminal Statistics (Scotland) 1972, Cmnd 5464, HMSO, Edinburgh, 1973.

Criminal Statistics, England and Wales 1973, Cmnd 5677, HMSO, 1974.

Young Adult Offenders, Report of the Advisory Council on the Penal System, HMSO, 1974.

Report of the Committee of Enquiry into the Care and Super-

vision Provided in Relation to Maria Colwell, HMSO, 1974.
Criminal Statistics (Scotland) 1973, Cmnd 5640, HMSO, Edinburgh, 1974.
Social Work in Scotland in 1973, Cmnd 5795, HMSO, Edinburgh, 1974.
The Children and Young Persons Act 1969, Eleventh Report from the Expenditure Committee, House of Commons 1974-5, 534, HMSO, 1975.
Scottish Social Work Statistics 1973, Social Work Services Group, HMSO, Edinburgh, 1975.
The Legal System in Scotland, HMSO, 1975.
A Guide to the Rehabilitation of Offenders Act 1974, HMSO, 1975.
Criminal Statistics (Scotland) 1974, Cmnd 6081, HMSO, Edinburgh, 1975.
Child Care in England and Wales, Department of Health and Social Security, Cmnd 6147, HMSO, 1975.
Social Work in Scotland in 1974, Cmnd 6153, HMSO, Edinburgh, 1975.
Criminal Statistics England and Wales 1974, Cmnd 6168, HMSO, 1975.
Scottish Social Work Statistics 1974, Social Work Services Group, HMSO, Edinburgh, 1976.
Children and Young Persons Act 1969, Cmnd 6494, HMSO, 1976.
Criminal Statistics England and Wales 1975, Cmnd 6566, HMSO, 1976.
Criminal Statistics (Scotland) 1975, Cmnd 6631, HMSO, Edinburgh, 1976.

United States of America

Standards for specialized Courts dealing with Children. Children's Bureau, US Department of Health, Education and Welfare (HEW) US Government Printing Office, Washington, 1966.
W.H. Sheridan, Standards for Juvenile and Family Courts (HEW) US Government Printing Office, Washington, 1966.
Crime in a Free Society, Report of the President's Commission on Law Enforcement and the Administration of Justice, US Government Printing Office, Washington, 1967.
W.H. Sheridan, Legislative Guide for Drafting Family and Juvenile Court Acts (HEW) US Government Printing Office, Washington, 1971.
Instead of Court, National Institute of Mental Health (NIMH), US Government Printing Office, Washington, 1971.
The Juvenile Court - a status report (NIMH), US Government Printing Office, Washington, 1971.
Community based Corrections Programs (NIMH), US Government

Printing Office, Washington, 1971.
Diversion from the Criminal Justice System (NIMH), US
Government Printing Office, Washington, 1971.
The Challenge of Youth Service Bureau, Youth Development
and Delinquency Prevention Administration (YDDPA) (HEW) US
Government Printing Office, Washington, 1973.
Better Ways to Help Youth (YDDPA) (HEW) US Government Print-
ing Office, Washington, 1973.
Diverting Youth from the Correctional System (YDDPA) (HEW)
US Government Printing Office, Washington, 1974.

BOOKS AND ARTICLES

ABEL-SMITH, B. and STEVENS, R., 'Lawyers and the Courts',
Heinemann, 1967.
ABEL-SMITH, B., et al., 'Legal Problems and the Citizen',
Heinemann, 1973.
ABBOT, G. (ed.), 'The Child and the State', Chicago, Uni-
versity of Chicago Press, 1938.
ADAM, G. et al., 'Juvenile Justice Management', Springfield,
Thomas, 1973.
ADDAMS, J., et al., 'The Child, the Clinic, and the Court',
New York, New Republic Inc., 1925.
ALEXANDER, P., Of Juvenile Courts and Justice, 'National
Probation and Parole Association Yearbook', New York,
National Probation and Parole Association, 1967.
ALLEN, F.A., Criminal Justice, Legal Values and the Reha-
bilitative Ideal, 'Journal of Criminal Law and Criminology',
50 (226), 1959.
ALLEN, F.A., 'The Borderline of Criminal Justice', Chicago,
University of Chicago Press, 1964.
ALPER, P.S., 40 Years of the Juvenile Court, 'American
Sociological Review', 26, 1961.
ANDREWS, C., Intermediate Treatment, 'Social Service News',
3 (1), 1972.
ANDREWS, C., Intermediate Treatment: how it works in prac-
tice, 'Social Service News', 1 (9), 1971.
ANTONIO, D.G., 'Scots Law', Collins, 1968.
APTER, D., 'Ideology and Discontent', New York, Free Press,
1964.
ARNAD, W., Race and Ethnicity relative to other factors in
Juvenile Court Disposition, 'American Journal of Socio-
logy', 72, 1973, p. 211.
ARNOLD, W.R., 'Juveniles on Parole', New York, Random
House, 1970.
ASHTON, E.T., Care, Protection and Control, 'New Law Jour-
nal', 118, 1968.
ASHTON T. and YOUNG, A.F., 'British Social Work in the

Nineteenth Century', Routledge & Kegan Paul, 1956.
ATTLEE, C., 'The Social Worker', Bell, 1920.
AUBREY, M., The Future of Juvenile Courts, 'Criminal Law Review', 1965.
AUGUSTUS, J., 'A Report on the Labors of John Augustus', Boston, Wright and Hardy, 1852.
AYSCOUGH, H., 'When Mercy Seasons Justice', Church of England Temperance Society, 1923.
BABINGRA, A., 'A House in Bow Street', Macdonald, 1969.
BAGOT, J.H., 'Juvenile Delinquency', Jonathan Cape, 1961.
BALFOUR, C., On becoming a children's panel member, M.A. Thesis, University of Aberdeen, 1975.
BARKER, T.B., 'War with Crime', Longmans, Green & Co., 1889.
BARR, H. and O'LEARY, E., 'Trends and Regional Comparisons in Probation', HMSO, 1966.
BAYH, B., Juveniles and Justice - 10 Building Blocks, 'Trial', September/October 1971.
BAYH, B., A Time for Improvement in the Juvenile Justice System, 'Juvenile Court Judges Journal', 22, 1971, p. 31.
BAZELON, D.L., Beyond Control of the Juvenile Court, 'Juvenile Court Judges Journal', 21, 1970, p. 43.
BEARD, C.A., 'The Office of the Justice of the Peace in England', New York, Burt Franklin, 1904.
BECKE, S., et al., 'Children Still in Trouble', Institute for the Study and Treatment of Delinquency, 1973.
BECKER, H., 'Outsiders', New York, Free Press, 1966.
BEGGS, T., 'An Inquiry into the Extent and Causes of Juvenile Depravity', Charles Gilpin, 1849.
BELL, M., 'Coping with Crime', New York, National Probation and Parole Association, 1937.
BELL, M. (ed.), 'Guide for Juvenile Court Judges', New York, National Probation and Parole Association, 1957.
BENNETT, M., The Voluntary Field, 'Child Care News', 94, 1970.
BERLINS, M. and MANSELL, G., 'Caught in the Act', Penguin Books, 1974.
BEST, G., 'Mid-Victorian Britain', Panther, 1973.
BEVAN, H.K., 'The Law Relating to Children', Butterworths, 1973.
BLOCH, H.A. and FLYNN, F.T., 'Delinquency: The Juvenile Offender in America Today', New York, Random House, 1956.
BLUMBERG, A.S., The Practice of Law as a Confidence Game, 'Law and Society Review', 1 (2), 1967, p. 1.
BLUMBERG, A.S., 'Criminal Justice', Chicago, Quadrangle Books, 1967.
BLUMBERG, A.S., 'The Scales of Justice', Chicago, Aldine Publishing Co., 1970.
BOSANQUET, C.B.P., 'Aspect of the Social Problem',

Macmillan, 1895, New York, Kraus reprint, 1968.

BOSANQUET, C.B.P., 'London: Some Account of its Growth, Charitable Agencies and Wants', Hatchard & Co., 1868.

BOSANQUET, H., 'Social Work in London, 1869-1912', New York, Dutton & Co., 1914.

BOSS, P., 'Social Policy and the Young Delinquent', Routledge & Kegan Paul, 1967.

BOTTOMS, A.E., On the decriminalization of English Juvenile Courts, in R. Hood (ed.), 'Crime, Criminology and Public Policy', Heinemann, 1974.

BOTTOMS, A.E., et al., Children, Young Persons and the Courts, 'Criminal Law Review', 1970.

BRACE, C.L., 'The Dangerous Classes of New York', New York, Wynkoop & Hallenbeck, 1872.

BRACE, C.L., 'Proceedings of the Conference of Charities and Corrections', Boston, 1976.

BRECKENRIDGE, S., 'Public Welfare Administration in the United States', Chicago University Press, 1938.

BRENNAN, W.C. and KHINDUKA, S.K., Role Expectations of Social Workers and Lawyers in the Juvenile Court, 'Crime and Delinquency', 17, 1971, p. 191.

BRIGGS, I.G., 'Reformatory Reform', Longmans, Green & Co., 1924.

BRITISH ASSOCIATION OF SOCIAL WORKERS, 'Intermediate Treatment', BASW, 1974.

BROWN, H., In the interest of A, B, and C, 'Juvenile Court Judges Journal', 16 (3), 1965, p. 120.

BROWN, L.B., 'Ideology', Penguin Books, 1973.

BROWN, L.N., The Legal Background to the Family Court, 'British Journal of Criminology', 6, 1966, p. 139.

BROWN, R.S., 'The Serjeants of the Peace', Manchester University Press, 1936.

BRUCE, N., Children's Hearings - A Retrospect, 'British Journal of Criminology', 15 (4), 1975.

BRUCE, N. and SPENCER, J., 'Face to Face with Families', Macdonald, Lothian, 1976.

BRUNS, F.J., 'Trends in Social Work, 1876-1956', New York, John Wiley, 1957.

BURTON, J.H., 'Narrative from Criminal Trials in Scotland', Chapman & Hall, 1852.

CARLEBACH, J., 'Caring for Children in Trouble', Routledge & Kegan Paul, 1970.

CARLEN, P., 'Magistrates' Justice', Martin Robertson, 1976.

CARMICHAEL, K., Developments in Scottish Social Work, 'Applied Social Studies', 1, 1969, p. 35.

CARPENTER, J.E., 'The Life and Work of Mary Carpenter', Macmillan, 1879.

CARPENTER, M., 'Juvenile Delinquents, their Condition and Treatment', reprinted New Jersey, Patterson Smith Publishing Corporation, 1970.

CARPENTER, M., 'Reformatory Schools', C. Gilpin, 1851 and Woburn Press, 1968.

CARR, L.J., Most Courts have to be Substandard, 'Federal Probation', XIII (3), 1949.

CARR-SAUNDERS, A.M., MANHEIM, H. and RHODES, E.C., 'Young Offenders: An Inquiry into Juvenile Delinquency', Cambridge University Press, 1942.

CARSON, W. and WILES, P., 'The Sociology of Crime and Delinquency in Britain', vol. I, Martin Robertson, 1971.

CARTER, R., The pre-sentence report and the decision making process, 'Journal of Research in Crime and Delinquency', 4, 1967, p. 203.

CARTER, R.M. and WILKINS, L.J., 'Probation and Parole', New York, John Wiley, 1970.

CAVENAGH, W.E., What Kind of Court or Committee, 'British Journal of Criminology', 6, 1966, p. 123.

CAVENAGH, W.E., 'Juvenile Courts, the Child and the Law', Baltimore, Penguin Books, 1967.

CENTRAL COUNCIL FOR EDUCATION AND TRAINING IN SOCIAL WORK, 'The Social Worker in the Juvenile Court', CCETSW, 1974.

A CHAIRMAN OF QUARTER SESSIONS, The Lay Justices: Some Criticisms and Suggestions, 'Criminal Law Review', 1961, p. 656.

CHAPMAN, J., Intermediate Treatment, 'New Society', 6 August 1970.

CHASE, E., Schemes and Visions: a suggested revision of juvenile sentencing, 'Texas Law Review', 51, 1973, p. 613.

CHUTE, C.L., Juvenile Court in Retrospect, 'Federal Probation', XIII (3), 1949.

CHUTE, C.L. and BELL, M., 'Crime, Courts and Probation', New York, Macmillan, 1956.

CICOUREL, A.V., 'The Social Organization of Juvenile Justice', New York, John Wiley, 1962.

CLARK, D., Personality characteristics of applicants and members of Children's Panels, unpublished paper, 1975.

CLOWARD, R.A. and OHLIN, L.E., 'Delinquency and Opportunity', Chicago, Free Press, 1960.

COGAN, N., Juvenile Law before and after the entrance of parens patriae, 'South Carolina Law Review', 22, 1970, p. 147.

COHEN, A., 'Delinquent Boys', Chicago, Free Press, 1955.

COHEN, A.K., 'Deviance and Control', Englewood Cliffs, Prentice-Hall, 1966.

COHEN, A.K., An Evaluation of Gault, 'Indiana Law Journal', 43, 1968, p. 489.

COHEN, F., A Lawyer looks at Juvenile Justice, 'Criminal Law Bulletin', 7 (6), 1971.

COHEN, S., It's all right for you to talk, in R. Bailey

and M. Brake, 'Radical Social Work', Edward Arnold, 1975.

COLE, L., 'Our Children's Keepers', New York, Grossman, 1972.

COLE, S., Lawyers in the Juvenile Court, 'Crime and Delinquency', 13, 1967, p. 488.

COLLEGE OF LAW LECTURES, 'Children and the Courts', College of Law, 1976.

COLLINS, P., 'Dickens and Crime', Bloomington, Indiana University Press, 1968.

COOK, B., Sentencing Behaviour of Federal Judges: Draft Cases 1972, 'Criminal Law Review', 42, 1973, p. 618.

COUCH, A.J., Diverting the Status Offender from the Juvenile Courts, 'Juvenile Justice', 25, 1976, p. 18.

COULL, J. and MERRY, E., 'Principles and Practice of Scots Law', Butterworth, 1971.

COXE, S., Lawyers in the Juvenile Court, 'Crime and Delinquency', 13, 1967, p. 488.

CROXTON, T.A., The Kent Case and its Consequences, 'Journal of Family Law', 1, 1967.

CULBERTSON, R., Commitment Practices in Indiana Juvenile Courts, 'Juvenile Justice', 24 (4), 1974, p. 25.

DANELSKI, D., The Influence of the Chief Justice in the Decision Making Process in W.F. Murphy and C.H. Pritchett, 'Courts, Judges and Politics', New York, Random House, 1974.

DAVIDSON, H.A., That other Helping Profession, 'American Journal of Psychiatry', 122, 1965, p. 691.

DAVIS, K.C., 'Discretionary Justice', St Paul, West Publishing Co., 1965.

DAVIS, M., 'Probationers in their Social Environment', HMSO, 1969.

DAY, S.P., 'Juvenile Crime', J.F. Hope, 1858.

DE TOQUEVILLE, A., 'On the Penitentiary System in the United States', Carbondale Ill., South Illinois University Press, 1964.

DEMBITZ, N., Justice for Children, 'American Bar Association Journal', 60, 1974, p. 588.

DICKENS, C., '44 Reprinted Pieces', Boston, Estes and Lauriat, 1895.

DOLBEARE, K., The Federal District Courts and Urban Policy, in J. Crossman and J. Tanenhaus, 'Frontiers of Judicial Research', New York, John Wiley, 1969.

DOUGLAS, W.O., Juvenile Courts and Due Process of Law, 'Juvenile Court Judges Journal', 19 (1), 1968.

DUNHAM, H.W., The Juvenile Court: Contradictory Orientations in Processing Offenders, 'Law and Contemporary Problems', 23, 1959, p. 508.

DUSTER, T., 'The Legislation of Morality', Free Press, 1970.

ELDEFONSO, E., 'Law Enforcement and the Youthful Offender', New York, John Wiley, 1973.

ELIOT, T.D., 'The Juvenile Court and the Community', New York, Macmillan, 1914.

ELKIN, W.A., 'English Juvenile Courts', Routledge & Kegan Paul, 1938.

EMERSON, R.M., 'Judging Delinquents', Chicago, Aldine, 1969.

EMPEY, L.T. and RABOW, J., The Provo Experiment in Delinquency Rehabilitation, 'American Sociological Review', 26, 1961, p. 679.

ENGELS, F., 'The Condition of the Working Class in England', Panther, 1969.

ERIKSON, E., 'Young Man Luther', New York, Norton, 1958.

ERIKSON, E., 'Insight and Responsibility', New York, Norton, 1964.

FAUST, F.L. and BRANTINGHAM, P., 'Juvenile Justice Philosophy', St Paul, West Publishing Co., 1974.

FELDMAN, J., The prosecutors special task in juvenile delinquency, 'Illinois Bar Journal', October, 1970, p.146.

FENNER, B., 'Raising the Veil', Boston, 1856.

FELKENS, G.T., 'The Criminal Justice System', Englewood Cliffs, Prentice-Hall, 1973.

FINKELSTEIN, M., et al., 'Prosecution in the Juvenile Courts', US Department of Justice: Law Enforcement Assistance Administration, Washington, US Government Printing Office, 1973.

FLACKETT, J., Juvenile Offenders in the Community, 'Howard Journal', 14, 1974, p. 22.

FLEXNER, B. and BALDWIN, R., 'Juvenile Courts and Probation', New York, Century Co., 1914.

FLEXNER, B., et al., 'The Child, the Family and the Court', US Department of Labor, Children's Bureau Publication, no. 193, 1929.

FLEXNER, B. and OPPENHEIMER, R., 'The Legal Aspects of the Juvenile Court', US Department of Labor, Children's Bureau Publication, no. 99, Washington, US Government Printing Office, 1922.

FORD, D., 'Children, Courts and Caring', Constable, 1975.

FORT, W.S., Looking Ahead in Juvenile Corrections, 'Juvenile Court Judges Journal', 16, 1965, p. 61.

FOX, S.J., 'Modern Juvenile Justice', St Paul, West Publishing Co., 1972.

FOX, S.J., 'The Scottish Panels: an American Viewpoint on Children's Right to Punishment', paper given to Panel Members' Summer School, June 1974.

FOX, S.J., The Reform of Juvenile Justice: The Child's Right to Punishment, 'Juvenile Justice', 25, 1974, p. 2.

FOX, S.J., Juvenile Justice Reform: Innovations in Scotland, 'American Criminal Law Review', 12, 1974, p. 61.

FOX, S.J., Juvenile Justice Reform: A Historical Perspective, 'Stanford Law Review, 28, 1970, p. 1187.

FOX, S.J., Philosophy and the Principles of Punishment in the Juvenile Court, 'Family Law Quarterly', 8, 1976, p. 313.

FRASER, M., 'Children in Conflict', Penguin Books, 1974.

FREEMAN, M.D.A., 'The Legal Structure', Longmans, 1974.

FREEMAN, M.D.A., 'The Children Act 1975', Sweet & Maxwell, 1976.

FRENCH, S., The Evolution of the Justices Clerk, 'Criminal Law Review', 1961, p. 688.

FRY, M. and RUSSELL, C., 'A Notebook for the Children's Court', Howard League, 1945.

FULBROOK, J., et al., 'Tribunals: A Social Court?', Fabian Tract 427, Fabian Society, 1973.

GARNETT, W.H.S., 'Children and the Law', John Murray, 1911.

GILMAN, M. and LOW, A., 'Training for Juvenile Probation Officers', US Department of Health, Education and Welfare, US Government Printing Office, Washington, 1962.

GLUECK, S., 'The Problem of Delinquency', Cambridge, Mass., Riverside Press, 1959.

GLUECK, S. and E., 'Towards a Typology of Juvenile Offenders', New York, Grune and Stratton, 1970.

GOLDMAN, S., Voting Behaviour: U.S. Court of Appeals, 1961-64, 'American Political Science Review', 60, 1966, p. 374.

GOLDMAN, S., Voting Behaviour on the U.S. Courts of Appeals Revisited, 'American Political Science Review', 69, 1975, p. 491.

GOLDMAN, S. and JAHNIGE, J.P., Systems Analysis and the Judicial System, 'Polity', 3, 1971, p. 334.

GOLDSTEIN, J., et al., 'Beyond the best interests of the child', New York, Free Press, 1973.

GOODMAN, L., 'Clarke Hall and Morrison's Law relating to Children and Young Persons', eighth edition, Butterworth, 1972.

GOODMAN, L., 'Notes on Juvenile Court Law', ninth edition, Bary Rose, 1973.

GORDON, G.H., Social Work (Scotland) Bill, 1968, 'The Scots Law Times', 3 May 1968.

GOUGH, A.R. and GRILL, M.A., The Unruly Child and the Law: Toward a Focus on the Family, 'Juvenile Court Judges Journal', 23, 1972, p.9.

GOULDNER, A., The Sociologist as Partisan, 'American Sociologist', 13 (2), 1968.

GOULDNER, A., The Politics of Mind, 'Social Policy', 2 (6), 1972.

GRANT, J., Leadership for Children's Panels, 'Focus', 22, 1973.

GRANT, J.P., Juvenile Justice - Part 3 of the Social Work Scotland Act, 'Juridical Review', 149, 1971.

GRANT, J.P., The Legal Safeguards for the Rights of the Child and Parents in the Children's Hearing System,

'Juridical Review', 209, 1975.
GREEN, E., 'Judicial attitudes to Sentencing', Macmillan, 1961.
GREENBLATT, M., et al., 'The Patient and the Mental Hospital', Chicago, Free Press, 1957.
GREENE, N. and ESSELSTYN, T.C., The Beyond Control Girl, 'Juvenile Justice', 23 (3), 1972.
GRIFFITHS, A., 'The Chronicles of Newgate', Chapman & Hall, 1884.
GRIFFITHS, J., Ideology in Criminal Procedure, 'Yale Law Journal', 79, 1970, p. 359.
GUNHUT, M., 'Juvenile Offenders before the Courts', Clarendon Press, 1956.
GRUNZMAN, P., Pre-sentence reports, 'Iowa Law Review', 52, 1972, p. 161.
HADDEN, T.B., A Plea for Punishment, 'Cambridge Law Journal', 1965, p. 117.
HALDANE, J.D., Children's Panel Advisory Committees, 'British Journal of Criminology', 11, 1975, p. 394.
HALL, W. Clarke, 'Children's Court', Allen & Unwin, 1926.
HANDLER, J., The Juvenile Court and the Adversary System, 'Wisconsin Law Review', 7, 1965.
HANDLER, J., 'Coercion in the Caseworker Relationship', Institute for Research on Poverty, University of Wisconsin, 1970.
HANDLER, J., 'The Coercive Social Worker', Chicago, Rand McNally, 1973.
HARRIS, B., Children's Act in Trouble, 'Criminal Law Review', 1972, p. 670.
HARRIS, B., The local authority social worker and the courts, 'Local Government Chronicle', 27 April 1973.
HARRISON, J.F.C., 'The Early Victorians, 1832-51', Panther, 1973.
HARTMANN, H.L., Interviewing Techniques in Probation and Parole, 'Federal Probation', XXVII (1), 1963.
HAWES, J., 'Children in Urban Society', Oxford University Press, 1971.
HAWKER, G., 'Magistrates in the Crown Courts', University of Birmingham, Institute of Judicial Administration, 1974.
HAXBY, D., Examiner of Children in Trouble, 'The New Law Journal', 8 May 1969.
HAZARD, G., Limitations in the Uses of Behavioural Sciences in the Law, 'Case Western Reserve Law Review', 19, 1967, p. 71.
HEALY, W., Thoughts about Juvenile Courts, 'Federal Probation', XIII (3), 1949, p. 16.
HEASMAN, C., 'Evangelicals in Action', Geoffrey Bles, 1962.
HEWAT, Lord, The Treatment of the Young Offender, 2nd Clarke Hall Lecture, 1935.

HILL, F. Davenport, 'Children of the State', Macmillan, 1889.

HILL, M., 'The Sociology of Public Administration', Weidenfeld & Nicolson, 1972.

HILL, M. and CORNWALLIS, C., '2 Prize Essays on Juvenile Delinquency', Smith & Elder, 1853.

HINDE, R.S., 'The British Penal System, 1773-1950, Duckworth, 1951.

HOBHOUSE, Rosa, 'Benjamin Waugh', C.W. David & Co. Ltd., 1939.

HOFFMAN, C.W., Organization of Family Courts, 'The Child the Clinic and the Court', New York, New Republic Inc., 1925.

HOGARTH, T., 'Sentencing as a human process', Toronto, University of Toronto Press, 1971.

HOLDEN, D.A., 'Child Legislation', Butterworth, 1970.

HOLMES, T., 'Known to the Police', Edward Arnold, 1908.

HOOD, R., 'Sentencing in Magistrates Courts', Stevens, 1962.

HOOD, R., 'Sentencing the Motoring Offender', Heinemann, 1972.

HOPSON, D., Introduction, 'Indiana Law Journal', 43, 1968, p. 18.

HOROWITZ, I.L. and LIEBOWITZ, M., Social Deviance and Political Marginality, 'Social Problems', 15, 1968, p. 280.

HORSLEY, J.W., 'How Criminals are Made and Prevented', T. Fisher Unwin, 1913.

HORSLEY, J.W., 'Jottings from Jail', T. Fisher Unwin, 1887.

HOUSTON, D. (ed.), 'Social Work in the Children's Hearings System', Glasgow and Edinburgh Universities' Committee for Further and Advanced Training in Social Work, 1975.

HOWARD, J., 'State of the Prisons', Warrington, 1780.

HOYLE, W., 'Crime in England and Wales in the 19th Century', Effingham, Wilson & Co., 1876.

HURLEY, T.D., Origin of the Illinois Juvenile Court Law in Addams, 'The Child, the Clinic and the Court', 1925.

JACKSON, R.M., 'The Machinery of Justice in England', Cambridge University Press, 1972.

JACKSON, R.M., 'Enforcing the Law', Penguin Books, 1972.

JONES, H., 'Crime and the Penal System', University Tutorial Press, 1962.

JORDAN, W., The Probation Service in the 'Sixties, 'Social and Economic Administration', 5, 1971, pp. 125-66.

JUSTICE EDUCATION AND RESEARCH TRUST, 'The Prosecution Process in England and Wales', Justice Education and Research Trust, 1970.

KAHAN, B.J., The White Paper, 'British Journal of Criminology', 6, 1966, p. 159.

KARLEN, D., 'Anglo American Criminal Justice', Oxford University Press, 1967.

KEATING, P., 'Into Unknown England', Fontana, 1976.
KILBRANDON, Lord, Children in Trouble, 'British Journal of Criminology', 6, 1966, p. 112.
KILBRANDON, Lord, The Scottish Reforms, 'British Journal of Criminology', 8, 1968, p. 235.
KING, D.B., '100 Injustices to the Child', St Louis University School of Law, National Juvenile Law Centre, 1971.
KNELL, B., Capital Punishment, 'British Journal of Delinquency', 5, 1965, p. 200.
KOLKER, D., The Test Case and Law Reform in the Juvenile Justice System, 'Yale Review of Law and Social Action', 1, 1971, p. 64.
LAMB, C.M., Exploring the Conservatism of Federal Appeals Court Judges, 'Indiana Law Journal', 51, 1974, p. 257.
LARSON, J.F., Identifying Court Needs, 'Juvenile Court Judges Journal', 20, 1969, p. 91.
LATHROP, J., The Background of the Juvenile Court in Illinois, in Addams, 'The Child the Clinic and the Court', 1925.
LAVER, J., 'Manners and Morals in the Age of Optimism', New York, Harper & Row, 1966.
LEAGUE OF NATIONS CHILD WELFARE COMMITTEE, 'Auxiliary Services of Juvenile Courts', Allen & Unwin, 1931.
LEAGUE OF NATIONS CHILD WELFARE COMMITTEE, 'Organisation of Juvenile Courts', Allen & Unwin, 1935.
LEE, J.M., Modern History of the Appointment of Lay Magistrates, 'Criminal Law Review', 1961, p. 678.
LEESON, C., 'The Probation System', P.S. King, 1914.
LEESON, C., 'Notes for New Magistrates', Magistrates Association, 1935.
LEMERT, E.M., Legislating Change in the Juvenile Court, 'Wisconsin Law Review', 1967, p. 421.
LEMERT, E.M., 'Human Deviance, Social Problems and Social Control', Englewood Cliffs, Prentice-Hall, 1972.
LEMERT, E.M., 'Instead of Court', Washington, National Institute for Mental Health, US Government Printing Office, 1971.
LENROOT, K., The Evolution of the Juvenile Court, 'Annals of the American Academy', 105, 1923, p. 213.
LEVIN, J., Children and Young Persons Act, 1969, 'Solicitors Journal', 114, 1970, p. 179.
LEVIN, M. and SARRI, R., 'Juvenile Delinquency: a comparative analysis of Legal Codes in the United States', East Lancing, University of Michigan, National Assessment of Juvenile Corrections, 1974.
LINDSAY, B.B., Colorado's Contribution to the Juvenile Court in Addams, 'The Child the Clinic and the Court', 1925.
LINDSAY, B.B., The Juvenile Court of the Future, 'Proceedings of the National Conference of Social Workers', Chicago, Chicago University Press, 1925
LINDSEY, E., The Juvenile Court Movement from a Lawyer's Standpoint, 'Annals of the American Academy', 52, 1914, p.141.

LOU, H.H., 'Juvenile Courts in the United States, Chapel
Hill, University of North Carolina Press, 1927.
LOW, S., 'The Charities of London', Samson Low, 1850.
LUBOVE, R., 'The Professional Altruist', Cambridge, Mass.,
Harvard University Press, 1968.
LUDWIG, F., 'Youth and the Law', Brooklyn, Foundation Press,
1955.
McCULLOCH, O.C., 'The Tribe of Ishmael (Kallikuks)', Pro-
ceedings of the National Conference of Charities and Correc-
tion, Washington, 1888.
MacCUNE, S. and WALTHER, R., Juvenile Judges in the United
States, 'Crime and Delinquency', 11, 1965, p. 384.
McDONOUGH, J.B., et al., 'Juvenile Court Handbook', South
Hackensack, Rothmans Co., 1970.
MacEWAN, J.N.S., Powers and Duties of Local Authorities with
regard to Children, 'The Scots Law Times', 26 March 1971.
MacFADERN, W., Changing Concepts of Juvenile Justice, 'Crime
and Delinquency', 17, 1971, p. 136.
McHARDY, L., An Assessment of Juvenile Probation Services,
'Juvenile Justice', 24 (2), 1974, p. 41.
MACK, J.W., The Juvenile Court, 'Harvard Law Review', 23,
1909, p. 104.
McNEEL, A., Caird, 'The Cry of the Children', Blackwood
& Sons, 1849.
MacRAE, F., The English Probation Training System, 'British
Journal of Delinquency', 8, 1958, p. 210.
MAGISTRATES ASSOCIATION, 'Speakers' Notes', Magistrates
Association, 1975.
MAHONEY, A.R., The Humanity of Probation Officers, 'Federal
Probation', XXXVI (3), 1972.
MAHONEY, A.R., The Effect of Labelling upon Youths in the
Juvenile Justice System - a review of the Evidence, 'Law
and Society', 8, 1974, p. 583.
MANNHEIM, H., 'Social Aspects of Crime in England between
the Wars', Allen & Unwin, 1940.
MANNHEIM, H., et al., Magisterial Policy in the London Juven-
ile Courts, 'British Journal of Delinquency', 8, 1957, p. 13.
MANNHEIM, H., Some aspects of Judicial Sentencing Policy,
'Yale Law Journal', 67, 1958, p. 961.
MARKS, et al., 'The Lawyer, the Public and Professional
Responsibility', Chicago, American Bar Foundation, 1972.
MARTIN, E.W., 'Comparative Development in Social Welfare,
Allen & Unwin, 1972.
MARTIN, F. and MURRAY, K. (eds), 'Children's Hearings',
Scottish Academic Press, Edinburgh, 1976.
MARTIN, J.P. and WILSON, G., 'The Police, a Study in
Manpower', Heinemann, 1969.
MAY, D., Delinquency Control and the Treatment Model,
'British Journal of Criminology', 11, 1971, p. 359.

MAY, D. and SMITH, G., Policy Interpretation and the Children's Panels, 'Applied Social Studies', 2, 1970, p. 91

MAY, D. and SMITH, G., Aberdeen City Children's Panel, 'British Journal of Social Work', 1, 1971, p. 5.

MAYHEW, H., 'London Labour and the London Poor', Griffin Bohn & Co., 1862.

MAYHEW, H. and BINNY, J., 'Criminal Prisons of London and Scenes of Prison Life', reprint of Economic Classics, New York, Augustus M. Kelley, 1968, first edition, 1862.

MAYS, J.B., 'Crime and its Treatment', Longmans, 1970.

MEAD, G.H., The Psychology of Punitive Justice, 'American Sociological Review', 23, 1918, p. 577.

MENNINGER, K., 'The Crime of Punishment', New York, Viking Press, 1968.

MENSCHER, S., The Influence of Romanticism on 19th Century British Social Work, 'Social Service Review', 38, 1964, p. 174.

MILES, W.A., 'Poverty, Mendicity and Crime', Shaw & Sons, 1839.

MILLER, D., 'Growth to Freedom', Tavistock, 1964.

MILLER, F.W., et al., 'Criminal Justice Administration and Related Processes', Mineola, Foundation Press, 1971.

MILLER, J.G., The Dilemma of the Post Gault Juvenile Court, 'Family Law Quarterly', 3, 1969, p. 229.

MILLER, W.B., Ideology and Criminal Justice Policy, 'Journal of Criminal Law and Criminology', 64 (2), 1973, pp. 141-62.

MILTON, F., 'The English Magistracy', Oxford University Press, 1967.

MIREHOUSE, J., 'Crime and its Causes', W.J. Cleaver, 1840.

MOIR, E., 'The Justice of the Peace', Penguin Books, 1969.

MORAN, F.A., New Light on the Juvenile Court and Probation, 'National Probation and Parole Association Yearbook', New York, National Probation and Parole Association, 1930.

MORRIS, A., Scottish Juvenile Justice: a critique, in R. Hood (ed.), 'Crime, Criminology and Public Policy', Heinemann, 1974.

MORRIS, A., A Criminal Law in Practice, 'National Conference on Teaching and Research in Criminology', 54, July 1973.

MORRIS, A., Children's Hearings in Scotland, 'Criminal Law Review', 1972, p. 693.

MORRIS, A., et al., Progress Report on Children's Panels, 'Scotsman', 13 June 1973.

MORRIS, R., WHITE, R. and LEWIS, P., 'Social Needs and Legal Action', Martin Robertson, 1973.

MORRIS, T., 'The Criminal Area', Routledge & Kegan Paul, 1957.

MORRISON, A., 'A Child of the Jago', MacGibbon & Kee, 1969.

MORRISON, W.D., 'Juvenile Offenders', New York, D. Appleton & Co., 1897.

MUMFORD, G.H.F., 'A Guide to Juvenile Court Law', Shaw & Sons, 1970.

MURRAY, G. and ROWE, A., Children's Panels: Implications for the Future, 'Policy and Politics', 1, 1974, p. 327.

NAGEL, S., Political Party Affiliations and Judges' Decisions, 'American Political Science Review', 55, 1961, p. 843.

NAGEL, S., Judicial Backgrounds and Criminal Cases, 'Journal of Criminal Law and Criminology', 53, 1962, p. 333.

NAGEL, S., 'The Legal Process from a Behavioural Perspective', Ontario, Irwin Dorsey, 1969.

NATIONAL ADMINISTRATION CONFERENCE ON CRIMINAL JUSTICE STANDARDS, 'Community Crime Prevention', Washington, US Government Printing Office, 1973.

NATIONAL CONFERENCE OF COMMISSIONERS ON UNIFORM STATE LAWS, 'Uniform Juvenile Court Act', Chicago, 1968.

NATIONAL COUNCIL ON CRIME AND DELINQUENCY, 'Guides for Juvenile Court Judges', second edition, Paramus, New Jersey, National Council on Crime and Delinquency, 1963.

NATIONAL COUNCIL ON CRIME AND DELINQUENCY, Jurisdiction over status offences should be removed from the Juvenile Court. A policy statement, 'Crime and Delinquency', 21, 1975, p. 97.

NATIONAL COUNCIL ON CRIME AND DELINQUENCY, 'Model Rules for Juvenile Courts', Paramus, New Jersey, National Council on Crime and Delinquency, 1963.

NATIONAL PROBATION ASSOCIATION, 'John Augustus', New York, National Probation Association, 1939.

NEALE, W.D., 'Juvenile Delinquency in Manchester', Gavin Hamilton, 1840.

NELSON V. HEYNE, 'Amicus Curae Brief', National Juvenile Law Centre, St Louis, 1972.

NORMAN, S., 'The Youth Service Bureau', Paramus, National Council on Crime and Delinquency, 1972.

NOYES, A.D., Has Gault changed the Juvenile Court Concept? 'Crime and Delinquency', 16, 1970, p. 158.

OLIVER, I.T., The Metropolitan Police Bureau Scheme, 'Criminal Law Review', 1973, p. 499.

OWEN, D., 'English Philanthropy', Cambridge, Mass., Bellknapp Press of Harvard University, 1964.

OWEN, R., 'Report to the County of Lanark', V.A.C. Gartree

(ed.), Pelican Books, 1970.

PACKMAN, J., 'The Child's Generation', Blackwell & Robertson, 1975.

PAGE, L., 'Justice of the Peace', Faber & Faber, 1936.

PALEY, J. and THORPE, D., 'Children: Handle with Care', National Youth Bureau, 1974.

PARKER, G.E., Some Historical Observations on Juvenile Courts, 'Criminal Law Quarterly', 9, 1967, p. 467.

PARKER, H., 'View from the Boys', David & Charles, 1974.

PARSLOE, P., et al., Social Work as Taught, 'New Society', 4 March 1976.

PATERSON, J., Lay Bodies and Social Workers, 'Social Work Today', 3 (2), 1972.

PATTHERD, A.W. and McCLEAN, J.E., Decision Making in Juvenile Courts, 'Criminal Law Review', 1965, p. 699.

PAULSEN, M., Fairness to the Juvenile Offender, 'Minnesota Law Review', 61, 1957, p. 549.

PAULSEN, M., Juvenile Courts and the Legacy of '67, 'Indiana Law Journal', 43, 1968, p. 523.

PAULSEN, M., The Child, the Court and the Commission, 'Juvenile Court Judges Journal', 18, 1967, p. 79.

PERRY, F., 'Information for the Court', Cambridge, Mass., Institute of Criminology, 1973.

PIERCE, B.K., 'A Half Century with Juvenile Delinquents', New York, Appleton & Co., 1869.

PIERCE, D., Crime and Society in London 1700-1900, 'Harvard Library Bulletin', 20 (4), 1972.

PHILLIPSON, M., 'Sociological Aspects of Crime and Delinquency', Routledge & Kegan Paul, 1971.

PICKETT, R.S., 'The House of Refuge', Syracuse, Syracuse University Press, 1969.

PILIAVIN, I. and BRIAR, S., Police Encounters with Juveniles, 'American Journal of Sociology', 70, 1964, p. 206.

PINCHBECK, I. and HEWITT, M., 'Children in English Society', Parts I & II, Routledge & Kegan Paul, 1973.

PLATT, A.M., et al., In Defense of Youth, 'Indiana Law Journal', 43, 1968, p. 636.

PLATT, A.M., 'The Child Savers', Chicago, Chicago University Press, 1969.

PODGORECKI, A., et al., 'Knowledge and Opinion about Law', Martin Robertson, 1973.

POLANYI, M., 'The Logic of Liberty', Routledge & Kegan Paul, 1957.

POLIER, J.W., Future of the Juvenile Court, 26 (2), 1975, p. 3.

POLK, K., Delinquency Prevention and the Youth Service Bureau, 'Criminal Law Bulletin', 7 (6), 1971.

POUND, R., 'Social Control Through Law', Hamden Conn., Archon Books, 1968.

POUND, R., 'The Limits of Effective Legal Action', address before the Pennsylvania Bar Association, 27 June 1916.

POUND, R., 'Interpretations of Legal History', New York, Macmillan, 1923.

POUND, R., The Rise of Socialized Justice, 'National Probation and Parole Yearbook', New York, National Probation and Parole Association, 1942.

PRITCHETT, C.H., 'The Roosevelt Court', New York, Macmillan, 1948.

PYFER, J., The Juvenile's Right to Receive Treatment, 'Family Law Quarterly', 6, 1972, p. 279.

QUINTON, R.F., 'Crime and Criminals 1876-1910', Longmans, Green & Co., 1910.

RADZINOWICZ, L., 'A History of the English Criminal Law', Stevens, 1948.

RADZINOWICZ, L., 'Penal Reform in England', P.S. King, 1940.

RENDLEMAN, D.R., Juvenile Court Jurisdiction, 'Journal of Urban Law', 48, 1970, p. 89.

RENDLEMAN, D.R., Parens Patriae: From Chancery to Juvenile Court, 'South Carolina Law Review', 23, 1970, p. 205.

RENTON, R. and BROWN, H., 'Criminal Proceedings according to the Law of Scotland', fourth edition, Green, 1972.

RITCHIE, M. and MACK, J., 'Police Warnings', University of Glasgow, 1974.

ROBERTSON, A., Penal Policy and Social Change, 'Human Relations', 22, 1969, p. 547.

ROBERTSON, R. and TAYLOR, L., 'Deviance, Crime and Socio-Legal Control', Martin Robertson, 1973.

ROSE, A.G., 'The Struggle for Penal Reform', Stevens, 1961.

ROSENHEIM, M., Youth Service Bureaux: A Concept in Search of Definition, 'Juvenile Court Judges Journal', 20, 1969, p. 69.

ROSENHEIM, M. and SKOLER, D.K., The Lawyer's Role in Intake and Detention stages of Juvenile Court Proceedings, 'Crime and Delinquency', 14, 1965, p. 167.

ROSENHEIM, M. (ed.), 'Justice for the Child', New York, Free Press, 1962.

ROTHMAN, D., 'The Discovery of the Asylum', Boston, Little Brown, 1971.

ROWE, A.J.B., 'Initial Selection for the Children's Panels in Scotland', Bookstall Publications (undated).

ROWNTREE REPORT, 'Social Work in Scotland: Report of a Working Party on the Social Work (Scotland) Act, 1968', University of Edinburgh, 1969.

SANDERS, W.B., Early Beginnings of the Juvenile Court Movement in England, 'National Probation Association Yearbook', 58, New York, National Probation and Parole Association, 1965.

SARRI, R.S., The Rehabilitation Failure, 'Trial', September/

October 1971, p. 18.

SCHEFF, J.O., 'Being Mentally Ill', Chicago, Aldine, 1966.

SCHOOLMAKER, M.H. and BROOKS, J.S., Women in Probation and Parole, 'Crime and Delinquency', 21, 1975, p. 109.

SCHORNHORST, T., The Waiver of Juvenile Court Jurisdiction: Kent Revisited, 'Indiana Law Journal', 43, 1968, p. 665.

SCHRAG, C., 'Crime and Justice: American Style', Washington, National Institute of Mental Health, 1971.

SCHRAM, G.L., The Judge Meets the Boy and his Family, 'National Probation Association Yearbook, 38, New York, National Probation and Parole Association, 1945.

SCHUBERT, G., 'The Judicial Mind', Evanston, Northwestern University Press, 1965.

SCHUBERT, G., 'The Judicial Mind Revisited', Oxford University Press, 1974.

SCHUBERT, G., 'Judicial Policy Making', Glenview, Scott Foresman & Co., 1974.

SCHULTZ, J.L., The Cycle of Juvenile Court History, 'Crime and Delinquency', 19, 1973, p. 457.

SCHUR, E.M., 'Labelling Deviant Behaviour', New York, Harper & Row, 1971.

SCHUR, E.M., 'Radical Intervention', Englewood Cliffs, Prentice-Hall, 1973.

SCOTT, H., 'The Concise Encyclopedia of Crime and Criminals', New York, Hawthorne Books Inc., 1961.

SCOTT, P.C., Child, Family Young Offender Cmnd 2742, 'British Journal of Criminology', 6, 1966, p. 105.

SCOTT, P., Juvenile Delinquency - The Juvenile's View, 'British Journal of Delinquency', 9, 1959, p. 200.

SEED, P., 'The Expansion of Social Work in Britain', Routledge & Kegan Paul, 1973.

SENNETT, R., 'The Uses of Disorder', New York, Alfred A. Knopf, 1970.

SHEARS, C.C., Legal Problems Peculiar to Children's Courts, 'American Bar Association Journal', 48, 1962, p. 719.

SHELDON, C.H., 'The American Judicial Process', New York, Dodd Mead & Co., 1974.

SHERIDAN, W., The Gault Decision and Probation, 'Indiana Law Journal', 43, 1968, p. 655.

SHERIDAN, W., 'Legislative Guide for Drafting Family and Juvenile Court Acts', US Children's Bureau, 1969.

SHERIDAN, W., 'Standards for Juvenile and Family Courts', New Jersey, National Council of Crime and Delinquency, 1966.

SIEGLER, J., Exclusive Jurisdiction in the Juvenile Court, in M. Bell (ed.), 'National Probation Association Yearbook', New York, National Probation and Parole Association, 1937.

SKOLER, D.L., The Right to Counsel and the Role of Counsel in Juvenile Court Proceedings, 'Indiana Law Journal', 43, 1968, p. 558.

SKOLER, D.L. and TENNEY, C.W., Attorney Representation in the Juvenile Court, 'Journal of Family Law', 4, 1964, p. 77.

SMITH, A.D., Young Offenders Institutions in Scotland, 'The Scots Law Times', 26 January 1968.

SMITH, J.C., The Personnel of the Criminal Law in England and the United States, 'Cambridge Law Review', 1955, p. 80.

SNYDER, E., The Impact of the Juvenile Court Hearing on the Child, 'Crime and Delinquency', 17, 1971, p. 180.

SNYDER, E., The Supreme Court as a Small Group, 'Social Forces', 36, 1958, p. 232.

SOCIETY OF FRIENDS, 'The Struggle for Justice', New York, Hill and Wang, 1971.

SPARKS, R.F., Sentencing by Magistrates in P. Halmos (ed.), 'Sociological Studies of the British Penal Services', University of Keele, 1965.

SPARKS, R.F., The Depraved are not just Deprived, 'New Society', 24 July 1969.

STAPLETON, V., A Social Scientist's View of Gault, 'Yale Review of Law and Social Action', 1, 1971, p. 72.

STAPLETON, V. and TEITELBAUM, L.E., 'In Defense of Youth', New York, Russell Sage, 1972.

STARK, H., Alternatives to Institutionalization, 'Crime and Delinquency', 13, 1967, p. 323.

STEVENSON, O., 'Claimant or Client?', Allen & Unwin, 1973.

STONE, O., Hard Cases and New Law for Children in England and Wales, 'Family Law Quarterly', 8, 1974, p. 351.

SUSSMAN, F.B., 'Law of Juvenile Delinquency', New York, Oceana Publications.

TAMILIA, P., Neglect Proceedings and the Conflict between Law and Social Work, 'Duquesne Law Review', 9, 1971, p. 579.

TAPPEN, P., 'Juvenile Delinquency', New York, McGraw-Hill Book Co. Inc., 1949.

TEETERS, N.K., Institutional Treatment of Juvenile Delinquency, 'Nebraska Law Review', 29, 1950, p. 577.

TEETERS, N.K. and REINEMANN, J.O., 'The Challenge of Delinquency', Englewood Cliffs, Prentice-Hall, 1950.

TENNEY, C.W., The Utopian World of the Juvenile Court, 'Annals of the American Academy', 383, 1969, p. 101.

THOMAS, D.A., The Control of Discretion in the Administration of Criminal Justice in R. Hood (ed.), 'Crime, Criminology and Public Policy', Heinemann, 1974.

THOMPSON, A., 'Punishment and Prevention', J. Nisbet & Co., 1957.

TILLICK, P., 'Love, Power and Justice', Oxford University Press, 1960.

TITMUSS, R., Welfare Rights, Law and Discretion, 'Political Quarterly', 42 (2), 1971.

TOBIAS, J., 'Nineteenth Century Crime in England', New York, Barnes & Noble, 1972.

TOBIAS, J., 'Crime and Industrial Society in 19th Century, Pelican Books, 1972.

TRATTNER, W., 'From Poor Law to Welfare State', Collier Macmillan, 1974.

TREADWELL, W.S., The Lawyer in Juvenile Court Dispositional Proceedings, 'Juvenile Court Judges Journal', 16, 1965, p. 109.

TROJAENDOICZ, R.C., 'Juvenile Delinquency, Concepts and Control, Englewood Cliffs, Prentice-Hall, 1973.

TURNER, E.S., 'Roads to Ruin', Baltimore, Penguin Books, 1966.

UNITED NATIONS, 'Comparative Study of Juvenile Delinquency', New York, 1952.

UNITED NATIONS, 'Probation and Related Measures', New York, 1951.

ULMER, S.S., Toward a Theory of Sub Group Formation in the U.S. Supreme Court, 'Journal of Politics', 27, 1965, p.133.

VAN WATERS, M., The Juvenile Court from the Child's Viewpoint, in J. Addams, 'The Child, the Clinic and the Court', 1925.

VEREKER, C., The Politics of Welfare in 'New Thinking about Welfare', Association of Social Workers, 1966.

VINES, K., Federal District Court Judges and Race Relations in the South, 'Journal of Public Law', 26, 1964, p. 338.

VOSS, H.L. 'Society, Delinquency and Delinquent Behaviour', Boston, Little Brown, 1970.

WADDY, H.T., 'The Police Court and its Work', Butterworth, 1925.

WAITE, E.F., The Outlook for the Juvenile Court, 'Annals of the American Academy', 105, 1923, p. 229.

WALKER, D.M., 'The Scottish Legal System', third edition, W. Green, 1969.

WALKER, N., 'Crime and Punishment in Britain', Edinburgh University Press, 1965.

WATSON, J., 'British Juvenile Courts', Longmans Green & Co., 1948.

WATSON, J., The Juvenile Court Today and Tomorrow, 11th Clarke Hall Lecture, 1951.

WATSON, J., 'The Child and the Magistrate', Jonathan Cape, 1965.

WATSON, J., 'Which is the Justice?', Allen & Unwin, 1969.

WATSON, J., The Children and Young Persons Act, 1969, 'Solicitors Journal', 114, 1970, p. 9.

WATSON, J., 'The Juvenile Court: 1970 Onward', Shaw &

Sons, 1970.

WATSON, J. and AUSTIN, P.M., 'The Modern Juvenile Court', Shaw & Sons, 1975.

WAUGH, B., 'The Gaol Cradle', Isbister & Co., 1875.

WEBB, P.R.M., The Training of New Magistrates, 'Criminal Law Review', 1965, p. 252.

WEEKS, H.A., 'Youthful Offenders at Highfields', Ann Arbor Press, 1963.

WHEELER, S. and COTTRELL, L.S., 'Juvenile Delinquency', Russell Sage, 1966.

WHITAKER, B., 'The Police', Penguin Books, 1964.

WHITLATCH, W.G., Towards an Understanding of Juvenile Court Process, 'Juvenile Justice', 23 (3), 1972, p. 2.

WHITTAKER, D. and LIEBERMANN, D., 'Psychotherapy Through the Group Process', Tavistock Press, 1965.

WHITTAKER, J., 19 Innovations in Delinquency Institutions, 'Child Care Quarterly', 2, 1973, p. 14.

WILES, P., 'The Sociology of Crime and Delinquency in Britain', vol. II, Martin Robertson, 1976.

WILKINS, L.T. and CHANDLER, A., Confidence and Competence in Decision Making, 'British Journal of Criminology', 5, 1965, p. 22.

WILLIAMS, J. Hall, 'The English Penal System in Transition', Butterworths, 1970.

WILLS, D., 'A Place Like Home', Allen & Unwin, 1970.

WILMOT, Sir E., 'A Letter to the Magistrates of England', Hatchard, 1827.

WILSHIRE, L., 'The Vale of Berkeley', Robert Hale, 1956.

WINES, F.H., 'Punishment and Reformation', New York, Thomas Y. Crowell and Company, 1895.

WINNICOTT, D.W., 'The Maturational Process and the Facilitating Environment', New York, International University Press, 1965.

WINSLOW, R., 'Crime in a Free Society', Belmont, Dickerson, 1969.

WINTERS, G.R., 'Judicial Selection and Tenure', Chicago, American Judicature Society, 1973.

WIZNER, S., The Defense Counsel: Neither Father, Judge, Probation Officer or Social Worker, 'Trial', September/ October 1971.

WOOLLEN, E., The Indiana Board of Children's Guardians, 'National Conference on Charities and Corrections', 1901.

WOODROOFE, K., 'From Charity to Social Work in England and the United States', Routledge & Kegan Paul, 1962.

WOOTTON, B., 'Crime and the Criminal Law', Stevens, 1963.

WOOTTON, B., The Juvenile Courts, 'Criminal Law Review', 1961, p. 669.

WOOTTON, B., White Paper on Children in Trouble, 'Criminal Law Review', 1968, p. 465.

YOUNG, D.J., Justice for Children, 'Juvenile Court Judges Journal', 21, 1970, p. 67.
YOUNGHUSBAND, E., The Dilemma of the Juvenile Court, 'Social Service Review', March 1959.
ZEHLER, R., One Judges View of the Juvenile Court, 'Juvenile Court Judges Journal', 21, 1971, p. 113.